Post Keynesian and Ecological Economics

Dedicated to John Kenneth Galbraith, who from the very beginning was concerned about protecting quality of life on this planet; and two sisters, Rosie Kerry and Angela Winthrop, who in their own way understood the relationship between quality of life and the environment.

Post Keynesian and Ecological Economics

Confronting Environmental Issues

Edited by

Richard P.F. Holt

Southern Oregon University, USA

Steven Pressman

Monmouth University, USA

and

Clive L. Spash

Commonwealth Scientific and Industrial Research Organisation (CSIRO), Australia

Edward Elgar

Cheltenham, UK • Northampton, MA, USA

Published by
Edward Elgar Publishing Limited
The Lypiatts
15 Lansdown Road
Cheltenham
Glos GL50 2JA
UK

Edward Elgar Publishing, Inc.
William Pratt House
9 Dewey Court
Northampton
Massachusetts 01060
USA

A catalogue record for this book
is available from the British Library

Library of Congress Control Number: 2009933366

ISBN 978 1 84720 668 8

Printed on FSC approved paper
Printed and bound in Great Britain by Marston Book Services Ltd, Oxfordshire

Contents

Figures

Tables

Contributors

Sabine Bietz is a PhD candidate at the Department of Consumer Behaviour and Consumer Policy at the University of Calw, Germany. Her main research interests are consumer behaviour and sustainable development.

Jerry Courvisanos is Associate Professor of Innovation and Entrepreneurship at the Centre for Regional Innovation and Competitiveness in the School of Business, University of Ballarat, Australia. He has published many articles on the environment and on Post Keynesian investment theory, including *Investment Cycles in Capitalist Economies* (Edward Elgar, 1996).

Peter E. Earl is Associate Professor of Economics at the University of Queensland, Australia. He is the author or editor of 17 books, including *Money Matters: A Keynesian Approach to Monetary Economics*, with Sheila Dow (Martin Robertson, 1982), *The Economic Imagination: Toward a Behavioural Analysis of Choice* (Wheatsheaf Books, 1983) and *Information, Opportunism and Economic Coordination* (Edward Elgar, 2002). From 2001 to 2004 he was co-editor of the *Journal of Economic Psychology*.

Mario Giampietro is a Research Professor at the Institute of Science and Technology for the Environment – Universitat Autonoma Barcelona, Spain. He has been a visiting scholar at Cornell University, Wageningen University, the European Commission Joint Research Center at Ispra, University of Wisconsin Madison, Penn State University, and Arizona State University. He has published more than 150 papers and is the author of *Multi-Scale Integrated Analysis of Agro-ecosystems* (CRC Press, 2003), and co-author of *The Jevons Paradox and the Myth of Resource Efficiency Improvements* (Earthscan, 2008).

John Gowdy is Rittenhouse Teaching Professor of Humanities and Social Science at Rensselaer Polytechnic Institute, Troy, New York, and President-Elect of the International Society of Ecological Economics. He is the author of several books including *Sustainability and Firms* (Edward Elgar, 1998), *Paradise for Sale*, co-authored with Carl McDaniel (University of California Press, 2000) and *Frontiers in Ecological Economic Theory and Application*, with Jon Erikson (Edward Elgar, 2007).

Richard P.F. Holt is Professor of Economics at Southern Oregon University. He has authored and edited a number of books and journal articles including the prize-winning *The Changing Face of Economics: Conversations with Cutting Edge Economists*, with David C. Colander and J. Barkley Rosser, Jr (University of Michigan Press, 2004). He has published with Steven Pressman *A New Guide to Post Keynesian Economics* (Routledge, 2001), and *Empirical Post Keynesian Economics* (M.E. Sharpe, 2006). They are working on a third volume that will finish their trilogy on Post Keynesian economics, *Post Keynesian Economics and Public Policy*.

James Juniper is a Lecturer in Economics and an Associate of the Centre for Full Employment and Equity at the University of Newcastle, Australia. His research interests include systems theory, quantitative finance, Continental philosophy, Post Keynesian macroeconomics and regional development.

James Kahn is the John F. Hendon Professor of Economics and Director of the Environmental Studies Program at Washington and Lee University in Lexington, Virginia. He is also director of a US–Brazil consortium under the auspices of the Brazilian Ministry of Education and the US Department of Education. He is the author of *Economic Approach to Environment and Natural Resources* (3rd edition, South-Western, 2004) and editor, with Anna Alberini, of *Handbook on Contingent Valuation* (Edward Elgar, 2006).

Marc Lavoie is Professor of Economics at the University of Ottawa, Canada. He has been a Visiting Professor at the universities of Bordeaux, Nice, Rennes, Dijon, Grenoble, Limoges, Lille, Paris-Nord and Paris-1, as well as Curtin University in Perth, Australia. He has written a number of books, including *Foundations of Post-Keynesian Economic Analysis* (Edward Elgar, 1993), *Introduction to Post-Keynesian Economics* (Palgrave Macmillan, 2006), and *Monetary Economics: An Integrated Approach to Money, Income, Production and Wealth* (Palgrave Macmillan, 2007) with Wynne Godley.

Kozo Mayumi is a Professor at the University of Tokushima, Japan. He is the author of *The Origins of Ecological Economics: The Bioeconomics of Georgescu-Roegen* (Routledge, 2001) and *The Jevons Paradox and the Myth of Resource Efficiency Improvements*, with Blake Alcott, Mario Giampietro and John Polimeni (Earthscan, 2008).

Andrew Mearman is Senior Lecturer in Economics at Bristol Business School, University of the West of England. He has published on economic methodology in journals such as *Oxford Economic Papers*, the *Cambridge Journal of Economics* and the *Review of Social Economy*.

Richard B. Norgaard is a member of the faculty of the University of California, Berkeley. In 2006 he received the Kenneth E. Boulding Award, which honours individuals making major contributions to interdisciplinary issues. He is co-author or co-editor of several books, and has published over 200 articles in environmental and ecological economics, environmental sociology, environmental epistemology and other fields. He is the author of *Development Betrayed: The End of Progress and a Coevolutionary Revision of the Future* (Routledge, 1994).

Steven Pressman is Professor of Economics and Finance at Monmouth University in West Long Branch, NJ. He also serves as co-editor of the *Review of Political Economy*, and as associate editor and book review editor of the *Eastern Economic Journal*. He has published more than 120 articles in refereed journals and as book chapters, and has authored or edited 15 books, including *Alternative Theories of the State* (Palgrave Macmillan, 2006) and *50 Major Economists*, 2nd edition (Routledge, 2006).

Jesus Ramos-Martin is Assistant Professor in the Department of Applied Economics and Researcher at the Institute for Environmental Science and Technology at the Autonomous University of Barcelona. He has been lecturer at FLACSO (Ecuador), organizes the biannual Iberoamerican Congress on Development and Environment, and is a member of the editorial board of the *Iberoamerican Journal of Ecological Economics*.

Lucia Reisch is Professor for Intercultural Consumer Behaviour and Consumer Policy at Copenhagen Business School, Denmark. She is editor of *Ethical-Ecological Investment: Towards Global Sustainable Development* (IKO, 2001) and co-editor of *The Ecological Economics of Consumption* (Edward Elgar, 2005).

Alexandre Rivas is Full Professor (Professor Titular) in the Departamento de Economia e Análise at the Universidade Federal do Amazonas in Brazil. He is also a Collaborating Professor at Washington and Lee University in Lexington, Virginia, and a member of the advisory board to a joint project of the University of the United Nations and the Banco do Brasil. He is the director of a US–Brazil consortium under the auspices of the Brazilian Ministry of Education and the US Department of Education.

J. Barkley Rosser, Jr is Professor of Economics and Kirby L. Cramer, Jr Professor of Business Administration at James Madison University, in Harrisonburg, Virginia. He is also editor of the *Journal of Economic Behavior and Organization*. Among his more than 100 publications are *From Catastrophe to Chaos: A General Theory of Economic Discontinuities*,

2nd edition (Springer, 2000), *Comparative Economics in a Transforming World Economy* 2nd edition, with Marina V. Rosser (MIT Press, 2004) and an edited volume, *Complexity in Economics* (Edward Elgar, 2004).

Heinz Schandl is leading research on resource use dynamics and sustainability transitions at the Commonwealth Scientific and Industrial Research Organisation (CSIRO) at Canberra, Australia. He has published on resource use dynamics in historical UK and contemporary Southeast Asia and Latin America as well as on global resource use patterns and the role of systems innovation for sustainability transitions.

Robert H. Scott, III is Assistant Professor of Economics and Finance at Monmouth University in West Long Branch, NJ. He received his PhD in Economics from the University of Missouri, Kansas City. His main research interests are credit cards, financial literacy and ecological economics.

Clive L. Spash is an Economics Professor and Science Leader within the Sustainable Ecosystems Division of the Commonwealth Scientific and Industrial Research Organisation (CSIRO), Canberra, Australia. He is editor-in-chief of *Environmental Values*, and former co-editor of *Environment and Planning C: Government and Policy*. His more than 100 publications include *Greenhouse Economics: Value and Ethics* (Routledge, 2002), and *Alternatives for Environmental Valuation* (Routledge, 2005), co-edited with Michael Getzner and Sigrid Stagl. From 1996 to 2006, he served as Vice-President and then two terms as President of the European Society for Ecological Economics.

Arild Vatn is Thor Heyerdahl Professor at the Department of International Environment and Development at the Norwegian University of Life Sciences (UMB). He was awarded the UMB Research Prize in 2002, and the Joint European Association for Evolutionary Political Economy (EAEPE) and Association for Evolutionary Economics (AFEE) Veblen 150 prize in 2007 for his book *Institutions and the Environment*. He is the current President of the European Society of Ecological Economics. He is also Head of the Board for the Research Program 'Environment 2015' under the Norwegian Research Council.

Tim Wakeley is a Senior Lecturer in Economics, Griffith University, Australia. He works on Schumpeterian and evolutionary economics, and his work explores the relevance of heterodox approaches to economic problems. He is also co-author of *Business Economics: A Contemporary Approach* with Peter Earl (McGraw Hill, 2005).

PART I

Introduction

1. Post Keynesian and ecological economics: alternative perspectives on sustainability and environmental economics

Richard P.F. Holt and Clive L. Spash

INTRODUCTION

For some time now the standard neoclassical economic model has been criticized from numerous directions. It has been criticized for assuming that people are solely rational and selfish, while in reality it seems that diverse inclinations seem to drive human behavior.[1] Another problem is the assumption of perfectly competitive markets as well as the existence of pervasive future markets to deal with the long-run consequences of present decisions; yet such markets do not exist. From these assumptions, neoclassical analysis then demonstrates the existence of a stable and optimal equilibrium. It concludes that government policies cannot make us better off. In short, like Dr Pangloss in Voltaire's *Candide*, we are supposed to live in the best of all possible worlds – a result that seems to be contradicted by our daily experiences.

These problems are quite prevalent when neoclassical economics seeks to analyze the environment and issues surrounding sustainability. Ecological economists have pointed out these problems by stressing the interaction between individual, social, ecological and economic life, as well as the long-term consequences of the complex choices we make today. For example, they have criticized the assumption of rational consumer choice since many environmental consequences of human decisions will remain unknown for many years. Furthermore, they have also questioned traditional methods of measuring and estimating values related to the quality of life, non-market goods, sustainability and social welfare.

Post Keynesians, too, have criticized the standard economic model. They have developed a notion of social rationality, in which habits and herd behavior can create bubbles and lead to serious economic problems. Using path-dependent models, rather than equilibrium models, they have explained the persistence of high unemployment in developed countries. Also, Post Keynesians have emphasized that the future is uncertain, rather than known with some probability distribution, and they have stressed that government policy is needed to prevent and solve economic problems.

Despite many differences in subject matter and approach, ecological and Post Keynesian economists have a great deal in common. Both criticize the mechanistic equilibrium models used in neoclassical economics. Both oppose the so-called 'value-free' methodology and analysis used by mainstream economics. Both reject the standard economic assumptions regarding how people behave; and both reject the neoclassical conclusion that free markets always lead to optimal outcomes.

The following chapters show how and where ecological economics and Post Keynesian economics share common ground concerning environmental problems. They also shed light on how these two schools can learn from one another. This is important for Post Keynesians, who have for the most part ignored microeconomic policy issues such as education, crime and the environment. Ecological economics has neglected methodological issues and might reflect upon Post Keynesian work in this area (see Chapter 2 by Andrew Mearman). There are also common areas for debate as to how evolving and changing complex systems should be taken into account (see Chapter 11 by J. Barkley Rosser, Jr). The role of mathematical formalism then becomes an issue in both schools, along with the importance of institutions (Greenwood and Holt, 2008).

Some identifiable differences also exist between these two schools of thought. Post Keynesians focus on promoting economic growth, while ecological economists emphasize the negative environmental consequences of growth. Post Keynesians focus on intra-generational distribution while ecological economists stress intergenerational distribution. Finally, Post Keynesians, with the notable exception of John Kenneth Galbraith, have ignored the important question of what really determines the quality of life. (See Chapter 3 by Clive Spash and Heinz Schandl, and Chapter 6 by Arild Vatn for more on the similarities and differences between the Post Keynesians and ecological economics.)

We hope that this book will spark a dialog over such issues between Post Keynesians and ecological economists (and others) on environmental issues and sustainable development, besides providing a critique of the neoclassical approach to the environment. To better understand what follows the next sections of this chapter provide a brief overview of these two schools, highlighting how they differ from mainstream economics and some common themes found in both. Finally, we give summaries of the different chapters in the book.

ECOLOGICAL ECONOMICS AND THE MAINSTREAM

In the late 1960s and early 1970s ecological economics seemed to be pushing the boundaries of economic analysis and heading away from the mainstream. By turning to materials balance theory, ecological economists brought in the laws of thermodynamics to economics as an alternative to the neoclassical model (Kneese et al., 1970). During this time Georgescu-Roegen (1971) wrote an influential book on the importance of entropy for the economy. The book questioned the feasibility of economic growth over the long run and suggested that economic development policy needed fundamental reform. His interpretation of classical entropy, along with lessons from materials balance theory, raised a range of concerns that ecological economists believed were important:

- The size and growth of populations and the pressure that they put on social, economic and ecological systems needs to be understood.
- The impact and rate of change that human and economic systems have on all living systems can be uncertain and possibly irreversible – time needs to be taken seriously.
- The need to go beyond substitution effects of capital in neoclassical economics, and recognize the necessity and role of all types of accumulated capital (that is, natural and social) on the well-being and sustainability of the economy, environment and society.
- Endless economic growth is unsustainable both socially and environmentally.
- The implicit value associated with growth that more is always better needs to be questioned.
- Economics cannot and should not be separated from ethical judgements, particularly in regard to the impact of those living today on future generations and the health of the planet.
- Nature has an intrinsic value.

Ecological economists characterized the mainstream view of the economy as a scene out of the Wild West, populated by cowboys exploiting resources, chucking their waste on the ground and riding away to infinite horizons where fresh resources could always be found; this was contrasted with looking at our planet, Earth, as a closed system like a spaceship (Boulding, 1966; see Chapter 5 in this volume by Robert Scott). Economic growth was seen as positively misleading in terms of the consequences for human society (Mishan, 1969) with the limits to growth highly profiled in a study by a team of scholars at the Massachusetts Institute of Technology (Meadows et al., 1972). Herman Daly (1977) championed the concept of a steady-state economy as a means to avoid environmental disaster. From the late 1960s to early 1980s ecological economists were able to establish a strong theoretical and empirical grounding to their field, which provided some cutting-edge work in economics. They also raised a series of interesting and important questions that were previously ignored by the majority of economists.

The response of the mainstream to this work was mixed. There was recognition of externalities and social costs associated with environmental degradation. Also the need to put value on environmental non-market goods to achieve adequate cost–benefit analysis associated with natural resources and the environment was acknowledged. This led to some important work by both mainstream and ecological economists from the 1970s to 1980s that tried to determine and measure different types of values associated with the environment. Valuation in cost–benefit analysis developed new methods such as travel cost, hedonic pricing, and contingent valuation. The travel cost method was the earliest to be more fully developed (Clawson and Knetsch, 1966), while contingent valuation followed later opening a whole new research agenda (Cummings et al., 1986). Primary data collection from face-to-face interviews gave results that questioned the economic model of human psychology and motivation (Spash, 2008). The theory behind values expanded from pure use to option, existence and bequest values (Krutilla, 1967; Krutilla and Fisher, 1978). This led to discussions over the ethical basis of economics (Kneese and Schulze, 1985; Schulze and Brookshire, 1982; Schulze et al., 1981). Climate change and the treatment of future generations were also topics on the valuation agenda (d'Arge, 1979; d'Arge et al., 1982). All this exciting work led to some important research breakthroughs in environmental economics.

Yet by the 1980s the entire thrust of this work towards a new and challenging research agenda seemed to have been narrowed by the mainstream. Environmental issues again were confined as a subdiscipline associated with resource and environmental economics. Topics had been tamed and controlled through equilibrium analysis, and reinforced by the teaching methods employed by graduate programs and what was considered acceptable economic model-building by key journals. It seemed that the response of mainstream economics to the concerns of ecological economists is that neoclassical economics can do the job. Mainstream economists simply asserted that, from its optimization models and welfare theory, neoclassical economics is able to produce theoretical explanations of how environmental problems can be evaluated. They argued that most environmental problems are anomalies correctable by taxes or tradable permit markets.

There is no need to go beyond a worldview of rational utility-maximizing agents and profit-maximizing firms. Resources are considered generally substitutable and, where they might run out, price changes are expected to stimulate new backstop technologies and resources. Where resources are overexploited, this can be corrected by imposing private property rights. Discounting takes care of future generations. Environmental values can all fit within a utilitarian framework, even including the existence of life and any value deemed intrinsic to an entity. Overall the environment and its problems can fit within the existing neoclassical theory where self-regulating markets function perfectly as the all-embracing solution.

Frustration with this outlook and methodology was growing and by the late 1980s ecological economists finally established their own association, the International Society for Ecological Economics (ISEE). A main difference between ecological economics and the mainstream is its interdisciplinary and pluralistic focus. Richard Norgaard (1989, p. 37) in the first issue of the association's journal *Ecological Economics* brought this point home:

> Ecology consists of numerous approaches to understanding natural systems: energetics, population biology, food-web models, hierarchy theory to mention just a few. Within ecology, field knowledge and the reporting of new observations are well respected. Economics, on the other hand, is dominated by one pattern of thinking and standard of 'proof', the market model and econometrics. Within economics, field knowledge and observations *per se* are little valued. Agreement on a correct method is frequently taken as an indication of the maturity of a science. The argument is developed in this paper that all the aspects of complex systems can only be understood through multiple methodologies. The agreement on method within economics, however, seems to reflect stronger pressures within the discipline for conformity than for truth relative to ecology. Since ecological economics seeks to understand a larger system than either economics or ecology seeks to understand, a diversity of methodologies is appropriate and pressures to eliminate methodologies for the sake of conformity should be avoided.

Most ecological economists look at ecological economics as an interdisciplinary and pluralistic school where knowledge in the field changes and progresses from the interaction and learning from different subject areas. This goes beyond just economics learning from ecology, but encompasses the need to explore areas such as philosophy, social psychology, and political science. One must understand the integrated and dynamic relationships that exist between these different areas. In addition, the role of the natural sciences in ecological economics changes in light of research in the social sciences as found in post normal science (Funtowicz and Ravetz, 1993) and sociological science–policy analysis (Wynne, 1994). Such an interdisciplinary approach requires understanding the key concepts and language of other disciplines and how they perceive and analyze the world. This provides additional and new ways, outside of economics, of gathering and analyzing information about the world around us. The primary benefit of this approach is recognizing that *problems* should be the focus of concern rather than *techniques* which restrain the type and form of concepts used in analysis. The pluralism that comes from the interdisciplinary method means seeing problems from different, equally valid perspectives. This does not mean all perspectives are accepted – all perspectives need to be explored through empirical and analytical rigor.

Even though there is an interdisciplinary commitment by ecological economists, there are differences within the school of what its range and focus should be. The divide seems to be mostly between one camp in the United States and the other in Europe (Spash, 1999). Some have argued that this represents the pluralism within the school.

DIFFERENCES AND DIVISIONS AMONG ECOLOGICAL ECONOMISTS

A core group of ecologists – including Bob Costanza (former ISEE President), Brian Walker, Paul Ehrlich, David Pimentel, and Carl Folke – seem to be closer to the mainstream and associate with economic theorists such as Ken Arrow, Joseph Stiglitz, Karl-Groan Maler, and Partha Dasgupta. Charles Perrings, a physicist who became an ISEE president, showed even closer ties to mainstream economics by advocating the use of abstract mathematical modeling of neoclassical resource economics (Perrings, 1987; see also the collected works by Perrings, 1997). The ISEE's journal, *Ecological Economics*, originally controlled by Costanza and dominated by Americans, had mainstream economists on its board and published articles well within the neoclassical realm. However, since the arrival of a new editor in 2008 this situation has begun to change.

In the United States the field seems to have become identified with two dominant ideas – monetary valuation of ecosystems services and a steady-state economy – primarily associated with two people, Bob Costanza and Herman Daly respectively. Regardless of the importance of this work, some have argued that such close ties to the mainstream and the narrowing of the subject areas in the field undermines the breadth and depth of ecological economics. Some have argued that this limiting view of ecological economics is driven by American institutional circumstances and a perceived necessity to use market rhetoric. In response, mostly from European ecological economists, some have shown a desire to go back to what they consider to be the cutting-edge work of the 1970s by ecological economists such as Georgescu-Roegen. These works, they believe, provide a much broader field of research for ecological economics. This has led a group of ecological economists to an area they call *social ecological economics*, so as to identify the interdisciplinary and socio-economic breadth of ecological economics.

SOCIAL ECOLOGICAL ECONOMICS

Social ecological economics goes beyond standard economic theory and focuses on the interconnection of power with environmental and institutional arrangements. Economics, environment, and politics are intertwined, so that any study of economics is political economy. In ecological economics such a framework can be found in the work of former ISEE Presidents Joan Martinez-Alier (2002) and Richard Norgaard (1994). The method in this framework moves beyond a simple belief in mechanistic cause–effect relationships, something that was criticized by both Kapp (1978 [1950]) and Georgescu-Roegen (1979). Economic, political, and environmental systems are seen as dynamic evolving structures, which involve biological and not just physical interactions. This leads to an interest in biological concepts and metaphors, in comparison to those from physics which has become the dominant comparator and methodological influence in economics.

Most prominent among the biological/ecological concepts are ideas of sustainability, resilience, and co-evolutionary development (Gowdy, 1994; Norgaard, 1981, 1987, 1988). In an evolving system, concepts of equilibrium are abstractions for convenience to describe specific states on a path of change. This can be linked to ecosystems as cycles of energy and materials organization, accumulation, destruction, and release (Holling, 1986). At the same time, not all attempts to merge economics and biology are accepted; particularly those of the Chicago School have been rejected (by another ISEE President, John Gowdy, 1987). Among the alternative approaches within ecology and biology, the non-reductionist approaches are to be favored over the atomistic and mechanistic alternatives found in the biology of Richard Dawkins.

Rejecting atomistic and mechanistic explanations as universal truths also leads to opening-up the Pandora's Box of the individual. Rather than regarding the human as some essentially irreducible atomic structure, which should remain unquestioned, the realm of motivation of individuals is revealed and explored. Psychology can then offer tremendous potential for insight into behavior, but only if economists are prepared to learn from, rather than dominate, the subject. Hence Earl (2005) draws the distinction between *economic psychology*, where economists dominate psychological concepts, and *psychological economics*, where they learn from those concepts. Economic psychology consists of economists (for example, Gary Becker from the Chicago School) taking topics from psychology and placing them in the context of constrained optimization or game theory, or psychologists adopting the conceptual framework of mainstream economics. Psychological economics, on the other hand, 'seeks to use inputs from psychology to obtain an enhanced understanding of, and/or an improved ability to predict, behaviour in respect of areas that have normally been viewed as the preserve of economics' (Earl, 2005, p. 911). This is the same methodological outlook as described here for ecological economics – that is, challenging economic approaches which have resisted learning from other disciplines.

Ecological economists believe that with psychological economics, as compared to economic psychology, understanding the nature and consequence of human decision-making becomes richer and more complex. Lexicographic preferences no longer appear as a strange exception to the rule of gross substitution but a relatively normal approach to choice, which may be motivated by non-utilitarian ethics, strong uncertainty, or satisficing behaviour. The needs of individuals can be differentiated from positional affluence. Social norms provide a link between the individual and the societal levels and the role of institutions.

These various insights have direct relevance for how economic growth is perceived to operate as a means for improving the human condition. The ecological economics literature addressing consumption has connected critiques of consumer manipulation by corporations (Galbraith, 1979; Kapp, 1978 [1950]), and the psychological and social roles material consumption plays in a modern market economy (Reisch and Røpke, 2004; Røpke, 1999). The psychological treadmill of material throughput also raises concerns over the scale of growth (Daly, 1991, 1992). This is firmly related to the literature arising from thermodynamics and energy use with its implications for the physical functioning of systems (Georgescu-Roegen, 1971). Interest in this has been expressed through the development of industrial ecology (Ayres and Ayres, 1996), and the concept of an 'industrial metabolism' (Ayres and Simonis, 1994) or a socio-ecological regime (Schandl and Schulz, 2002; Sieferle, 2001). Creation of the modern energy-intensive economy is explained through historical analysis combined with the characterization of specific institutional and governance structures, demographic and spatial patterns of land use, infrastructure networks, and technology. Economic industrial development can then be seen as dependent upon exploiting key non-renewable fuel sources while creating ever-expanding waste streams.

Ecological economics challenges approaches to economics that aim to limit the use of ideas from ecology. Those ideas arose strongly in the 1960s and 1970s, but the momentum was lost until the early 1990s. Ecological economics itself has changed over the last twenty years from just linking ecology and economics to putting forward a range of ideas which are critical of modern economies. They have done this by an interdisciplinary endeavor which requires serious reflection upon world views, concept, metaphors, and models. The field is starting to synthesize ideas and also to reach out to other schools of economic thought – Post Keynesian economics being one of them.

POST KEYNESIAN ECONOMICS AND THE MAINSTREAM

As John King (2002) notes, Post Keynesian economics begins with *The General Theory of Employment, Interest and Money* by John Maynard Keynes (1936). *The General Theory* challenged the foundations of neoclassical economics, explained how and why great depressions are possible, and set forth policy recommendations to deal with important economic problems. While this work is macroeconomic in nature, it contains a number of key principles that can be applied to microeconomic problems in general and to environmental problems specifically. Four principles form the basis of Post Keynesian economics and distinguish it from neoclassical economics: uncertainty, historical time, social rationality, and the importance of income effects. Let's look at each one of these.

Uncertainty

Uncertainty refers to the fact that the future cannot be known as a result of past experiences. As Keynes (1937, p. 213) noted:

> The game of roulette is not subject, in this sense to uncertainty . . . the expectation of life is only slightly uncertain. Even the weather is only moderately uncertain. The sense in which I am using the term is that in which the prospect of a European war is uncertain, or the price of copper and the rate of interest twenty years hence, or the obsolescence of a new innovation, or the position of private wealth owners in the social system in 1970. About these matters there is no scientific basis on which to form any calculable probability whatever. We simply do not know.

In an uncertain world 'animal spirits' or expectations drive the investment decision, and since such behavior can undergo radical transformation, sharp economic fluctuations are possible.

J. Barkley Rosser, Jr (2001) points out that Post Keynesians have two arguments for the prevalence of uncertainty. First, Brian Loasby (1976) and George Shackle (1955, 1972, 1974) note that the world itself is unpredictable and constantly changing; we never know when things will change or how they will change. Moreover, past evidence provides no guidance when events happen infrequently or when we are dealing with situations that extend far into the future. Paul Davidson (1982–83, 1988, 1991, 1996) argues that uncertainty is a characteristic of a non-ergodic world, or the real world in which we live. Systems are ergodic if both their key parameters and structure remain stable over time. In this case, we can extrapolate from the past to the future. Non-ergodic systems experience structural change or parameter changes over time, which means that rational agents cannot figure out what the future is going to be like.

Second, some Post Keynesians (Arestis, 1996; Carabelli, 1988) see uncertainty arising because real-world outcomes depend on the behavior of many other people. The problem is that individual behavior depends on what we expect others to do, and we can never be certain about the behavior of others. Perhaps the best description of this is Keynes's (1936, p. 156) famous beauty contest – where we try to figure out not the most beautiful contestant, but the one that others will think is the most beautiful, knowing that others are also making such calculations. For this reason, our behavior changes based on our expectations of what other people will do. Everyone else is in the same boat and proceeds in the same fashion.

The first view of uncertainty appears in the contributions to this volume of John Gowdy et al. (Chapter 10) and Richard Norgaard (Chapter 4), which have ecosystem models with cycles of energy and materials organization, accumulation, destruction, and release. James Juniper (Chapter 12) and Jerry Courvisanos (Chapter 14) bring out the consequences of the second view of uncertainty in connection with business decisions on environmental innovation and investment policy for sustainable development. They show how group behavior can have a cumulative effect: it can lead to major breakthroughs in environmental investments, or it can result in long-term damage to the environment.

Historical Time

Because the world and individual choices are constantly changing, Post Keynesians hold that economies do not head toward some equilibrium (Robinson, 1974; Kaldor, 1985). Instead, economies evolve over time, and economists must focus on this process. To consider historical time means a commitment to understanding how economic processes function in the real world. History matters in the sense that the past influences subsequent outcomes. This differs markedly from the neoclassical Arrow–Debreu–Mackenzie model, based on logical time, where agents plan for all present and future economic activities, and all economic outcomes are determined simultaneously at a single instant (Holt and Setterfield, 1999). The system moves effortlessly with no track of the processes involved.

While logical time is essentially spatial and mechanical, historical time is social, environmental, and behavioral. Historical time is a unidirectional sequence of events, which puts the present in the context of what has gone on beforehand. This allows for the possibility that 'history matters', in that the past has an influence on subsequent outcomes (Holt, 2005).

As Georgescu-Roegen (1971) pointed out, unlike logical time, historical time is irrevocable; we move strictly from the present to the future. In historical time, if we make a mistake we cannot go back in time and make a better decision. Decisions made now cannot be reversed, except at a great cost. The long period is thus a sequence of paths taken in the short period and does not exist independently of these paths. One famous example of the importance of historical time is the adoption of the QWERTY keyboard, which slowed down typing. When people typed on manual typewriters, individual keys would sometimes hit each other and stick together when one typed too quickly. Under these circumstances a keyboard layout that slowed down typing made sense. Once everyone learned to type on such a keyboard, however, it made sense to continue using it, even when computers replaced typewriters and there was no longer any reason to slow down typists in order to keep keys from jamming (David, 1985).

Social Rationality

We noted above that neoclassical economics sees people as knowing all the options available to them, and the probabilistic outcomes of each choice, and then making decisions to maximize their utility. In contrast, Post Keynesians see individuals confronting uncertainty when they have to make decisions. When people are not sure what they want and what they want to do, it is sensible for them to look around when making decisions and follow the lead of others. For this reason, Post Keynesians have focused on habits and social factors when explaining how people behave.

This work is important for understanding consumer behavior in a world where consumption and individual choices impact upon our environment and the well-being of the planet (see Chapter 9 by Lucia Reisch, Clive Spash and Sabine Bietz). For example, when deciding whether to buy a new car I can choose to buy a family car or a sport utility vehicle (SUV). I might prefer buying a sedan because it is more fuel-efficient than an SUV. However, sedans do not do well in crashes with SUVs. So if there are lots of SUVs on the road, then that is what I will want and that is what I will buy. The problem here is that my preferences are strongly influenced by the decisions of others.

Going further, Post Keynesians have questioned whether the notion of individual rationality actually yields optimal outcomes in the real world, or whether there is a social rationality that makes everyone better off (Pressman, 2004). The difference between individual rationality and social rationality is clearest in the prisoner's dilemma, which shows how two individuals pursuing their own interests wind up in a less than optimal situation. In the prisoner's dilemma, two accused men are captured and put into separate rooms. If neither confesses to their crime, they are forced to go through a lengthy and expensive trial but are likely to get acquitted and go free. If both confess, they each get moderate prison terms. If one confesses but the other does not, then the one who confesses gets off without any penalties while the other prisoner faces a long jail term.

Prisoner's dilemmas are common in everyday life. They are the heart of the free-rider problem. Like the prisoner who confesses, the free-rider does not pay to support community services that everyone regards as desirable, such as clean air and safe streets, figuring that everyone else will contribute and that one less contribution to the common good will make no difference overall. The aggregate outcome, if free-riding is prevalent, is that we lack things that everyone desires because people fail to pay for them on an individualistic basis. This opens the door for government policy: taxes to support public goods and environmental regulations to halt human-induced climate change.

Income Effects

Following Abraham Maslow in psychology, Post Keynesians recognize that people seem to form a hierarchy of needs, with some needs more important than others (see Chapter 7 by Marc Lavoie). At the bottom is the need for survival – we need food, we need shelter, and we need clothing. Next come needs for comforts and social interaction. Finally, there are needs for self-actualization and improvement. As our income increases, and our survival is no longer in jeopardy, we concern ourselves with higher needs such as comforts and friends. This lexicographic ordering limits the ability of prices or substitution effects to change behavior and helps establish the primacy of income effects.

Neoclassical economists see substitution effects as of paramount importance, sometimes to the exclusion of any income effects. Economies are seen as supply-constrained, and therefore price changes and incentives become important to assure that scarce resources get used efficiently. In contrast, and for reasons noted above, Post Keynesians see income effects as more important than substitution effects (Davidson, 2005, p. 459). This is why Post Keynesians focus on income and spending as necessary for full employment, and creating a virtuous cycle of economic and income growth. However, income effects have a larger import than just promoting growth. One consequence of the primacy of income effects is that we cannot rely on the price system to get things right or lead to optimal outcomes. In the real world, prices reflect market power and current short-term perspectives only. They are also affected by speculation. Because prices do not reflect scarcity, we cannot count on prices to deal with current overutilization of resources or to protect the planet from the enhanced greenhouse effect. To take just one example, since the people who will be most affected by human-induced climate change are not alive today, their preferences cannot be taken into account and they cannot spend their money to make sure that a viable planet exists in the future. For the same reason, we cannot rely on current interest rates to discount the future appropriately so that future generations avoid climate problems. Since we cannot rely on the market to get prices right, we must rely on government action to protect the environment. Peter Earl and Tim Wakeley (in Chapter 8) apply this analysis to the case of automobiles and explain that, when it comes to pollution and safety, the government must establish standards to keep our air clean and our cars safe. James Kahn and Alexandre Rivas (in Chapter 13) make a similar argument with respect to sustainable development in rural Amazonia.

POST KEYNESIAN ECONOMICS AND THE ENVIRONMENT

Post Keynesians believe that neoclassical economics with its current methodological approach is *limited* in its ability to analyze the problem of sustainable development in particular and environmental issues in general. The traditional neoclassical approach to environmental issues and sustainable development works from three primary assumptions: 1) reasonable market valuations can be made with non-market environmental goods for cost–benefit analysis; 2) environmental externalities and other forms of market failure associated with the environment can be internalized and corrected by incentive-based policies; 3) different types of capital can be substituted for each other to achieve sustainable development. Post Keynesian economics, with its focus on the role of institutions, radical uncertainty, historical time and its criticism of gross substitution, questions the comprehensiveness of these three assumptions. This does not mean that mainstream economics cannot deal with many environmental issues, but its methodology limits its ability to deal with many of the complexities associated with environmental problems, which can lead to bad public policy.

For example, with the first assumption mentioned neoclassical economics usually gives value on non-market goods by contingent valuation. But what if these surveys do not represent preferences and relative scarcities? The Post Keynesian method of pricing that looks at social practices might be more appropriate, which take into consideration price mark-ups, procedural rationality, and separability of needs. The second assumption is rejected because of radical uncertainty. This undermines the neoclassical policy of environmental modeling, forecasting, and management, which are based on calculating and predicting levels of risk that are needed for incentive-based policies. The Post Keynesian view of radical uncertainty provides them with more options to deal with environmental policies in the real world as they develop models of complex nonlinear dynamics and can use applications of the precautionary principle to derive policies.

The final assumption of substitutability of capital takes us to the Cambridge controversy discussed decades ago by Geoff Harcourt and Joan Robinson (Harcourt, 1972).Within the neoclassical model, time is dealt with by discounting. This raises issues of pricing capital – the ability to come up with an efficient interest rate. Besides the pricing of capital, the Cambridge controversy also dealt with the issue of aggregation of capital (Winnett, 2003, pp. 122–6). The controversy provides insights into the environmental debate concerning a 'weak' or 'strong' definition of sustainability by raising two important questions: a) how do we measure capital and can it be aggregated, and b) what is the substitution potential and effects between different kinds of capital. This leads to a discussion of our ability to aggregate all types of capital which is important in defining sustainability. If you cannot adequately aggregate different types of capital, the neoclassical model has difficulties with allocation and efficient use of resources based on asset valuations and substitution as advocated by the Hartwick–Solow rule, which predicts the optimum extraction and substitution rate needed to sustain all types of capital and resources for sustainability.

Let us now review the different chapters in the book. Some will advocate that Post Keynesian economics is better suited to incorporate sustainability and grasp the real dimensions of environmental problems facing our world today than neoclassical economics.

INDIVIDUAL CONTRIBUTIONS TO THE VOLUME

The contributions that follow were written by both Post Keynesian and ecological economists. These chapters point out numerous links between these two schools and also provide penetrating insights into how more links can be established. Many of these ideas go beyond just showing a connection between ecological and Post Keynesian economics and provide insights for mainstream environmental economics. In the past, we believe, many of these ideas have been blocked from the mainstream for ideological or methodological reasons. But there are signs of change within the profession as cutting-edge economists are questioning the holy trinity of rationality, greed and equilibrium and moving into the innovative work of purposeful behavior, enlightened self-interest and sustainability (Colander et al., 2004a, 2004b, 2010). The following chapters capture some of that change.

Chapter 2, by Andrew Mearman, deals with recent developments in Post Keynesian methodology and their implications for ecological economics. It focuses on realism and ontology, open systems, the implications of ontology for uncertainty, and arguments for pluralism of method. Mearman then discusses how these methodological views affect our understanding and study of ecological problems. This means that our concepts such as natural capital may need to be reconsidered, and tools that rely on long-term predictability or certainty must be questioned. The chapter implies that one must be sceptical about current methods employed in environmental economics, including long chains of deduction and mathematical modelling, as well as concepts such as equilibrium and optimization.

In Chapter 3 Clive Spash and Heinz Schandl discuss some areas of overlap and some areas of disagreement between Post Keynesian and ecological economics. Both schools recognize the importance of historical time and that the future is uncertain, and both schools recognize that institutions matter. In contrast to these areas of agreement, the chapter also raises questions about whether the Post Keynesian focus on economic growth misses the most important message of ecological economics: that economic growth has serious negative consequences for the environment and for society.

In Chapter 4 Richard Norgaard discusses some of the problems with contemporary environmental economics. This subfield within neoclassical economics was designed to help fine-tune the economy in response to environmental challenges. However, Norgaard argues, the problems of human-induced climate change and ecosystem transformation make it clear that the economy needs to be set on a whole new track.

Unfortunately, standard economic analysis provides little guidance on how to do this. Economists have been strong defenders of the economic status quo, and their defense relies on complex, highly fragmented and contradictory myths. On a more positive note, Norgaard hopes that an assessment of the standard economic approach to the environment, along the lines of the *Intergovernmental Panel on Climate Change and Millennium Ecosystem Assessment*, can help us understand how traditional economic analysis blinds us to environmental problems and supports the economic status quo.

In Chapter 5 Robert Scott discusses the contributions of Kenneth Boulding, an early figure behind the development of modern ecological economics. Boulding recognized that the environment is a dynamic system and that it encompasses the economy, rather than being a part of the economy. Boulding identified the Earth as a closed, finite system that must be managed in order to sustain human life and the economy. He adopted a transdisciplinary approach to studying the economics of the environment that drew on many social and hard sciences. The chapter then goes on to argue that many of the key tenets of ecological economics established by Boulding are largely consistent with those of Post Keynesian economics – particularly the importance of uncertainty and historical time in decision-making, and redefining economic growth so that it takes into consideration environmental sustainability.

Chapter 6, by Arild Vatn, explores similarities and differences across three heterodox economics traditions: Post Keynesian, ecological and institutional economics. All three traditions developed in reaction to deficiencies in mainstream economics and have much in common. They are all systems-oriented, they emphasize complexity and uncertainty, they base their models on bounded rationality, they emphasize incommensurable and lexicographic value structures, they see preferences as endogenous to the economic system, they emphasize that substitution possibilities are restricted, and they share an interest in studying the role of power in economic processes. Nevertheless, the three schools have some fundamental differences. The greatest conflict, according to Vatn, seems to be in the Post Keynesian focus on economic growth as a way to solve urgent problems, while ecological economists explore the limits to growth, seeing growth as a potential cause of problems.

In Chapter 7, Marc Lavoie sets forth the Post Keynesian theory of consumer choice. This theory arises from a multitude of influences, including socio-economics, psychology, marketing specialists, and individuals such as Herbert Simon and Georgescu-Roegen, who were aware of the complexity of our environment. It also arises from the disparate clues left by the founders of Post Keynesian economics. Despite its neglect among

Post Keynesians, Lavoie shows that there exists a Post Keynesian theory of consumer choice, based on the principles of procedural rationality; satiable needs; separability, growth and subordination of needs; non-independence, and heredity.

Chapter 8, by Peter Earl and Tim Wakeley, looks at how to reduce greenhouse gas emissions from automobiles; however, its arguments can be applied to other areas as well. This chapter argues that government intervention in the form of standards is a more effective way to reduce the environmental consequences of consumption than changing relative prices. In the mainstream view, environmental policy focuses on overcoming market failures and allowing the price mechanism to generate an efficient set of prices. One problem with this view is its presupposition of rational choice and its assumption that the initial distribution of property rights has been settled fairly. In addition, as Keynes (1936, Chapter 19) argued, freeing up relative prices was no guarantee that coordination problems would be solved.

In Chapter 9, Lucia Reisch, Clive Spash and Sabine Bietz point out the challenges to designing institutions that can move us towards a more sustainable economy. These authors explore how behavioral changes in everyday consumption patterns might be addressed. They do this by presenting a case study called Project Balance, which involves an attempt to improve interest in sustainable behavior in Germany using the mass media. The aim of this project was to raise the level of engagement with sustainable consumption issues among those who were poorly informed and disinterested. The study monitored and provided analysis from media, marketing, and consumer research perspectives. The authors report initial consumer research results and discuss some of the implications.

Chapter 10 by John Gowdy, Mario Giampietro, Jesus Ramos-Martin and Kozo Mayumi claims that economic theory is currently in a state of disarray because neoclassical welfare economics collapsed in the face of empirical evidence that *Homo economicus* offered a poor description of actual human behavior and led to erroneous predictions and policy disasters. In response, this chapter extends the Post Keynesian model of production to include the biophysical nature of human activity. The energy and mineral bonanza of the twentieth century put the issue of biophysical limits on the back burner for neoclassical and heterodox economists alike. However, that is changing with issues of resource scarcity and environmental degradation. They describe a new approach to the study of economic production called 'Multi-Scale Integrated Analysis of Societal Metabolism'. They then report an application of the method to the case of China making a transition to a sustainable modern economy.

In Chapter 11 J. Barkley Rosser, Jr considers the implications of complex ecological economic dynamics from a Post Keynesian perspective. Rosser argues that catastrophic, chaotic, and other complex dynamics reinforce the conceptual foundations of the Keynesian notion of uncertainty. He also shows that predator–prey models can be linked to Post Keynesian macrodynamic models. He then shows how these can be linked to ecological models, which include fisheries, forestry, lake dynamics, and global climatic–economic dynamics.

Chapter 12 by James Juniper draws on the work of Michael Porter, which addresses the potential for corporations to meet stringent environmental regulations and at the same time improve their competitive advantage. The work of Porter needs to be linked with two other strands of research to make a case for the viability of stringent environmental regulations. First, the literature on smart or responsive regulation argues that regulation is needed to provide pressure to innovate and to promote innovation that is environmentally friendly. Second, the Post Keynesian literature argues that government deficit spending is necessary to guarantee that there will be demand for environmentally friendly consumer goods. Such deficit spending would help achieve full employment and adequate demand by guaranteeing (largely) full-time jobs within the public sector.

In Chapter 13 James Kahn and Alexandre Rivas attempt to bridge the gap between ecological economics and Post Keynesian economics by looking at how ecological services, social capital and human capital can help achieve sustainable development in a developing country. The chapter argues that when the importance of environmental capital is recognized, one must look at the growth process in a fundamentally different way, especially when considering the economic development of indigenous and traditional peoples. This chapter contributes to the Post Keynesian perspective by showing that the consideration of environmental capital, its potentially irreversible destruction and the non-substitutability of other types of capital for environmental capital, leads to important path-dependency problems. The contributors' model is illustrated with case studies from the Rio Negro region of Amazonas, Brazil.

Finally, Chapter 14 by Jerry Courvisanos introduces a dynamic satisficing framework based on the work of Adolph Lowe and Michał Kalecki. The first half of this chapter argues that optimization strategies fail to address two failures at the core of capitalism: the fundamental instability in economic activity and the inappropriate use of the technology embedded in the capital structures. This undermines any effective investment policy towards sustainable development, but provides an opportunity for a major contribution from a non-optimal perspective. The second part of this chapter uses Post Keynesian principles to set forth some steps toward a sustainable development investment policy. It emphasizes that optimality needs to be replaced by satisficing for future development that guides and supports broad economic–ecological institutional settings. Clear ecological goals set for the long-term future are a prerequisite in this framework.

NOTE

1. Work in this area of psychological and irrational behavior has mostly been carried out by economic research in behavioral economics. Recent examples would include Richard H. Thaler and Cass R. Sunstein, *Nudge: Improving Decisions About Health, Wealth and Happiness* (Yale University Press, 2008) and George A. Akerlof and Robert J. Shiller, *Animal Spirits: How Human Psychology Drives the Economy, and Why It Matters for Global Capitalism* (Princeton University Press, 2009).

REFERENCES

Arestis, P. (1996), 'Post-Keynesian economics: towards coherence', *Cambridge Journal of Economics*, **20**, 111–35.
Ayres, R.U. and L.W. Ayres (1996), *Industrial Ecology: Towards Closing the Materials Cycle*, Cheltenham, UK and Northampton, MA, USA: Edward Elgar.
Ayres, R.U. and U.E. Simonis (eds), (1994), *Industrial Metabolism: Restructuring for Sustainable Development*, Tokyo: United Nations University Press.
Boulding, K. (1966), 'The economics of the coming spaceship earth', in H. Jarrett (ed.), *Environmental Quality in a Growing Economy*, Baltimore, MD: Johns Hopkins University Press, pp. 3–15.
Carabelli, A. (1988), *On Keynes's Method*, London: Palgrave Macmillan.
Clawson, M. and J.L. Knetsch (1966), *Economics of Outdoor Recreation*, Baltimore, MD and London: Johns Hopkins University Press.
Colander, D., R.P.F. Holt and J.B. Rosser, Jr (2004a), *The Changing Face of Economics: Conversations with Cutting Edge Economists*, Ann Arbor, MI: University of Michigan Press.
Colander, D., R.P.F. Holt and J.B. Rosser, Jr (2004b), 'The changing face of mainstream economics', *Review of Political Economy*, **16** (4), 485–99.
Colander, D., R.P.F. Holt and J.B. Rosser, Jr (2010), *European Economics at a Crossroads*, Cheltenham, UK and Northampton, MA, USA: Edward Elgar.
Cummings, R.G., D.S. Brookshire and W.D. Schulze (eds) (1986), *Valuing Environmental Goods: An Assessment of the Contingent Valuation Method*, Totowa, NJ: Rowman & Allanheld.
Daly, H. (1977), *Steady-State Economics*, San Francisco: W.H. Freeman.
Daly, H. (1991), 'Towards an environmental macroeconomics', *Land Economics*, **67** (2), 255–9.
Daly, H. (1992), *Steady-State Economics*, 2nd edn, London: Earthscan.
d'Arge, R.C. (1979), 'Climate and economic activity', in *Proceedings of the World Climate Conference*, Geneva: World Meteorological Organization, pp. 652–81.
d'Arge, R.C., W.D. Schulze and D.S. Brookshire (1982), 'Carbon dioxide

and intergenerational choice', *American Economic Association Papers and Proceedings*, **72** (2), 251–6.
David, P. (1985), 'Clio and the economics of QWERTY', *American Economic Review*, **75**, 332–7.
Davidson, P. (1982–83), 'Rational expectations: a fallacious foundation for studying crucial decision-making processes', *Journal of Post Keynesian Economics*, **5**, 182–97.
Davidson, P. (1988), 'A technical definition of uncertainty and the long-run non-neutrality of money', *Cambridge Journal of Economics*, **12**, 329–37.
Davidson, P. (1991), 'Is probability theory relevant for uncertainty?', *Journal of Economic Perspectives*, **5**, 129–43.
Davidson, P. (1996), 'Reality and economic theory', *Journal of Post Keynesian Economics*, **18**, 479–508.
Davidson, P. (2005), 'The Post Keynesian school', in B. Snowdon and H. Vane (eds), *Modern Macroeconomics: Its Origins, Development and Current State*, Cheltenham, UK and Northampton, MA, USA: Edward Elgar, pp. 451–73.
Earl, P. (2005), 'Economics and psychology in the twenty-first century', *Cambridge Journal of Economics*, **29** (6), 909–26.
Funtowicz, S.O. and J.R. Ravetz (1993), 'Science for the post-normal age', *Futures*, **25** (7), 739–55.
Galbraith, J.K. (1979), *The New Industrial State*, Harmondsworth, UK: Penguin.
Georgescu-Roegen, N. (1971), *The Entropy Law and the Economic Process*, Cambridge, MA: Harvard University Press.
Georgescu-Roegen, N. (1979), 'Methods in economic science', *Journal of Economic Issues*, **13** (2), 317–28.
Gowdy, J.M. (1987), 'Bio-economics: social economy versus the Chicago school', *International Journal of Social Economics*, **14** (1), 32–42.
Gowdy, J. (1994), *Coevolutionary Economics: The Economy, Society and the Environment*, Dordrecht: Kluwer.
Greenwood, D. and R. Holt (2008), 'Institutional and ecological economics: the role of technology and institutions in economic development', *Journal of Economic Issues*, **42** (2), 445–52.
Harcourt, G.C. (1972), *Some Cambridge Controversies in the Theory of Capital*, Cambridge: Cambridge University Press.
Holling, C.S. (1986), 'The resilience of terrestrial ecosystems: local surprise and global change', in W. Clark and R. Munn (eds), *Sustainable Development of the Biosphere*, Cambridge: Cambridge University Press, pp. 292–317.
Holt, R. (2005), 'Post-Keynesian economics and sustainable development', *International Journal of Environment, Workplace and Employment*, **1** (2), 174–86.
Holt, R. and M. Setterfield (1999), 'Time', in P. O'Hara (ed.), *Encyclopedia of Political Economy*, London: Routledge, pp. 1158–61.
Kaldor, N. (1985), *Economics without Equilibrium*, Armonk, NY: M.E. Sharpe.
Kapp, K.W. (1978 [1950]), *The Social Costs of Business Enterprise*, 3rd edn, Nottingham: Spokesman.
Keynes, J.M. (1936), *The General Theory of Employment, Interest and Money*, London: Macmillan.
Keynes, J.M. (1937), 'The general theory of employment', *Quarterly Journal of Economics*, **51**, 209–23.
King, J. (2002), *A History of Post Keynesian Economics since 1936*, Cheltenham, UK and Northampton, MA, USA: Edward Elgar.

Kneese, A.V., R.U. Ayres and R.C. d'Arge (1970), *Economics and the Environment: A Materials Balance Approach*, Washington, DC: Resources for the Future.
Kneese, A.V. and W.D. Schulze (1985), 'Ethics and environmental economics', in A.V. Kneese and J.L. Sweeney (eds), *Handbook of Natural Resource and Energy Economics, Volume I*, Amsterdam: Elsevier, pp. 191–220.
Krutilla, J.V. (1967), 'Conservation reconsidered', *American Economic Review*, **57** (4), September, 777–86.
Krutilla, J.V. and A.C. Fisher (1978), *The Economics of Natural Environments: Studies in the Valuation of Commodity and Amenity Resources*, Baltimore, MD: Johns Hopkins University Press.
Loasby, B. (1976), *Choice, Complexity and Ignorance*, Cambridge: Cambridge University Press.
Martinez-Alier, J. (2002), *The Environmentalism of the Poor: A Study of Ecological Conflicts and Valuation*, Cheltenham, UK and Northampton, MA, USA: Edward Elgar.
Meadows, D., D. Meadows, J. Randers and W. Behrens III (1972), *The Limits to Growth*, New York: Universe Books.
Mishan, E. (1969), *Growth: The Price We Pay*, London: Staples Press.
Norgaard, R. (1981), 'Sociosystem and ecosystem coevolution in the Amazon', *Journal of Environmental Economics and Management*, **8**, 238–54.
Norgaard, R. (1987), 'Economics as mechanics and the demise of biological diversity', *Ecological Modelling*, **38**, 107–21.
Norgaard, R. (1988), 'Sustainable development: a co-evolutionary view', *Futures*, **20**, 606–62.
Norgaard, R. (1989), 'The cast for methodological pluralism', *Ecological Economics*, **1**, 37–57.
Norgaard, R. (1994), *Development Betrayed: The End of Progress and a Coevolutionary Revisioning of the Future*, London: Routledge.
Perrings, C. (1987), *Economy and Environment*, Cambridge: Cambridge University Press.
Perrings, C. (1997), *Economics of Ecological Resources: Selected Essays*, Cheltenham, UK and Northampton, MA, USA: Edward Elgar.
Pressman, S. (2004), 'The two dogmas of neoclassical economics', *Science & Society*, **68**, 483–93.
Reisch, L. and I. Røpke (2004), *The Ecological Economics of Consumption*, Cheltenham, UK and Northampton, MA, USA: Edward Elgar.
Robinson, J. (1974), *History versus Equilibrium*, London: Thames Polytechnic.
Røpke, I. (1999), 'The dynamics of willingness to consume', *Ecological Economics*, **28** (3), 399–420.
Rosser, J.B. (2001), 'Uncertainty and expectations', in R. Holt and S. Pressman (eds), *A New Guide to Post Keynesian Economics*, London and New York: Routledge, pp. 52–64.
Schandl, H. and N. Schulz (2002), 'Changes in the United Kingdom's natural relations in terms of society's metabolism and land use from 1850 to the present day', *Ecological Economics*, **41** (2), 203–21.
Schulze, W.D. and D.S. Brookshire (1982), 'Intergenerational ethics and the depletion of fossil fuels', in J. Quirk, K. Terasawa and D. Whipple (eds), *Coal Models and their Use in Government Planning*, New York: Praeger, pp. 159–78.
Schulze, W.D., D.S. Brookshire and T. Sandler (1981), 'The social rate of discount

for nuclear waste storage: economics or ethics', *Natural Resources Journal*, **21** (4), 811–32.
Shackle, G. (1955), *Uncertainty in Economics and Other Reflections*, Cambridge: Cambridge University Press.
Shackle, G. (1972), *Epistemics and Economics*, Cambridge: Cambridge University Press.
Shackle, G. (1974), *Keynesian Kaleidics*, Edinburgh: Edinburgh University Press.
Sieferle, R.P. (2001), *The Subterranean Forest: Energy Systems and the Industrial Revolution*, Cambridge: White Horse Press.
Spash, C.L. (1999), 'The development of environmental thinking in economics', *Environmental Values*, **8** (4), 413–35.
Spash, C.L. (2008) Contingent valuation design and data treatment: if you can't shoot the messenger, change the message', *Environment & Planning C: Government & Policy*, **26** (1), 34–53.
Winnett, Adrian (2003), 'Environmental economics', in J.E. King (ed.), *The Elgar Companion to Post Keynesian Economics*, Cheltenham, UK and Northampton, MA, USA: Edward Elgar, pp. 122–6.
Wynne, B. (1994), 'Scientific knowledge and the global environment', in M. Redclift and T. Benton (eds), *Social Theory and the Global Environment*, London: Routledge, pp. 169–89.

PART II

Methodology and History of Thought

2. Recent developments in Post Keynesian methodology and their relevance for understanding environmental issues

Andrew Mearman

INTRODUCTION

Until quite recently, Post Keynesian economics has had relatively little to say about the economics of the environment (Mearman, 2005a, 2005b). Much of this new work stems from a methodological critique of neoclassical economics, borrowing heavily from the philosophy of science as well as economic methodology, and from increased awareness of and concern for the environment.

The methodological developments are located in three main literatures, all of which have a potential impact on how Post Keynesians understand environmental issues. First, the recent rediscovery of Keynes's writings on philosophy and ethics have led to a fresh interpretation of his economics. Especially important is the *Treatise on Probability* (Keynes, 1921), which contains a critique of existing theories of probability and develops an alternative theory. This work has led to a better understanding of methodology, of uncertainty, and of assorted theoretical issues, such as the role and existence of money in the economy.

Two literatures, both inspired by Keynes, are more controversial. These are not universally accepted by Post Keynesians, many of whom regard them as incorrect, or at best distracting from theoretical and empirical work.

Babylonianism,[1] developed principally by Sheila Dow, holds that science does not search out great truth claims; rather, the aim of theory is explanation and understanding. The nature of reality, comprising organic, complex and open systems, dictates that complete explanations are impossible. The Babylonian approach shares much with that of Keynes. Indeed, Keynes's approach might be described as Babylonian; he even used the term to describe Newton's actual approach to scientific enquiry (Keynes,

1972a, p. 364). However, it should be noted that many Post Keynesians view Babylonianism with suspicion, claiming it is insufficiently rigorous, eclectic and incoherent (Davidson, 2003–04; Dow, 2005; Holt, 2007).

Even more controversial has been Critical Realism, a philosophy developed by Roy Bhaskar (1978, 1979). Bhaskar provided an argument for a reality existing independent of our present conception of it, which has depth, and is open. Observable events and experiences, the initial focus of science, are thus the products of causal mechanisms operating 'beneath' the observable surface reality. Both the social and natural sciences seek to identify these mechanisms. Critical Realism has been brought to economics by Tony Lawson (1997, 2003). It shares many concerns of Keynes and Babylonianism. Its main contribution to economics has been to urge that a greater prominence be given to ontology. Lawson (1997) uses Critical Realism to argue against mathematical and statistical techniques (except in highly unlikely circumstances). There are, of course, critiques of Critical Realism; one prominent criticism is that it is unable to inform empirical work (Downward, 2003).

This chapter examines these methodological developments and draws out their implications for a Post Keynesian economics of the environment. It is beyond the scope of this chapter to argue for a single Post Keynesian methodology for environmental economics or to contrast this with existing alternatives, such as (neoclassical) environmental economics or (non-neoclassical) ecological economics.[2] Rather, we consider several common themes that straddle the Post Keynesian methodological literatures: (1) a focus on realism and ontology; (2) a view that reality is organic and comprises complex 'open systems'; (3) how recent methodological developments reinforce the Post Keynesian concept of uncertainty; and (4) the implications for choice of method, specifically arguments for pluralism and the mixing of methods. Each of these will be considered in turn and related to a Post Keynesian economics of the environment.

REALISM AND ONTOLOGY

There is considerable debate about the extent of realism (as opposed to subjectivism) in Keynes's theory of probability (Keynes, 1972b; Bateman, 1987); but both Babylonianism and Critical Realism adopt the precept of both common sense and scientific realism that there is a reality existing independent of our particular investigation of it. They agree that while it is reasonable to argue that our perceptions of reality, our actions upon it, and our understanding of it, are complex, there is a reality to be studied. It would seem strange to argue that tigers or ecosystems or pollution are social constructions. Yes, our understanding of them is mediated by social activity; for example, our concern for, and actions towards, tigers reflect the value put on them by society.[3] But that is not the same as claiming that our theories about them actually create them. Nevertheless, it is worth restating this basic realist principle because of the influence of constructivist thought in economics, which sometimes argues that reality is purely a social construct with no material element. A Post Keynesian environmental analysis must take this realism seriously, which means engaging in ontological analysis.

Recognizing the importance of ontology reinforces the Post Keynesian belief that theories should be realistic – they must refer to real things and have some basis in reality. In that sense, Post Keynesian economics shares one of the main strengths of ecological economics, which is that an understanding of the object of knowledge and of ecological concepts informs economic concepts. Existing economic concepts are rejected if they are unable to illuminate ecological factors. Post Keynesians claim that its realism is an advantage in environmental economics. Orthodox treatments accept that there is a reality, but are less concerned that their theories are realistic; they are happy to use convenient fictions, such as the notion of a rational economic person maximizing their utility. A similar concern for realism exists in ecological economics. For example, Gowdy (2007) argues that models of the consumer in environmental analysis should capture behavioural regularities supported by experimental results.

How might this affect a Post Keynesian economics of the environment? The capital controversy of the 1950s and 1960s (see Harcourt, 1972) provides a suggestion. The controversy focused on the possibility of an aggregate production function, and on the possibility of valuing aggregate capital and the profit rate independently. This debate showed that calculating capital stock depends on the profit rate, which itself depends on the valuation of the capital stock. As a result, aggregate capital stock was considered infeasible along with aggregate production functions. While the capital controversy centred on several theoretical curiosa, an essential element of the debate was an ontological concern about whether capital was homogeneous and perfectly malleable in historically reversible ways. Neoclassical economists advocated such a conception, whereas Post Keynesians argued that capital is more inflexible and heterogeneous.

The capital controversy may have implications for the concept of natural capital. 'Natural capital' is a term developed mainly by ecological economists. It means: 'the whole endowment of land and resources available to us, including . . . the ecological life-support systems that make economic activity . . . possible' (Harris, 2002, p. 122).[4] Natural capital may be useful for measuring whether natural resources and ecosystems are being eroded, and therefore whether development is sustainable. Ecological economists also distinguish between critical and non-critical natural capital, to stress how crucial some resources are (Spash and Clayton, 1997, p. 148).

From the perspective of the capital controversies, however, we must question the notion of natural capital since it attempts to measure the aggregate stock of a vast number of heterogeneous objects. While man-made capital is reproducible in an identical form, natural capital is not. Further, when some natural capital is critical, and other natural capital is not, how could they be compared and measured? The natures of natural capital and man-made capital might be so different as to render them incommensurate. Likewise for different types of natural capital.[5] Further problems arise in trying to value such a stock. All this creates difficulties for environmental analysis. Such criticisms significantly undermine further concepts, such as weak sustainability, which holds that man-made physical and natural capital can be easily substituted. Weak sustainability is undermined as a concept, because it holds that a decrease in natural capital should be compensated for by an increase in physical capital. However, if the two types of capital are essentially different, it is difficult to see how they could be compared and even further how we could substitute one for another.

ORGANICISM AND OPEN SYSTEMS

Realism also has implications for studying the environment: particularly in relation to organicism and open systems. As his work on probability evolved, Keynes adopted an organic ontology. Drawing on Winslow (1993), we can imagine Keynes's ontology as involving internal (necessary) relations. An internal relation is one in which an entity A is defined (partly) in terms of another entity B. Thus, we can talk of internal relations between polluter, pollutant and polluted, predator and prey, input and output, invader and invaded, and so on. Social examples of internal relations include landlord–tenant, master–slave and employer–employee. Babylonianism also explicitly adopts organicism. There may be parallels between this literature and ecological economics; for example, Norgaard (1984, p. 169) notes that neoclassical approaches assume the separability of factors of production.

The concept of organicism has now been superseded by the concept of open systems. While Post Keynesians freely use the term 'open systems', its meaning is far from clear and varies considerably among users. Indeed, there are a number of different treatments of open systems, all with distinct advantages. Their nature is discussed further below. Open systems are

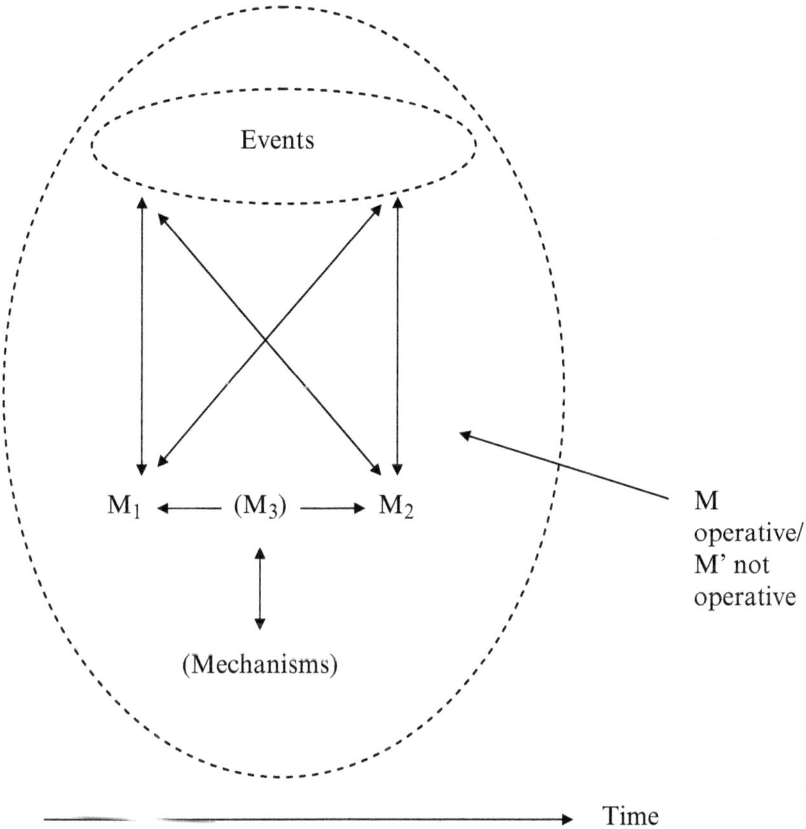

Figure 2.1 An open-system ontology

consistent with organicism, with Keynes's position, with Babylonianism, with Critical Realism, and with other Post Keynesian perspectives such as Davidson's work on nonergodicity, complexity theory and general systems theory.

Figure 2.1 displays a possible way to conceptualize open systems. This example is only illustrative; it is perhaps most useful as a vehicle for discussing some of the main characteristics of open systems and their implications.

The system has a boundary, which is permeable and shows how system throughput is normal and necessary for the system's survival. The permeable boundary allows the impact of external causal factors to be felt inside the system. There is no assumption that external factors can be excluded, and so the objects inside the system are not isolated. In contrast, economics tends to treat outside factors as an inconvenience for their models. This is justified as a necessary abstraction, but in fact they make assumptions that deny the nature of the system in question.

Systems are sets of entities and the relations between them. From organicism, we know that some relations may be internal; and from complex adaptive systems, we know that some relations may be internal, while others are external. Because the system moves through time, entities within the system evolve over time, as do relations between them. Furthermore, over time the entities may act in different ways, combine in different ways and create new emergent phenomena. The history of the system therefore matters in understanding its current state. For this reason, the system is shown with a time arrow. Of course, the importance of history to economic analysis has been emphasized by Post Keynesian economists (for example, Robinson, 1980). Similarly, ecological economics has stressed history – for instance through the co-evolution of systems (Norgaard, 1984, 1988).

As stated above, one aspect of recent work in Post Keynesian methodology has been to shift the focus of analysis onto ontological concepts, such as structure and mechanism. In the system being discussed, the entities found may be structured. These structured entities may be very different from each other in nature. For example, a human and a fish are both structured entities but are very different. Causal mechanisms or processes (such as M_1 and M_2 in Figure 2.1) may be contained within these structures. They may act independently, or (and perhaps differently at different times) in combination, creating events. Other events also may trigger mechanisms to operate; this is why the vertical arrows shown in Figure 2.1 are two-way arrows. Furthermore, the objects may be internally related (or organic), and this relationship itself may have a causal function (M_3). For example, in trying to explain fish stocks, one mechanism may be the actions of the fisherman and another mechanism the actions of other fish; these relationships affect the final outcome.

However, these mechanisms may not always operate. Mechanisms inside the system may operate intermittently, thereby creating uncertainty about and within the system. Similarly, mechanisms outside the system may not always operate to affect the system. In the diagram, M/M' represents the on-(M)-and-off (M') nature of mechanisms. Thus, there is a focus on potentialities and not just actualities. In addition, the ways in which causal mechanisms combine also change over time.

Another important concept is ontological depth. Causal mechanisms lying beneath the level of events operate to change the system. Conceptualizing the nature of reality in this way has specific implications. First, the ecological dimension of the economy is clearly acknowledged. Given that the open system contains depth, it must automatically include the ecological. It is therefore incorrect to envisage the economic and the ecological as separate spheres (see Figure 2.2a), as is common in environmental economics. The concept of depth also enriches all the approaches seeking to embed the economic within the ecological (see Figure 2.2b). In formulations such as Figure 2.2b, reality could be flat: the economy draws from the ecology which surrounds it. Depth requires us to think of the economic as embedded in and (at a higher level) emergent from the ecological. That still allows one to envisage the economic reacting back on the ecological. For this reason we draw the two-way arrows in Figure 2.2c.

Moreover, beneath the mechanisms shown in the diagram, there are further levels. Economic events are determined by combinations of economic mechanisms, but also political, social and psychological mechanisms, which are in turn all affected by the biological, chemical and physical mechanisms. Therefore, any ecological feature or event is complexly determined by a range of causal mechanisms located at various layers of reality. Take the pollution of a river. One can construct a causal sequence as a story of how the pollution occurred and what its effects were. A physical process of production has created a toxic effluent. This is partly a product of the physical and chemical mechanisms (and hence engineering). The economic mechanisms are those causing (in the sense of a temporal causal sequence) a particular productive technology to be chosen. Class relations may also affect the choice of technology. The physical and chemical output also affects the biological nature of the river and humans. The chemical in the river harms organic elements in the river, such as fish, and anything else that consumes the water or the fish. The pollution may cause ill health and the loss of enjoyment from activities related to the river, such as swimming or fishing. The fact that the pollution is noticed is the result of social mechanisms that value rivers and create institutional structures for monitoring them. The impulse to act against pollution is, in turn, partly psychological and partly cultural (it may emanate from religious or other cultural norms).

This story is familiar to economists. What does the concept of ontological depth add? Principally, it impels comprehending the pollution as not merely a causal sequence of events, in which an event occurs and leads directly to another event (like one billiard ball striking another), but in terms of layers of reality with different causal mechanisms. Further, the higher layers in the overall structure, such as the economic, are dependent on lower levels such as physical structure; but they also have their own properties which are emergent from the lower.

This conceptual framework provides a broader and deeper apparatus for understanding reality than those approaches that focus on the economic as a separate entity. It is impossible to ignore the bigger picture in

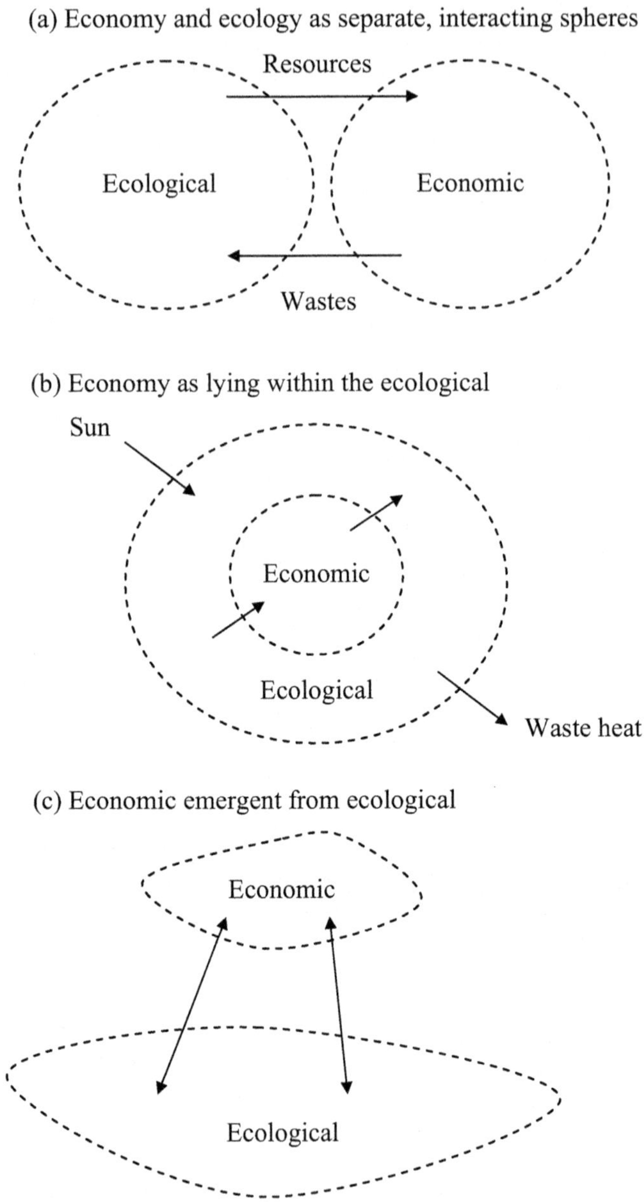

Sources: (a) See, for example, Common (1988, p. 13, Fig 1.4); (b) adapted from Harris (2002, p. 8, Fig. 1.2).

Figure 2.2 The economic and the ecological: contrasting conceptions

explaining an apparently economic effect. Such a wider view is crucial in dealing with highly complex ecological issues. That does not mean that an economist must understand every detail of every aspect at every layer of reality, but neither can all these layers be ignored. An economist informed by this view must pay more attention to the interaction between the economy and ecology.

Methodologically this has important implications. Most of the time, economists ignore the underlying physical to focus on the economic, and claim that this is a necessary abstraction. However, taking ecological considerations into account, this abstraction is clearly not justified. Every production decision has irreducible ecological dimensions and implications. It could even be argued that classical economists recognized this (Christensen, 2005). As an aside, methodologically this could mean that an economic analysis of the environment is necessarily interdisciplinary; it must take information from other disciplines to inform its own judgements. Further, the lessons from methodological developments such as those found in Kuhn (1962) and Babylonianism, as well as arguments for pluralism, suggest that strategies of economic imperialism are unlikely to be successful.

However, analysis in terms of depth and causal mechanisms means that it is important to focus on mechanisms, and their potential activity and effects (and their interaction with other mechanisms). This changes the policy focus. The key ontological questions are: (1) Which mechanisms exist? (2) How are mechanisms triggered? and (3) Can structures be created with mechanisms that produce better outcomes?

That is not to say that the framework described here is without flaws. The concept of depth does not let us determine the mechanisms that are most important. Clearly, when applied to the environment, this is crucial. Some mechanisms may be crucial to life, or death, and thus there is a hierarchy of mechanisms to consider. There is an analogy here with lexicographic preferences, which imply that substitutability between goods is not complete (van den Bergh et al., 2000; Gelso and Peterson, 2005). Lexicographic preferences are a staple of Post Keynesian consumer theory (see Lavoie, 1992, *passim*).

The ontology outlined may have other implications for economics generally, and for an economics of the environment specifically. For example, the concept of equilibrium appears problematic. Equilibrium has been a concern of Post Keynesians since at least Kregel (1976) and Robinson (1974). Equilibrium encompasses multiple, very different senses, including expectations being met, a balance of forces, an equality of two quantities and no tendency to change. While some meanings of the term (for example, 'stability') are easier to support in an open system (if only because people act to create stability), others are weak. It might be possible for individual expectations to be met, but only by luck because the current actions of agents make the construction of probability distributions very difficult (see below). Similarly, given emergence, it is difficult to conceive of equilibrium as the end of an economic process. Questioning the concept of equilibrium also raises questions about economics. In the context of the environment, many concepts are thrown into doubt. For example, all notions of optimization must be questioned. This has a considerable impact on environmental economics, and even on ecological economics (where optimum is a less popular concept, but still used).

UNCERTAINTY

The second implication of recent methodological work for the study of the environment concerns uncertainty. It is clear that environmental analysis and decision-making are dogged by uncertainty. All economists would accept that. However, Post Keynesians have long taken a particular view on uncertainty – that it is non-probabilistic. This point is well established in Paul Davidson's work (1994), which stresses the non-ergodic nature of the world. Davidson claims that through crucial decisions (those that are irreversible or difficult to reverse) future possibilities are changed, and thus probability distributions for future events are impossible to formulate. That has implications for economic modelling and for the economy. It explains the existence of money as something people seek to hold as a store of wealth during uncertain times (Keynes, 1936, Chapter 17); and it means that individual agents make decisions based not on rational calculation, but often on a whim. Davidson's view is itself rooted in Keynes's work on probability. Recent developments in Post Keynesian methodology have refocused attention on Keynes and provide ontological support for his views.

Keynes's theory of probability is based on the formation of a logical relation between an a priori reasonable hypothesis and evidence related to that hypothesis. Consider a prediction about the rate of economic growth in the UK 20 years from now. This cannot be derived from a past frequency distribution because the conditions under which the past frequencies occurred no longer hold. Long-term prediction in particular is therefore difficult. Hence, Keynes's (1937, pp. 213–4) comment that: 'the prospect of a European war is uncertain, or the price of copper and the rate of interest twenty years hence . . . About these matters there is no scientific basis on which to form any calculable probability whatever. We simply do not know.' Keynes's probability is concerned 'with what it is rational to believe given the evidence' (Lawson, 1985, p. 118), rather than with what is 'out there'. Agents are held to form, on the basis of induction, a degree of rational belief in a hypothesis, which itself is formed by analogy. Although Keynes (1921) did not define uncertainty, for him, and *contra* mainstream economics, uncertainty is not a probabilistic concept. Probability helps define uncertainty, since there is a correspondence between certainty and knowledge of a probability relation, and therefore uncertainty can be defined as the absence of such knowledge.

Agents form probability estimates about outcomes but also a weight, similar to a degree of confidence (not to be confused with the statistical concept of confidence interval – see Franklin, 2001), that they have in those estimates. If a probability carries a low weight, that probability is likely to be unstable. Keynes (1936, p. 148) notes that:

> The state of long-term expectation, upon which our decisions are based, does not solely depend, therefore, on the most probable forecast we can make. It also depends on the *confidence* with which we make this forecast – on how highly we rate the likelihood of our best forecast turning out quite wrong.

Keynes's theory of probability, and its subsequent interpretation and expansion, provide a theory of action – agents consider likelihood plus confidence, or probability plus weight. When weight is low, Keynes argues, investors will be driven by factors such as convention, whims, 'animal spirits', imagination (Carvalho, 1988, p. 76) and ethics (Runde, 1990). As Dow (2004) argues, Keynes places an emphasis on judgement in decision-making in uncertain environments. She offers monetary policy through committees of decision-makers, such as those in central banks, as an example.

The distinction between probabilistic risk and non-probabilistic uncertainty has influenced ecological economists (Spash and Clayton, 1997; Spash, 2007). It supports the view that environmental futures cannot have probabilities attached to them based on past relative frequencies, given that in open systems ecological entities are evolving in non-random ways. For example, the notion of a feedback loop suggests that rising levels of carbon dioxide lead to irreversible changes in the ecosystem (such as the oceans producing their own net carbon dioxide). This changes the basis of life. Under such circumstances, simply extrapolating from past instances (even with some stochastic adjustment) is flawed. Such arguments have parallels in complexity theory. In complex adaptive systems, agents adapt to new circumstances, often creating new rules and routines and mechanisms that govern future behaviour, thereby creating emergent phenomena. Thus, although the present and future are rooted in each other and in the past, in the past it would have been difficult to predict the future. In the language of non-ergodicity, past frequency distributions would have different averages than current or future ones.

Furthermore, it could be argued that even with a logical theory of probability, there is no basis for constructing a probability for some ecological outcome. Or, to be more precise, one could not construct a probability distribution in which one has much confidence because the available evidence is likely to be small relative to our ignorance about the problem. Events far in the future are difficult to predict; attempting to make forecasts about the economy 20 years from now is fruitless (Keynes, 1937). For example, it would seem impossible to construct a probability distribution of the effects of peak world oil production (Campbell, 2003), which include economic reorganization and social dislocation. But what is the probability of any one of these outcomes, or even of counteracting events or mechanisms, such as the ability of individuals to sustain themselves without access to oil? Such variables appear beyond estimation; certainly past data provide little support for any estimate, however precise.[6]

In economics, uncertainty affects theory. The Arrow and Debreu (1954) model of general equilibrium requires the existence of a complete set of futures markets. These would simply not exist in the world pictured here. The problems are specifically acute for environmental problems. The conventional analysis of pollution suggests that there may be an optimal amount of pollution. A typical analysis of pollution calculates marginal private and social costs and benefits of units of pollution and production. The contrast between social and private involves the recognition of externalities. Moreover, the calculation of costs and benefits requires, for accuracy, that future costs and benefits are taken into account. However, those future effects are unknown. They would need to be estimated probabilistically, but the arguments above suggest that the relevant probability distributions may not even exist.

These problems plague all cost–benefit analyses, the most popular tool employed by environmental economists. The pervasiveness of uncertainty leads to methodological objections to cost–benefit analysis (Harris, 2002, pp. 111–14; Keat, 1997; Gowdy, 2007; Hansson, 2007; Spash, 2007) – agents are not equipped with the information to calculate future benefits and weigh them against future costs. Such an approach assumes methods of projecting the future, which uncertainty would suggest have dubious reliability. Further, cost–benefit analysis usually rests on there being a discount factor so that future costs and benefits can be viewed in current terms. Such discount factors are subjective and psychological and reflect one's attitude to the future. However, they also reflect a prediction of how our current actions might affect the future and therefore what rate of discount would be safe and reasonable for us to assume; thus, our ability to predict becomes relevant. For policy analysis, from a realist perspective, one would prefer that discount factors had some objective anchor. It may be possible to employ random discount factors, simulations, sensitivity analysis and the like to the problem, but without much confidence that this will improve the prediction and valuation of future outcomes. Of course, the same analysis applies to cost-effectiveness analysis, which avoids the problems of comparing costs and benefits, but still must engage in calculation of the future and its translation into present values.

UNCERTAINTY ABOUT METHODS

For Dow, no one method can be relied upon a priori. Babylonianism is organic in its practice. Investigations evolve, often in unpredictable ways, and perhaps halt, to start again from a different point. Science is trial and error, not in the sense of moving incrementally to a perfect theory, but in trying out theories and taking elements from one and parts from another to tell a story. Thus, Babylonianism holds that there is unlikely to be a single set of axioms, or a single theory, which can explain a set of phenomena. Theories beginning from different assumptions and different paradigms, therefore, must be respected and explored (Feynman, 1965).

Babylonianism also advocates theories whose assumptions form and content bear some relation to reality. It holds that atomistic theories are less likely to be successful than organic theories. However, atomistic theories should not be thrown out because they might throw some light on reality, particularly if there are parts of it which are more atomistic. However, simple theories that are deduced from simple axioms are problematic.[7] Reflecting the concerns of Marshall and Keynes about long chains of deductions from axioms, Babylonianism regards such logical leaps to be somewhat fanciful (Dow, 2005, p. 387). This is partly because, due to uncertainty about the world, there is no set of axioms that we can be (reasonably) certain about, and also because deductions assume that no other interfering factors will change the conclusion.[8]

The analysis of an ecosystem is a case in which the identification of a single set of driving axioms is problematic. As illustrated above, pollution is complex, and so we need several different strands of reasoning and evidence to understand its causes. On the issue of climate change, although models generally predict a dire future, there are a range of models and therefore different predictions. Different models contain different assumptions and different causal mechanisms. Fallible theories and the incomplete nature of modelling make it unlikely that any single theory could be 'the' model of climate change. Support for this view is given implicitly by studying the behaviour of major decision-makers, such as central banks, who may use one main structural model and support this by using a set of auxiliary models. The problems associated with modelling and forecasting those economic systems in the fairly short term are likely to be much greater in models attempting to capture climate change and its effects (for an illustration, see Spash, 2007).

There are grounds for further pessimism. Keynes's methodological objections to Tinbergen suggest that modern econometric techniques have severe limitations (but see Brady, 1988). For Keynes, the assumptions of the uniformity of nature and fixed coefficients undermine the usefulness of econometrics in an organic reality. Econometrics assumes an independence of observations, and this in turn assumes an atomic rather than organic reality. This critique has been embraced by Davidson, by Critical Realism and by Dow. All argue against traditional methods of economic analysis, driven by econometrics, because they rely on closed systems.

Such arguments can appear rather sceptical and even nihilistic. What can we as agents do? Facing uncertainty about the world and about which methods to use, researchers and policy-makers require a basis for action. One possible route is to adopt the 'precautionary principle', a view commonly held in ecological economics. The precautionary principle holds that humanity should 'strive for minimum interference with the operation of natural systems, especially where we cannot predict long-term effects' (Harris, 2002, p. 131). Advocating the precautionary principle can be understood in the context of uncertainty, open systems and the limited prospects of developing knowledge in such environments. However, critics of the precautionary principle might argue that it is merely a way of avoiding or suspending judgement and analysis. This is not strictly fair, because precaution, judgement and analysis are connected; indeed, precaution often follows the others.

A Post Keynesian approach would be to apply judgement directly and base action on that. One way that confidence in a course of action may be increased (and the weight of argument increased) is to gather more evidence. However, this cannot be a simple inductive exercise of generalizing from a number of cases, or counting similar instances. Rather, Keynes saw benefit in negative analogy; that is, gathering evidence in unlike situations. If a finding occurred in a range of contexts, it was more likely to be true. According to Dow (2005, p. 387), Keynes employed an ordinary or human logic, in which we use 'judgement to combine direct knowledge, indirect (theoretical) knowledge, conventional knowledge, and animal spirits or intuition' to make decisions. None of this guarantees greater accuracy; neither does it claim faux precision.

PLURALISM

Babylonianism and Critical Realism argue that methods should be tailored to the reality they are studying; however, given the complexity of the environment, it is difficult to be confident that the correct method has been chosen. For this and other reasons, there have been many recent calls for pluralism. Inevitably, there are many definitions of pluralism (Salanti and Screpanti, 1997). Pluralism can be defined as the advocacy of plurality. This can operate on various levels. One can envisage a plurality of realities, or a fragmented, complex reality in which there is a plurality of heterogeneous types of entity. Given that, and given the difficulties in establishing knowledge in those environments, one can advocate a plurality of methodological approaches (including some that make prediction their standard for theoretical success and others that eschew this standard) and of methods. Significantly, ecological economists have also argued for pluralism (Martinez-Alier et al., 1998).

Given the difficulty of choosing the correct method, some authors have argued that several methods be combined. Downward and Mearman (2007) argue for mixed-methods research. Mixed methods combine, in a single investigation, multiple data types, theoretical accounts, methods and methodologies. Downward and Mearman (2008) contend that economic agents, such as the Bank of England, use mixed methods as a response to the uncertainty they face. Using mixed methods has implications for environmental economics. As with all economics, environmental economics has a quantitative and formal bias. Mixed methods see this bias as misplaced. Rather, consistent with Keynes's concept of weight, different methods and data illuminate different parts of reality and add to the weight of the argument.

There is a parallel here with multi-criteria analysis, which is sometimes referred to as 'multi-criteria evaluation' or 'multi-attribute utility analysis' (Stirling, 1997). Multi-criteria analysis attempts to gather together pieces of evidence from different perspectives to aid decision-making in complex environments. As its name suggests, it tries to avoid the problems with attempting to make optimization decisions based on a single criterion. However, multi-criteria analysis has a quantitative bias, since it attempts to generate an algorithm that quantifies all the evidence (Martinez-Alier et al., 1998; Stirling, 1997; Stirling and Mayer, 2001). A mixed-methods approach would see this final step as unnecessary. Rather, following Keynes, evidence would be presented in its raw quantitative and qualitative form, and decision-makers would then use their judgement in drawing conclusions.[9] How this would be operationalized requires further investigation. However, it is unlikely that any kind of formulaic response would be suitable. Rather, each investigation requires its own context-specific response. This is not eclecticism; some methods will be better than others in different contexts, and some methods will be better per se (modelling versus reading tea leaves). But this approach recognizes that complex environments require complex investigation. This takes us back to Keynes's human logic.

CONCLUSION

This chapter has discussed some recent developments in Post Keynesian methodology and their implications for an economic analysis of the environment. Sceptics and other critics might ask: 'So what?' Many of the arguments made here have been foreshadowed, often within Post Keynesian economics. That is true; however, the recent work has codified the earlier work. Further, a critic may say that the recommendations above are light and weak. Again, that is true; methodological arguments are necessarily vague. Yet vagueness may be a virtue in uncertain environments. To paraphrase Keynes, it is better to be vaguely right than precisely wrong. Furthermore, recent methodological work has highlighted the problem of prescriptive methodology. Thus, the developments in a Post Keynesian methodology should act only as suggestions for practice, not rules. Any useful developments in a Post Keynesian economics of the environment will emerge from theoretical and empirical work, albeit with the assistance of methodology. Much of the theoretical apparatus already exists; the new methodology will assist future work.

This chapter also has identified some key features of a Post Keynesian economics of the environment, which is rooted in the methodology of the approach. A Post Keynesian environmental economics would embrace realism; ontological reflection; an ontology of depth, layers and emergence; an ontology of uncertain openness, history and change; a scepticism about current methods, including long chains of deduction, mathematical modelling, econometrics and concepts such as equilibrium and optimization; and a recognition that ordinary logical thought might require weighing different types of evidence drawn from a variety of locations and methods.

Finally, there are many overlaps between the Post Keynesian approach to economics, especially its methodological positions and recommendations, and ecological economics. This commonality is much more than a shared opposition to neoclassical environmental economics. To be sure, that opposition is shared; but the dialogue beginning between Post Keynesian economics and ecological economics will likely lead to an array of positive developments (Holt, 2005). Furthermore, the ground is shared without making either approach redundant. Ecological economists have already drawn on Post Keynesian influences, for instance on natural capital and on uncertainty; conversely, Post Keynesians can learn much from the practical and theoretical developments in ecological economics, for instance on multi-criteria analysis.

NOTES

1. Dow (2005) prefers the term 'structured pluralism' to Babylonianism. The former conveys the pluralism she advocates, but eschews eclecticism. Dow feels that Babylonianism has become associated with eclecticism (despite her many statements to the contrary). Since Babylonianism is better known, it shall be retained here.
2. This distinction is rather blunt but common (Harris, 2002). It is beyond the scope of the chapter to explore either environmental or ecological economics in detail, or the distinction between them. Generally, environmental economics tends to be neoclassical, while ecological economics does not.
3. Many realists argue for a moral realism; that is, a morality existing independent of us, in the same way that objects might (Mearman, 2009).
4. Spash and Clayton (1997) note that there are many definitions of natural capital and that none of the available definitions is particularly effective.
5. Martinez-Alier et al. (1998) argue that there is only weak comparability between objects considered in ecological analysis. This case applies also to natural and non-natural capital. Holland (1997) argues that the distinction between natural and man-made capitals is complicated, even unsustainable. For example, cultivated nature is partly natural, partly man-made. Holland argues further that the distinction between weak and strong sustainability is flawed.
6. It could be said that such scenarios are characterized by ignorance; that is, not knowing the possible outcomes of processes. Under uncertainty, the possible outcomes could be known, even if no probability could be attached to them. See Stirling (1997) and Faber et al. (1996, Chapter 11) for further discussion.
7. There are limits to this argument. Some effects may be easy to identify and predict (such as pouring excess chemicals into a river); however, Babylonianism urges caution about making strong causal claims.
8. It should be noted that the decision to reject axiomatic thought has been controversial among Post Keynesians. Davidson (2003–04) has argued that Post Keynesians must adopt an axiomatic framework to compete with mainstream approaches. However, Dow (2005) argues against this, and suggests that Davidson's use of the word 'axiom' should not be taken in the same way as is it used in mainstream approaches. Specifically, Post Keynesian axioms should be empirically grounded and not lead to long chains of logic reasoning.
9. A similar procedure occurs under multi-criteria mapping (Stirling, 1997; Stirling and Mayer, 2001). Multi-criteria mapping is seen as eschewing any analytical fix, such as those allegedly attempted by cost–benefit analysis. This claim deserves further investigation, since multi-criteria mapping retains concepts such as utility maximization (across criteria) (Stirling, 1997, p. 200) and 'linear additive weighting' (Stirling and Mayer, 2001, p. 535), which retain a quantitative bias.

REFERENCES

Arrow, K. and G. Debreu (1954), 'The existence of an equilibrium for a competitive economy', *Econometrica*, **22**, 265–90.

Bateman, B. (1987), 'Keynes's changing conception of probability', *Economics and Philosophy*, **3**, 97–120.
Bhaskar, R. (1978), *A Realist Theory of Science*, Brighton: Harvester.
Bhaskar, R. (1979), *The Possibility of Naturalism*, Hemel Hempstead: Harvester.
Brady, M. (1988), 'J.M. Keynes's position on the general applicability of mathematical, logical, and statistical methods in economics and social science', *Synthese*, **76** (1), 1–24.
Campbell, C. (2003), 'When will the world's oil and gas production peak?', in R. Douthwaite (ed.), *Before the Wells Run Dry: Ireland's Transition to Renewable Energy*, Dublin: Feasta Books, pp. 30–44.
Carvalho, F. (1988), 'Keynes on probability, uncertainty and decision-making', *Journal of Post Keynesian Economics*, **11** (1), 66–81.
Christensen, P. (2005), 'Recovering and extending classical and Marshallian foundations for a Post Keynesian environmental economics', *International Journal of Environment, Workplace and Employment*, **1** (2), 155–73.
Common, M. (1988), *Environmental and Natural Resource Economic: An Introduction*, London: Longman.
Davidson, P. (1994), *Post Keynesian Macroeconomic Theory*, Aldershot, UK and Brookfield, VT, USA: Edward Elgar.
Davidson, P. (2003–04), 'Setting the record straight on a history of Post Keynesian economics', *Journal of Post Keynesian Economics*, **26** (2), 245–72.
Dow, S.C. (2004), 'Uncertainty and monetary policy', *Oxford Economic Papers*, **56** (3), 539–61.
Dow, S.C. (2005), 'Axioms and Babylonian thought: a reply', *Journal of Post Keynesian Economics*, **27** (3), 385–91.
Downward, P. (ed.) (2003), *Applied Economics and the Critical Realist Critique*, London: Routledge.
Downward, P. and A. Mearman (2007), 'Retroduction as mixed-methods triangulation: reorienting economics into social science', *Cambridge Journal of Economics*, **31** (1), 77–99.
Downward, P. and A. Mearman (2008), 'Decision-making at the Bank of England: a critical appraisal', *Oxford Economic Papers*, **60** (3), 385–409.
Faber, M., R. Manstetten and J. Proops (1996), *Ecological Economics: Concepts and Methods*, Cheltenham, UK and Brookfield, VT, USA: Edward Elgar.
Feynman, R. (1965), *The Character of Physical Law*, Cambridge, MA: MIT Press.
Franklin, J. (2001), 'Resurrecting logical probability', *Erkenntnis*, **55** (2), 277–305.
Gelso, B. and J. Peterson (2005), 'The influence of ethical attitudes on the demand for environmental recreation: incorporating lexicographic preferences', *Ecological Economics*, **53** (1), 35–45.
Gowdy, J. (2007), 'Toward an experimental foundation for benefit–cost analysis', *Ecological Economics*, **63**, 649–55.
Hansson, S. (2007), 'Philosophical problems in cost–benefit analysis', *Economics and Philosophy*, **23**, 163–83.
Harcourt, G. (1972), *Some Cambridge Controversies in the Theory of Capital*, Cambridge: Cambridge University Press.
Harris, J. (2002), *Environmental and Natural Resource Economics: A Contemporary Approach*, New York: Houghton Mifflin.
Holland, A. (1997), 'Substitutability: or, why strong sustainability is weak and absurdly strong sustainability is not absurd', in J. Foster (ed.), *Valuing Nature*, London: Routledge, pp. 119–34.

Holt, R.P.F. (2005), 'Post-Keynesian economics and sustainable development', *International Journal of Environment, Workplace and Employment*, **1** (2), 174–86.
Holt, R.P.F. (2007), 'What is Post Keynesian Economics?', in M. Forstater, G. Mongiovi and S. Pressman (eds), *Post Keynesian Macroeconomics: Essays in Honour of Ingrid Rima*, London: Routledge, pp. 89–107.
Keat, R. (1997), 'Values and preferences in neo-classical environmental economics', in J. Foster (ed.), *Valuing Nature*, London: Routledge, pp. 32–47.
Keynes, J.M. (1921), *A Treatise on Probability*, London: Macmillan.
Keynes, J.M. (1936), *The General Theory of Employment, Interest and Money*, London: Macmillan.
Keynes, J.M. (1937), '*The General Theory*: fundamental concepts and ideas', *Quarterly Journal of Economics*, **51**, 209–23.
Keynes, J.M. (1972a), 'Newton the man', *The Collected Writings of John Maynard Keynes*, Vol. 10, London: Macmillan.
Keynes, J.M. (1972b), 'F.P. Ramsey', *The Collected Writings of John Maynard Keynes*, Vol. 10, London: Macmillan.
Kregel, J. (1976), 'Economic methodology in the face of uncertainty: the modelling methods of Keynes and the Post Keynesians', *Economic Journal*, **86**, 209–25.
Kuhn, T. (1962), *The Structure of Scientific Revolutions*, Chicago, IL: University of Chicago Press.
Lavoie, M. (1992), *Foundations of Post Keynesian Economic Analysis: New Directions in Modern Economics*, Aldershot, UK and Brookfield, VT, USA: Edward Elgar.
Lawson, T. (1985), 'Keynes, prediction and econometrics', in T. Lawson and M.H. Pesaran (eds), *Keynes' Economics: Methodological Issues*, Sydney: Croom Helm, pp. 116–33.
Lawson, T. (1997), *Economics and Reality*, London: Routledge.
Lawson, T. (2003), *Reorienting Economics*, London: Routledge.
Martinez-Alier, J., G. Munda and J. O'Neill (1998), 'Weak comparability of values as a foundation for ecological economics', *Ecological Economics*, **26**, 277–86.
Mearman, A. (2005a), 'Post Keynesian economics and the environment: introduction to the mini-symposium', *International Journal of Environment, Workplace and Employment*, **1** (2), 121–30.
Mearman, A. (2005b), 'Why have Post Keynesians had (relatively) little to say on economics of the environment?', *International Journal of Environment, Workplace and Employment*, **1** (2), 131–54.
Mearman, A. (2009), 'Realism', in J. Peil and I. van Staveren (eds), *The Handbook of Economics and Ethics*, Cheltenham, UK and Northampton, MA, USA: Edward Elgar, pp. 433–40.
Norgaard, R. (1984), 'Coevolutionary development potential', *Land Economics*, **60** (2), 160–73.
Norgaard, R. (1988), 'Sustainable development: a co-evolutionary view', *Futures*, **20** (6), 607–20.
Robinson, J. (1974), 'History versus equilibrium', *Indian Economic Journal*, **21** (3), 202–13.
Robinson, J. (1980), 'Time in economic theory', *Kyklos*, **33** (2), 219–29.
Runde, J. (1990), 'Keynesian uncertainty and the weight of arguments', *Economics and Philosophy*, **6**, 275–92.

Salanti, A. and E. Screpanti (eds) (1997), *Pluralism in Economics*, Cheltenham, UK and Lyme, NH, USA: Edward Elgar.
Spash, C. (2007), 'The economics of climate change impacts à la Stern: novel and nuanced or rhetorically restricted?', *Ecological Economics*, **63**, 706–13.
Spash, C. and A. Clayton (1997), 'The maintenance of natural capital: motivations and methods', in A. Light and J. Smith (eds) *Space, Place and Environmental Ethics*, London: Rowman & Littlefield, pp. 143–74.
Stirling, A. (1997), 'Multi-criteria mapping: mitigating the problems of environmental valuation?', in J. Foster (ed.), *Valuing Nature*, London: Routledge, pp. 186–210.
Stirling, A. and S. Mayer (2001), 'A novel approach to the appraisal of technological risk: a multicriteria mapping study of a genetically modified crop', *Environment and Planning C: Government and Policy*, **19**, 529–55.
van den Bergh, J., A. Ferrer-i-Carbonell and G. Munda (2000), 'Alternative models of individual behaviour and implications for environmental policy', *Ecological Economics*, **32** (1), 43–61.
Winslow, E.J. (1993), 'Organic interdependence, uncertainty, and economic analysis', *Economic Journal*, **103**, 1173–82.

3. Challenges for Post Keynesian growth theory: utopia meets environmental and social reality

Clive L. Spash and Heinz Schandl

INTRODUCTION

The methodological approach of Post Keynesian economics (PKE) has been explained by Paul Davidson (1981) as involving 'historical and humanistic models' which, while abstract, aim for descriptive realism. More specifically he regards three propositions as constitutive of PKE. First, the economy is a process in historical time. This emphasizes the time taken for production and consumption, that knowledge is asymmetric and incomplete with the past revealed and the future hidden, and that failing to account for time in economic models makes them irrelevant. Second, uncertainty and surprises are unavoidable which makes expectations central to understanding economic decisions. Uncertainty refers to ignorance of the future and should not then be equated with risk assessment of uncertain but knowable futures. Different people have different histories and experiences and so expectations. This inherent variety adds heterogeneity and plural perspectives to economic agents. Third, economic and political institutions play an important role in determining economic outcomes. Thus, PKE is concerned about the distribution of income as a basic struggle by individuals for control of their destinies and between various groups and social organizations.

Each of these three elements can also be found in ecological economics.[1] First, the importance of the economy's historical path is revealed by analysis of energy and materials use over the last few hundred years and the related concept of industrial metabolism (Ayres and Simonis, 1994; Schandl and Krausmann, 2007; Schandl and Schulz, 2002). Second, concern has been expressed over the epistemology of ignorance and uncertainty (Faber et al., 1992). Spash (2002b) defines uncertainty as 'strong' involving ignorance and indeterminacy as opposed to 'weak' and merely being a set of potential but known probabilistic futures. This conceptualization can be traced back to Keynes (1988 [1921]) and Knight (1921); although in developing the concept of strong uncertainty Spash (2002b) makes more substantive use of Loasby (1976), Funtowicz and Ravetz (1990) and Wynne (1992). Third, the economy–environment nexus has been described as essentially one of political economy (Brennan, 2008; O'Neill, 1993; Spash, 1995). Institutional analysis (outside game theory) is recognized as absent from orthodox economic approaches and politics is ignored or hidden. Ecological economics recognizes politics and institutions as key to our understanding of resource and environmental problems and the potential ways out of the current state in which we find modern economies (Martinez-Alier, 2002; Söderbaum, 1999; Spash and Villena, 1999; Vatn, 2005). However, the struggle within the political economy can be seen as going well beyond the PKE concern for income distribution among currently existing voices in the body politic. In ecological economics the exploitation and treatment of others spreads to the inclusion of many silent voices such as children, future generations and non-humans and how they might be represented (O'Neill, 2001). This brings together environmental ethics, political science and social psychology as necessary to inform a revision of how socio-economic systems can be understood.

Thus, while ecological economics is more interdisciplinary and has a broader perspective, there appear general areas for agreement across a range of concerns expressed as falling within PKE and ecological economics. Common ground clearly arises in criticizing orthodox approaches to economics. Both see policy problems requiring new approaches and better analytical tools. There is a mutual concern that human well-being is inadequately approached as a quasi-utilitarian concept based upon individual preferences. Both express the need for a more realistic model of human psychology and of the world in which we live. In PKE there have been some notable minority interests in psychological and behavioural theories relating to consumption and market structures (for example, Earl, 1990; Earl, 2005), and there is the related work of Galbraith (1969 [1958], 1978) which addresses itself to the political power and behaviour of the modern corporation. Orthodox economics is also believed by both Post Keynesians and ecological economists, but for different reasons, to exclude consideration of factors which create instability in social and economic systems.[2] Whether this is enough common ground for a collaborative effort towards a new economics remains to be seen.

Indeed, where a divide can be clearly discerned is in terms of the objects of attention. PKE appears, at least to the 'outsider', largely a macroeconomic enterprise which has spread into methodology. PKE seems to have been primarily concerned with effective demand, unemployment, inflation, interest rates and money as a means of economic management. Ecological economics is concerned with environmental degradation, loss of species, damage to ecosystems' structure and functioning, the basic limits on economic activity imposed by physical laws, the role of money in perverting environmental values and the means by which human society can operate in harmony with nature. PKE has almost totally failed to pay attention to the environment until more recently (Holt, 2005; Mearman, 2005), and has neglected limits to growth.[3] Ecological economics is particularly weak on macroeconomic issues, and indeed if anything has tended to use economic equilibrium theories and concepts of capital which are inconsistent with some of its basic premises about systems functioning derived from ecology (for example, Holling, 1986). A more heterodox macroeconomic approach sharing basic methodological concerns would therefore be a significant step forward. However, the role and meaning of macroeconomic growth is a core area where disagreement seems most likely. Although emphasizing distributional concerns, PKE, like mainstream economics, assumes growth is good and more is better. Rather than questioning growth and capital accumulation the concern is for how to achieve more of the same.

Economic growth is then discussed, in what follows, as a topic upon which divergence between PKE and ecological economics exists and any collaboration will need to focus. In the next section we employ a historical analysis of the industrial revolution to show how dependent growth has been upon exhaustible energy sources and the exploitation of other countries. A picture is painted of an internationally divisive economic system, which creates material affluence for the minority, gross inequity in resource use, and fails to increase human well-being beyond some minimum level. The global environmental and social prognosis is seriously worrying and the social–ecological–economic regime is one which cannot be sustained for long.[4] Exploring how Keynesian economics has characterized such issues reveals its inadequacies at reflecting reality

A problem then arises as to how economists should respond. One approach is to adjust the existing theories to include aspects of the environment. Hence the concepts of natural capital, green accounting and adjusted gross domestic product (GDP) measures have arisen, hand in hand with monetary valuation of non-traded entities characterized as 'goods and services'. These are attempts to make the environment part of the capitalist system without any major disruption to the theoretical approach or the fundamentals of the system itself. Capital accumulation, innovation, technology and growth remain unquestioned in a framework expanded to market trading and monetary valuation of everything from human life to carbon atoms in the atmosphere. We argue that this is totally inadequate.

If PKE is to help then reflection is required upon a different type of future and how it might be achieved. Envisioning potential futures is, of course, a utopian exercise, but one even rational people like Keynes knew was important. After providing a historical perspective on growth, we discuss Keynes's own vision of the future. This adds an important perspective to his more traditional views on the role of economic growth. The material presented also indicates some need for those following in his footsteps to reflect upon the type of society they themselves envision as desirable. We conclude with some remarks as to where all this might leave those economists amongst us striving for a fairer world in which economics as a discipline is more realistic about social problems (for example, inequity, poverty, domination of others), human psychology and environmental interactions.

A HISTORICAL PERSPECTIVE ON GROWTH

In this section we employ the concept of a socio-ecological regime as introduced by Sieferle et al. (2006).[5] This links a specific mode of production, distribution and consumption with the biophysical properties of a socio-economic system and the related patterns of society–nature interactions. The approach allows transitions in economic development over time to be understood through material and energy components.

Most of human history has been spent in agrarian societies that were unable to grow beyond a certain limit. Over 10 000 years these systems shared a number of similarities with regard to their socio-ecological characteristics. The resource base was a controlled solar energy system. Societies had to tap into flows of renewable energy mainly from biomass. As a consequence, land use, human time and the amount of available energy were intrinsically dependent upon one another. Land-based resource utilization was associated with decentralized systems and infrastructure. Technologies for energy conversion were limited. This imposed low mobility and confined the transport of bulk materials because of the high energy costs. Most importantly, growth and innovation were ultimately constrained by the amount of suitable land and labour available to meet a variety of energy needs (that is, nutrition, transport and process heat).

Any surplus was distributed unequally between a rich but small ruling class and the vast majority of relatively poor peasants. Although agrarian societies had to ensure a certain level of sustainability of their main activities, a number of environmental and social problems typically occurred. These 'sustainability' problems included soil erosion and declining soil fertility, land degradation and deforestation, energy scarcity, wildlife and habitat loss, and social inequality.

Industrialization produced a transition in the agrarian socio-metabolic regime. This occurred for the first time in the United Kingdom (UK) by a unique combination of institutional change, population growth, improvements of land-use practices and an energy transition (Krausmann et al., 2008; Schandl and Schulz, 2002). The energy transition involved the emergence of a new technology cluster around coal, iron ore and the steam engine (Ayres, 1990; Gruebler, 1998). Sieferle (1982, 2001) describes the large stocks of fossilized biomass as a subterranean forest which provided the energy basis of physical growth during the Industrial Revolution. The shift to mining of coal, instead of harvesting woodlands, was the first step in the process of decoupling energy supply from land use and the photosynthetic cycle (Krausmann et al., 2008). Simultaneously, the coal-based industrial regime created a surge in demand for human labour, and population growth concentrated in new towns around the coalfields. Intensive coal use also produced severe and contentious environmental and health problems.

During the nineteenth century and until the middle of the twentieth century the urban-industrial centres, powered by fossil fuels and the use of non-renewable resources, co-existed with a rural matrix surprisingly untouched as an energy system by the new regime. Two centuries of British industrial development left the rural periphery essentially under the pre-industrial conditions of the agrarian regime. For some time the dual economy involved a modern urban-industrial sector trading in markets and a traditional agrarian sector based around socially structured exchange (Lutz, 1984). There was, for example, no labour market in rural areas due to various institutions binding labour to the parish from which subsistence support was paid (see Polanyi, 1944). This co-existence of regimes restrained British industrial development because population growth driven by the urban-industrial sector could not be supported by food production in the agrarian sector. Agriculture was confined to modernization within its traditional bounds. In 1846 the repeal of the Corn Laws was a major landmark in the UK, opening its markets to foreign producers by removing import tariffs, and by the early 1880s food imports surpassed domestic food production. This shift in food supply, from home production to imports, further decoupled the energy system from domestic land use and contributed to economic growth and material prosperity (Pomeranz, 2000).

The use of territories and labour from outside the UK for supplying food, and other raw materials, appears to have been novel at such a large scale. However, this was only a partial answer: the newly cultivated lands, most notably in the Midwest of America, were overly exploited and gradually became impoverished so that yields had steadily declined by the end of the nineteenth century (Cunfer, 2005). It was only after another socio-ecological transition in the 1950s that the traditional agricultural constraint was effectively dealt with.

Coal was replaced as the main energy carrier and a new resource–technology cluster – oil, gas, electricity, the internal combustion engine and electric motors – allowed for unprecedented levels of material throughput. This transition involved the industrialization of agriculture and so another step in delinking energy production and land use. The technologies (mechanization and agrochemicals) that became available boosted agricultural yields and labour productivity. The previous rules for agricultural production – to produce at a positive return upon energy invested – profoundly changed and agriculture became a net consumer of energy due to the use of fossil fuels embedded in inputs (for example fertilizers) and for running machinery. The traditional limits to growth imposed by the agrarian regime no longer applied in developed industrial economies (Grigg, 1992).

A growth constellation emerged in the 1950s built around the welfare state, a compromise between capital and labour, introducing an era of mass production and consumption. The welfare system neutralized the relationship between unemployment and salaries. This can be seen as having eased the way for the modern industrial sector to absorb the agricultural sector, with a majority of the informal agricultural workforce being integrated into the formal labour market. The modern industrial sector was supplied with both a labour force and consumers for its products. In the pre-Second World War era the direct consumptive role of households and private citizens had been comparatively small. The period from 1950 to 1973 in the UK showed a rapid increase in per capita energy consumption. Relative energy prices declined markedly (Pfister, 2003; Smil, 2003) and household consumption became a major driver of overall energy use. Previously, most of the growth in energy consumption had been determined by the size of energy-intensive industries and the transportation network.

As Table 3.1 shows, departing from the agrarian regime and moving into an industrial regime caused a massive increase in the use of energy and natural resources (by a factor of 3–5 per capita and 10–30 per hectare). Simultaneously, in accord with the laws of thermodynamics, waste and emissions (for example, sulphur dioxide, nitrous oxide, carbon dioxide, particulates) increased. Demographic change was characterized by reduced reproduction rates, increased life expectancy, urbanization and agricultural decline. Over 250 years of transition the UK population density rose from 34 to 247 people per km^2, and energy supply from 63 to 190 GJ per capita. The industrial transition introduced new resources, technologies and institutional arrangements with respect to the exploitation of finite

Table 3.1 Metabolic profiles of the agrarian and industrial socio-ecological regime

	Historical agrarian regime	Industrial regime	Growth factor
Energy use per capita (GJ/cap)	40–70	150–400	3–5
Material use per capita (t/cap)]	3–6	15–25	3–5
Energy use per area (GJ/ha)	<30	<600	10–30
Material use per area (t/ha)	<2	<50	10–30
CO_2 emissions per capita (t/cap)	<2	8–20	4–10

Source: Krausmann et al. (2008).

stocks of fossil fuels and minerals, and saw a reduced relative share of biomass in overall material flows. Infrastructure was increasingly centralized and a range of energy conversion technologies allowed for high mobility and long-distance transport of bulk materials.

While the change from an agrarian to industrial regime has been achieved in most Western economies, such transitions are still ongoing in industrially developing countries and have been surprisingly recent in many others (Schandl et al., 2009). The transition has brought Western society unprecedented levels of economic growth and material consumption across a range of socio-economic classes. However, this has been achieved at large environmental cost including pollution of water, air and land, alteration of atmospheric composition, irreversible resource depletion and biodiversity and habitat loss. Such negatives are often referred to as temporary and/or necessary evils. Starting in the mid-1970s energy use in the UK was reduced, due to deindustrialization and efficiency gains stimulated by rising oil prices, seemingly offering the hope of a less damaging post-industrial society. However, this decline cannot be taken at face value because it conceals the shift of industrial production to other countries and the resulting energy-intensive global transportation of goods. Just as land in other countries was used to supply food in the first stage of transition, so today are energy, materials and environmental capacity. Indeed, the social and environmental costs of the material- and energy-intensive lifestyle of citizens in industrialized countries have long been supported by less industrially developed economies. However, those countries are now undergoing their own industrial transformation at a speed and scale never experienced before (Schandl et al., forthcoming). The nineteenth-century UK supply-side 'solution' of exploiting foreign lands through imperial enterprise fails as a general blueprint by which agricultural and resource bottlenecks can be bypassed. One person's empire is another's domination. As the industrial transition spreads this will create new global social and environmental problems and tensions over who gets to use the diminishing resource base.

THE REALITY OF GROWTH: KEYNES AND AFTER

Keynes summarized his economic theory in one sentence when he stated:

> During the nineteenth century, the growth of population and of invention, the opening-up of new lands, the state of confidence and the frequency of war over the average of (say) each decade seem to have been sufficient, taken in conjunction with the propensity to consume, to establish a schedule of the marginal efficiency of capital which allowed a reasonably satisfactory average level of employment to be compatible with a rate of interest high enough to be psychologically acceptable to wealth-owners. (Keynes, 1978 [1936], p. 307)

This might be paraphrased as: economic growth requires sufficient aggregate demand (whether by war or other means) so that consumption maintains employment and prices can be fixed to allow rates of return which satisfy owners of capital. Confidence and psychology are important to the extent that they support the economic system in maintaining consumption and investment.

This picture fails as a sketch of reality because there are no imperial powers striving by warfare to gain and maintain control of natural resources to supply the economy. Actually there are no environmental problems or resource constraints. Indeed Keynes (1978 [1936], p. 381) in discussing war cites just two causes: (1) dictators, and similar warmongers; and (2) economic causes, specified as population growth and the competitive struggle for markets in which to sell goods, that is, export-led growth. Thus:

> if nations can learn to provide themselves with full employment by their domestic policy (and, we must add, if they can also attain equilibrium in the trend of their population), there need be no important economic forces calculated to set the interest of one country against that of its neighbours. (Keynes, 1978 [1936], p. 382)

Perhaps in an age of British empire questioning resource abundance, or how supply was achieved, seemed unnecessary, and Keynes was after all well embedded in the establishment (for example, the civil service, Indian Office, Treasury, Cambridge University; see Pressman, 2006). While PKE has added concern about social conflict, in terms of the negotiations between employers or corporations and employees or unions (Arestis,

1992, p. 89), there has been neglect of the industrial–military complex, as well as conflict over resources between regions and states. Today, for example, the largest per capita consumer nations can be observed fighting to maintain control over the lands supplying diminishing supplies of oil. More than this, the basic picture of the economy is totally inadequate if the social and environmental impacts of ever-expanding energy and materials growth are ignored. An apologia for Keynes is his primary concern for unemployed resources so that achieving a fully employed economy seemed enough of a problem without worrying too much about dealing with resource scarcity, environmental degradation or the world once full or near full employment was achieved.[6]

There is less excuse for PKE, which has persisted in this partial and limited view of reality for half a century. For example, Arestis (1992, p. 102) presents a modified flow diagram which summarizes the PKE economy. This repeats the failure of mainstream orthodox economic texts in having no resource base, nor any environment into which wastes must go or from which amenities might flow. A fully employed, low-inflation, positive-growth economy is apparently an equally desirable human society regardless of whether it entails emitting toxic waste into the water supply and pollutants into the air, and depleting the resource base, or a pristine environment with minimal non-renewable resource use. Infinite natural resources, unlimited carrying capacity and waste treatment available at no cost are the implicit 'stylized facts'.

What makes this worse, though, than the same neglect by mainstream economists is PKE's methodological claim to be based upon a realist position (most commonly associated with Lawson, 1989, 1997). As Arestis (1992, pp. 94) states: 'Theories, then, should represent economic reality as accurately as possible. Post-Keynesian theory is very much based on this premise and has as its primary objective an explanation of the real world as observed.' In which case PKE scholars need to get out more and do some observing. Even some neoclassical resource economists (for example, Maler, 1974) have recognized the embedded character of the economy in an environmental system. Yet two decades later Arestis summarized the state of the art in PKE without any environmental interactions.

During the 1960s and 1970s critiques arose questioning macroeconomic growth in terms of environmental and social impacts (Hirsch, 1977; Meadows et al., 1972; Mishan, 1969). In the 1970s economists linked fundamental aspects of the physical laws of thermodynamics to economic growth models (Georgescu-Roegen, 1971; Kneese et al., 1970). This clarified the relationship between resource consumption and waste (nothing can be created nor destroyed, so all that is consumed becomes waste) and the degradation of energy (flowing from useful to useless forms under the entropy law). In an economic discipline with no concept of the environment or capacity constraints, and where efficiency is the sole operational criterion, there is no concern for the scale of the economy or the impact of human activity on natural systems. Daly expressed this in terms of the need for a steady-state economy (Daly, 1977), and an equivalent of the Plimsoll line for economic activity to be drawn as an indicator of excessive material throughput (Daly, 1991).[7]

Yet the creation of environmental problems by market economies was explicitly recognized even decades earlier than the above literature (Polanyi, 1944), and in its modern institutional form (Kapp, 1950). In particular, Kapp (1950) wrote his environmental analysis of business enterprise (covering both private and planned economies) which explained in detail how costs were passed on to others in order to create an apparent 'surplus'. In contrast to the now commonly cited 'externality theory' he did not describe these costs as 'external' because they are an integral part of the economic system and all-pervasive, not one-off anomalies due to negligence. Kapp (1976) also argued for regarding economic systems as open socially and physically, for explicit recognition of value premises and acknowledging basic needs, and against the 'mechanics of self interest'. This might have been expected to strike a chord with at least those PKE theorists claiming an institutional approach. Unfortunately Hodgson seems to stand alone both in linking PKE to institutional economics (1988) and in showing awareness of Kapp and the economic history of thought which made the connection to the environment (Hodgson, 1997).

This failure is a shame because PKE would seem well placed to address the environment due to its acceptance of open systems, instability, strong uncertainty, social conflict, needs, lexicographic preferences and the importance of corporate power in controlling resources. Yet PKE appears to have been resistant to paying serious attention to environmental problems, bringing it into an unwelcome parallel with mainstream macroeconomics. Employment, inflation and increasing demand seem to exclude any environmental considerations and criticism of growth theory.

Let us take, hopefully not unfairly, Arestis's (1992) book on PKE as our prime example.[8] There seems to be some tension between recognition of the writings critical of the modern affluent society, and the Keynesian promotion of full employment as the societal goal. Interestingly, the critical work on affluence by Galbraith (1969 [1958]), undoubtedly a member of the PKE community (Galbraith, 1978), gets little attention. Arestis (1992, pp. xiii–xiv) states that his aim is to clarify the limits of mainstream theory described by Galbraith, but then merely makes a few references to corporate power, citing none of Galbraith's major works and instead just briefly mentioning two articles.

Growth goes unquestioned apparently because there is a 'reserve army of unemployed' and the theories of imperfect competition embedded in PKE predict excess capacity and hence no scarcity of resources, or at least capital (Arestis, 1992, p. 97). In essence:

> The conception of economics in this system is no longer the study of how scarce resources are allocated to finite needs. It is, instead, the study of how actual economic systems are able to expand their outputs over time by producing and distributing the resulting social surplus. (p. 90)

> Post-Keynesian analysis recognizes the possibility of 'insufficient demand' rather than concentrating on scarcity of resources, so that 'effective demand' assumes a central position. (p. 97)

> The long-run analysis is concerned with the determination of the warranted rate of growth, and therefore the conditions required for a steady rate of expansion. (p. 105)

So, on this interpretation of PKE, the underlying tenets are set up to exclude environmental issues because there are no resource constraints and the goal is an ever-expanding material growth path for consumption and production.

This seems to fit well with Bruntland-type 'sustainable development' which replaced the hard line of limits to growth. Sustainability as 'development' has been used to encapsulate a range of amorphous concepts in order to allow economic growth with a friendly face. Rhetorical arguments over the need for development have justified traditional industrialization and spreading the market model while avoiding the need to address key social and environmental issues seriously. This is not to deny value in the concept of sustainability and some of the related literature (see Sneddon et al., 2006), but progress in questioning the meaning of development (for example Norgaard, 1994), recognizing limits and transforming economics and government policy has been limited. The main concern has remained having the economic cake and eating it, or rather continually making bigger cakes while ignoring the limited availability of ingredients and the need to handle the inevitable waste products that result from producing and consuming ever more cake. Of course who gets to eat the cake is another issue.

The lie of economic growth is the fact that billions of people remain materially impoverished. As the United Nations Development Programme (2008, p. 25) notes:

> There are still around 1 billion people living at the margins of survival on less than US$1 a day, with 2.6 billion – 40 percent of the world's population – living

> on less than US$2 a day . . . The 40 percent of the world's population living on less than US$2 a day accounts for 5 percent of global income. The richest 20 percent accounts for three-quarters of world income . . . Income inequality is also rising within countries. Income distribution influences the rate at which economic growth translates into poverty reduction. More than 80 percent of the world's population lives in countries where income differentials are widening.

Thus, despite economic growth, there is gross inequity across and within countries; for example, 497 people rank as billionaires controlling personal fortunes amounting to 7 per cent of world GDP.[9] The promise that economic growth will raise the standards of living and the well-being of all is not borne out by the facts. That gross inequity fails to spill over more often into civil strife is more surprising.

Potential unrest would seem to have been averted in Western economies by the welfare state, which Keynes must be credited with having helped establish. However, as Dryzek (1992, p. 32) notes, there is tension within the welfare state, and something of a Keynesian policy dilemma because it both supports and criticizes capitalism, for example controlling boom–bust cycles while criticizing and removing 'market incentives' in the form of unemployment and bankruptcy. Adding environmental concerns reveals further contradictions in policy goals:

> To the extent that states cannot simply export or displace ecological problems, environmental conservation will be established more firmly as an additional imperative. And this establishment can only add to the contradictions of the Keynesian welfare state. There is a clear conflict with accumulation – the deleterious environmental effects of economic growth are now well understood. And to claim that one needs the fruits of growth to pay for environmental cleanup is absurd, given that *all* of this growth would produce negative effects on the environment, whereas only a *small part* of it could be siphoned off for cleanup. (Dryzek, 1992, p. 32)

There is theoretical support for Dryzek's contention because 'sustainable' growth defined in economic terms provides no constraint on undermining ecosystems sustainability, and so can prove to be positively harmful (Common and Perrings, 1992). New forms of increasing economic production and consumption, which avoid such problems, are the hope of sustainable development and the promise of technocentric optimists.

NATURE AS CAPITAL, TECHNOLOGY AS SAVIOUR

The standard counter to environmental problems is to claim that technology will provide solutions, inputs (including capital) are perfectly substitutable and new forms of resources will arrive, like manna from heaven, to replace those exhausted. Our historical analysis shows why such positions arise, but also why they are fallacious. Technology–resource clusters have arisen which seemingly surpass previous constraints, but what remains are the fundamental relationships to physical laws, energy use and the environment. Economies cannot grow in the long run by exploiting finite material and energy supplies and degrading the functioning of ecosystems. A problem for PKE and ecological economics is then how to address the necessary reformulation of economics and policy.

One popular suggestion has been to treat various aspects of environmental and social systems as 'capital' in order that they should have equal footing with the more traditional man-made stuff. Everything from mountains to butterflies to the very carbon of which we are constituted is meant to be some form of 'capital' which is then to be given a price in order to be 'valued'. The aim is to squeeze everything into a capitalist framework. Numerous problems arise including treatment of non-economic environmental values, refusals to trade, respect for non-humans and protection of nature on non-consequentialist grounds (Spash and Clayton, 1997).[10] Raising something as obscure as the 'Cambridge capital controversy' hardly seems worthwhile as no one using 'natural capital' seems particularly worried about measuring the immeasureable.

The aim is to impose an overarching concept of capital and to apply monistic welfare measures in the form of money and GDP. For example Ekins (1992), amongst others, has advocated the idea of capital incorporating a whole range of different concepts (that is, environment, social institutions and organization, human knowledge, physical man-made items) in order to achieve the adjustment of standard economic growth theory. From the family to the furnace all seems to be eligible for categorization as capital. In short, a useful environmentalist's metaphor has become a tool for 'taking nature into account'. Next step nature is just another asset on the corporate balance sheet and ready to be traded off in the national income accounts, for example the increasing output of computer games, DVDs, mobile phones or whatever gizmo is in fashion, compensates for the loss of species, habitat and ecosystems functions.[11] This merely results in various non-equivalent concepts being subsumed under an inappropriate title as if standard theory might then be applied to resolve all our problems.

In considering how meaningless and yet powerful is the designation of nature as capital, think of the following examples. Copyrighting genes means companies are created, genetic code identified and stock value accumulated. Nothing has been invented or innovated, merely rights captured in a legal system supporting private ownership and rent-seeking. What might be regarded as public information is now a corporate capital asset. Alternatively, consider controlling carbon in a cycle for which balances cannot be accurately (or perhaps even inaccurately) estimated. Create some arbitrary notion of carbon capital stock and pollution offsets, and then start trading. Pre-existing and previously planted forests suddenly have added commercial value. Firms which are shutting down old equipment suddenly get certificates of carbon offset and make money selling non-existent future emissions (for more detail see Lohmann, 2006). No more carbon has been removed from the cycle than would have occurred otherwise, but 'natural capital' has been made tangible for the economic system and the financial speculators have a new multi-billion-dollar market in which to play.[12] Then there are species which just become items for optimal use and even optimal extinction (for example, as suggested by Swanson, 1994). After all they are just assets in the marketplace.

Here then lies the crux of the capitalist market system and its 'solutions'. Rent is captured and costs passed along to others. Value exists in trade enforced by private property rights. In this context the environment is at best valued as an asset for use in the production of something, anything, that can be captured, priced and traded. Technology, tourism or trinkets – it makes no difference, as long as you can sell it. This also leads to the promotion of the synthetic over the natural because rents are easier to capture: for example fish farms, or genetically modified crops. The market dominates all other forms of human exchange, management and interaction.

Ludwig et al. (1993) point out that large and immediate prospects of gain generate political and social power that facilitates unlimited exploitation. The rich variety of cultures and indigenous management of resources is something which has been eradicated by empire-building, colonization and corporate globalization. Where traditions still exist they are either ignored or regarded as inferior to modern economic systems of 'efficient' resource use. Resources are then repeatedly overexploited often to the point of collapse or extinction. However, in discussing such overexploitation, Ludwig et al. (1993) fail to identify the drivers as having become more predominant in recent human history. This seems especially the case during the European settler period in the Americas, where social rules and norms on resource use were either absent or easily broken (for example the beaver rush, cattle rush, land rush, gold rush, oil rush). Yet, as natural scientists, their recommendations do not claim that expert judgement will provide the solution either. Learning, or science, is unable to prevent the problem because complexity precludes standard experimental approaches (that is, reductionism, control and replicates), especially for large-scale systems. As systems worsen the situation is masked by natural variability.

Despite the history of collapses there remains no scientific consensus on the causes of failure. Ludwig et al. (1993) therefore recommend caution and more specifically attention to: human motivation; acting before scientific consensus; recognizing scientists and their judgements are subject to political pressure; distrusting claims of sustainability (especially where problems of population growth and excessive resource use are ignored); and confronting uncertainty.

The inability of normal scientific method to address environmental problems is something which also has implications for how sustainable futures are perceived by economists, and the role technology plays. Much faith is placed at the door of innovative science embodying knowledge in man-made capital stock to provide 'solutions'. Economists post-Jevons have tended to rely on the promise of technology as the get-out clause relieving them from the need to worry about such things. For Jevons (1965 [1865]) made much of what would happen when coal was exhausted, and the failure of his more dire predictions helped spur the confidence of economists and politicians in backstop technologies and signals from the price system. Today human systems are riding on a precarious wave of ever-advancing technologies of which we have very little ability to predict how they may turn out.

If experiments on, say, a terminator gene using genetic modification are conducted, partial ignorance means accidental release could be devastating. Society has become committed to a new path. Decision stakes are high but concealed, and if the experiment is replicated by hundreds of laboratories, social commitment increases along with indeterminacy. The danger is meant to be controlled by preventative and precautionary measures embedded in social customs expressed via scientific process. Yet the clear-cut case of the laboratory experiment being a core area of low systems uncertainty and low stakes seems highly questionable. Indeed this is more likely to be the claim characterized by corporations wishing to avoid safety testing and regulation, who conduct research on and supply products and processes (for example, nuclear power, synthetic chemicals, genetically modified crops, nanotechnology, microwave transmission) exhibiting features of strong uncertainty.

Narrowly motivated (for example profit- or power-seeking) enterprises can be expected to prefer an approach which fails to show danger as opposed one which aims to reveal that danger. For example, a water quality bioassay can place a fish next to an outfall pipe. The fish survives, so the pipe is assumed clean. However, there is a major difference between selecting the hardiest species available and placing it upstream and selecting a highly vulnerable species and placing it downstream. Hence we hear from biotech companies that they have conducted hundreds of experiments and found no evidence of harm; but were they typically minimizing the chances rather than actively looking for harm? As we enter the information age with all-pervasive microwave technology – with its transmission of frequencies for mobile phones and community Wi-Fi systems at ranges and with population exposure levels never tested (Anslow, 2008) – we may wonder where the next environmental or health problem will arise. In addition, the social changes entailed by such technologies go unremarked, and are accepted as if inevitable, despite being fundamental to the way in which humans operate, communicate and interact.

Indeterminacy of knowledge is something Wynne (1992) explains as endemic in science and technology. He sees the accumulation of scientific knowledge as involving the 'exogenizing' of significant uncertainties which then become invisible; this built-in ignorance becomes part of the basic assumptions underlying theories and models. As society makes commitments (that is, the social stakes rise) on the basis of that knowledge, problems arise. Scientific knowledge is particularly blind to the boundary conditions on the applicability of the existing framework of knowledge to new situations. As Wynne (1992, p. 115) elaborates: 'This institutionalized exaggeration of the scope and power of scientific knowledge creates a vacuum in which should exist a vital social discourse about the conditions and boundaries of scientific knowledge in relation to moral and social knowledge.' This call for social discourse is also something found in the concept of post-normal science which has been advanced within ecological economics by Funtowicz and Ravetz (1992, 1993).[13]

Funtowicz and Ravetz (1992, 1993) offer an insightful critique of normal science which provides guidance on alternative ways in which environmental problems might be better addressed. They combine both an analytical approach for assessing the quality of scientific information, and the idea of an extended peer community including people likely to be affected. The latter is important in light of limits to knowledge being clouded by professional training and the prevalence of value conflicts over environmental issues.

Normal science is effectively regarded as bound to a limited range of cases where decision stakes and strong uncertainty are low (for example, experimentation in the laboratory). This mission-driven approach is contrasted with post-normal science being issue-driven and applicable where stakes are high and uncertainty strong. Between these two extremes is the whole area of research consultancy. The strength of traditional science is regarded as having been due to abstraction from uncertainty in knowledge and values. While successful in the past the approach is not seen as relevant to the present environmental crisis. Here facts are uncertain, values in dispute, stakes high and decisions urgent: 'New methods must be developed for making our ignorance usable. For this there must be a radical departure from the total reliance on techniques, to the exclusion of methodological, societal or ethical considerations that has hitherto characterized traditional "normal science"' (Funtowicz and Ravetz, 1993, p. 743). The conclusion is strikingly similar to that of Wynne (1992). There is a recognized need for participatory approaches to environmental, science and technology issues. How practical new methods, following a post-normal science approach, can be applied to actual policy problems is starting to become clearer (see van der Sluijs et al., 2005).

Addressing our uncertain future requires opening up the decision space and engaging with the body politic. The conjunction of ideas from economics, ecology and science technology assessment provide a challenging agenda. For economics to be relevant to modern environmental and social problems requires rethinking the role of technology and science, rethinking the treatment of nature, avoiding oversimplistic categorizations (for example, nature as capital), and showing some regard for where socio-economic systems have come from and are heading.

FUTURITY

Where socio-economic systems are taking us seems to have fallen off the economist's agenda, along with political economy. An interesting reflection upon the future was made by Keynes (1930) himself. He described the world of a developed economy 100 years in the future. This would be a leisure society, because needs would have been met by general productivity increases:

> The *pace* at which we can reach our destination of economic bliss will be governed by four things – our power to control population, our determination to avoid wars and civil dissensions, our willingness to entrust to science the direction of those matters which are properly the concerns of science, and the rate of accumulation as fixed by the margin between our production and our consumption; of which the last will easily look after itself, given the first three. (Keynes, 1930, p. 98)

The growth path was already set within the context of the modern economy and (despite the recession) Keynes was observant enough to recognize this and the ongoing social-metabolic transition through which he was living. For example, he predicted the imminent industrialization of agriculture (Keynes, 1930, p. 37). Only maintaining the stability and pace of change then seemed necessary for the 'economic problem' to be solved. This is a modernist vision of a stable society driven by faith in science and technology to improve production techniques, and through compound interest to accumulate capital stock.

However, for Keynes, the 'economic problem' itself is not one of ever-increasing material living standards or a stable growth expansion path into the never-ending future. The economic problem is to remove the struggle for meeting subsistence needs; something which has a definable, if debatable, endpoint:

> Now it is true that the needs of human beings may seem to be insatiable. But they fall into two classes – those needs which are absolute in the sense that we feel them whatever the situation of our fellow human beings may be, and those which are relative in the sense that we feel them only if their satisfaction lifts us above, makes us feel superior to, our fellows. Needs of the second class, those which satisfy the desire for superiority, may indeed be insatiable; for the higher the general level, the higher still are they. But this is not so true of the absolute needs – a point may soon be reached, much sooner perhaps than all of us are aware of, when these needs are satisfied in the sense that we prefer to devote our further energies to non-economic purposes. (Keynes, 1930, p. 96)

Keynes is describing a very different role for economic growth than is current today, that is, a means to an end rather than a goal in itself.

Unfortunately, attempting the impossible task of satisfying the relative needs he describes has become the dominant modus operandi of industrialized economies. The issue is one described by Hirsch's (1977) theory of social limits to growth, that is, the failure of increased material living standards to satisfy human desires or increase welfare based upon positional goods. A similar line of reasoning also informs hedonic critiques of income growth (Easterlin, 1974, 1995, 2003), where the non-economic drives well-being (for example, friendship, marriage, health, meaningful employment). Productivity increases have failed to transform into Keynes's vision of reduced work hours or a society devoted to 'non-economic purposes'.

Worse still, the medicine to get to the blissful situation is to maintain capital accumulation, which requires behaviour that Keynes describes as basically unethical and undesirable: greed, usury and the desire for ever more money. Keynes wanted such behaviour finally to be removed. That is, on solving the economic problem:

> We shall be able to rid ourselves of many of the pseudo-moral principles which have hag-ridden us for two hundred years, by which we have exalted some of the most distasteful of human qualities into the position of the highest virtues. We shall be able to afford to dare to assess the money-motive at its true value. The love of money as a possession – as distinguished from the love of money as a means to the enjoyments and realities of life – will be recognised for what

> it is, a somewhat disgusting morbidity, one of those semi-criminal, semi-pathological propensities which one hands over with a shudder to the specialists of mental disease.
>
> . . . But beware! The time for all this is not yet. For at least another hundred years we must pretend to ourselves and to everyone that fair is foul and foul is fair; for foul is useful and fair is not. Avarice and usury and precaution must be our gods for a little longer still. For only they can lead us out of the tunnel of economic necessity into daylight. (Keynes, 1930, p. 97)

He is recommending the blind pursuit of future wealth, ignoring our actions' 'own quality or their immediate effects on our own environment' (Keynes, 1930, p. 97). The prescription also requires that we value the useful over the good. This unpleasant society was one through which Keynes believed we should transition in two generations.

Once the economic system reached high enough material standards to meet absolute needs, Keynes foresaw the problems of a leisure society arising. He recognized the need for behavioural transition in an affluent society from work to leisure. This he described as 'a fearful problem for the ordinary person', made worse 'if he no longer has roots in the soil or in custom or in the beloved conventions of a traditional society'. Keynes feared that affluence, in removing the drive for work as a meaning to life, would leave no apparent idea of how 'the art of life itself' should be conducted (Keynes, 1930, p. 97), and he noted the depressing and disastrous examples of the wealthy.

Just 20 years after Keynes (1930) penned his words Kapp (1950) published *The Social Costs of Private Enterprise*, pointing out many of the pitfalls facing modern economic systems and the society they create. Economic growth to accumulate capital as a means of getting to Keynes's utopia seems simultaneously to destroy the possibility of ever getting there. This has as much to do with the social and psychological character of industrial consumer society as with the environmental havoc it brings. The problem Keynes had underestimated was the extent to which the system of growing material affluence would become addictive and uncontrollable, instil the negative values he recognised and yet fail to meet the goals he set out.

Keynes never foresaw the problem of reversing patterns of human behaviour created by generations of consumerism, or how powerful institutions would be created to perpetuate a system which he assumed to be transitory. The ability to produce with increased efficiency leads to increases in the scale of production, not meeting the same needs with fewer inputs; a problem recognized by Jevons (1965 [1865]) and which has recently been given some new attention (this has been termed the Jevons paradox; see Polimeni et al., 2008). Greater production and lower prices mean greater quantities are sold. Those for whom the economic problem was actually long ago solved continue to consume ever-growing quantities of energy and materials. The consumer society encourages large loans and mortgages pushed by financial institutions. People work more hours to service the loans to consume more at the behest of modern corporations. Modern material fantasy worlds, flaunting of status, self-obsession with looks, aging and fashion – these are the common pursuits of the affluent. The rise of corporate power using brand-driven advertising is expressed through low product durability, fast food, supermarkets, superstores and super-convenient consumption. Support your nation's economy with larger cars with more gadgets, and ever more 'stuff' from ever-changing product lines. The twenty-first-century motto might be: 'Keep the customer dissatisfied'.

This leaves a rather different 'fearful transition' to be faced now, but one which still involves addressing the economic problem at the global scale. Modern society has created no less work, has failed to address inequality, has not been increasing self-reported happiness and has left the majority of humanity in poverty. Rather than leading us 'out of the tunnel', we seem to have lost our way in the darkness due to the pretence that foul is fair and fair is foul.

Interestingly Keynes's musings on the leisure society strike a chord with the utopian vision of Morris (1993 [1890]). They share identification of the problems of diminishing available work, and the meaning of a worthwhile life without competition and the need to struggle for survival. The difference is that Morris saw his utopia as requiring a social revolution, sharing of wealth, removal of money and profit motive and a transition requiring human social, institutional and behavioural change. Keynes wanted to solve material needs using capitalism, and worry about dismantling the system later – a worthy desire when many starve and suffer poverty, but as 80 years of intervening growth have shown, growth alone achieves gains for the few, not the many. Martinez-Alier (2002) notes that the poor sell cheaply so they are the most susceptible to exploitation in the market capitalist system, too often losing control and watching the destruction of the very environmental systems upon which they have sustained themselves for generations.

The means to achieve something of what Keynes envisioned may have been within our grasp if population had been controlled, science contained and growth changed qualitatively in form and moderated in scale. Perhaps some smoother transition might have been planned to a less materially and energy-intensive system of production which more equitably met basic needs. Yet, since the anti-trust movement of the early 1900s, there has been little sign of mainstream economic or political will to challenge significantly or seriously the institutions addicted to growth which prevent redistribution and degrade the environment. That these institutions create economic, social and environmental instability will become ever more apparent, and a societal reaction can therefore eventually be expected, but for many (especially those suffering environmental degradation and poverty) this appears already long overdue.

How we aim for utopia seems to end up being more important than actually getting there. For example, Keynes underestimated the potential for war to stimulate aggregate demand, boost 'business' and achieve full employment. Writing relatively shortly after the Second World War, Hansen (1953, p. 229) notes: 'For most advanced democratic countries, full employment has become a settled policy more quickly than Keynes had believed possible or indeed than would have been possible except for the war and its aftermath.' Avoiding the ongoing waste and misery of wars and weaponry is, as they say in Australia, a 'no-brainer'. Yet wars provide jobs and throughput of materials which are conveniently and quickly destroyed, allowing more throughput and so a 'virtuous' cycle of growth and employment. Technology is stimulated by the drive for ever more efficient means of destruction. Clearly not all paths are equally desirable even if they achieve a goal quickly or 'efficiently'.

That there are many paths to the same goal means making choices and that involves judgement, not blind faith in markets or growth. There are also many criteria upon which to make such choices. To advocate an economic system that you acknowledge as unethical and psychologically pathological, with no plan for control, remedy or escape seems at least irresponsible. The fact is that economic and social systems entail and instil in people certain values, and those should be desirable values which are regarded as positive attributes for current and future generations. The values of the consumerist society are at best highly suspect and at worst self-destructive.

The writings of Galbraith reflect many of the concerns raised with respect to the direction of growth and quality of modern society (see reviews by Dunn and Pressman, 2005, 2006). His description of private affluence explains the favouritism shown towards private goods and their supply, leading to public squalor and environmental degradation (Galbraith, 1969 [1958]). Excessive supply of private goods and mass consumerism is linked to corporate power as wielded through advertising and marketing. His response, to achieve the 'good society', is to limit the power of corporations which operate outside the realm of market competition and are run by a planning process controlled by professional managers (the technostructure). Contrary to economic theory the wealth of the managerial class is derived from their economic power rather than their hard work (that is, marginal productivity). There is some irony in the rhetoric of the largest corporations with their advocacy of free market systems when they themselves are centrally planned. These organizations define public interest in their own light and are integrally linked to the military, causing excessive spending on weapons and related systems. They have the power to control prices and the resources to mould public opinion. Consumerism is then an artefact of their power, used through advertising to equate happiness with purchasing private goods.

Galbraith advocated sources of countervailing power such as unions and government regulation, for example limiting the claims of the military industrial complex. Small producers in the real 'market sector' are disadvantaged and therefore need policies to correct the balance of power; their workers being liable to poverty need support, for example minimum wages. Placing the burden of response on a strong state means also improving democratic processes as government is otherwise captured by the technostructure. Individual workers and citizens have little power in the face of conspicuous consumption reinforced by advertising, leading to low savings and high indebtedness. Explanations for the neglect of public goods and psychic accommodation to mass poverty combine to make Galbraithian analyses highly relevant to modern environmental problems. Despite being a PKE supporter of maintaining effective demand, Galbraith did at least question what might compose national output (1969 [1958], pp. 128–9). Thus, while not environmentally focused (unlike Kapp), the works of Galbraith might help to provide a bridge between PKE and ecological economics.

CONCLUSION

The Keynesian statement, 'in the long run we are all dead', is often taken out of context to imply no need for long-term planning so that short-term growth and 'full employment' can be pursued and future generations left to look after themselves. Keynes's (1971, p. 65) original point was a criticism of the belief in idealized long-run self-equilibrating solutions in the context of inflationary problems. Similarly, the idea of unemployment as temporary cyclical or sectoral phenomena can be seen as having been confounded along with Say's Law by the unemployment of the 1920s and 30s.[14] Just waiting for systems to correct themselves in the long run to some imagined equilibrium was an inadequate response. Such idealized free market responses are commonly given in retort to concerns over resource depletion. Keynes's response that action is required now can equally be applied to the arguments of environmental sceptics that natural systems will prove self-equilibrating in the long run: for example ozone holes will disappear, systems will adjust to human-induced climate change. Rejecting the blind faith in benign equilibrating systems leads to calls for government intervention as the only obvious countermeasure. Yet, how the institutions of government will control and change economic systems, and avoid substantive harm to natural ones in the process, is far from clear. Merely managing the situation fails to address the overall path upon which socio-economic systems have been set.

The dominant acceptance of a growing materialistic consumer society is what must be questioned and is brought into question by its failure to address and ability to exacerbate major social and environmental problems. Neoliberal governments, of the type typical in Western society in recent times, then seem the least likely to respond appropriately given their proximity to the technostructure. Their institutional responses promote rather than address corporate power, and diminish rather than increase a sense of community values and respect for others. Others (human and non-human) are for the consumer just competitors in a struggle for 'goods and services', and for the firm assets to be exploited. There appears no room in the modern economic system for beings with feelings, direction, ability to flourish or moral standing.

Recognizing the importance of issues of globalization and global environmental change requires a broadening of the economic research perspective. It requires acknowledging that, in a biophysical sense, all economic activities are embedded in ecosystems and therefore have to respect environmental and resource use constraints. Limits to growth play no role in PKE. The approach remains very much in line with orthodox macroeconomics in the failure to take the laws of thermodynamics seriously or to include their implications in long-term growth policy.

That 'traditional' economic growth is unsustainable can be illustrated by paying attention to the historical pattern of growth in the UK over the last 250 years. The change in energy utilization came about in two stages. First, between 1830 and 1890, the implementation of the coal, iron, steel and steam engine resource–technology cluster enabled the UK economy to operate at almost twice the level of energy availability of other economies. Second, around the 1950s oil, electricity and the internal combustion engine took over as the main drivers underpinning growth. Economic growth has been essentially concerned with the exploitation of finite non-renewable material and energy resources.

The UK example has been followed by many other countries, resulting in remarkably similar resource use patterns, social structures and trajectories at the end of the twentieth century. During the industrial transition, a structurally coupled socio-ecological regime is established that closely links economic growth to natural resource use. Despite contemporary notions of post-industrial, service or information societies there has been no dematerialization in terms of natural resource use. In the historic transition, industrial materials (fossil fuels, ores and mass minerals) added to biomass materials without replacing them. The increased relative importance of the service sector in many industrial economies has actually increased natural resource flows.

Certain aspects of industrial transition have been a topic for PKE, and other economists, namely employment, salaries, and mass consumption and production. The focus has been on the means by which economic prosperity could be enhanced and mass unemployment and its undesirable social and economic consequences avoided. The biophysical aspects of transition have long been neglected. Assuming unlimited substitutability and benign technological change produces a fantasy world to justify the industrial socio-ecological regime continuing in its current mode. The literature on the socio-ecological regime helps recognition of the fact that the modern industrial economy is transitory in character and a relatively recent occurrence in human history, rather than a stable long-term structure in equilibrium.

Addressing the current environmental crisis requires a new economic revolution allowing major services – such as transport and mobility, construction and housing, nutrition, water and energy use – to be organized in very different ways from today's socio-technical individualistic solutions. Such a transition would need to happen while a large part of the world is in the midst of trying to achieve the old industrial transition. It would require deliberately redirecting investment and institutional change. Lacking organizations and institutions operating at the appropriate temporal and geographic scales means that globally humanity is ill equipped to guide a sustainability transition. That governments are susceptible to capture by the technostructure makes their response equally dubious.

Proposed 'solutions' to environmental problems have included minor adjustments to GDP measures, adding some extra environmental 'goods and services' into market pricing and widening the already troubled concept of capital. These approaches fail to address the fundamental concerns raised; nor do they address key drivers of the economic system or their implications for society, human psychology or the environment. The rush to innovate and replace creates discontent while spreading the depth and scale of interventions into natural systems with unknown and unknowable consequences. An inherent characteristic of the scientifically and technologically driven throughput society is the propensity to increase strong uncertainty in terms of social indeterminacy and partial ignorance. To avoid an environmental collapse points us toward breaking the growth–technology–consumption complex in an intelligent way to improve society. Open social discourse has then been identified as an important part of any process whereby the role of technology and new information might be reconsidered. This can be seen as one part of the necessary challenging and questioning of the modern industrial state through increasing democracy.

A focus on growth and employment seems to miss the point of economic activity. Throughput is not an end in itself; the having and consuming of more 'stuff' does not alone increase 'happiness'. Employment can be demeaning, exploitative and self-destructive or it can be fulfilling, rewarding and give great meaning to a person's life. If economics aims to increase well-being in society then it must go beyond such bland aggregates as employment and growth. Keynes achieved great things as an economist, but the socio-economic system he advocated as a temporary measure to reach economic bliss seems to have spread and made seem virtuous the 'semi-criminal, semi-pathological propensities' of which he warned. A new political economy must question the reason for consumption and production activity and the qualitative aspects of the system, not just focus on potential quantitative end goals. A new revolution in macroeconomic thought also then seems necessary.

NOTES

1. When referring to ecological economics we maintain the meaning in European terms of a new field outside the orthodox economic tradition and which is more than merely economics and ecology combined (see Spash, 1999).
2. PKE sees orthodox belief in long-run stability in an unfettered market system as leading to policies which are irresponsible, for example as in the 1930s with respect to unemployment. Ecological economics sees orthodox economics as having created the myth of never-ending and ever-increasing production and consumption which is destroying the ecosystems which support economic and social systems.
3. A search of the *Journal of Post Keynesian Economics* on the ISI database reveals 1312 articles of which there is just one on an environmental topic, and that relates to oligopoly in the oil industry but does attempt connections to environmental policy and sustainable development (Roncaglia, 2003).
4. A new approach to economics offers the hope of a planned transition, but lock-in to political and economic structures seems to make crisis management more likely as the need for change is denied by various vested interests protecting their power base.
5. A socio-ecological regime is characterized by specific institutional and governance structures, by demographical patterns, spatial patterns of land use, infrastructure networks and technology. This approach regards key regulators as positive and negative feedbacks moulding and constraining the regime. A socio-ecological regime is always associated with a specific pattern of material and energy use (metabolic profile) and of human activity (time allocation profile). While regimes allow for incremental change, a transition process may be introduced resulting in a qualitatively different regime if a critical set of variables or characteristics transcends regime boundaries.

6. Note that Keynes did raise population stabilization as an issue. However, this has also failed to make a Keynesian or PKE agenda.
7. Space precludes entering into a discussion of steady-state economics. Suffice to say that the concept of a steady-state seems to fall well within the constructs of equilibrium theory and stability rejected by PKE, ecosystem ecologists and many ecological economists. Daly's point on scale and his environmental concerns stand independent of his recommended solution which does at least address the need to control exponential material and energy growth.
8. As Davidson (1981) makes clear there are divergent PKE schools, but none of the differences he notes would seem to bear on the points made here with respect to reasons for the neglect of environmental issues.
9. This statistic is taken from the following website which cites sources for many similar and disturbing facts on global poverty and inequity: see http://www.globalissues.org/TradeRelated/Facts.asp, accessed 28 July 2008.
10. Raising something as obscure as the 'Cambridge capital controversy' hardly seems worthwhile as no one using 'natural capital' seems particularly worried about measuring the immeasurable.
11. The concept of incommensurability is a highly relevant consideration (see Aldred, 2006; O'Neill, 1993; 1997) as well as the difference between creating harm and good (Spash, 2002a).
12. On the basis of Keynes's concerns over the role of speculators in standard stock markets, his opinion on this new innovation with respect to the potential for increasing international economic instability would have been most interesting.
13. Interestingly Ravetz (1995) has also published in the *Journal of Post Keynesian Economics*.
14. Say's Law is the belief that supply creates its own demand, which was put forward by Ricardo in 1803 on the basis of his reading of French economist J.B. Say (Stewart, 1979, p. 26).

REFERENCES

Aldred, J. (2006), 'Incommensurability and monetary valuation', *Land Economics*, **82** (2), 141–61.
Anslow, M. (2008), 'The gathering brainstorm: Wifi', *Ecologist* (January), 43–8.
Arestis, P. (1992), *The Post-Keynesian Approach to Economics*, Aldershot, UK and Brookfield, VT, USA: Edward Elgar.
Ayres, R.U. (1990), 'Technological transformations and long waves. Part 1', *Technological Forecasting and Social Change*, **37**, 1–37.
Ayres, R.U. and U.E. Simonis (eds) (1994), *Industrial Metabolism: Restructuring for Sustainable Development*, Tokyo: United Nations University Press.
Brennan, A.J. (2008), 'Theoretical foundations of sustainable economic welfare indicators: ISEW and political economy of the disembedded system', *Ecological Economics*, **67** (1), 1–19.
Common, M. and C. Perrings (1992), 'Towards an ecological economics of sustainability', *Ecological Economics*, **6**, 7–34.
Cunfer, G. (2005), *On the Great Plains: Agriculture and Environment*, College Station, TX: Texas A&M University Press.
Daly, H.E. (1977), *Steady-State Economics*, San Francisco, CA: W.H. Freeman.
Daly, H.E. (1991), 'Towards an environmental macroeconomics', *Land Economics*, **67** (2), 255–9.

Davidson, P. (1981), 'Post Keynesian economics: solving the crisis in economic theory', in D. Bell and I. Kristol (eds), *The Crisis in Economic Theory*, New York: Basic Books, pp. 151–73.

Dryzek, J.S. (1992), 'Ecology and discursive democracy: beyond liberal capitalism and the administrative state', *Capitalism, Nature and Socialism*, **3**, 18–42.

Dunn, S.P. and S. Pressman (2005), 'The economic contributions of John Kenneth Galbraith', *Journal of Post Keynesian Economics*, **17** (2), 161–209.

Dunn, S.P. and S. Pressman (2006), 'The lasting economic contributions of John Kenneth Galbraith, 1908–2006', *Journal of Post Keynesian Economics*, **29** (2), 179–90.

Earl, P.E. (1990), 'Economics and psychology: a survey', *Economic Journal*, **100** (402), 718–55.

Earl, P.E. (2005), 'Economics and psychology in the twenty-first century', *Cambridge Journal of Economics*, **29** (6), 909–26.

Easterlin, R.A. (1974), 'Does economic growth improve the human lot? Some empirical evidence', in P.A. David and M.W. Reder (eds), *Nations and Households in Economic Growth: Essays in Honor of Moses Abramovitz*, New York: Academic Press, pp. 98–125.

Easterlin, R.A. (1995), 'Will raising the income for all increase the happiness for all?', *Journal of Economic Behavior* and *Organization*, **27** (1), 35–47.

Easterlin, R.A. (2003), 'Explaining happiness', *PNAS*, **100** (19), 11176–83.

Ekins, P. (1992), 'A four-capital model of wealth creation', in P. Ekins and M. Max-Neef (eds), *Real-life Economics: Understanding Wealth Creation*, London: Routledge, pp. 147–55.

Faber, M., R. Manstetten and J.L.R. Proops (1992), 'Humankind and the environment: an anatomy of surprise and ignorance', *Environmental Values*, **1**, 217–41.

Funtowicz, S.O. and J.R. Ravetz (1990), *Uncertainty and Quality in Science for Policy*, Dordrecht: Kluwer Academic Publishers.

Funtowicz, S.O. and J.R. Ravetz (1992), 'Risk management as a post-normal science', *Risk Analysis*, **12** (1), 95–7.

Funtowicz, S.O. and J.R. Ravetz (1993), 'Science for the post-normal age', *Futures*, **25** (7), 739–55.

Galbraith, J.K. (1969 [1958]), *The Affluent Society*, Boston, MA: Houghton Mifflin.

Galbraith, J.K. (1978), 'On Post Keynesian Economics', *Journal of Post Keynesian Economics*, **1** (1), 8–11.

Georgescu-Roegen, N. (1971), *The Entropy Law and the Economic Process*, Cambridge, MA: Harvard University Press.

Grigg, D.B. (1992), *The Transformation of Agriculture in the West*, Oxford: Blackwell.

Gruebler, A. (1998), *Technology and Global Change*, Cambridge: Cambridge University Press.

Hansen, A.H. (1953), *A Guide to Keynes*, New York: McGraw-Hill.

Hirsch, F. (1977), *Social Limits to Growth*, London: Routledge & Kegan Paul.

Hodgson, G.M. (1988), *Economics and Institutions: A Manifesto for a Modern Institutional Economics*, Cambridge: Polity Press.

Hodgson, G.M. (1997), 'Economics, environmental policy and the transcendence of utilitarism', in J. Foster (ed.), *Valuing Nature? Ethics, Economics and the Environment*, London: Routledge.

Holling, C.S. (1986), 'The resilience of terrestrial ecosystems: local surprise and global change', in W.C. Clark and R.E. Munn (eds), *Sustainable Development of the Biosphere*, Cambridge: Cambridge University Press, pp. 292–317.

Holt, R.P.F. (2005), 'Post-Keynesian economics and sustainable development', *International Journal of Environment, Workplace and Employment*, **1** (2), 174–86.

Jevons, W.S. (1965 [1865]), *The Coal Question: An Inquiry Concerning the Progress of the Nation and the Probable Exhaustion of Our Coal-Mines*, New York: Augustus M. Kelley.

Kapp, K.W. (1950), *The Social Costs of Private Enterprise*, New York: Shocken.

Kapp, K.W. (1976), 'Nature and significance of institutional economics', *Kyklos*, **29** (2), 209–32.

Keynes, J.M. (1930), 'Economic possibilities for our grandchildren', *Nation and Athenaeum*, **48** (11 and 18), 36–7, 96–8.

Keynes, J.M. (1971), 'A tract on monetary reform', *The Collected Writings of John Maynard Keynes*, Vol. 4, London: Macmillan.

Keynes, J.M. (1978 [1936]), *The General Theory of Employment, Interest and Money*, London: Macmillan.

Keynes, J.M. (1988 [1921]), *A Treatise on Probability*, London: Macmillan.

Kneese, A.V., R.U. Ayres and R.C. d'Arge (1970), *Economics and the Environment: A Materials Balance Approach*, Washington, DC: Resources for the Future.

Knight, F. (1921), *Risk, Uncertainty and Profit*, Boston, MA: Houghton Mifflin.

Krausmann, F., H. Schandl and R.P. Sieferle (2008), 'Socio-ecological regime transitions in Austria and the United Kingdom', *Ecological Economics*, **65** (1), 187–201.

Lawson, T. (1989), 'Abstraction, tendencies and stylised facts: a realist approach to economic analysis', *Cambridge Journal of Economics*, **13**, March, 59–78.

Lawson, T. (1997), *Economics and Reality*, London: Routledge.

Loasby, B.J. (1976), *Choice, Complexity and Ignorance: An Inquiry into Economic Theory and the Practice of Decision-Making*, Cambridge: Cambridge University Press.

Lohmann, L. (2006), 'Made in the USA: a short history of carbon trading', *Development Dialogue*, **48** (September), 31–70.

Ludwig, D., R. Hilborn and C.J. Walters (1993), 'Uncertainty, resource exploitation, and conservation: lessons from history', *Science*, **260** (5104), 17, 36.

Lutz, B. (1984), *Der kurze Traum immerwährender Prosperität*, Frankfurt: Campus.

Maler, K. (1974), *Environmental Economics: A Theoretical Inquiry*, Baltimore, MD: Johns Hopkins University Press.

Martinez-Alier, J. (2002), *The Environmentalism of the Poor: A Study of Ecological Conflicts and Valuation*, Cheltenham, UK and Northampton, MA, USA: Edward Elgar.

Meadows, D.H., D.L. Meadows, J. Randers and W.W. Behrens III (1972), *The Limits to Growth*, New York: Universe Books.

Mearman, A. (2005), 'Why have post-Keynesians had (relatively) little to say on the economics of the environment?', *International Journal of Environment, Workplace and Employment*, **1** (2), 131–54.

Mishan, E.J. (1969), *Growth: The Price We Pay*, London: Staples Press.

Morris, W. (1993 [1890]), *News from Nowhere*, London: Penguin Books.

Norgaard, R.B. (1994), *Development Betrayed: The End of Progress and a Coevolutionary Revisioning of the Future*, London: Routledge.

O'Neill, J.F. (1993), *Ecology, Policy and Politics: Human Well-Being and the Natural World*, London: Routledge.
O'Neill, J.F. (1997), 'Value, pluralism, incommensurability and institutions', in J. Foster (ed.), *Environmental Economics: A Critique of Orthodox Policy*, London: Routledge.
O'Neill, J.F. (2001), 'Representing people, representing nature, representing the world', *Environment and Planning C: Government and Policy*, **9** (4), 483–500.
Pfister, C. (2003), 'Energiepreise und Umweltbelastung. Zum Stand der Diskussion über das "1950er Syndrom"', in W.E. Siemann (ed.), *Umweltgeschichte Themen und Perspektiven*, Munich: C.H. Beck.
Polanyi, K. (1944), *The Great Transformation*, New York, USA and Toronto, Canada: Rinehart & Company.
Polimeni, J.M., K. Mayumi, M. Giampietro and B. Alcott (2008), *The Jevons Paradox and the Myth of Resource Efficiency Improvements*, London: Earthscan.
Pomeranz, K. (2000), *The Great Divergence: China, Europe and the Making of the Modern World Economy*, Princeton, NJ: Princeton University Press.
Pressman, S. (2006), *Fifty Major Economists*, London: Routledge.
Ravetz, J. (1995), 'Economics as an elite folk science: the suppression of uncertainty', *Journal of Post Keynesian Economics*, **17** (2), 165–84.
Roncaglia, A. (2003), 'Energy and market power: an alternative approach to the economics of oil', *Journal of Post Keynesian Economics*, **25** (4), 641–59.
Schandl, H., M. Fischer-Kowalski, C. Grünbühel and F. Krausmann (2009), 'Socio-metabolic transitions in developing Asia', *Technological Forecasting and Social Change*, **76** (2), 267–81.
Schandl, H. and F. Krausmann (2007), 'The great transformation: a socio-metabolic reading of the industrialization of the United Kingdom', in M. Fischer-Kowalski and H. Haberl (eds), *Socioecological Transition and Global Change: Trajectories of Social Metabolism and Land Use*, Cheltenham, UK and Northampton, MA, USA: Edward Elgar, pp. 83–115.
Schandl, H. and N. Schulz (2002), 'Changes in the United Kingdom's natural relations in terms of society's metabolism and land use from 1850 to the present day', *Ecological Economics*, **41** (2), 203–21.
Sieferle, R.P. (1982), *Der unterirdische Wald. Energiekrise und industrielle Revolution*, Munich: C.H. Beck.
Sieferle, R.P. (2001), *The Subterranean Forest: Energy Systems and the Industrial Revolution*, Cambridge: White Horse Press.
Sieferle, R.P., F. Krausmann, H. Schandl and V. Winiwarter (2006), *Das End der Fläche. Zum sozialen Metabolismus der Industrialisierung*, Cologne: Böhlau.
Smil, V. (2003), *Energy at the Crossroads: Global Perspectives and Uncertainties*, Cambridge, MA: MIT Press.
Sneddon, C., R.B. Howarth and R.B. Norgaard (2006), 'Sustainable development in a post-Brundtland world', *Ecological Economics*, **57** (2), 253–68.
Söderbaum, P. (1999), 'Values, ideology and politics in ecological economics', *Ecological Economics*, **28** (2), 161–70.
Spash, C.L. (1995), 'The political economy of nature', *Review of Political Economy*, **7** (3), 279–93.
Spash, C.L. (1999), 'The development of environmental thinking in economics', *Environmental Values*, **8** (4), 413–35.
Spash, C.L. (2002a), *Greenhouse Economics: Value and Ethics*, London: Routledge.

Spash, C.L. (2002b), 'Strong uncertainty: ignorance and indeterminacy', *Greenhouse Economics: Value and Ethics*, London: Routledge, pp. 120–52.

Spash, C.L. and A.M.H. Clayton (1997), 'The maintenance of natural capital: motivations and methods', in A. Light and J.M. Smith (eds), *Space, Place and Environmental Ethics*, Vol. 1, Lanham, MD: Rowman & Littlefield Publishers, pp. 143–73.

Spash, C.L. and M. Villena (1999), 'Exploring the approach of institutional economics to the environment', Discussion Paper No. 11, Cambridge: Department of Land Economics, University of Cambridge.

Stewart, M. (1979), *Keynes and After*, Harmondsworth: Penguin.

Swanson, T.M. (1994), *The International Regulation of Extinction*, London: Macmillan.

United Nations Development Programme (2008), *Human Development Report 2007/2008: Fighting Climate Change: Human Solidarity in a Divided World*, Basingstoke: Palgrave Macmillan.

van der Sluijs, J.P., M. Craye, S. Funtowicz, P. Kloprogge, J. Ravetz and J. Risbey (2005), 'Combining quantitative and qualitative measures of uncertainty in model-based environmental assessment: the NUSAP system', *Risk Analysis*, **25** (2), 481–92.

Vatn, A. (2005), *Institutions and the Environment*, Cheltenham, UK and Northampton, MA, USA: Edward Elgar.

Wynne, B. (1992), 'Uncertainty and environmental learning: reconceiving science and policy in the preventive paradigm', *Global Environmental Change* (June), 111–27.

4. The environmental case for a collective assessment of economism

Richard B. Norgaard

INTRODUCTION

Environmental economics emerged over the latter half of the twentieth century to fine-tune the economy, perhaps defensible in its early years, but it is now obvious that we need a major economic adjustment. Since 1900, the human population has increased four times, from some 1.6 billion to about 6.7 billion. During the same period, the global market economy has increased by about a factor of 25, from less than US$2 trillion to about US$50 trillion per year. Science and technology have made this possible, fossil hydrocarbons and ecosystem degradation feed the 'affluenza', while corporate advertising and public infrastructure promote ever more consumption and waste. The realization that our children will suffer from climate change, biodiversity loss and reduced ecosystem services is slowly convincing many that we need to change dramatically how we interact with each other and nature. Taking on such a major adjustment will require that we deconstruct the economic myths, the 'economism', that has kept the economy on course in spite of the mounting social and environmental evidence.

In spite of the vast differences between rich and poor, academics and farm workers, and the political and economic perspectives people hold, people function together in a global economy in amazing synchrony. Roughly half of the people in the world are absolutely dependent on the actions of others through a complex economic system. Some among the other half of the global population who are not so enmeshed in the world's economy are actively protesting against its inequities at meetings of the World Trade Organization. A few are violently opposing postmodern culture as a whole, drawing attention to their wrath by flying airliners into the World Trade Center. At the beginning of the third millennium, the economy is central to daily human life and people's concerns for the future.

Let me, for the moment, distinguish between an economy that is 'out there' and the complex of myths that people, both individually and in order to act together, have developed to aid them in living within the economy. This distinction is roughly parallel to nature as a reality of its own and the complex of myths that traditional peoples hold about nature and their relation to nature. In traditional societies, myths provide explanations for natural phenomena, facilitate individual and collective decisions, and give meaning and coherence to life. Modern people, and what can now only be understood as postmodern, also require comparable beliefs about the world around them, a world that is largely economic. I refer to this complex of myths as economism. Of course, the economy that is 'out there' and economism have coevolved. While traditional people's beliefs affected how they interacted with and thereby were a selective force upon natural evolution, their populations were relatively small compared to the natural world that evolved for millennia before them. Not so the economy. The economy and economism are not separate at all in time frames of a decade.

BACKGROUND

Historically, people characterized environmental problems as individual bad things that needed to be changed. Sewage needed to be carried further away or treated, smoke stacks needed to be taller or combustion technologies changed, and lead needed to be used more carefully if at all. In this framing, environmental problems are resolved by regulating releases or mandating the replacement of technologies. Questions of technological possibilities were central, and scientists and engineers reigned over the environmental policy process through the 1960s.

By the 1960s, the practice of cost–benefit analysis had improved and economic arguments began to dampen engineers' dreams of manifest destiny in the development of water, transport, and other systems. Economists began to portray pollution and other environmental questions in economic terms. Economists at Resources for the Future played a central role in laying the foundation for this transition of thinking about the benefits and costs of environmental protection (Clawson and Knetsch, 1966; Kneese and Bower, 1968). Within this context, without questioning the economic system or system of myths within which values were expressed, economists began to estimate environmental values within a broad argument that there are optimal levels of environmental quality. Engineers were still needed to find least-cost approaches to pollution control, but economists positioned themselves, in a process that was of course ultimately political, as holding the formula for optimally balancing the interests of polluters and pollutees. Four decades later, this economic mindset dominates public and political discussions, though not political outcomes, from the provision of local ecosystem services to the solutions for global climate change. Yet, while some environmental conflicts are partially being resolved through markets, new environmental problems continue to emerge. While trying to fine-tune the environmental dial through market-based approaches, global drivers of environmental change have dramatically worsened. To change tracks, we have to acknowledge that the whole institutional structure and system of beliefs through which we now perceive, understand, discuss, weigh and react to environmental problems is wholly inadequate.

Like fish trying to grasp the nature of water, getting a clear picture of the economy and its role in the current human trajectory is going to be difficult. Half of the world's population is deeply immersed in the economic system, playing specialized roles, connecting to each other through markets. Specialization in both scientific understanding and experiential understanding makes it more and more difficult for a single individual to begin to see and understand the system as a whole. Furthermore, the economy is increasingly becoming people's lens on reality. Things are important in accordance with how people relate to them through the economy. The 'diamond and water paradox' has been forgotten, and the current level and share of things in our household budgets and gross national product has become a measure of importance. Changing prices signal abundance or scarcity, telling people not only what to consume or conserve but in which areas to seek education, invest capital and transform the land. And now in science as well (certainly among conservation biologists), market valuation techniques are becoming an essential way of not only expressing value to the public but also for aggregating environmental impacts in scientific analyses. The economy has become our window on the world through which we understand nature. Supporting this perspective, filling in the missing details, people have developed what I will refer to as economism, a set of beliefs constituting a secular religion guiding the remnants of our modern hopes for human progress: material, moral and scientific.

From the perspective of the economic priests who extol proper, formal ways of thinking about the economic system and some of the most important decisions people make, privately and publicly, the economy and the values people express through it are simply 'given'. Of course, people can see that the economy is rapidly evolving over time, in part in response to the preaching of economists. With the signals of environmental degradation becoming overwhelming, it makes little sense simply to keep trying to adjust incentives within the existing economic system. It is time to question openly and collectively the system within which people are privately and publicly making decisions. But doing so leaves people with serious problems of 'footing'; that is, on what do we stand?

Seeing the whole economic system, including how it has affected the path people's values have taken, is by no means easy. As the spottiness of my own argumentation in this current effort shows, my own 'glimpses' do not combine into a clear view. As a society, we will need to take a critical look into the system, putting our respective insights together, and then building something new. It will take time and cooperation, but a central message of this chapter is that those who are morally concerned about the environmental transformations under way and the future of humanity may be able to enrich and strengthen their voices by collectively calling for an assessment of economism and working together to understand it.

ECONOMISM

'Economism' refers to the mix of popular, political and policy mythology as well as practical beliefs that help us understand and rationalize the economy and how we live within it. People share some of these beliefs globally; other beliefs people adapt to fit particular national and regional situations; while yet others serve specific groups, including economists. Economism is to the formal models of the discipline of economics as environmental beliefs are to ecology and environmental science more generally. Just as selected parts, sometimes old remnants, of environmental science help inform and justify environmental beliefs, both those advocating conservation and those espousing development, bits of the logic and findings from the discipline of economics help inform economism, whether politically left or right. Our more conserving-oriented environmental beliefs influence funding for environmental science, and how environmental scientists choose between frameworks, the ways in which they interpret their results and how they speak to the public. Similarly, technologically optimistic environmental beliefs influence a more technologically optimistic community of biologists and natural scientists, how they are funded and how they communicate to the public. While distinctions between environmentalism and environmental science, and between technological optimism and technology-driven science are commonly recognized, the term 'economism' and its relationship to economic theory and the body of knowledge of economists are only beginning to be discussed. Others have used the term 'economism', but it is a new concept to most people, even in academe. The academic discipline of economics is so tightly bound by and infused with economism that distinctions are more difficult than those between environmental beliefs and science. One important distinction is that few environmental scientists use their science to justify, to rationalize the rightness of, the current state of the environment. Economists regularly take the distribution of income as a given and thereby reach conclusions that defend the status quo. In this sense, almost all economics is advocacy science. Thus economism is not only the better word to describe the role of economics in our lives, but also an important entry point to understanding the discipline and profession of economics.

For purposes of elaboration, economism can be divided into multiple interactive realms of beliefs. First, there is academic economism: the beliefs guiding the careful choice of equations, data, methods and words that appear in academic articles, and the beliefs guiding the disciplinary dynamics that lead to a few articles and the economists who write them being important while most are not. Second, there is the acculturation of students, from the lessons about markets in secondary school on to the training of those who graduate with doctoral degrees in economics. Acculturation also includes the beliefs embedded in the general interest material about the economy appearing in the popular press and in books. Third, there are the beliefs influencing how economists work professionally, interacting with those who need their services, in governmental policy and implementation processes, as well as in the corporate sector. Fourth, there is the popular political economic discourse on ends and means. And, fifth, there is people's everyday solid, albeit particular, empirical evidence grounded in their participation in the economy and the broader, fuzzy beliefs that help fit what highly specialized capitalists, landowners and laborers know into a larger sense of reality. Living within a highly fragmented, market-linked, nearly global economy rather than, for example, in a nearly self-sufficient community of near subsistence farms, demands and facilitates different explanations and rationales among different actors. We should expect economism, like the economy, to be highly differentiated even while the multitude of myths work together.

We can see separate realms. What is taught as basic economics bears little relationship to the diversity of the explorations of the small proportion of innovative economists, many at the best universities, who are questioning economic conventions and exploring new paths (Colander et al., 2004). The ethereal mathematical abstractions of academic economics bear little relation to the commonsense understanding of laborers working in a globalized economy. And yet there are strong feedbacks between these different realms as well as selective processes affecting their evolution over time. The theory of exchange of products, incorrectly used by capitalists, politicians and academic economists to justify freeing one factor of production – capital – so that it is globally mobile, has transformed everyday economic life. The variety and price of goods, as well as wages and employment opportunities in developing economies, as well as profits, wages and employment security in developed economies, are all transformed by late twentieth century developments in economism. In this sense, the different realms of economism cannot be disentangled.

The importance of economism and the ways it has become integral to modern, and now postmodern, life is also critical. Our global economy is a product of economic reasoning, albeit using highly selected and sometimes incorrect parts of economic reasoning. A great many individual decisions, some with deep moral implications, are now determined by income and prices. We perceive and understand 'reality' from our particular positions in the economy and through the economy to the positions of others and a world of resources and ecosystem services. Our hopes for the future are frequently reduced to merely economic portrayals of material progress. Economism is our secular religion within which we engage in political discourse about values and through which we describe our relations to each other and our overall position in the world. In short, today economism functions as have religions throughout history.

Let me elaborate this further with a particular example around which my broader argument will build. Since 1990, with the rise in concern over environmental sustainability, natural scientists, especially conservation biologists, have become increasingly engaged in debates over the course of development and the implementation of new development strategies. Within these debates, while defending biodiversity and ecosystem integrity, they found monetary valuation strategically very attractive. Describing the value of nature in monetary terms did not necessarily fit their personal values and relations to nature. However, for younger biologists who have been acculturated in economism since their youth, monetary valuation, with its emphasis on summing individual values, seems to present fewer conflicts than it does for older biologists with a stronger sense of moral discourse in politics before economism dominated, and also a stronger sense of a public good. But young and old feel they are driven to address biodiversity loss and ecosystem integrity through what they think is, and portray as, economics. Identifying the contradictions of this particular new interest in economic valuation provides a way of identifying why we cannot use purportedly objective economic techniques to get us out of a predicament that economism has been central to getting us into.

Conservation biologists share the objective of conserving biological diversity, and this objective defines their academic and professional careers. While they personally value biodiversity 'for its own sake' or because they hold life sacred in some way or another, they also have come to believe that the majority of people will never appreciate the richness of life as they do. Nature films have vastly increased the public's awareness, but conservation biologists have concluded that to get through media barriers and engage in the rough and tumble of real politics, money talks louder than our attraction to the cute and fuzzy or our public sense of the complex, delicate dynamics of nature. Thus just as engineers in America at mid-twentieth century in the era of large water projects were drawn to learn economics and contribute to the practice of cost–benefit analysis, so biologists are drawn into learning some economics and contributing to its application today in the discourse on the value of ecosystem services, as well as the possibility of saving ecosystems through payments for their services.

Economics textbooks present the human predicament as largely a problem of imperfect markets. We misuse the environment because there are not markets for pollution or ecosystem services. As a consequence, the prices generated in imperfect markets lead people to make choices about interacting with the environment that are not in the public interest. Market prices need to be corrected by including all of nature's services. Cost–benefit analyses used in public decisions also need to include values that are not currently reflected in markets. So, to a large extent, the problem is portrayed as one of getting the prices right so that the right decisions are made. And getting the prices right is portrayed as a technical difficulty to be overcome by doing economics well. Hence conservation biologists are busily learning economic theory.

In fact, however, conservation biologists are simply learning economism. Economic theory is much more complicated and raises far more interesting questions than it answers, and what real theory says about values provides the strongest levers for conservation biologists.

In 1838, the French mathematician Augustin Cournot determined that markets could equilibrate at multiple efficient combinations of prices and quantities depending on how rights to factors of production are initially assigned between people (Cournot, 1963 [1897]). English mathematical economists rediscovered the same phenomena several decades later. The field of welfare economics flourished between the 1930s and 1960s. In this subdiscipline, economists derived the conditions necessary for deriving public values from existing prices. It was also instrumental to reaching a professional consensus around rationalizations for presuming that those conditions were reasonable approximations of reality for the purposes of doing cost–benefit analysis (Eckstein, 1958). The assumptions and rationales made some sense for considering the costs and benefits of individual public investments in an era when global environmental constraints were not yet of concern, and the belief that progress would lead to a more equalitarian society was strong. And then the assumptions became established as practical working doctrine (Harberger, 1971). The assumptions and rationales make no sense at all for thinking about global-scale phenomena driven by climate change, biodiversity loss or ecosystem transformation. They make no sense in an era when progress through the 'control of nature' has so clearly failed and income inequality is increasing.

The sustainability debate is fundamentally about ethics, about whether our descendants have a right to an environment more or less like the one we have, or at least the right to an environment that is changing at a manageable speed. And when rights are reassigned, market prices, even interest rates change (Howarth and Norgaard, 1992). The key point is that value systems beyond economics must be tapped to ponder whether we want to give future generations more rights. Conservation biology can help inform this moral decision, and conservation biologists have taken a personal stand on the issue. When conservation biologists resort to economism, they vastly simplify the scientific information they can convey about ecosystems and undercut their own values. During the rise of popular concern over sustainability, even the economics profession accepted the point that sustainability is a matter of rights and ethics beyond economics. But as public concern with sustainability peaked and became just one of many concerns, this acceptance by economists was followed by a concerted, deceptive effort to show that the conventional way economics models the future and its related assumptions about valuing the future were quite adequate after all (Portney and Weyant, 1999). The veil of economism was once again pulled in front of economics.

The fact that efficient market prices depend on the distribution of rights to capital, land and education and other factors affecting income has been known within economics for nearly two centuries. Thus, on the one hand, economists quickly point out when challenged that they themselves have thoroughly identified this relationship, usually expressed in a tone implying that others have no right to even point this out. Yet, on the other hand, in practice the economics profession works very effectively with economism, ignoring the fact that past moral choices with respect to the distribution of rights affect the nature of value expressed in markets today.

I am not arguing that we can have a rational society guided simply by objective evidence and pure reason. Even if we had a community of extremely bright scientists working with models that were coherent across the sciences, unlimited computing power and incredible amounts of data, we would still need myths by which the vast majority of people could live. Rather, I am arguing that environmental science provides sufficient clear evidence that economism as a system of myths by which to operate is destroying the environment, threatening present and future populations, and likely ending human culture as we have known it. Further, in my experience from within economics, economists are the first to defend economism over reason and evidence.

ECONOMISM AND THE POSTMODERN SOCIO-ECOLOGICAL PREDICAMENT

I have already introduced the term 'postmodern' and use it with some trepidation, but it provides an important lens on economism. Only the very rich have a mastery over their private lives that fits the modern dream. To be sure, those in the middle class and above have incredible material access, but it provides them with but temporary command or pleasure (Brekke and Howarth, 2000). Rather, most people are on a material treadmill, running faster while staying in place or even slipping behind. Similar to the term 'postmodern', I introduce the term 'command' deliberately. Command over nature was a central idea in the rise of modern natural philosophy and its unfolding as science and technology (Merchant, 1980), while command over one's life was a defining point in the rise of individualism and materialism in modern moral philosophy (Norgaard, 1994). Markets bring us new options, but the specialization required to earn more to stay engaged in the expanding economy robs us of more general skills and the options associated with exercising them. Economists emphasize the joys of choice, and choice is central to economism. Our choices, however, do not lead to control over what we get in the medium to long run. When what we choose makes little difference, the economic emphasis on choice loses meaning and life itself loses meaning. Thus one strand of my argument is that the transition from modern to postmodern is closely related to the transition from the sense that modern science and economics would soon bring us control over our lives, to the sense that command will forever remain beyond our grasp. And fruitless grasping for meaning through efforts to get command of one's life is a symptom of postmodernism.

The rise of utopian hopes, and fall in the delusion of control, is recent. The hopes for science and progress ignited in the nineteenth century seemed to be coming true in the twentieth through very rapid change. Improved technologies, complemented by advances in science, allowed humanity to reduce its immediate dependence on energy from the sun and coevolve a whole new economy around technologies fueled by fossil hydrocarbons (Norgaard, 1994). Tremendous scientific advances, economic growth and increased access to material goods seemed to validate a gain in command. In spite of the First World War, the Great Depression, the Second World War, and the emergence of nuclear weapons and the Cold War, hubris was high at mid-century as we prepared to develop the world as a whole.

Rapidly changing times, however, are inherently risky. To a large extent, what we think of as command over nature through modern technologies, our new approach to environmental management, has been a process of pushing problems to a new environmental medium, to a greater distance, or to a future time so that for a while the problems go unseen. With fast rates of change, however, the period of not being seen has shortened into periods of individual memory. In a world of instant communication and globalization, pollution pushed aside is soon discovered again. There is also a greater likelihood in rapidly changing times that lags in ecological adjustments and the crossing of unforeseen thresholds, combined with lags in detection and policy response, will leave us in devastating situations. Many of the scientists collectively trying to understand climate change, where environmental system lags are critical, to say nothing of social system lags, see humanity as being in a very dangerous situation (Baer and Mastrandrea, 2006; Spratt and Sutton, 2008). Conservation biologists see many of the world's ecological systems as being on the verge of collapse due to rapid increases in population and material consumption, while the modest policy corrective actions now being contemplated are completely inadequate to stem the destruction (Millennium Ecosystem Assessment, 2005). The inland Sacramento–San Joaquin Delta between California's capitol city, Sacramento, and the San Francisco metropolitan region is one of the most scientifically studied areas of the world, yet ecologists admit that today they can say little more about the dynamics of its various fisheries than they could in 1980. The dynamics are simply too complex and changing; and this is before they factor in more rapid rates of sea level rise and new invasives inherent in future climate and associated ecosystem changes (Healey et al., 2008).

The myth that we can learn how to master nature to consume ever more has given way to the myth of sustainable development, that we can learn how to live with nature and all consume at least a significant amount. But scientists working 'where the rubber hits the road' with respect to ecosystems management and restoration are worried because they comprehend, command and control so little. The delusions of command through science and technology parallel those in the personal lives we lead.

There are moral parallels to the way we have technologically displaced environmental problems that then come back to haunt us in new forms. Adam Smith's great discovery that individual greed serves the public good through markets helped to reduce mercantilism, to reduce and disperse economic power sanctioned by the state, for a while. But it also allowed us to rationalize individually whatever we do within the economy. The geographical expansion of markets meant that the effects of our activities were becoming further and further distant. The substitution of market relations for activities that occurred within the home and between friends reduced diverse relationships and moral obligations, the basis of community, to mutual greed. Then economic development became equated with human progress, a concept previously derived from moral progress (Bury, 1932). Eventually market logic, though now more economism than logic, also became the model for the public sector itself and is now the basis of political discourse among the masses (Brown, 1994; Frank, 2000). Managing problems through economic morality pushes the problems out of sight and into the future. Conveniently, economic assumptions provide moral blinkers as well.

One consequence of subjecting problems to economism is that we have not been able to carry on the broader moral discussion needed to guide the economy to address the inequities inherent in economic development, climate change and ecosystem destruction. The inequities are now compounding the environmental difficulties. The rich with incredible global material access cannot see, or refuse to acknowledge, the implications of their richness while the poor, merely to survive, are driven to destroy the few environmental services they can access locally. More importantly, corporations exercise power, setting the rules of the market for the short-run interests of executives and stockholders, while the citizenry romps in imagined free market idyll (Reich, 2007).

At the same time, however, some scientists and engineers are arguing we will soon reap untold benefits from bioengineering and nanotechnology, commanding the natural and man-made environment to support ecstatic lives of health and wealth. Social theorists and ethicists counter-argue that we are neither organized nor morally prepared to discuss and address the ethical issues inherent in bioengineering (reviewed in Norgaard, 2004; Sandel, 2007). Imagine the disparities and moral challenges that will arise as bioengineering is applied beyond disease correction to human improvement itself. If we continue to pursue free market ethics, the rich will have first access to producing super-children, leaving the masses inevitably to become 'substandard'. Clearly, some serious thinking about moral choices in a modern economy is desperately needed.

While those exalting in the transformative powers of new technologies (Kurzweil, 2005) and those pondering the dynamics of the socio-ecological system (Millennium Ecosystem Assessment, 2005) see the future remarkably differently, most people do not think much about the future at all. Of course, they think about how they might improve their own well-being and that of their family within the economic system in which they are embedded. The engagement of the masses in the economy, their inability to disengage and see what is happening to us as a whole and how we might best guide systemic change, is a major part of the problem too. Of course this is not new. Throughout history, only a few have ever taken on the burden of looking ahead for the whole. But the ideal of democratic societies where each participates in determining the direction for all remains laudable and lauded. Indeed some, including me, argue that discursive democracy still provides some hope (Dryzek, 1990, 2000; Norgaard, 2007). Yet within the gap between reality and ideal, powerful interests have done their best to manipulate both the values and the understanding of individuals.

In retrospect, we can now see that worrying about the future and rethinking our moral order were never on the horizon of the modern expedition. Quite the contrary, we were on the path to utopia; the future need only be hastened toward. As the drudgery of life lessoned, theologians imagined people facing fewer material temptations and having more time to be religious, while secular modernists saw people increasingly involved in the artistic life where moral issues are parsed and sophistication grows. Rather than worrying about the future, we lost our ability to even seriously think about the future or question whether we were fulfilling our obligations to our progeny. On the path of progress, knowledge and values improve, things increase or become more advanced, perhaps the order of accumulation is uncertain, and morality can slip backward, but the path is to completeness, fulfillment. How can there be a different science or moral order?

A significant change in how we interact with each other and nature will be technically very difficult. We fully occupy the globe, and this means that any mistakes in the transition will come at the cost of further ecosystem transformation with fewer and fewer opportunities for recovery. Experimentation is difficult because our socio-economic and ecological systems are tightly coupled. People's livelihoods are highly interdependent in what has become a truly global economy. To complicate the difficulties further, we live in rapidly changing times, socially and ecologically. For these reasons, strong, informed environmental and economic governance are absolutely necessary in order to shift toward sustainability while not crashing either our ecological or our socio-economic systems.

Yet strong informed governance is more elusive than ever. Our knowledge remains highly fragmented in relation to scientific disciplines and bureaucratic boundaries while it is becoming ever more specialized in relation to economic roles and interests. This makes communication, shared understanding and collective governance increasingly difficult. A corporate-controlled media trivializes social and ecological analysis into 'infotainment' while supporting further consumption. Free market ideology promotes individual over collective choice and has been used to shrink both the role of government and our expectations for its quality. To compound problems further, material inequality is increasing within and between nations, further narrowing future options while challenging the possibilities of effective governance arising in order to reach them.

In the absence of strong, coherent political governance, market prices provide the dominant feedback signals. Markets, however, are not the self-governing dream espoused by many economists. They are incomplete, insensitive to social and ecological complexities, and give little heed to the future. A naive reliance on markets without adequate laws, regulations and mores to guide market actors surely accounts for much of the gravity of the human condition.

As faith in secular material progress fades, as belief in the commanding possibilities of science, technology and rational governance shrivels, religions are once again providing individuals with a sense of destiny and their position in a whole system. Religious beliefs, however, are hardening and diverging around original sacred texts rather than becoming more tolerant and converging around common moral concerns with the future of humanity. Indeed, a few splinter religious groups within every religious tradition are beginning to challenge the corporatized remnants of modern social order, some violently.

The resilience of progressive religion, rise of evangelicalisms and resurgence of fundamentalism provide the biggest surprises for many observers of modernity. Religion can be defined as a system of narratives, symbols and rituals that situate individuals in a larger whole, providing a basis for understanding reality holistically while also supporting ethical norms (Bellah, 2001). Many of the differences between religious systems are with respect to how they explain the nature of life, while there is relatively more homogeneity in the moral orders they espouse. This led many, secularists and religious, to argue in the nineteenth century that, as science developed a unified view of nature and where people fitted in the scheme of things, people would shed religious explanations of natural phenomena and their position with respect to nature. The increase in informed rationality and systemic understanding would progressively reduce the scope of religion to simply a moral sphere. And this would provide the conditions for religions to converge around their common moral teachings.

This secularist explanation of the future of religion, of how it would adapt to progress, was widely accepted. Every major religious tradition has progressive branches that accept science, actively reinterpret historic texts to fit modern times, and promote ecumenical and interfaith efforts to work together around common moral concerns. They also accept the separations between church, state and science, and hence rarely engage in moral politics or raise questions about science in public discourse. But while progressive religious traditions are clearly present, they have steadily lost followers over the past half-century. Fundamentalist believers of diverse religious traditions never went away, but their leaders and followers have long stayed out of active social discourse and politics, until recently. Within this gap between a shrinking progressive tradition and fundamentalism, a new movement steadily gained ground, starting largely in North America during the 1930s. Evangelicals read the bible literally, though selectively, and hold modern beliefs that allow them to accept modern technology and economic institutions, while engaging intensely in social commentary about individual morality. Then, unlike either progressives or fundamentalists, many evangelicals began actively to engage in politics and personally enter the halls of power during the 1980s (Lindsay, 2007). Some also openly questioned the monopoly that science holds on true descriptions of natural phenomena in general and evolutionary accounts of 'the descent of man' in particular. In retrospect, we can see that science has not developed the coherent story that most people apparently need to feel comfortably situated in a larger order. So now we see educated people, even some scientists, reading religious texts literally and choosing religious explanations about life over scientific ones. In the process, religious differences have also become accentuated (Smith, 1998; Almond et al., 2003).

There is a strong interplay between the fragmentation, devaluing and fall of science in the public sphere and the fragmentation and revaluing of religion, especially the rise of strict readings of religious texts, in the public sphere. Modern science has long been connected to a narrative of progress through the comprehension, command and control of nature. In practice, without having made a concerted effort to build toward shared public goals, modern science has proved remarkably incomplete, myopic, frequently disastrous in practice and in various ways unfulfilling. Environmental movements, while informed by science and until recently strictly working in the realm of the secular, have been instrumental in debunking the progressive narrative with respect to the comprehension of and command over nature. The environmental movement, having its own sense of the wholeness of nature, has been a very effective critic of fragmented sciences and science-driven agencies. The environmental movement and environmental scientists, however, have not been able to build a coherent system of science and management to replace the fragmented approach of the progressive era that they have successfully critiqued (Norgaard, 1994, 2008; Norgaard and Baer, 2005a).

The creation story of science and explanations of our place in the universe are apparently too rich and humbling for many people. Largely in response to the ecological crisis, selected scientific explanations of our place in the world, without the narrative of human progress through complete comprehension, command and control of nature, are now being synthesized with religious traditions in a way that may provide meaning for the many some day (Berry, 2006; Swimme, 1996; Tucker, 2003).

Few expected modernity to unfold into dramatically divergent views and yet collective impotence through unity in economism. It is difficult to imagine a combination of social trajectories more unfavorable for seriously addressing our environmental challenges, whether taking a technological option perspective or a moral order perspective. Economism plays a critical role in holding us together, rushing between work and shopping mall with amazing synchrony, yet remaining passive politically.

Nevertheless, within this dismal overall picture, key groups of scientists have learned how to bring their diverse expertise together to assess the gravity of the human predicament from an environmental and technological perspective. We need to learn from this process to undertake an assessment of economism in postmodernity.

COLLECTIVE ASSESSMENTS, DECONSTRUCTING ECONOMISM, AND BUILDING SUSTAINABILITY

Scientists with both the Intergovernmental Panel on Climate Change (IPCC) (2007) and the Millennium Ecosystem Assessment (MA) (2005) are clearly spelling out the technological implications of the complex environmental challenges we face, and the weaknesses of existing organizational structures for addressing them. Similar collective learning efforts are under way, focusing on different issues and working at different geographical and political scales. Yet governments, corporations and individuals have responded only modestly at best to these scientists' collective portrayal of the human predicament. Indeed, to a large extent their findings are treated simply as the perspective of yet another special interest. We are beginning to see some, but still inadequate, movement with respect to climate change, while the richness of the shared understandings of scientists with respect to our dependence on natural systems more generally are not being broadly accepted.

The ways in which we perceive and understand reality, however, are not easily separated from the economism that dominates the moral order guiding how we care. And so the apparent disinterest in the collective scientific portrayals of the seriousness of the human condition leads to the question of whether we simply do not care about the future of humanity and nature, or we do not have adequate moral systems to both inform and express our care. Of course both are certainly true to some extent, as well as mutually reinforcing. Just as importantly, the feedbacks between care and knowing go both ways. This suggests that a collective assessment of economism could prove complementary with scientific environmental assessments in the transition to a sustainable future for humanity and nature.

One of the interesting aspects of the IPCC and MA is the differing extents to which they have forced participating economists to confront how they are embedded in economism. From the beginning, the IPCC process has been surrounded by a 'theoretical' debate over the nature of costs, and especially interest rates (DeCanio, 2003). The IPCC process, however, has not been open to dissenting economists or social scientists in general. The physical scientists who initiated the IPCC process seemed to be more comfortable with the certainty provided by the range of conventional economic thinking, narrowed within economism, than with the open contestation of the social sciences as a whole (Spash, 2002). Not having been invited into the IPCC process, a broader social science community set out to work on its own (Rayner and Malone, 1998). Yet in an atmosphere of open liberal debate, alternative economic arguments have been reviewed in the IPCC process. The arguments that Clive Spash put forward with respect to a sustainability approach or that Howarth and I put forward with respect to the rights of future generations and the use of overlapping generation models were reviewed in the second IPCC assessment and then ignored (Pearce et al., 1996). Thus the dominant assumptions made in the culture of economism have held sway, keeping the role of economics in IPCC assessments and economic outcomes tightly bounded. The report issued by Sir Nicholas Stern (2007) created as much controversy (Nordhaus, 2007; Spash, 2007) as it did because it broke through some of the conventions of economism and reached a different economic conclusion.

The Millennium Ecosystem Assessment proved to be a much more open forum that readily confronted economism. Participants from developing countries repeatedly pointed out that the values of environmental services were heavily weighted by who had the income to pay for them. Hence, the importance of different ecosystem services reflected the tastes and concerns of the rich more than the poor. The dollars of rich ecotourists spent on international airfares are weighted the same as the dollars of the poor spent on bus fares to get to work. Thus MA participants readily saw how markets to save trees to sequester carbon, for example, are being established in poor nations where the poor are 'willing' to stop using forests because the rich have the economic power to buy up the rights of the poor to stop them from using other ecosystem services of the forest. As a consequence, carbon sequestration is cheaper than it would be in a world with less income disparity. The rich can continue to drive their sport utility vehicles (SUVs) because the poor are willing to forego using their forests for little. Once this was made clear within the MA process, it was very difficult to use prices generated in markets as neutral values. In short, the open participatory process of the MA began to deconstruct economism.

Another major contradiction of economic valuation appeared in the Millennium Ecosystem Assessment. Several scientists noticed that for there to be any rationality to relying on stated preferences or behavior to derive the values of environmental services, one would have to assume that lay people were sufficiently informed of the very complexities the MA scientists were struggling to understand. This assumption contradicted the objective of the MA to provide much-needed knowledge to the public and policy-makers. In short, as with the problem of measuring resource scarcity by looking at prices over time (Norgaard, 1990), the problems of using monetary values to weight phenomena are tightly embedded in the very socio-economic system driving the problems of ecosystem degradation that the MA sought to understand in order to design better socio-economic policies. This contradiction highlights how difficult it is to understand nature without looking through the economy with the aid of economism.

Both modern science and the modern moral order are highly fragmented. 'Mix and match' characterizes our approach, both as individuals and as nations, to discussing technical options and their moral implications. Addressing technical options boils down to a battle over multiple frameworks and metaphors from the natural sciences, while in discussing moral implications we battle between diverse sacred and utilitarian perspectives and narratives. Let me be very clear that I have no hopes that either the natural sciences or moral philosophy will soon be integrated through some meta model that shows us how the fragments of each come together into a seamless whole. Quite the contrary: economism provides some of the glue needed to hold the fragments together, to the extent that they are held together. Deconstructing economism will expose more fragmentation.

The scientific community is reasonably successfully addressing the fragmentation of science by bringing thousands of scientists from diverse disciplines together to assess complex issues like climate change and ecosystem degradation. The sciences are not integrated in this process. Rather, the implications of the diverse fragments are explored, and reasonable judgments about the whole are reached among the steady, long-term participants in the process. Lesser, shorter-term participants also make breakthroughs, bridging particular barriers that open their minds to new research questions and interpretations that bridge disciplines (Wilson and Howarth, 2002; Norgaard and Baer, 2005b). While diverse sectors of the economy follow the separate technological options provided by different fragments of science, the multi-scientist assessments try to look at the whole picture and identify superior technological directions from a more united scientific perspective. From both the climate and the ecosystem assessments, we hear calls for substantial changes, new technological paths.

Yet these calls from the scientific community go unheeded to a large extent because they clash with the comfortable rationalizations of economism, and because our deeper moral concerns are not tapped in political debates with powerful interests cloaked in economism. To change the track of the economy substantially to assure a sustainable, desirable future, we need to work with our moral fragmentation in a similar way as scientists have dealt with the fragmentation of science. We need to construct socially a new context for serious moral discussion to move towards sufficient shared moral judgment to make big changes. We need to step back consciously from the economism that satisfies our current moral needs within the economy that is off-track, and discuss what is really important, and what not.

Integrated environmental assessments provide some interesting lessons for thinking about an assessment of economism and our system of morals. Here I identify four. First, bring the full range of voices to the table. Though environmental scientists generally and ecologists in particular tend to be concerned about the future, they always bring technological optimists into the environmental assessment process. Similarly, any effort to understand economism needs to include those who think everything is going fine, and those who do not, from economists, secular moral philosophers, theologians and sociologists, among others. By including scholars who think we are moving in favorable directions into the assessment process, we can seriously engage our differences as well as arrive at a fuller understanding of how economism works. Serious libertarians, neoclassical economists, avowed socialists and Marxists must be included along with economic sociologists, economic anthropologists, historians, psychologists and political theorists, as well as theologians and scholars from a broad range of religious perspectives. The whole point is to span differences that are reflected in the community at large and then provide an environment in which the incompleteness of separate myths helps move the participants toward a new understanding of how economic beliefs and structures affect moral perceptions, analysis and decisions.

Second, participants should expect and look forward to learning with each other. This is difficult in scientific assessments. Many scientists feel that any incongruities in understanding between the disciplines are due to deficiencies in the thinking of others. No doubt this will be more of a problem in an assessment of economism, especially one focusing on the moral outcomes of economism. And so participants need to be selected for a predilection for learning, and weeded out if they prove too dogmatic. It is absolutely essential that people be prepared both to teach others what they take to be central and to learn from others as well. Each participant has to have a clear sense that together they can reach a deeper understanding of how economism misguides modernity.

Third, participants should not come to the assessment process hoping to discover some underlying consistent interpretation of economism that will lead to a new construction and some sort of moral unity. The process of assessment will highlight troubling differences between participants, some that participants had not considered before, and many of these will remain after the process is over. A narrow agenda might need to be agreed upon that is aimed at particular issues relevant to environmental and cultural sustainability. To the extent that agreement is found, it is reached through shared human judgment, rather than the discovery of a model and meta-ethics that unites all in their interpretation of economism. Most importantly, agreement on the moral implications of a discussion about climate change, for example, can sometimes be reached even while particular rationales, or ordering of the rationales, may differ. Fragmentation will continue to exist, but hopefully inappropriate fragments will be weeded out as well.

Fourth, in fact we can expect the assessment process to intensify a sense of both unity and disunity in our understanding and interpretation of economism. Ecologists in the MA came to realize that there are greater differences between what they had become accustomed to thinking about as similar ecosystems, greater than they typically present in textbooks and lectures. It proved considerably more difficult to make general arguments about ecosystems in the company of ecologists from supposedly similar ecosystems. How economism works in conjunction with authoritarian and democratic societies, let alone for example Catholicism and Islam, which also have multiple traditions and tremendous variation across regions and between groups within regions, will make it very difficult to generalize about how economism works and affects moral arguments. Yet even as greater differences come to the fore, shared understanding can be reached with respect to the importance of economism, the moral condition and new directions needed.

CONCLUSION

From within economism, the economic system and beliefs we hold, we cannot conceive of how we could possibly reduce greenhouse emissions by 80 percent from 1990 levels by 2050. Conventional economic analyses suggest that it pays to cook the planet; that investing in whatever technological change arises will benefit people more than providing future generations with a stable climate. Some hope that, by getting started on reducing those greenhouse gases that can be easily reduced, reductions will become easier and easier over time. While getting started will certainly help, my own sense is that we will have to move beyond economism to a more suitable belief system to keep from cooking humanity and nature as we have known them.

REFERENCES

Almond, Gabriel A., R. Scott Appleby and Emmanuel Sivan (2003), *Strong Religion: The Rise of Fundamentalisms around the World*, Chicago, IL: University of Chicago Press.

Baer, Paul and Michael Mastrandrea (2006), *High Stakes: Designing Emissions Pathways to Reduce the Risk of Dangerous Climate Change*, London: Institute for Public Policy Research.

Bellah, Robert N. (2001), 'Habit and history', *Ethical Perspectives*, **8** (3), 156–67.

Berry, Thomas (2006), *Evening Thoughts: Reflections on Earth as a Sacred Community*, Mary Evelyn Tucker (ed.), Berkeley, CA: University of California Press.

Brekke, Kjell Arne and Richard B. Howarth (2000), 'The social contingency of wants', *Land Economics*, **76** (4), 493–503.

Brown, Peter G. (1994), *Restoring the Public Trust: A Fresh Vision of Progressive Governance in America*, Boston, MA: Beacon Press.

Bury, John B. (1932), *The Idea of Progress*, New York: Macmillan.

Clawson, Marion and Jack L. Knetsch (1966), *Economics of Outdoor Recreation*, Baltimore, MD: Johns Hopkins University Press.

Colander, David, Richard P.F. Holt and J. Barkley Rosser, Jr (2004), 'Introduction', in D. Colander, R.P.F. Holt and J.B. Rosser, Jr (eds) *The Changing Face of Economics: Conversations with Cutting Edge Economists*, Ann Arbor, MI: University of Michigan Press, pp. 1–26.

Cournot, Augustin (1963 [1897]), *Researches into the Mathematical Principles of the Theory of Wealth*, Nathaniel T. Bacon (trans.), Homewood, IL: Richard D. Irwin.

DeCanio, Stephen J. (2003), *Economic Models of Climate Change: A Critique*, New York: Palgrave Macmillan.

Dryzek, John S. (1990), *Discoursive Democracy: Politics, Policy, and Political Science*, Cambridge: Cambridge University Press.

Dryzek, John S. (2000), *Deliberative Democracy and Beyond: Liberals, Critics, Contestations*, Oxford: Oxford University Press.

Eckstein, Otto (1958), *Water-Resource Development: The Economics of Project Evaluation*, Cambridge, MA: Harvard University Press.

Frank, Thomas (2000), *One Market under God: Extreme Capitalism, Market Populism, and the End of Economic Democracy*, New York: Doubleday.

Harberger, Arnold (1971), 'Three postulates for applied welfare economics', *Journal of Economic Literature*, **9** (3), 785–97.

Healey, Michael, Michael Dettinger and Richard B. Norgaard (2008), *The State of Bay-Delta Science 2008: A Summary for Policymakers and the Public*, Sacramento, CA: CALFED Science Program.

Howarth, Richard B. and Richard B. Norgaard (1992), 'Environmental valuation under sustainable development', *American Economic Review*, **82** (2), 473–7.

Intergovernmental Panel on Climate Change (IPCC) (2007), *Climate Change 2007*, Cambridge: Cambridge University Press.

Kneese, Allan V. and Blair T. Bower (1968), *Managing Water Quality: Economics, Technology, Institutions*, Baltimore, MD: Johns Hopkins University Press.

Kurzweil, Ray (2005), *The Singularity is Near: When Humans Transcend Biology*, New York: Penguin.

Lindsay, D. Michael (2007), *Faith in the Halls of Power: How Evangelicals Joined the American Elite*, Oxford: Oxford University Press.

Merchant, Carolyn (1980), *The Death of Nature: Women, Ecology, and the Scientific Revolution*, New York: Harper & Row.

Millennium Ecosystem Assessment (2005), *Ecosystems and Human Well-Being*, Washington, DC: Island Press.

Nordhaus, William (2007), 'Critical assumptions in the Stern review on climate change', *Science*, **317** (13 July), 201–3.

Norgaard, Richard B. (1990), 'Economic indicators of resource scarcity: a critical essay', *Journal of Environmental Economics and Management*, **19**, 19–25.

Norgaard, Richard B. (1994), *Development Betrayed: The End of Progress and a Coevolutionary Revisioning of the Future*, London: Routledge.

Norgaard, Richard B. (2004), 'Posthuman enough?', *Bioscience*, **54** (3), 258–62.

Norgaard, Richard B. (2007), 'Deliberative economics', *Ecological Economics*, **63** (2–3), 375–82.

Norgaard, Richard B. (2008), 'Finding hope in the millennium ecosystem assessment', *Conservation Biology*, **22** (4), 862–9.

Norgaard, Richard B. and Paul Baer (2005a), 'Collectively seeing complex systems: the nature of the problem', *BioScience*, **55** (11), 953–60.

Norgaard, Richard B. and Paul Baer (2005b), 'Collectively seeing climate change: the limits of formal models', *BioScience*, **55** (11), 961–6.

Pearce, D.W., W.R. Cline, A.N. Achanta, S. Frankhauser, R.K. Pachuari, R.S.J. Tol and P. Vellinga (1996), 'The social costs of climate change: greenhouse damage and the benefits of control', in J.P. Bruce, H. Lee and E.V. Haites (eds), *Climate Change 1995: Economic and Social Dimensions of Climate Change*, Cambridge: Cambridge University Press, pp. 183–224.

Portney, Paul R. and John P. Weyant (1999), *Discounting and Intergenerational Equity*, Washington, DC: Resources for the Future.

Rayner, Steve and Elizabeth L. Malone (1998), *Human Choice and Climate Change*, 4 vols, Columbus: Battelle Press.

Reich, Robert B. (2007), *Super Capitalism: The Transformation of Business, Democracy, and Everyday Life*, New York: Knopf.

Sandel, Michael J. (2007), *The Case Against Perfection: Ethics in the Age of Genetic Engineering*, Cambridge, MA: Belknap Press of Harvard University Press.

Smith, Christian (1998), *American Evangelicalism: Embattled and Thriving*, Chicago, IL: University of Chicago Press.

Spash, Clive L. (2002), *Greenhouse Economics: Value and Ethics*, London: Routledge.
Spash, Clive L. (2007), 'The economics of climate change à la Stern: novel and nuanced or rhetorically restricted?', *Ecological Economics*, **64** (4), 706–13.
Spratt, David and Phillip Sutton (2008), *Climate 'Code Red': The Case for a Sustainability Emergency*, Fitzroy, Australia: Friends of the Earth.
Stern, Nicholas (2007), *The Economics of Climate Change: The Stern Review*, Cambridge: Cambridge University Press.
Swimme, Brian (1996), *The Hidden Heart of the Cosmos: Humanity and the New Story*, Maryknoll, NY: Orbis.
Tucker, Mary Evelyn (2003), *Worldly Wonder: Religions Enter their Ecological Phase*, Chicago, IL: Open Court.
Wilson, Matthew A. and Richard B. Howarth (2002), 'Discourse-based valuation of ecosystem services: establishing fair outcomes through group deliberation', *Ecological Economics*, **41**, 431–43.

5. The Post Keynesian/ecological economics of Kenneth Boulding[1]

Robert H. Scott, III

> Anyone who believes exponential growth can go on forever in a finite world is either a madman or an economist. (Boulding, 1966, p. 3)

INTRODUCTION

On 8 March 1966 at the sixth Resources for the Future Forum on Environmental Quality in a Growing Economy, Kenneth Boulding (1966) presented his now famous paper 'The economics of the coming spaceship earth'. This paper, arguably, marks the beginning of modern ecological economics. In it, Boulding castigates neoclassical economists for ignoring the environment in their models. As Ehrun Kula (1998, p. 4) accurately states, Boulding's paper 'must be one of the most thought-provoking pieces written on the environment this century'. Robert Heilbroner (1975, p. 77) called it a 'classic'. Its importance is mostly due to the fact that until this time mainstream economists were largely silent about how the economy impacts upon the environment (as well as how the environment impacts upon the economy). Boulding's article made it clear that the environment is important, and also made it clear that economists could no longer ignore it in their analyses.

In the 1970s, due to growing national interest in environmental issues (resulting in the first Earth Day and creation of the Environmental Protection Agency in the USA) mainstream neoclassical economists developed two subfields to study the environment: (1) environmental economics; and (2) natural resource economics. Today most mainstream economists use the term 'environmental economics' to encompass both subfields.

Environmental economics studies the effects (or inclusions) of economic activity on the environment: water pollution, air pollution and toxic waste leakage. All these effects are harmful, but some to a larger degree than others. Natural resource economics studies the economic effects of resources (or elements) taken out of the environment for economic uses, such as through mining, logging and commercial fishing. Both subfields weigh the costs of environmental degradation against the economic benefits of greater economic growth and resource use. But because it is unlikely that someone can accurately assess future environmental costs in the present (environmental effects are often immeasurable until many years, or decades, later), environmental economists often discount the true economic impact of environmental degradation, which makes the economic benefits seem larger than they actually are (Spash, 1999).

Both environmental economics and natural resource economics adhere to several mainstream principles. First, they believe technology will develop quickly enough to solve any environmental problems that may arise. Second, they support the idea that the free market will solve all environmental problems (a green invisible hand); therefore, they promote small government with limited (or no) regulations. Third, they think economic growth equates to economic development and is thus always desirable.

Mainstream economists view the environment as a mere extension of the economy. Their models generally ignore the long-term environmental impact of economic activities (for example, water pollution) and instead include the environment as an afterthought to growth constraints. Their anthropocentric perspective separates humans from the ecological system; therefore the economy, as a social construction, is also removed from the environment.

Boulding (1966, 1978) criticizes this anthropocentrism and argues that any discussion of the economy must presuppose environmental importance (and environmental dominance). This belief has important implications for how economists should view economic growth. Mainstream economists encourage economic growth at almost any cost. They see growth as the primary solution to social and economic problems (poverty, inequality and crime). But Boulding believed economic growth is unlikely to solve many of the problems (economic, social and environmental) caused by a capitalist system. Instead, he argued for a more fair and equitable social construction revolving around enhancing people's living standards.

Mainstream economists also conflate economic growth and economic development. Their growth models (for example, the Solow growth model) classify the environment as an open system of endless bounty, and thus disregard its value when making economic decisions. These models are constrained by population growth and technological improvement in the long run, but they ignore the environmental resources needed to sustain this growth, and waste-producing outputs due to growth. For Boulding (1966, 1978), economic growth is a quantitative measure of increased production while economic development is a qualitative measure of living standards – much in the way that John Kenneth Galbraith (1996, 1998) and Amartya Sen (1984, 1985) view growth. Thus, an increase in economic growth does not imply (nor necessarily lead to) better living standards – in fact, rapid uncontrolled economic growth will likely lead to large income and wealth inequalities and environmental problems (such as we are now seeing in China). The costs of such growth far outweigh the benefits, which makes this type of growth unsustainable (Daly, 1999). Ecological economics was born from these principal disagreements with mainstream economics, and the potential negative long-term effects of decisions made using mainstream ideology.

Post Keynesians have written little on environmental issues. However, a few Post Keynesians have been drawn into discussions concerning the environment. Richard Holt (2005) argues that Post Keynesians need to start studying the environment, but he never applies Post Keynesian theory to specific environmental problems. Andrew Mearman (2007) argues that Post Keynesians share many theoretical (and ideological) views with green economics (an offshoot of ecological economics), but his work falls short of making suggestions as to how the two views can be meshed to create new policies. His research, therefore, is largely limited to explaining why Post Keynesians should start studying the environment. But Boulding's ecological research has what Post Keynesians' work so far lacks, which is the conviction that economists must look at the environment differently today and pay careful attention to how the economy influences the environment. Specifically, Boulding acknowledges the earth as a closed system (and thus limited); he, therefore, promotes environmental sustainability for the long-run good of both the environment and the economy. For example, he believes we must address problems associated with our growing population, and that energy consumption is the root of many of our environmental problems. Boulding also provides suggestions for addressing these problems (and others).

This chapter presents a summary of Boulding's contributions to the development of modern ecological economics. The next section identifies the similarities between Post Keynesian economics and the ecological economics as developed by Boulding. Then, several Post Keynesian ecological economic public policy solutions are discussed that encourage environmental sustainability and protection while minimizing harmful consequences of economic growth. The principal findings of this chapter are summarized in the concluding section.

BOULDING'S ECOLOGICAL ECONOMICS

Boulding was one of the founders of the International Society for Ecological Economics (ISEE) formed in 1988. The ISEE was created 'to advance understanding of the relationships among ecological, social, and economic systems for the mutual well-being of nature and people' (www.ecoeco.org). It publishes the journal *Ecological Economics*. The ISEE also confers biennially the Kenneth Boulding Memorial Award. The work of the award recipient is supposed to represent the objectives of the ISEE in the spirit of Boulding's transdisciplinary scholarship.

Boulding first started writing about ecological economic issues in 1958 when he started conceptualizing society as an ecological system. He observed that firms were interconnected with one another. There was more cooperation than competition among them in the system. So, instead of viewing each firm as separate, he started seeing them as part of a larger whole, where each was dependent on all others for survival. He then broadened this view to explain how our economy is likewise interconnected with the environment, and that the two must cooperate to achieve a level of sustainability that allows for long-run economic growth without ruining the environment.

However, it was his 'spaceship' article that cemented his commitment to bringing the environment into economic analysis. In this article, Boulding castigates the mainstream for their failure to consider the environment's importance in studying the economy. Boulding goes on to present many reasons why the environment should be important to economists. He believes that economics represents, in large part, an attempt to understand the interdependence between the economy and the environment. Moreover, Boulding views the environment as encompassing the economy. The economy, therefore, is not the entire system, but rather a subsystem that is beholden to the larger ecosystem. This perspective is contrary to the neoclassical belief that the economy is the principal system within which all others fit.

Boulding's 'spaceship' article was a clarion call for all economists to begin considering the limitations of planet earth, and to start incorporating the effects that economic decisions have on the environment. He argued that earth had finally reached an exhaustive point where there were no new lands to inhabit. No longer could people think of their world as illimitable (open). Boulding states that earth is a closed system, which he compares to a spaceship. In Boulding's spaceship regular attention must be paid to population growth, energy use, and the use and disposal of all other resources. If spacemen pay no mind to how best to use their inputs and account for outputs, then the environment becomes unstable, potentially leading to their extinction (or crisis at minimum). To mainstream economists, however, the environment is considered an open system of unlimited resources. This anachronistic view is a holdover from times when economic models were oversimplified to account for our inability to model accurately a macrodynamic system (Boulding, 1978).

According to Boulding (1966, p. 4): 'Economists . . . have failed to come to grips with the ultimate consequences of the transition from the open to the closed earth.' An open system is one where 'the outputs of all parts of the system are linked to the inputs of other parts' (1966, p. 4). In a closed system, no inputs come from outside and no outputs go outside the system (outside does not exist). Boulding claims that mainstream economists' open system perspective can be analogized to that of a 'cowboy economy'. This analogy generates images of frontier plains (abundant unexplored free territories) and 'is associated with reckless, exploitative, romantic, and violent behavior, which is characteristic of open societies' (Boulding, 1966). For Boulding this romantic view of undiscovered plains is naive today because there are no more undiscovered plains on earth. As such, Boulding's closed system economy that he calls a 'spaceship' is the earth.

In the cowboy economy, growth via consumption and production is desirable. The more an economy consumes, the more is produced, the higher is its Gross Domestic Product (GDP), and the better off everyone becomes (Boulding, 1966, 1978). No consideration is given to pollution or the degradation of resources (or other long-run effects) in the cowboy economy. Conversely, in the spaceship economy, it is desirable to minimize throughputs. The success of this economy is not measured by maximizing consumption and production; rather, success is measured by increasing 'the nature, extent, quality, and complexity of the total stock of capital, including in this the state of the human bodies and minds included in the system' (Boulding, 1966). The spaceship economy is consequently better off with lower levels of production and consumption. And technology is valuable when it lessens harmful outputs by using fewer (or the same amount of) inputs without destabilizing the system – socially, economically or environmentally.

All living things are open systems because they take inputs to live (air, food, water) and give off outputs in the form of carbon dioxide and waste. Open and closed systems rely on three classes of inputs and outputs: matter, energy and information. Boulding states that the economy is open with regard to all three classes. And all three are dependent on each other; or, more generally, 'everything depends on everything else' (Boulding, 1978, p. 224). However, not all are accounted for by economists; therefore, Boulding (1966, p. 5) states:

> Thus we see the econosphere as a material process involving the discovery and mining of fossil fuels, ores, etc., and at the other end a process by which the effluents of the system are passed out into noneconomic reservoirs – for instance, the atmosphere and the oceans – which are not appropriated and do not enter into the exchange system.

Energy is either renewable (sunlight, heat, water) or non-renewable (fossil fuels), and both types are used 'to move matter from the noneconomic set into the economic set or even out of it again' (Boulding, 1966, p. 5). Advanced economies use significant amounts of non-renewable resources to increase the amount of energy throughput far above the amount of renewable energy stock available. This results in an increase in economic production (and throughput). But this boost is temporary because energy in this system adheres to the Second Law of Thermodynamics: in a closed system, energy disperses over time, and work (production) is only possible at the point of entropy where less concentrated energy is useful. Entropy represents a steady state where pure energy has dissipated enough to become useable. In order to have a sustainable energy stock, it is necessary to learn how to use renewable energies effectively. This is necessary because eventually non-renewable energies (fossil fuels) will be extinguished. Using more renewable resources now will also reduce (perhaps eliminate entirely) the end amount of damage caused by pollution from outputs produced by using fossil fuels and nuclear fission (Boulding, 1978, pp. 293–5; Georgescu-Roegen, 1971).

According to Boulding (1966), of the three classes of inputs and outputs, information (knowledge) is the most important to humans. He argues that matter is only significant when it becomes a part of human knowledge. The production of knowledge is necessary for human development, and the more knowledge a society possesses the greater is its economic progress. Knowledge, therefore, evolves in the ecosystem where it lets people organize energy and materials for effective use (Boulding, 1978, p. 225). But, Boulding argues, there may be an eventual limit to this evolution, which implies that technology will, contrary to neoclassical beliefs, fail to solve important social, environmental and other problems (Boulding, 1966, 1978). At what point technology will fail to provide solutions is impossible to predict, but the world is currently creating environmental problems at rates faster than existing science can solve (Daly, 1999).

For example, Boulding believed the effects of population growth deserved significant attention because it is growing at an unsustainable rate (he does argue that we do not know a priori what should be the steady-state population level – but we have to pay much more attention to population growth and start measuring its impact on living standards) (Boulding, 1964; 1971b, pp. 137–42; 1978, pp. 298–9). He provides three theorems to explain the result of population growth. First is 'The Dismal Theorem', which states if human misery is the only measure of population growth then the world will expand until it is so miserable that it will eventually reduce its population. Second is 'The Utterly Dismal Theorem', which asserts that any technical advancement will only relieve misery for a short while. Ultimately it only serves to increase the number of people – and period of – suffering until maximum misery is achieved and population is reduced to a non-miserable level. Last is 'The Moderately Cheerful Form of the Dismal Theorem', that encourages finding a way other than misery to check population growth. It is necessary to measure earth's capacity for population sustainability so that maximum misery is avoided. Boulding was possibly the first person to consider tradable reproductive rights as a practical method for controlling population (a concept today being applied to the trading of pollution emission credits in the private sector) (Boulding, 1964, 1950, 1978; McFarling, 2002). Herman Daly (1996, p. 119) elaborates Boulding's point by stating: 'The eventual necessity of a steady-state population has been evident to many for a long time. What holds for the population of human bodies must also hold for the populations of cars, buildings, livestock, and each and every other form of physical wealth that humans accumulate.' Daly, like Boulding, argues that an increasing population harms the lower classes because it raises the unskilled labor supply, thus keeping wages low (or pushing them lower). They both see population as having a principal influence on people's well-being. However, little research has been done in this area, even as the population expands to new record highs worldwide.

POST KEYNESIAN LINKS WITH BOULDING'S ECOLOGICAL ECONOMICS

Boulding worked under Joseph Schumpeter (who was also Hyman Minsky's professor and mentor) at Harvard, and Frank Knight at Chicago. His first journal article was accepted by John Maynard Keynes for publication in the *Economic Journal* in 1931; so, early in Boulding's intellectual development were influences furthering his detachment from mainstream economics toward a (what we may now label) Post Keynesian (pluralistic, transdisciplinary) view of the world. While Boulding's work has received positive reviews from Post Keynesians (for example McFarling, 2002; Wray 1994, 1997), his ecological economics research has thus far gone unnoticed by them. This section begins to rectify this oversight.

Boulding and Post Keynesians vehemently dispute the core principles of mainstream economics. Four principal theoretical concepts that Post

Keynesians and Boulding share include: (1) the role of uncertainty in decision-making; (2) acknowledging that the economy exists in historical time (rather than logical time); (3) recognizing the environmental (social and psychological) impact of economic growth – specifically that growth does not necessarily lead to higher living standards; and (4) open systems analysis.

First, they believe that uncertainty plays a critical role in decision-making. Boulding adopted his definition of uncertainty from Knight, as did the Post Keynesians (Davidson, 1982, 1991). According to Knight (1921), it is important to differentiate between risk that is mathematically calculable and uncertainty which is incalculable. Keynes (1973, pp. 113–14) makes his view of uncertainty clear when he wrote:

> By 'uncertain' knowledge, let me explain, I do not mean merely to distinguish what is known for certain from what is only probable. The game of roulette is not subject, in this case, to uncertainty. Even the weather is only moderately uncertain. The sense in which I am using the term is that in which the prospect of a European war is uncertain, or the price of copper and the rate of interest twenty years hence . . . About these matters there is no scientific basis on which to form any calculable probability whatever. We simply do not know.

Boulding (1971c, p. 160) echoes Knight and Keynes when he states that 'under imperfect markets . . . there is a double uncertainty – we are not only uncertain as to the future, but we are uncertain even as to the present parameter of the market functions'. For Post Keynesians and Boulding, because the future is unknowable we must carefully weigh our decisions, but we will never know a priori the probability of any decision's result(s). This is especially disconcerting with issues relating to the environment – we have only one, for in spaceship earth there is nowhere else to go. Because humans rely on a stable natural environment to survive, it is essential to take measures to ensure environmental protection (if for no other reason than out of our own self-interest).

Mainstream economists are largely interested in prediction and establishing economic laws based on risk (or chance propositions) (Spash, 1999). However, for Boulding, uncertainty surrounds all decisions that influence the environment (and therefore the economy too). Most mainstream modeling techniques (that is, cost–benefit analysis) collapse under uncertainty, which is especially the case when making economic decisions that directly (or indirectly) influence the environment because it is indispensable and not substitutable.

According to Post Keynesians, the real world is a dynamic, largely unpredictable system that is non-ergodic (Boulding, 1978, p. 225; Davidson, 1982, 1991, 1994). Post Keynesians use the term 'non-ergodic' to explain our inability to use past experiences to predict future outcomes accurately – it is thus impossible to calculate risk probabilistically – including problems related to the environment. This means that cost–benefit analysis, which is popular among mainstream environmental economists for decision-making, is irrelevant to Post Keynesians because it is impossible to price the future value of something today with any degree of certainty. Decisions based on cost–benefit results are made with limited (or no) knowledge of future (end) results. Decisions that affect the environment (directly or indirectly) may, therefore, have long-term unintended consequences; so, careful planning and oversight are necessary to maintain environmental sustainability.

Second, Post Keynesians (and ecological economists) are interested in studying the real world in historical time (Lavoie, 2005). In historical time, decisions made today are not easily reversed in the future (if they can be reversed at all). For Boulding this is important because economic decisions not only affect the economy, but also the larger environment that supports it.

Mainstream economists analyze the economy in logical time. This allows them to perform static mathematical modeling (for example, general equilibrium analysis) that assumes away many environmental problems that could arise. This approach is rejected by Post Keynesians and Boulding because: (1) there is no reason to assume that one optimum equilibrium exists or that we will know what the optimum equilibrium is – even if we by chance reach it; (2) decisions made in logical time can be reversed easily without consequences (which is not the case in the real world); and (3) inputs and outputs in mainstream models produce no waste (externalities with unknown future costs) – effects such as pollution are unaccounted for. Boulding (1966) asserts that this open earth (cowboy economy) perspective is no longer the case. Because of population increases and technological advances people are spread throughout the world, resulting in no untouched regions to discover or exploit (or escape to). We must now find ways to use inputs efficiently (for example, renewable energy) so as to minimize harmful outputs and forget about modeling the economy and the environment in logical (cowboy) time.

Post Keynesians have long stressed that because the real world exists in historical time, economic analysis, if it is to be of any real value, must analyze how economies change over time. Historical time is irrevocable – moving constantly from an unchangeable past to an unknown future. Therefore, no equilibrium can exist in a system moving through historical time, which makes clean, static mainstream models irrelevant. Decisions made in historical time are more lasting (perhaps permanent). In studying the environment, Boulding (1966) adopts such a historical perspective;

specifically, he observed that: 'even if we concede that posterity is relevant to our present problems, we still face the question of time-discounting and the closely related question of uncertainty-discounting' (pp. 12–13). He further argues that this is 'perhaps the reason why conservationist policies almost have to be sold under some other excuse which seems more urgent, and why, indeed, necessities which are visualized as urgent, such as defense, always seem to hold priority over those which involve the future' (p. 13). According to Boulding, therefore, environmental problems are largely the result of people's inability to comprehend problems in historical time.

Third, Boulding has a well-developed view of growth. For him the objective of economic policy should not be to maximize consumption or production, but rather to minimize it (Boulding, 1966). Boulding's focus on thermodynamics emphasizes his viewpoint that economic growth must be scrutinized, given constraints on what we know about the environmental impact of production resulting from the necessary inputs (resources, labor, and so on) and resulting outputs (waste and products). Besides, rapid growth, even if it were sustainable, does not directly result in better living standards.

Post Keynesians also believe it is wrong to promote economic growth at any cost because it will not lead to a better environment or a better economy. For example, Galbraith (1996, p. 83) notes that: 'environmental problems emerge from the impact of . . . production and consumption on the contemporary health, comfort, and well-being of the larger community'. He also argues that growth fueled by a free market system is in direct conflict with the goal of environmental protection. Furthermore, a 'sacrifice of freedom of decision and profit in order to protect the larger community or its unborn children is held to be an abridgment of the very freedom that produced economic success' (Galbraith, 1996, p. 85).

Fourth, because they use open systems analysis, Post Keynesians are able to accept the fact that the economy is complex, and that we cannot understand all the variables associated with its many operations. According to Boulding (1966, p. 4): 'all human societies [are] open systems'. He believes, therefore, that the environment is complex too, which due to the interconnections between the economy and the environment, results in an even more complex system. Therefore, static models such as cost–benefit analysis are too limited, and cannot adequately measure the present (or future) influence of economic activity on the environment. Barkley Rosser (2001) correctly states that various complex dynamics are present in ecologic–economic systems. Chaotic and catastrophic dynamic patterns are shown to be possible, along with other complex dynamics arising from non-linearity. Therefore, public policies in a complex system must set reasonable thresholds to avoid catastrophic system failure. These policies must also be flexible so that they can adjust to new information and institutional changes. Environmental stability is too important to risk making long-term policy mistakes – thus it is better to err by setting system thresholds too strictly rather than too loosely.

POLICY PRESCRIPTIONS

The three principal beliefs of Boulding and Post Keynesians discussed above lead to alternative environmental economic policy solutions that contrast sharply with those proposed by the mainstream. Most economic policy research in the United States that deals with the environment is conducted by conservative think-tanks: the Heritage Foundation, the Competitive Enterprise Institute and the Independent Institute. These think-tanks have become powerful policy-generating agencies (Beder, 2001).

To the displeasure of ecological economists they endorse neoliberal (libertarian) agendas that promote free markets and deregulation. Many of these organizations deny that an ecological threat exists. They believe technology will solve all environmental problems and that present environmental dilemmas are simply a necessary outcome of much-needed economic growth (for example, Bailey, 1995, 1999; Higgs and Close, 2005; Lomborg, 2001). In contrast, Boulding and Post Keynesians recognize the importance of social investment and government regulations in protecting the environment, which they believe is constantly under threat from free market forces. Stephen Dunn and Steven Pressman (2005, p. 162), writing about Galbraith, note that he believed 'that increasingly outmoded economic ideas misinform social policy in a way that supports the corporate power structure, to the detriment of wider society', and these ideas could 'make it easier for large firms to resist government regulation and shield firms pursuing practices that may be environmentally unsound'.

Boulding and Post Keynesians both recognize the importance of social (or government) investment. Social investment should be used to promote a better environment. For example, green buildings use recycled waste water, solar energy and green roofs to diminish operating costs and enhance work environments (more ambient light and cleaner air). Investment in green buildings is unlikely to occur in a major way until it is more strongly encouraged by government funding (for example, significant tax breaks for green practices). Adopting environmentally friendly production techniques is expensive. It is usually cheaper for businesses to use the institutionally standardized environmentally unfriendly inputs; but this maximizes harmful waste outputs, which become externalities for society. According to Keynes (1964 [1976], p. 317): 'Government is not to do things which individuals are doing already, and to do them a little better or a little worse; but to do those things which at present are not done at all' (quoted by Pressman, 1987, p. 17).

Post Keynesians see regulations as the central policy tool for solving problems in a capitalist system – and keeping new ones from occurring. Environmental regulation in the USA is largely upheld by the Environmental Protection Agency (EPA). The EPA is an organization designed for the benefit of everyone. In contrast, the free market model supported by the mainstream economists sector has thus far failed to ensure environmental protection. The free market is incapable of making the necessary 'regime switches' necessary to minimize environmental problems (Rosser, 2001). Only governments have the overarching authority, and capability, to 'adjust the system toward sustainable, eco-friendly, growth' (Rosser, 2001, p. 57).

Between 2004 and 2008 President George W. Bush's budgets reduced the EPA's research budget by more than 25 percent. And the EPA's overall budget has decreased at an annual rate of 3–6 percent. Bush's 2008 budget further cut the EPA's budget by more than 6 percent (roughly $500 million): a $35 million reduction in air quality management, a $31.3 million reduction in scientific investigation and research, and a more than $20 million reduction in research into and prevention of climate change. Bush's 2006 EPA budget reduced the EPA's library system funding by almost half (a $2 million cut), resulting in the closing of more than half of the EPA's 27 libraries located across the country (EPA, 2006). This loss greatly reduces researchers' ability to investigate environmental issues. At a time when environmental research and regulations should be at a record high (and given government priority), the EPA is facing severe financial constraints (Environmental and Energy Study Institute, 2007). Galbraith (1996) writes about the conflict between the free market and environmental protection that there 'is no escape from the role of government; it is for the larger community interest and its future protection that government and governmental regulation exist'. This sentiment is strongly shared by Boulding and Post Keynesians.

Post Keynesians' job creation strategies can benefit the environment. For example, Mathew Forstater (2003) proposes establishing an environmentally friendly Public Service Employment program to raise effective demand. However, instead of employing people to do production jobs that create more pollution (or hiring someone to dig a hole and another to fill it in) they will create jobs that endorse environmentally friendly goals. For example, collecting refuse, promoting recycling programs, beautifying areas (painting, rebuilding, landscaping), educating people about environmentally friendly practices, and so forth. These are jobs the private sector is unlikely to create because they have little profit potential, but they will likely result in positive social effects. This program could eventually result in attracting new businesses to once dilapidated areas by making them safe and clean.

For Boulding and Post Keynesians, unchecked economic growth cannot solve our economic problems. Rampant economic growth often creates more problems than it solves. Rethinking this issue includes addressing the environmental consequences of unregulated population growth – an issue of contentious debate. Boulding (and ecological economists generally) believe population must be managed (Daly, 1996). Conversely, mainstream economists argue in favor of the 'demographic transition hypothesis', which states that population will diminish as an economy grows (develops) (Daly, 1999, pp. 20–21, 46; Lomborg, 2001). This supports mainstream economists' belief that economic growth is the solution to almost everything. Ecological economists argue, however, that even if economic growth does show signs of slowing population growth, it does not work fast enough. Boulding believed tradable reproductive rights would lend flexibility to this sensitive subject. In his plan, people who want more children than the mandated limit can either buy (or be given) additional rights for more children. Herman Daly (1999, p. 113) suggests that more active family planning education and assistance will give people the power to control reproduction rates better. There are, however, religious and cultural issues that obfuscate Boulding's plan. Both Daly's and Boulding's plans could garner Post Keynesian support; but this issue requires further research before a clear solution can emerge.

CONCLUSION

Kenneth Boulding developed the foundation of modern ecological economics. His 'spaceship' article emphasizes the dependent relationship that exists between the economy and the environment. He believes mainstream economists incorrectly view the world as an open (cowboy) system, which subsequently ignores harmful outputs resulting from economic activities. Boulding, like Post Keynesians, is critical of mainstream economists' anthropocentric methodology, and argues that ecological economists must study the real world.

A future Post Keynesian ecological economics should embrace Boulding's transdisciplinary approach and start developing public policy strategies that account for the complexities and uncertainties inherent in the economy. Boulding and Post Keynesians think that a capitalist system is more likely to cause environmental problems than solve them.

It is necessary, therefore, to promote social investment in environmentally sustainable programs and reinforce institutions designed to protect the environment (for example, the EPA).

NOTE

1. An earlier version of this chapter was presented at the United States Society for Ecological Economics conference in New York, 25 June 2007. Financial support was provided by the Monmouth University Business Council.

REFERENCES

Bailey, R. (ed.) (1995), *The True State of the Planet*, New York: Free Press.
Bailey, R. (ed.) (1999), *Earth Report 2000: Revisiting the True State of the Planet*, New York: McGraw-Hill.
Beder, S. (2001), 'Neoliberal think tanks and free market environmentalism', *Environmental Politics*, **10** (2), 128–33.
Boulding, K.E. (1950), *A Reconstruction of Economics*, New York: Science Editions.
Boulding, K.E. (1964), *The Meaning of the Twentieth Century: The Great Transition*, New York: Harper & Row.
Boulding, K.E. (1966), 'The economics of the coming spaceship earth', in H. Jarrett (ed.), *Environmental Quality in a Growing Economy*, Baltimore, MD: Johns Hopkins University Press, pp. 3–15.
Boulding, K.E. (1971a), 'Income or welfare', in F.E. Glahe (ed.), *Kenneth E. Boulding: Collected Papers, Vol. 1*, Boulder, CO: Colorado Associated Press, pp. 263–74.
Boulding, K. E. (1971b), 'Foreword to T. R. Malthus, *Population: the First Essay*', in F.E. Glahe (ed.), *Kenneth E. Boulding: Collected Papers, Vol. 2*, Boulder, CO: Colorado Associated Press, pp. 137–42.
Boulding, K.E. (1971c), 'The present position of the theory of the firm', in F.E. Glahe (ed.), *Kenneth E. Boulding: Collected Papers, Vol. 2*, Boulder, CO: Colorado Associated Press, pp. 155–71.
Boulding, K.E. (1978), *Ecodynamics: A New Theory of Society Evolution*, Beverly Hills, CA: Sage Publications.
Daly, H. (1996), *Beyond Growth: The Economics of Sustainable Development*, Boston, MA: Beacon Press.
Daly, H. (1999), *Ecological Economics and the Ecology of Economics: Essays in Criticism*, Cheltenham, UK and Northampton, MA, USA: Edward Elgar.
Davidson, P. (1982), 'Rational expectations: a fallacious foundation for studying crucial decision-making processes', *Journal of Post Keynesian Economics*, **5** (2), 182–97.
Davidson, P. (1991), 'Is probability theory relevant for uncertainty? A Post Keynesian perspective', *Journal of Post Keynesian Economics*, **13** (1), 129–43.
Davidson, P. (1994), *Post Keynesian Macroeconomic Theory*, Aldershot, UK and Brookfield, VT, USA: Edward Elgar.
Dunn, S. and S. Pressman (2005), 'The economic contributions of John Kenneth Galbraith', *Review of Political Economy*, **17** (2), 161–209.

Environmental and Energy Study Institute (2007), 'EPA clean air and global climate change fy 2008', www.eesi.org/publications/Press%20Releases/2007/2.6.07_FY08_EPA_Budget.htm, 21 July.

Environmental Protection Agency (EPA) (2006), 'EPA fy 2007 library plan: national framework for the headquarters and regional libraries', www.epa.gov/natlibra/Library_Plan_National_Framework081506final.pdf, 15 August.

Forstater, M. (2003), 'Public employment and economic sustainability', *Journal of Post Keynesian Economics*, **25** (3), 385–406.

Galbraith, J.K. (1996), *The Good Society: The Humane Agenda*, New York: Mariner Books.

Galbraith, J.K. (1998), *The Affluent Society*, New York: Mariner Books.

Georgescu-Roegen, N. (1971), *The Entropy Law and the Economic Progress*, Cambridge, MA: Harvard University Press.

Heilbroner, R. (1975), 'Kenneth Boulding, *Collected Papers*: a review essay', *Journal of Economics Issues*, **9** (1), 73–9.

Higgs, R. and C. Close (eds) (2005), *Re-Thinking Green: Alternatives to Environmental Bureaucracy*, Oakland, CA: Independent Institute.

Holt, R.P.F. (2005), 'Post-Keynesian economics and sustainable development', *International Journal of Environment, Workplace and Employment*, **1** (2), 174–86.

Keynes, J.M. (1964 [1936]), *The General Theory of Employment, Interest, and Money*, New York: Harcourt Brace & World.

Keynes, J.M. (1973), *The Collected Writings of John Maynard Keynes, Vol. XVI, The General Theory and After: Defense and Development*, London: Macmillan.

Knight, F.H. (1921), *Risk, Uncertainty and Profit*, Boston, MA: Houghton Mifflin.

Kula, E. (1998), *History of Environmental Economic Thought*, New York: Routledge.

Lavoie, M. (2005), 'Post-Keynesian consumer choice theory for the economics of sustainable forest management', in S. Kant and A.R. Berry (eds), *Economics, Sustainability, and Natural Resources: Economics of Sustainable Forest Management*, Dordrecht: Springer, pp. 67–90.

Lomborg, B. (2001), *The Skeptical Environmentalist: Measuring the Real State of the World*, Cambridge: Cambridge University Press.

McFarling, R. (2002), 'A Post Keynesian appreciation of "A reconstruction of economics"', *Journal of Post Keynesian Economics*, **24** (4), 643–56.

Mearman, A. (2007), 'Post Keynesian economics and the environment: wake up and smell the burning coffee', *International Journal of Green Economics*, **1** (3–4), 374–80.

Pressman, S. (1987), 'The policy relevance of *The General Theory*', *Journal of Economic Studies*, **14** (4), 13–24.

Rosser, J.B. (2001), 'Uncertainty and expectations', in R. Holt and S. Pressman (eds), *A New Guide to Post Keynesian Economics*, New York: Routledge, pp. 52–64.

Sen, A.K. (1984), *Resources, Values and Development*, Cambridge, MA: Harvard University Press.

Sen, A.K. (1985), *Commodities and Capabilities*, Amsterdam: North Holland.

Spash, C. (1999), 'The development of environmental thinking in economics', *Environmental Values*, **8** (4), 413–35.

Wray, L.R. (1994), 'Kenneth Boulding's grants economics', *Journal of Economic Issues*, **28** (4), 1205–25.

Wray, L.R. (1997), 'Kenneth Boulding's reconstruction of macroeconomics', *Review of Social Economy*, **55** (4), 445–63.

6. Combining Post Keynesian, ecological and institutional economics perspectives

Arild Vatn

INTRODUCTION

The purpose of this chapter is to conduct a comparison of the three heterodox economic schools of Post Keynesian, ecological and institutional economics, and on this basis highlight a set of research areas where there seems to be some common ground. The broader aim is to support a process of developing a strong and coherent alternative to the dominant neoclassical perceptive of the behavior of human agents and the functioning of economic systems.

The focus of this book is to develop ideas at the intersection between Post Keynesian and ecological economics. In this chapter I also add some insights from institutional theory. This has a double motivation. First of all, including institutional perspectives will enrich the synthesis as it fills some important gaps in the cross-section between the other two positions. Secondly, ecological economics is a diverse heterogeneous school. Including the institutionalist perspective in the chapter provides a clarification of which 'kind' ecological economics this author considers the most promising.

Certainly, I am not the first to look for links across these schools. We see several efforts to compare or combine perspectives from Post Keynesian and institutional economics, for example, Keller (1983), Tymoigne (2003) and Ferrari-Filho and Cormago Conceicao (2004). Similarly, there is a substantial amount of literature produced by people who look at the interconnection between institutional and ecological economics, for example, Söderbaum (1994, 2000), Bromley (1998), Costanza et al. (2001), Lehtonen (2004), Paavola and Adger (2005) and Vatn (2005a, 2005b). Finally, there is a recent trend concerning papers that explore the interface between Post Keynesian and ecological economics, for example, Holt (2005), Mearman (2005a, 2005b) and Berr (2008) in addition to chapters in this book.

It should be emphasized that it is not only with regard to ecological economics that there is diversity of opinion of its heterogeneous nature. Institutional economics is split into two main positions: the 'classic' and the 'new' (Vatn, 2005a). The latter shares a lot of common ground with neoclassical economics and will not be covered here. In the case of Post Keynesianism, I observe also some variation, but will leave out references to the Sraffian position. Given these different views, special care will be taken in singling out not only common themes, but also disagreements.

The chapter is divided into two parts. First, I will offer a brief discussion of the core ideas of the three schools and identify where there is common ground and where there are important disagreements. Second, I will recognize two specific areas where I find it especially fruitful for the three to join forces. This concerns the theory of behavior and the interaction between the economic system and its environment. Within these areas there is both great potential and urgency for these three schools to produce advances.

CORE IDEAS OF THE THREE POSITIONS

When presenting core ideas of each position, I will work chronologically. Hence, I will start with the institutional school, continue with Post Keynesian economics and close with ecological economics. All three traditions were established very much as a reaction to neoclassical economics, and its lack of capacity to offer answers to pressing issues like economic and environmental crises. This fact is in itself an interesting basis for integration. It is especially fascinating to see how different problems addressed by the three have resulted in similar theories. The greater the similarities are, the larger the possibility to develop a general model that is robust.

Institutional Economics

Thorstein Veblen is considered the 'father' of institutional economics. His paper 'Why is economics not an evolutionary science?' (Veblen, 1898) is often acknowledged as marking the starting point of institutional economics. Veblen challenged the foundations of the evolving neoclassical paradigm as he crafted out his own position. This includes his understanding of the economy as an evolutionary system, where he emphasized that: 'The economic life history of the individual is a cumulative process of adaptation of means to ends that cumulatively change as the process goes on, both the agent and his environment being at any point the outcome of the past process' (Veblen, 1898, p. 391). He criticized the idea or assumption of the autonomous individual that is fundamental to the neoclassical paradigm, and saw institutions not only as formed by, but also forming individuals. Veblen was critical of what would later be called methodological individualism, but we observe that he was also critical of pure structural explanations.

Veblen saw preferences as endogenous to the social and economic system (Veblen, 1909). Hence, a critique of utilitarianism and neoclassical marginalism was laid out (Veblen, 1898, 1909). He moreover emphasized that consumption – at least among the rich – was a way to gain position in social hierarchies. More generally he accentuated the role of habits as a kind of social convention characterizing different classes (for example, Veblen 1970 [1899], 1969 [1923]). He also challenged vigorously the neoclassical understanding of private property, linking the concept to the issue of status and power rather than to scarcity and one's labor (Veblen, 1958 [1904]). Moreover, he criticized the neoclassical concept of capital – a critique based on understanding capital in physical terms, emphasizing the subsequent aggregation problems. Veblen emphasized that the shift from a 'money economy' to a 'credit economy', increased the role of a secondary market for credit. This created a new form of uncertainty linked to the expectations of investors – the speculators. Moreover, as markets expanded tremendously in the later decennial of the nineteenth century, mainly through changes in transportation opportunities, another kind of uncertainty appeared: that of uncertain demand. In Veblen's eyes the legal transformation and subsequent rise of the corporation in the 1890s in the United States was a response to these uncertainties. First the corporate trust appeared as a way to consolidate business in the face of uncertainties. Its development was, however, hampered by the Sherman Anti-Trust Act of 1890. The next 'solution' was found in changes in the legal basis of the corporation, including among other elements the right for a corporation to own stocks in other corporations.

The various themes raised by Veblen have been developed further by later scholars of the institutionalist tradition. Also new topics have been added. John R. Commons was less critical of the fundamental institutions of capitalism, seeing institutions as supporting various interests and handling conflicts. He was less interested in how institutions formed individuals, looking more at how institutions could create some harmony between conflicting interests in a world of resource scarcity (Commons, 1990 [1934]). Commons was a contemporary of Keynes,[1] working in a period where a lot of effort was put into increasing labor rights and to facilitating state intervention into an essentially corporatist-driven economy. These processes can moreover be seen as a reaction to the fact that corporations, in protecting their interests, forced various kinds of uncertainty upon the working class. Commons himself took an active part in the development of labor protection. It should finally be observed that even Commons was critical of the idea of the autonomous individual. He saw the economy as a relation between persons, not between persons and things. He therefore emphasized the importance of transaction. He was critical of the hedonist perspective of neoclassicism with its focus on concepts like marginal utility and time preferences, emphasizing instead the role of social constructs like rights, duties and ownership (Commons, 1931).

After the Second World War institutional economics lost much of its influence in US economics departments. We can, however, observe a revival from the 1980s through the work of, for example, Schmid (1987, 2004), Hodgson (1988, 1996, 2004), Bromley (1989, 2006), Tool (1995), Samuels et al. (1997) and Vatn (2005a).[2] These authors have emphasized very strongly the interdependencies between the actions of humans. In relation to that, the neoclassical model of autonomous individuals interacting only through trade has again been heavily challenged. Instead the idea of plural rationality (for example, Hodgson, 1988; Sjöstrand, 1995) and the parallel distinction between private and social preferences (for example, Swaney, 1987) have become core themes. This literature hence emphasizes that human behavior can be inspired by different kinds of motivations and that different institutional contexts, like the market or the community, appeal to different logics – those of private gain versus adherence to social norms, respectively.

Institutionalists have also taken up the concept of bounded rationality as developed by Herbert Simon (for example, Simon, 1957). The emphasis here has been on information costs and the fact that such costs make the idea of maximizing indefinable (Knudsen, 1993). Simply, if gathering and processing information is costly, agents are caught in infinite regresses concerning allocating time between further information gathering, processing and decision-making. Boundedness is next seen to introduce a kind of uncertainty that is different from standard risk as agents cannot know which perceptions drive the decisions of other agents. Analyzing these issues has again brought up the old Veblenian theme of habits or social conventions as capable of 'fixing' expectations.

The issue of information costs is taken further by including the concept of transaction costs (for example, Schmid, 1987; Bromley, 1989; Vatn, 2005a). These costs are defined as the costs of information gathering, contracting and controlling. They are the costs of running the economic system. Transaction costs are seen as system- or institution-specific and hence impair the validity of the welfare economic theorems of neoclassicism.

Finally, the concept of power plays a core role in institutional theory.

Power is seen foremost as structural, as embedded in the institutions of a society. As institutions form people and operate as rationality contexts, they also protect interests and secure their access to various benefit streams (Bromley 1989). Capitalist institutions are seen as on the one hand securing formal equality, but on the other producing de facto inequality.

Post Keynesian Economics

Describing Post Keynesian economics demands first a visit to Keynes. He is certainly most famous for *The General Theory of Employment, Interest and Money* (Keynes, 1936) – a volume which was a response to pressing issues of his time, especially unemployment, which he found orthodox theory unable to handle. His book had a large influence upon contemporary as well as later policies and intellectual developments. Where Veblen was a stark commentary, Keynes was, like Commons, engaged in policy reform.

The 1936 book also grew, however, out of a long-lasting engagement by Keynes with a set of fundamental theoretical issues. In his *A Treatise on Probability* (Keynes, 1921) he rejected that uncertainty could generally be reduced to risk, a position which was incompatible with the neoclassical stand and its emphasis on maximization and equilibrium. Instead there was an emphasis on cognitive limitations. There is a common theme to that of the institutionalists because Keynes also emphasized conventions as means for economic agents to reduce uncertainty by 'fixing' behavior. Hence, under normal conditions uncertainty, by the convention-making it stimulates, produces predictable regularities. In situations of crisis, when for some reason following convention does not help, uncertainty becomes a destabilizing force.

His concept of uncertainty was that of Knightian or radical uncertainty, that is, the impossibility of knowing all potential future states or future outcomes of an action.[3] While he saw the world as fundamentally uncertain, he also emphasized that institutions could themselves be the source of uncertainty. In his *A Treatise on Money* (1930), Keynes developed his view of money as non-neutral, that is, as more than a medium of exchange. The introduction of money changed the basis for choice and made the economy fundamentally different from the barter type. Moreover Keynes showed how growth of the institutional arrangements of money not only simplified transactions, but also changed the logic of the system. Money went from being an exchange medium to being essential for production. Keynes emphasized the uncertainties this created. He studied not only business where money is necessary for production and to make a profit, but also its use in the face of the uncertainties concerning future streams of remuneration.

In *The General Theory* the non-neutrality of both choice and money was then considered. Uncertainty was the basis for both, and the combination that made modern economies vulnerable to crises. Holding money was a way for agents to handle the uncertainties they faced. Economic crises (for example, unemployment) were, according to Keynes, caused by this strategy towards uncertainty reduction (for example, creating too low an aggregate demand). Hence, it was scarcity of demand, not scarcity of resources, that created problems in market economies. Such crises could be countered by macroeconomic policies, for example, by increasing public demand through investment and other public policies.

As Lavoie (1992) has emphasized, the project of Keynes was to establish a practical theory of procedural or bounded rationality, taking the variety of human limitations into account. Since bounded-rational individuals have to rely on collective experience, Keynes has been termed an organicist. Like Veblen he rejected the view that individuals were autonomous or isolated entities. They were rather to be seen as standing in relation to other parts of a system in which they operated. Certainly, he thought that people could reason and make deliberate choices. They did so, however, dependent on the structures in which they lived and were a part.

Though Keynes is considered to be the founder of Post Keynesianism, the school encompasses a rather heterogeneous group of scholars engaged in recovering and extending the ideas of Keynes (King, 2002). A typical way of grouping Post Keynesians is found in Hamouda and Harcourt (1988) and King (2002), distinguishing between the 'fundamentalist Keynesians', the 'Sraffians/neo-Ricardians' and finally 'the Kaleckians'.

Post Keynesians treat many of the same topics that Keynes introduced and developed. This concerns topics like uncertainty, historical and irreversible time (non ergodity), path-dependency and the issue of bounded rationality. Methodologically we observe elements of organicism, (critical) realism and open-system analysis, where the latter two capture rather recent trends. Moreover, Post Keynesians expanded their analysis into topics going well beyond those of Keynes, for example, economic growth, distribution and the effect of economic structures like monopolies.

Looking more specifically into the sub-positions emphasized above, we observe substantial differences across the above-mentioned topics and perspectives. Davidson, for example, follows the core Keynesian themes with his work on labor demand, on distribution and on money, for example, Davidson (1972). He defends the Keynesian and Post Keynesian position and distinguishes it from the neoclassical synthesis of Keynesian thinking.[4]

The 'Kaleckians' on the other hand focused more on the power structures of the economy and the political resistance against Keynesian ideas.

Again we observe an analysis seeing power foremost as a structural phenomenon, especially embedded in the monopolistic structures of existing market economies. Kalecki emphasized that full employment was a technical possibility through government intervention, but recognized that it was politically controversial as it would weaken the relative position of the capitalists, for example, Kalecki (1943).

While the dominant area of concern is with macroeconomics, there is also some work on microeconomics and choice theory. For example, the work of Lavoie on consumer theory (see, Lavoie, 1992; see also Lavoie's chapter in this book). He develops what he sees as a Post Keynesian model of choice including uncertainty and hence bounded or procedural rationality that accentuates the role of radical, or what he terms fundamental uncertainty. Similar to Knudsen (1993), he stresses the infinite regresses involved in trying to maximize under uncertainty, and how various socially constructed rules or conventions help individuals handle these difficulties.

Looking at the specificities of his model, we find that Lavoie emphasizes both the restricted substitutability between goods ('the principle of irreducibility') and the hierarchies of needs ('the principle of subordination') leading to a model with lexicographic preferences. In this way Lavoie emphasizes that people have needs that are fundamental and irreducible aspects of being a human in the sense of biological, psychological and social needs. Choices therefore have to be made on the basis of non-compensatory 'filtering' procedures. In this lies also a distinction between needs and wants, where wants (for example, beer) are substitutable only within lexicographically ordered needs (for example, drink). Specifically, he sees 'the concept of the opportunity cost [to] apply only to wants within a given category of needs' (Lavoie, 1992, p. 67). Emphasizing non-compensability between goods, the principle of irreducibility implies that prices have meaning only within groups of goods. Lavoie introduces the notion of incommensurability between goods or value dimensions, that is, the lack of a common term of denomination.

There are aspects of his model which are parallel to that of the institutionalists. First of all Lavoie accentuates that needs are socially dependent ('the principle of non-independence'). Next, and linked to this, he emphasizes the role of habits and rules of thumb when we choose between wants. Specifically, the concept of 'non-compensatory filtering procedures' is introduced as a way to describe how consumers go about reducing the amount of options down to a manageable number of alternatives.

Post Keynesians have for a long time been engaged in studies about how to foster economic growth. Recently, we observe a growing interest also for ecological sustainability, for example, Holt (2005), Mearman

(2005a, 2005b) and Berr (2008). This literature does look at the question of why Post Keynesians have shown so little interest in the growing environmental concerns. Mearman (2005a, p. 131) gives the reasons amongst contemporary Post Keynesians as being that they: 'have adopted a strategic focus on criticizing orthodox monetary and pricing theory; they have used static tools ill-equipped for analyzing the environment; and they have focused more on growth and full employment'. Holt (2005, p. 174), on the other hand, emphasizes that: 'Post Keynesian economics – with its focus on macro and policy outcomes, the role of institutions, uncertainty, historical time, and its criticism of gross substitution and ergodicity – has elements within its methodology that make it better suited to incorporate sustainability into its analysis than neoclassical economics.' This takes us directly to ecological economics, whose history is based on a similar understanding of the need to establish alternatives to orthodox environmental economics.

Ecological Economics

Compared to institutional economics, and to some extent Post Keynesian economics, ecological economics is very young. Certainly, we find important inputs leading to the creation of ecological economics at least to the 1950s with the establishment of systems ecology (for example, Odum, 1953). In the 1960s we observe an increased interest in environmental issues following from the rapid economic growth after the Second World War. Kenneth Boulding's article on 'spaceship earth' (Boulding, 1966) and the Meadows et al. (1972) volume *Limits to Growth* showed an increased worry over resource limitations. The same issue was raised at a more fundamental level by Georgescu-Roegen (1971) in his work on the implications of the law of entropy for the economic process. He saw a need for shifting the basis for economics in a direction that included biophysical reality. Similarly, Herman Daly emphasized the need for linking economics to its biophysical basis (Daly, 1968) and to find ways of establishing a steady-state economy (Daly, 1977). Finally, the development of general systems theory (for example, Prigogine, 1980) describing self-organizing dissipative systems should be mentioned as important for the emergence of ecological economics.

Ecological economics started very much as a society. According to Røpke (2004, 2005) this happened when ecologists looked to economists who were dissatisfied with neoclassical environmental economics. This led to the establishment of the journal *Ecological Economics* in 1987 and the International Society for Ecological Economics the year after.

Thus, ecological economics grew out of an engagement of several people[5] to develop an interdisciplinary form of cooperation better tackling the challenges raised by environmental degradations and the quest for sustainable development. A difference from the other two traditions visited in this chapter is that ecological economics did not grow out of a group of 'followers of a founding father'. The center of attraction was less a set of already defined ideas to be developed, but a process of establishing new ideas that still needed to be discovered.

The kinds of economists attracted to ecological economics represented a wide variety. Some can be defined as socio-economists, others are better characterized as institutional economists, and some are Marxists. Actually quite a substantial group of neoclassical environmental economists were also attracted to ecological economics.[6] This, of course, created some conflicts in efforts to define ecological economics and the goals of its society as it tried to establish a new forum to get beyond the perspectives of the mainstream.[7]

Ecological economics is concerned with the interrelations between the economic system and the ecological or biophysical processes on which it is based. It was explicitly acknowledged that mainstream economics did not capture the important physical dimension of economic systems. They were analyzed as systems of perpetuated internal circulation. From the beginning, ecological economists were strongly engaged in analyses of matter flows, for example, Kneese et al. (1970) and Daly (1977). In particular Daly put explicit emphasis on the interactions with the biospheric processes and on the scale of the economy relative to its ecological base. These initial contributions have been developed further in different directions. One concerns the construction of indicators measuring physical impacts of human consumption, for example, the MIPS[8] concept (Hinterberger et al., 1997), and the concept of ecological footprint (Rees and Wackernagel, 1994). Another concern was with 'social metabolism' as developed by Marina Fisher-Kowalski and colleagues, for example, Fisher-Kowalski and Weisz (1999). The latter links matter flows to the organization and dynamics of socio-economic systems.

The next development was the focus on complementarity rather than substitution as the dominant aspect of biophysical systems. The issue of restricted substitution possibilities again has a history that predates the formation of the society. The issue was highlighted in the early 1970s when *Limits to Growth* (Meadows et al., 1972) was attacked by mainstream economists like Dasgupta and Heal (1974) and Solow (1974) who claimed that there were no fundamental scarcity problems. Scarcity was only relative as there was always the opportunity of substitution. It is interesting that their argument was not based on empirical observation or on any evaluation of the law of entropy. It followed directly from assuming technologies where substitution elasticities between natural and human-made capital were defined as ≥ 1 (for example, Cobb–Douglas technology).[9] As in the case of the institutionalists and the Post Keynesians, there is a questioning of the unrealistic assumptions of neoclassical economics.

Also, ecological economists emphasized irreversibility, hence real or historic time and path-dependency. Like the Post Keynesians, the world is seen as non-ergodic, although this specific term is rarely used by ecological economists. Its evolutionary perspective goes beyond that of ecology as social systems are also seen to be open, self-organizing and hence evolutionary systems. Another core concept in ecological economics thinking is the concept of resilience as introduced by Holling (1973, 2001), emphasizing that ecological systems are adaptive and that a main feature is their ability to handle external shocks and hence their capacity to resist attractor shifts. The concept of resilience has been taken up in the study of social systems seeking to understand the capacity of socio-ecological systems to withstand external pressures and reorganize in the face of more fundamental challenges (for example, Folke, 2006). Finally, this has brought ecological economists to adapt concepts from complexity theory, emphasizing the multi-scale attributes of socio-ecological systems (for example, Giampietro, 2004) and the issue of ignorance, irreducible ignorance or Knightian radical uncertainty that is fundamental to these systems (for example, Funtowicz and Ravetz, 1993, 1994; Faber et al., 1996). Again the emphasis is on the insufficiency of capturing risk in what is going on, as there will be novelty involved concerning future states. Certainly, the question of developing policies for sustainability relates strongly to how the uncertainties involved are perceived. There is strong support among ecological economists for the precautionary principle and for instituting participatory processes in assessing consequences of various policies. In a situation with radical uncertainty, expert and citizen evaluations should be combined.

Not only is there an emphasis among ecological economists that market prices do not offer the right signals for securing sustainable use of environmental resources. Certainly, as the mainstream acknowledges, such prices are lacking for many of these resources or services. The distinct point developed by ecological economists is that environmental values might often be incommensurable internally and with other types of goods, for example, O'Neill (1993), Vatn and Bromley (1994) and Martinez-Alier et al. (1998). Hence, as with Post Keynesian consumer theory, there is a clear focus on lexicographic preferences, for example, Spash (1998, 2000). Ecological economists add one specific dimension to the understanding of the observation of such preferences. They emphasize the ethical dimensions involved in environmental choices, for example, O'Neill (1993),

Holland (1997) and Vatn (2000). One aspect in this is the emphasis on the intrinsic value of other species. Another is the focus on environmental goods as systems goods where actions are interdependent, that is, where the actions of one influence the opportunities for others.

Added to this, we observe interest in how institutions like rights, and power relations, influence: (1) access to resources (for example, Martinez-Alier, 1987); and (2) price estimates for environmental values based on contingent valuation (for example, Knetsch, 1994; Spash and Villena, 1998; Vatn, 2004; Spash, 2006). The way valuation is undertaken – the choice of value-articulating institutions – is seen as influencing which values will be emphasized and in which form they may be expressed (Jacobs, 1997). In relation to this, there is also a strong emphasis in ecological economics on the endogeneity of preferences.

While ecological economics started out by crafting its own type of 'macroeconomics', we also see a focus on the micro level with its interest in behavioral economics. This interest is still developing. There is a field we may call 'the ecological economics of consumption' (Reisch and Røpke, 2004). It takes the macro focus down to the level of consumer choice. Here we see links to both Veblen and Post Keynesians. There is also some work in ecological economics focusing on motivation and behavior, for example, Söderbaum (1994, 2000), van den Bergh et al. (2000), Siebenhüner (2000), Vatn (2005a, 2008) and Stagl (2007). Several of these efforts have a basis in institutional theory accentuating capacity restrictions and multi-rationality.

What is Common and Different?

The above discussion shows some striking similarities across the three schools. Certainly, there are internal differences. Nevertheless, most striking is what the three traditions share. Similarities start on the ontological level. All three traditions are systems-oriented, emphasizing relational aspects, hence understanding the motion of systems as dependent on the relations between the parts. Implicit in this is a critical attitude towards methodological individualism. All fit quite well within an 'organicist' as opposed to 'atomist' ontology. Moreover, we see a strong focus on open-systems theory and evolutionary, self-organizing dynamics. All three schools emphasize irreversibility and are engaged in developing models operating in real time.

More concretely, complexity and uncertainty is a core issue among the three. It enters in different ways though. Post Keynesians emphasize the uncertainty in human interaction and how the market introduces specific types of uncertainty where it becomes difficult for individual agents to anchor their expectations about future developments on past experiences. Ecological economists focus mostly on the uncertainty of ecological systems and the interplay between ecological and economic systems. It is, however, the same kind of uncertainty that is emphasized. It is foremost Knightian uncertainty whether it is termed radical uncertainty, fundamental uncertainty or irreducible ignorance. Both the Post Keynesians and the institutionalists emphasize behavioral conventions as ways that individuals and societies cope with such issues.

This takes us next to the model of the individual and the understanding of behavior and choice. Agents are seen as influenced by social or institutional systems. While we see this strongly with institutionalists, all three positions look at preferences as endogenous. Agents are, moreover, seen as being boundedly rational. This is the consequence of the complexity and uncertainty with restricted cognitive capacity that comes from bounded rationality. Moreover, there are elements in all schools of plural preferences – the emphasis on blocked trade-offs or incommensurabilities, and lexicographic preferences. The role of habits and conventions, and norms, is a pronounced feature especially of the institutional and Post Keynesian, but examples are also found among ecological economists. In all cases consumption patterns are very much understood as socially and institutionally conditioned. There is even a basis for a wider claim: that preferences and values are taken to be profoundly influenced by institutions. This is a basic tenet of institutionalism. It comes forward in Post Keynesianism through the insistence on the non-neutrality of money and in the emphasis on conventions and rules as social phenomena. Finally, ecological economists take the same position when insisting that, for example, valuation methods are institutional structures emphasizing different logics and value systems.

Complementarity and non-substitutability is a common thread across the three. It links directly to the observation of lexicographic preferences, and the Post Keynesian and Veblenian emphasis on the non-aggregability of different types of capital. Also there is the ecological economist emphasis on substitutability thresholds in the case of natural versus human-made capital. Here ecological economics adds to the story with its focus on resilience.

Finally, interests and power relations are important for all three schools. This thread surfaces differently, however, as power in institutional economics is a general feature of understanding both the establishment of institutions and their effects. Power is necessary both to make change and to coordinate action. In the Post Keynesian context power is seen as an effect of market structures. In the case of ecological economics, the main focus is on how power relations influence access to resources and the distribution of risk.

Given all these similarities, one must acknowledge that there is also at least one important area of difference. First of all, Post Keynesian economics has been concerned primarily with economic growth and the problem of unemployment due to scarcity of demand. Resource scarcity does not feature as important in Post Keynesian texts. Rather, it has been important to emphasize scarcity as socially constructed. This parallels areas of institutional economics where the focus has been on how the capitalist economy actually hampers technological change and hence growth. This topic appears very differently from within the ecological economics literature, where the main emphasis is on scale and non-substitutability between natural and human-made capital. More precisely, while this tradition emphasizes that many scarcities are socially constructed, for example, Martinez-Alier (1987) and Aguilera-Klink et al. (2000), the existence of real physical scarcity in the sense of weakened ecosystem resilience and impeded capacities to substitute between environmental resources is also strongly underlined. These scarcities are to a large extent due to the complementarities of living systems. The latter type dynamics is also observed in the Post Keynesian literature with its emphasis on complementarities between the needs of one specific living system, namely the human (cf. Lavoie above). So, while there are conflicts, these have more to do with focus – with different system delineations – than with fundamental disagreement on the way systems work.

DEVELOPING COMMON GROUND

This chapter is based on the idea that a more systematic development of common ground for Post Keynesian, ecological and institutional economics will offer great opportunities for all three schools. They not only share much the same base, but also have complementary insights which should be utilized. The aim of this section is to demonstrate this potential by looking at two of the core areas that have materialized from the above analysis: that of behavioral theory, and the theory of the economy–environment interface and dynamics.

Behavior

A vision for the three traditions would be to join forces in developing a common model for understanding human behavior that could form a more complete and consistent alternative to the neoclassical school. This is certainly a big endeavor, but the above discussion shows that there is basis for a common engagement. Trying to delineate some directions for such an effort, I would like to emphasize three interlinked focal points: those of uncertainty, incommensurability and endogenous preferences.

As we have seen, studying uncertainty is a feature of all three traditions. The focus and understanding seem to vary, though, as some authors appear to associate uncertainty with our capacity to handle mentally all the complexities we face, while others also emphasize that the world itself is characterized by radical uncertainty, that is, situations with genuine novelty. Moreover the Keynesian and Post Keynesian tradition focuses first of all on uncertainty within social systems. This is the dominant view also of institutional economics. Ecological economists, on the other hand, look at uncertainties pertaining first of all to the working of ecological systems and the interactions with socio-ecological systems.

Analyses of uncertainty have led to models of bounded rationality and satisficing behavior which, as we have seen, are taken up by representatives of all three traditions. There is a need to develop and understand this aspect of behavior further. First, the concept of bounded rationality is referred to, but often in a rather shallow way. The information problem that the individual faces is understood. What is lacking is an understanding of how people act in the face of information uncertainties. There are references to procedures, rules of thumb, habits and conventions. We have, however, not yet established how these institutions function. We have little insight into how they develop and change, despite referring to collective learning. Similarly, how they may solve the problem of fixing expectations and how they themselves might create new uncertainties and rigidities that may obstruct necessary change are still open questions.

Second, as emphasized by Dequech (2001), the present model of bounded rationality seems relevant only for situations where it is the restricted cognitive capacity which establishes the uncertainty. Principally, an optimal solution could then be foreseeable *ex ante* if this capacity was expanded, at least to some extent, through collective learning. If outcomes are truly novel or unimaginable, the present theory of bounded rationality does not offer a viable understanding. In the face of environmental degradation and change, it is important to increase our understanding of how people act in situations characterized by truly radical uncertainty and, next, what may foster our ability to change our rules in the face of new and challenging conditions.

A specific aspect of the above relates to the uncertainties established by interdependencies between human actions. This is an issue where the three traditions should be especially well equipped to advance and develop. All environmental problems are problems of interdependencies, as the environment is common to us. Being problems of interdependence, they are problems of coordination. One problem, of course, is persuading individuals to forego the gains of free-riding. Solving this problem demands, however, that agents are willing to trust that others will also cooperate. We have learned that communication (for example, the establishment of norms of appropriate conduct) may have the capacity to facilitate this (Ostrom, 2005). Still, there is no model that coherently explains what is observed and why coordination works well under certain conditions and not under others, often with similar circumstances.

Expanding the neoclassical model of individual rationality to include individual utility gains from acting 'nicely' is a direction that some have looked at, for example, Andreoni (1990), Frey (1997) and Ostrom and Walker (2003). I find these attempts interesting, but lacking. There is hence not only room, but also great need for advancements taking classical institutionalist and Post Keynesian perspectives further in this area. What I find especially important is the emphasis on the dynamics between institutions and individual action, which not only opens up for developing models where the interaction between the two is the focal point (Vatn, 2008), but it also offers the opportunity to study how uncertainties are constructed, transformed and made manageable through the establishment of institutions. This area of research can provide some new insights in developing models of cooperation that are needed in dealing with environmental coordination problems.

Another important area is the issue of incommensurability that is essential to all three traditions. It surfaces at different levels and in different forms and contexts. We have observed that consumption analyses (for example, Lavoie, 1992) reveal the existence of lexicographic preferences. The same choice concerns pertain to environmental issues (for example, Spash, 2000). Finally, we observe focus on complementarities as opposed to substitution possibilities in both consumption and production analyses across the three traditions. Two quite different issues seem to be involved. One relates to the biophysical level and the other to the ethical sphere.

The biophysical dimension concerns the fact that processes of consumption as well as production are characterized by technical and/or biological interdependencies. Hence, consumption is influenced by biological needs from a body constituted of a complex set of interacting processes. Being so, complementarity is the core characteristic. Similarly, substitution possibilities in humanly constructed production systems also include the functioning of the biosphere in various ways and cannot be well described by a model anchored in the idea of substitution only.

Concerning the ethical dimension, the issues are of another kind. These appear in situations where choices are interdependent, as previously emphasized. Such interlinkages are typical attributes of choices in the realm of the environment. The interconnections of the environment imply that we, by our very existence, will have to influence the opportunities for others. This may result in the development of norms about appropriate behavior which are not easily traded off against individual interests. They simply refer to what is the right thing to do in such conflicting situations. The problem structure does not lend itself to maximization and trade-offs (Vatn, 2000, 2005a).

Looking further into this, we observe many studies documenting that incommensurabilities exist between ethical and other issues. What is lacking is an understanding about how people choose when faced with such incommensurable values. There is a lot of work, not least in the field of multi-criteria analysis, looking at decision making with incommensurable values. Typically, such procedures transform values into forms that can be compared[10] or construct hierarchical decision procedures that facilitate making priorities between non-comparable values. While this kind of analysis is dominantly found within ecological economics, Post Keynesian and institutional thinking could help in clarifying the dynamics of such choice processes. What is lacking is an understanding of: (1) how well these procedures describe actual decision-making processes; and (2) what kind of reasoning people use to make sense of choices where values are incommensurable. Douglas (1986) argues that many difficult decisions do not lend themselves to individual ratiocination. They are, rather, offloaded to institutions. I think her point is valid. We lack, however, an understanding of how these institutions are constructed and changed. As Holland (2002) has emphasized, if people follow the logic of utility maximization, there is really no choice. The individual is commanded by what the maximization calculus reveals. Hence, real choice is about choosing between options that do not lend themselves to calculation or are at least not decided upon only by that calculation itself. So real choice is actually about incommensurabilities, and yet we know very little about how we go about choosing between such values.

The third aspect of a better model of human behavior and agency concerns that of endogenous preferences. This topic has gained a lot of attention lately, an interest that goes into the ranks of orthodoxy itself. All the way back to Veblen, endogeneity has been a central claim by different heterodox positions. It unites large fractions of the three schools included in this chapter. This area is, however, also an underexposed field of research. This concerns not least how preferences are influenced by economic and social processes. Certainly, there are elements of insights offered by the three schools themselves and the wider literature, for example, sociology, anthropology and psychology. Nevertheless, what we seem to be faced with is more like a series of weakly related observations than a systematic build-up of insights ready to be synthesized.

Studying endogeneity really implies studying the role of institutions. Their major role may actually be to form what could be called rationality contexts. The idea is that they support individuals not least in choosing whether individual or social rationality is expected. Looking to the role of institutions, making a systematic distinction between individual variation and institutional variation, may have the capacity to help build a more comprehensive and coherent theory for understanding endogenous preferences. Institutions may play a role along both dimensions. First, they influence individuals through different and continuously ongoing enculturation processes. Second, they also seem to have the capacity to help people sort out whether what is at stake in a concrete situation is accepted to be an individual as opposed to a social issue, and whether we can trust others to be willing cooperators in specific settings. Better insights into these issues will be of the utmost importance, not least for the formulation of policies in areas like consumer choice and environmental policy.

The Environment and the Economic System

While the Post Keynesian tradition emphasizes the instability and intragenerational distribution issues of modern capitalism, ecological economists are more focused on the effect of our economic system on the environment and on intergenerational distribution. Certainly, both these areas are very important sets of issues. Moreover, inter- and intragenerational distribution issues are clearly linked. Instability in the economic system may result in policies that are detrimental in the form of both unemployment and environmental degradation.

Nevertheless, as emphasized before, the dominant Post Keynesian solution of expanding demand is problematic when seen from an ecological economist perspective. This is acknowledged by Post Keynesians themselves as some have started to look into the issue of environmental degradation, for example, Mearman (2005a). On the other hand, Post Keynesians have a long-standing tradition in looking into the dynamics of economic systems or structures. This is also the case for institutionalists.

Joining forces here should focus on the relationships between economic structures and environmental destruction and preservation, respectively. The aim should be to develop ideas concerning institutions that could secure sustainability along its various dimensions, that is, the environmental, economic and social. From the ecological economics perspective, the issue is about the scale of the economy relative to its environmental underpinning. Seen from that angle, our institutions are found lacking. The present economic system demands growth to be economically and socially sustainable. Growth levels around 2 percent and beyond are used as the indication of a healthy economy. Low levels threaten the amount of investment and result in problems with accelerating unemployment. This is a well-known scenario from the Post Keynesian perspective clearly emphasized by the present financial crisis.

The problem is that we now realize that the very scale of economic activity makes it hard to use growth as a way to secure sustainability. Rather, it threatens severely to change the biophysical underpinning of the system in ways that endanger its economic and social functioning. Climate change and massive biodiversity losses are examples of this trend.

The neoclassical solution to these problems is the use of instruments to internalize the so-called externalities that environmental problems represent in this model. The problem is understood as a lack of markets to produce the necessary prices. Environmentally oriented institutionalists and ecological economists think differently about these issues. They see the problems rather as systems-dependent (Kapp, 1971). They cannot be handled well without more fundamental changes in the economic system itself. Some ecological economists have proposed to develop a comprehensive arrangement controlling the input of natural resources into the economy (Daly, 1997). Others have emphasized the need for altering (also) the more fundamental motivation structures of the economy (Princen, 1997; Vatn, 2008). Interestingly, some Post Keynesians have recently started to engage in this issue, too. One proposal concerns using macroeconomic measures like public investment control to facilitate necessary innovation (Courvisanos, 2005).

These are difficult issues because they are politically very sensitive. They demand a lot of innovative and creative thinking. As I see it, we seem to need substantial changes in the way the economic system is organized in order to make a sustainable future possible along all three dimensions – environmental, economic and social. Three issues seem of special importance.

First, making the economy less dependent on growth – actually securing the space there is for growth for those in greatest need – demands changes in the motivation system of the economy. This may imply less room for the profit motive and more emphasis on cooperative structures. Whether this can be solved by macroeconomic planning, by changing the rules of corporate business, by instituting social rationality as a basic element of business motivation, are all open questions. Maybe a better path involves a combination of approaches? A good start would be to begin challenging each other's ideas about this. As I see it, we are faced with very large and demanding structural changes and need to join forces in developing proposals that can be tested out in what can hopefully be a gradual change of the economy towards a structure that matches the coming challenges.

Second, these challenges will only partly be possible to determine *ex ante*. The kinds of uncertainties we now face are pervasive and will dominantly be of the radical type. While a successful transformation will reduce the pressures on the environment and hence the chances for substantial shifts in its dynamics, we will still have to face unexpected challenges. So, we do not only need to change motivation systems; we also need to think about how to make our systems more resilient in the face of challenges that will by necessity follow from the changes that are already under way. Here I see special potential for cooperation between the three traditions. Ecological economists are strongly engaged in understanding what characterizes resilient systems, but mainly at the local level and concerning primarily small-scale changes. Institutional and Post Keynesians possess insights related to scaling these problems up, better to see and understand the demands at national and international levels.

Third, there is a need to look more systematically at what determines consumer behavior and how the social construction of needs operates. Present economic structures seem to demand a willing consumer to avoid economic crises. People seem to have easily adapted to becoming restless consumers. At the same time, we do not seem to get happier by means of the tremendous increases in consumption (for example, Layard, 2005). Certainly, we may simply be back to Veblen. Beyond a certain level, consumption is about positioning oneself in social hierarchies. Economic growth may itself increase the relative income positions of some people, which actually increases dissatisfaction among others. Keynes emphasized that the 'economic problem' would soon be solved in that we would turn to more important issues than just securing our economic sustenance. It does not seem likely, however, that we will ever be satisfied as an effect of some physical, biological or psychological limit. We rather need to construct these limits by somehow breaking the logic of consumerism and finding ways to establish identity and meaning outside of that realm. Personally, I think this is impossible without at the same time changing the basic institutions of the economy. These issues are fundamentally linked and establish a very important, but also demanding, common ground for Post Keynesians, ecological and institutional economists to develop.

NOTES

1. They also communicated. According to King (2002, p. 226) Keynes wrote to Commons that: 'there seems to me to be no other economist with whose general way of thinking I feel myself in such general accord'.
2. It should be mentioned that, from the 1960s, the so-called New Institutionalist posi-

tion evolved. It was very much based on the neoclassical core, but included positive transaction costs into the analysis (for example, Coase, 1960; North, 1990).

3. There are different ways of distinguishing between the various categories of 'uncertainty'. Most typically risk is seen as known outcomes with known probabilities. Uncertainty then is characterized by lack of a probability distribution. Radical uncertainty is, finally, seen as situations where not all potential outcomes are even known.
4. Such an attempt is taken on by the so-called New Keynesian economists.
5. Core people in the process of establishing the journal and the society were ecologists like AnnMari Jansson and Robert Costanza, and economists like Herman Daly and Joan Martinez-Alier. Costanza was the first president of the society and the first editor of the journal.
6. Prominent examples of 'neoclassical ecological economists' are Partha Dasgupta, Karl-Göran Mäler and David Pearce. One might wonder about the motivation for their engagement. Based on Røpke (2004) I see at least two potential reasons. One was that when the first initiatives were taken by ecologists like AnnMari Jansson, they turned to top economists in the field, not being aware of the discussions within economics itself and not thinking about 'which kind of' economics could be the better basis for cooperation. They saw a need for interdisciplinary research and just looked for 'excellence'. The other reason was more related to the interest of environmental economists in engaging with forming the new society in the way they would like to see it. Certainly, it is hard to envision how the society for ecological economics could then be differentiated from that of environmental economics that was established in the 1970s.
7. For an instructive discussion of the distinctions between ecological economics and neoclassically inspired environmental economics, see Spash (1999).
8. MIPS = material input per unit of service.
9. This implies that the economy can be run on minimal inputs of energy and materials.
10. This looks very much like the way in which neoclassical economists reduce uncertainty to risk. It is a shift that is fundamentally at error with the underlying concept.

REFERENCES

Aguilera-Klink, F., E. Perez-Moriana and J. Sanchez-Garcia (2000), 'The social construction of scarcity: the case of water in Tenerife (Canary Islands)', *Ecological Economics*, **34** (2), 233–45.

Andreoni, J. (1990), 'Impure altruism and the donations to public goods: a theory of warm glow giving', *Economic Journal*, **100**, 467–77.

Berr, E. (2008), 'Keynes and the Post Keynesians on sustainable development', Working paper GRETHA UMR CNRS 5113, Cashiers du GEThA, no 2008-1, http://beagle.u-bordeaux4.fr/gretha/publications/2008/2008-01.pdf.

Boulding, K. (1966), 'The economics of the coming spaceship earth', in H. Jarret (ed.), *Environmental Quality in a Growing World*, Baltimore, MD: Johns Hopkins University Press, pp. 3–14.

Bromley, D.W. (1989), *Economic Interests and Institutions: The Conceptual Foundations of Public Policy*, Oxford: Basil Blackwell.

Bromley, D.W. (1998), 'Searching for sustainability: the poverty of spontaneous order', *Ecological Economics*, **24** (2–3), 231–40.

Bromley, D.W. (2006), *Sufficient Reason: Volitional Pragmatism and the Meaning of Economic Institutions*, Princeton, NJ: Princeton University Press.

Coase, R.H. (1960), 'The problem of social cost', *Journal of Law and Economics*, **3**, 1–44.
Commons, J.R. (1931), 'Institutional economics', *American Economic Review*, **21**, 648–57.
Commons, J.R. (1990 [1934]), *Institutional Economics: Its Place in Political Economics*, New Brunswick, NJ: Transaction Publishers.
Costanza, R., B.S. Low, E. Ostrom and J. Wilson (eds) (2001), *Institutions, Ecosystems and Sustainability*, Boca Raton, FL: Lewis Publishers.
Courvisanos, J. (2005), 'A post-Keynesian innovation policy for sustainable development', *International Journal of Environment, Workplace and Employment*, **1** (2), 187–202.
Daly, H.E (1968), 'On economics as a life science', *Journal of Political Economy*, **76**, 392–406.
Daly, H.E. (1977), *Steady-State Economics*, San Francisco, CA: W.H. Freeman & Company.
Daly, H. (1997), 'Reconciling internal and external policies for sustainable development', in O.K. Dragun and K. Jacobson (eds), *Sustainability and Global Environmental Policy*, Cheltenham, UK and Lyme, NH, USA: Edward Elgar, pp. 11–32.
Dasgupta, P.S. and G.M. Heal (1974), 'The optimal depletion of exhaustible resources', in *Review of Economic Studies, Symposium on the Economics of Exhaustible Resources*, Edinburgh: Longman, pp. 3–28.
Davidson, P. (1972), *Money and the Real World*, London: Macmillan.
Dequech, D. (2001), 'Bounded rationality, institutions, and uncertainty', *Journal of Economic Issues*, **35** (4), 911–29.
Douglas, M. (1986), *How Institutions Think*, Syracuse, NY: Syracuse University Press.
Faber, M., R. Mansetten and J. Proops (1996), *Ecological Economics: Concepts and Methods*, Cheltenham, UK and Brookfield, VT, USA: Edward Elgar.
Ferrari-Filho, F. and O.A. Carmago Conceicao (2004), 'The concept of uncertainty in Post Keynesian theory and in institutional economics', Paper, seminario 24/24-14/10/2004, University of Sao Paulo, http://www.econ.fea.usp.br/seminarios/artigos2/uncertainty.pdf.
Fisher-Kowalski, M. and H. Weisz (1999), 'Society as a hybrid between material and social realms: toward a theoretical framework of society–nature interaction', *Advances in Human Ecology*, **8**, 215–51.
Folke, C. (2006), 'Resilience: the emergence of a perspective for social–ecological systems analyses', *Global Environmental Change*, **16**, 253–67.
Frey, B.S. (1997), *Not Just For the Money: An Economic Theory of Personal Motivation*, Cheltenham, UK and Lyme, NH, USA: Edward Elgar.
Funtowicz, S. and J.R. Ravetz (1993), 'Science for the post-normal age', *Futures*, **25**, 735–55.
Funtowicz, S. and J.R. Ravetz (1994), 'The worth of a songbird: ecological economics as a post-normal science', *Ecological Economics*, **10** (3), 197–208.
Georgescu-Roegen, N. (1971), *The Entropy Law and the Economic Process*, Cambridge, MA: Harvard University Press.
Giampietro, M. (2004), *Multi-Scale Integrated Analysis of Agroecosystems*, London: CRC Press.
Hamouda, O.F. and G.C. Harcourt (1988), 'Post Keynesianism: from criticism to coherence', *Bulletin of Economic Research*, **40** (1), 1–33.

Hinterberger, F., F. Luks and F. Schmidt-Bleck (1997), 'Material flows vs. "natural capital": what makes an economy sustainable', *Ecological Economics*, **23**, 1–14.
Hodgson, G.M. (1988), *Economics and Institutions: A Manifesto for a Modern Institutional Economics*, Cambridge: Polity Press.
Hodgson, G.M. (1996), *Economics and Evolution: Bringing Life back into Economics*, Ann Arbor, MI: University of Michigan Press.
Hodgson, G.M. (2004), *The Evolution of Institutional Economics: Agency, Structure, and Darwinism in American Institutionalism*, London: Routledge.
Holland, A. (1997), 'Substitutability, or why strong sustainability is weak and absurdly strong sustainability is not absurd', in Foster, J. (ed.), *Valuing Nature? Economics, Ethics and Environment*, London: Routledge, pp. 119–34.
Holland, A. (2002), 'Are choices tradeoffs?', in D.W. Bromley and J. Paavola (eds), *Economics, Ethics and Environmental Policy. Contested Choices*, Oxford: Blackwell, pp. 17–34.
Holling, C.S. (1973), 'Resilience and stability of ecological systems', *Annual Review of Ecological Systems*, **4**, 1–24.
Holling, C.S. (2001), 'Understanding the complexity of ecological, economic and social systems', *Ecosystems*, **4**, 390–405.
Holt, R.P.F. (2005), 'Post-Keynesian economics and sustainable development', *International Journal of Environment, Workplace and Employment*, **1** (2), 174–86.
Jacobs, M. (1997), 'Environmental valuation, deliberative democracy and public decision-making', in J. Foster (ed.), *Valuing Nature? Economics, Ethics and Environment*, London: Routledge, pp. 211–31.
Kalecki, M. (1943), 'Political aspects of full employment', *Political Quarterly*, **14** (4), 322–31.
Kapp, K.W. (1971), *The Social Costs of Private Enterprise*, New York: Schocken Books.
Keller, R. (1983), 'Keynesian and institutional economics: compatibility and complementarity?', *Journal of Economic Issues*, **17** (4), 1087–95.
Keynes, J.M. (1921), *A Treatise on Probability*, London: Macmillan.
Keynes, J.M. (1930), *A Treatise on Money*, London: Macmillan.
Keynes, J.M. (1936), *The General Theory of Employment, Interest and Money*, London: Macmillan.
King, J.E. (2002), *A History of Post Keynesian Economics since 1936*, Cheltenham, UK and Northampton, MA, USA: Edward Elgar.
Kneese, A.V., R.U. Ayres and R.C. d'Arge (1970), *Economics and the Environment: A Materials Balance Approach*, Washington, DC: Resources for the Future.
Knetsch, J. (1994), 'Environmental valuation: some problems of wrong questions and misleading answers', *Environmental Values*, **3** (4), 351–68.
Knudsen, C. (1993), 'Equilibrium, perfect rationality and the problem of self-reference in economics', in U. Mäki, B. Gustafsson and C. Knudsen (eds), *Rationality, Institutions and 'Economic Methodology'*, London: Routledge, pp. 133–70.
Lavoie, M. (1992), *Foundations of Post-Keynesian Economic Analysis*, Aldershot, UK and Brookfield, VT, USA: Edward Elgar.
Layard, R. (2005), *Happiness: Lessons from a New Science*, New York: Penguin Press.
Lehtonen, M. (2004), 'The environmental–social interface of sustainable development: capabilities, social capital, institutions', *Ecological Economics*, **49**, 199–214.

Martinez-Alier, J. (1987), *Ecological Economics. Energy, Environment and Society*, Oxford: Basil Blackwell.
Martinez-Alier, J., G. Munda and J. O'Neill (1998), 'Weak comparability of values as a foundation of ecological economics', *Ecological Economics*, **26** (3), 277–86.
Meadows, D., D.L. Meadows, J. Randers and W.W. Behrends III (1972), *Limits to Growth: A Report for the Club of Rome's Project on the Predicament of Mankind*, New York: Universe Books.
Mearman, A. (2005a), 'Why have post-Keynesians had (relatively) little to say on the economics of the environment?', *International Journal of Environment, Workplace and Employment*, **1** (2), 131–54.
Mearman, A. (2005b), 'Post-Keynesian economics and the environment: introduction to the mini symposium', *International Journal of Environment, Workplace and Employment*, **1** (2), 121–30.
North, D.C. (1990), *Institutions, Institutional Change and Economic Performance*, Cambridge: Cambridge University Press.
Odum, E. (1953), *Fundamentals of Ecology*, Philadelphia, PA: W.B. Saunders Co.
O'Neill, J. (1993), *Ecology, Policy and Politics: Human Well-Being and the Natural World*, London: Routledge.
Ostrom, E. (2005), *Understanding Institutional Diversity*, Princeton, NJ: Princeton University Press.
Ostrom, E. and J. Walker (eds) (2003), *Trust and Reciprocity: Interdisciplinary Lessons from Experimental Research*, New York: Russell Sage Foundation.
Paavola, J. and N. Adger (2005), 'Institutional ecological economics', *Ecological Economics*, **53** (3), 353–68.
Prigogine, I. (1980), *From Being to Becoming: Time and Complexity in the Physical Sciences*, San Francisco, CA: Freeman & Co.
Princen, T. (1997), 'The shading and distancing of commerce: when internalization is not enough', *Ecological Economics*, **20**, 235–53.
Rees, W.E. and M. Wackernagel (1994), 'Ecological footprints and appropriated carrying capacity: measuring the natural capital requirements of the human economy', in A.M. Janson, M. Hammer, C. Folke and R Costanza (eds), *Investing in Natural Capital: The Ecological Economics Approach to Sustainability*, Washington, DC: Island Press, pp. 362–90.
Reisch, A. and I. Røpke (eds) (2004), *The Ecological Economics of Consumption*, Cheltenham, UK and Northampton, MA, USA: Edward Elgar.
Røpke, I. (2004), 'The early history of modern ecological economics', *Ecological Economics*, **50** (3–4), 293–314.
Røpke, I. (2005), 'Trends in the development of ecological economics from the late 1980s to the early 2000s', *Ecological Economics*, **55**, 262–90.
Samuels, W.J., S.G. Medema and A.A. Schmid (1997), *The Economy as a Process of Valuation*, Cheltenham, UK and Lyme, NH, USA: Edward Elgar.
Schmid, A.A. (1987), *Property, Power, and Public Choice: An Inquiry into Law and Economics*, New York: Praeger.
Schmid, A.A. (2004), *Conflict and Cooperation: Institutional and Behavioral Economics*, Oxford: Blackwell Publishing
Siebenhüner, B. (2000), 'Homo sustinens: towards a new conception of humans for the science of sustainability', *Ecological Economics*, **32** (1), 15–25.
Simon, H.A. (1957), *Models of Man*, New York: John Wiley & Sons.
Sjöstrand, S.-E. (1995), 'Towards a theory of institutional change', in J. Groenewegen, C. Pitelis and S.-E. Sjöstrand (eds), *On Economic Institutions:*

Theory and Application, Aldershot, UK and Brookfield, VT, USA: Edward Elgar, pp. 19–44.
Söderbaum, P. (1994), 'Actors, ideology, markets: neoclassical and institutional perspectives on environmental policy', *Ecological Economics*, **10** (1), 47–60.
Söderbaum, P. (2000), *Ecological Economics: A Political Economics Approach to Environment and Development*, London: Earthscan.
Solow, R.M. (1974), 'Intergenerational equity and exhaustible resources', in *Review of Economic Studies, Symposium on the Economics of Exhaustible Resources*, Edinburgh: Longman, pp. 29–45.
Spash, C.L. (1998), 'Investigating individual motives for environmental action: lexicographic preferences, beliefs, attitudes', in J. Lemons, L. Westra and R. Goodland (eds), *Ecological Sustainability and Integrity: Concepts and Approaches*, Dordrecht: Kluwer Academic Publishers, pp. 46–62.
Spash, C.L. (1999), 'The development of environmental thinking in economics', *Environmental Values*, **8**, 413–35.
Spash, C.L. (2000), 'Multiple value expression in contingent valuation: economics and ethics', *Environmental Science Technology*, **34**, 1433–8.
Spash, C.L. (2006), 'Non-economic motivation for contingent values: rights and attitudinal beliefs in the willingness to pay for environmental improvements', *Land Economics*, **82** (4), 602–22.
Spash, C.L. and M.G. Villena (1998), 'Exploring the approach of institutional economics to the environment', Environment Series Number 11, Department of Land Economy, University of Cambridge.
Stagl, S. 2007), 'Theoretical foundations of learning processes for sustainable development', *International Journal of Sustainable Development and World Ecology*, **14** (1), 52–62.
Swaney, J.A. (1987), 'Elements of a neoinstitutional environmental economics', *Journal of Economic Issues*, **21**, 1739–79.
Tool, M.R. (1995), *Pricing, Valuation and Systems. Essays in Neoinstitutional Economics*, Aldershot, UK and Brookfield, VT, USA: Edward Elgar.
Tymoigne, E. (2003), 'Keynes and Commons on money', *Journal of Economic Issues*, **37** (3), 527–45.
van den Bergh, J.C.J.M., A. Ferrer-i-Carbonell and G. Munda (2000), 'Alternative models of individual behavior and implications for environmental policy', *Ecological Economics*, **31** (1), 43–61.
Vatn, A. (2000), 'The environment as a commodity', *Environmental Values*, **9**, 493–509.
Vatn, A. (2004), 'Valuation and rationality', *Land Economics*, **80** (February), 1–18.
Vatn, A. (2005a), *Institutions and the Environment*, Cheltenham, UK and Northampton, MA, USA: Edward Elgar.
Vatn, A. (2005b), 'Rationality, institutions and environmental policy', *Ecological Economics*, **55** (2), 203–17.
Vatn, A. (2008), 'Institutions and rationality', in S. Batie and N. Mercuro (eds), *Assessing the Evolution and Impact of Alternative Institutional Structures*, London: Routledge, pp. 113–39.
Vatn, A. and D. Bromley (1994), 'Choices without prices without apologies', *Journal of Environmental Economics and Management*, **26**, 129–48.
Veblen, T. (1898), 'Why is economics not an evolutionary science', *Quarterly Journal of Economics*, **12**, 373–97.

Veblen T. (1909), 'The limitation of marginal utility', *Journal of Political Economy*, **17**, 620–36.
Veblen, T. (1958 [1904]), *The Theory of Business Enterprise*, New York: New American Library.
Veblen, T. (1969 [1923]), *Absentee Ownership and Business Enterprise in Recent Times: The Case of America*, Boston, MA: Beacon Press.
Veblen T. (1970 [1899]), *The Theory of the Leisure Class: An Economic Study of Institutions*, London: Unwin Books.

PART III

Consumers in Theory and Practice

7. Post Keynesian consumer choice theory and ecological economics

Marc Lavoie

INTRODUCTION

Post Keynesian consumer theory arises from a multitude of influences, including those of socio-economists, psychologists, marketing specialists, and individuals such as Herbert Simon (1962, 1976) and Georgescu-Roegen, who are or were fully aware of the complexity of our environment, as well as the disparate clues that were left by the founders of Post Keynesian theory, clues that turn out to be surprisingly consistent with each other.

Despite its apparent neglect, there exists a Post Keynesian theory of consumer choice, based on the indications left by the best-known and most productive Post Keynesian authors, such as Joan Robinson (1956, p. 251), Luigi Pasinetti (1981, p. 73), Edward Nell (1992, p. 396), Philip Arestis (1992, p. 124) and Bertram Schefold (1997, p. 327). These indications on consumer choice show a great degree of coherence, and in my opinion they fit tightly with the rest of Post Keynesian theory. The most detailed examination of a possible Post Keynesian consumer theory can be found in two books by Peter Earl (1983, 1986), and the motivations supplied above are quite apparent there. Other specific contributions to Post Keynesian consumer choice can be found in the works of Arrous (1978), Eichner (1987, Chapter 9), Drakopoulos (1990, 1992, 1994) and Lavoie (1992, Chapter 2), where a substantial amount of overlap with Earl's initial attempt at defining a specific Post Keynesian consumer choice vision is obvious. A neat, earlier exposition of a post-Keynesian consumer choice theory can be found in the recently translated work of Roy (2005).

I have shown that the common ground of Post Keynesian consumer theory can be represented by a set of six principles which have been presented in detail in Lavoie (1994, 2004, 2005), and to which I now add a seventh one. Most of the names of these heterodox principles of consumer behavior arise from the terms used by Georgescu-Roegen (1954, pp. 514–5). Separability is taken from Lancaster (1991), while non-independence is taken from Galbraith (1958). The principles are only listed here:

1. The principle of procedural rationality.
2. The principle of satiable needs.
3. The principle of separability of needs.
4. The principle of subordination of needs.
5. The principle of the growth of needs.
6. The principle of non-independence.
7. The principle of heredity.

A key consequence of these seven principles, in particular the principle of subordination, is that the utility index cannot be represented by a scalar any more, but rather by a vector, and that the notions of gross substitution and trade-offs, which are so important for neoclassical economics, are brought down to a minor phenomenon that only operates within narrow boundaries. This consumer theory does not rely on the Archimedes principle that 'everything has a price'. In particular, it is presumed that the principle of subordination, or hierarchy, is particularly relevant when dealing with moral issues, for instance, questions of integrity and religion or ecological issues.

Past work in ecological economics has shown indeed that a substantial proportion of individuals refuse to make trade-offs with material goods when biodiversity, wildlife or forests are concerned. This has implications for contingency value analyses, based on willingness to pay or willingness to accept compensation, that attempt to take into account the non-market value of ecology or forestry preservation. The claim made here is that post-Keynesian consumer choice theory is highly relevant to ecological economics, going beyond the critiques that can be addressed to *Homo economicus* from the standpoint of experimental economics (Gintis, 2000).

I was recently struck by an account of the relationship between North American Indians (Autochtones) and French and English settlers in the seventeenth century. Indians were initially trading pots, knives, guns, textiles, shirts and various useful products with French settlers, in exchange for beaver and other animal pelts. When the Indians met the English settlers, who were much better stocked from their homeland, they were offered twice the amount of goods for each pelt. At this higher price, neoclassical theory would then tell us that Indians would have increased their supply of pelts, working longer hours (as a result of the higher cost of leisure). But it turns out that the exact opposite occurred. Indians instead cut their supply of pelts by half, figuring that they now could obtain the necessities of life by reducing their hunting time by 50 percent (Havard and Vidal, 2003, p. 229). There was no substitution effect, only an income effect, as Post Keynesians would emphasize. This is certainly an enlightening story in a world concerned with excessive and wasteful consumer spending.

SOME COMMON THEMES

A quick survey of the literature on environmental economics demonstrates that the more radical environmental economists – ecological economists – have used all seven principles mentioned above in their effort to present a consumer choice theory that would be an alternative to the standard neoclassical model. The claim made here is that Post Keynesian consumer choice theory is highly relevant to ecological economics, and that indeed ecological economists have already provided models of consumer behaviour which rely, unknowingly except for Kant (2003), on a Post Keynesian theory of behaviour.

It should first be pointed out, as explained by Holt (2005), that many of the themes evoked by Post Keynesian economists are ranked highly by ecological economists. First and foremost, there is the precautionary principle associated with fundamental uncertainty. When information is lacking, business people act prudently. They usually postpone taking decisions that might increase the probability of bankruptcy of their institution. The same principle should be applied to environmental issues. In doubt, no decision that increases the probability of an environmental catastrophe should be taken. This concern with true uncertainty has been underlined by Vatn and Bromley (1995, p. 18), van den Bergh et al. (2000, p. 57) and Ravetz (1994–95). It also involves another Keynesian concept, that of the 'weight of an argument', which Georgescu-Roegen (1966, p. 266) called the 'credibility' of a statement: the degree of confidence in assessed probabilities does and should affect decision-making.

Second, there is the heredity principle, or a variant of what I have called the principle of non-independence. Preferences are endogenous and context-specific, as Kant (2003) would like them to be described by consumer theory. 'Utility depends on past experience, the duration and intensity of past experience, and the length of time that has passed since the relevant experience took place' (Gowdy, 1993, p. 235). Habit formation can be seen as a particular case of path-dependency (Zamagni, 1999, p. 117). In this framework, the theory of choice reflects the complexities of human nature rather than the mathematical requirements of tractability. As Crivelli (1993, p. 119) points out, 'the longest standing invocation of hysteresis seems to be in the context of the theory of choice', and Georgescu-Roegen's heredity principle is a case example of hysteresis. The path taken by consumers will have permanent effects on future choices. This, linked to the other feature of the principle of non-independence, that is, the fact that advertising and fads have an impact on the choices made by individual consumers, reinforces the arbitrary nature of consumer choices and the possibility of intransitive preferences and multiple equilibria. Indeed,

Gowdy (1993, p. 235) claims that the heredity principle is tied to the large discrepancies that have been observed between willingness to pay and willingness to accept in contingent valuation studies. Gowdy argues that agents will be less likely to give up some environmental landscape that they have had the opportunity to experience.

A third theme which is common to both ecological economists and Post Keynesian economists is that of multidimensional choice. This point was made very early on by Bird (1982, p. 592), who argued that in contrast to neoclassical economics, 'the choice between alternative environmental policies must necessarily therefore be made in more than one dimension'. This theme is a recurrent one among the proponents of sustainable forest management. Bengston (1994, pp. 523–5) for one claims that: 'the multidimensional or pluralist perspective maintains that held values cannot be reduced to a single dimension and that all objects cannot be assigned value on a single scale – values are inherently multidimensional'. This is certainly an important feature of socio-economics (Etzioni, 1988), and it has been endorsed by several ecological economists such as Vatn and Bromley (1995, p. 9), who have called it the 'incongruity' problem.

Martinez-Alier et al. (1998) make an interesting distinction. They represent the idea of multidimensions under the name of 'weak comparability'. When there exists a common unit of measurement across plural values, usually a monetary one, one can speak of strong comparability. When such a common rod does not exist, one speaks of weak comparability. The latter implies incommensurability. Martinez-Alier et al. (1998) claim that no value is superior to another. We are in a zone where no preference can be ascertained beforehand. Multi-criteria evaluation techniques must be brought in to disentangle conflict and multidimensional elements of choice. The value that will actually appear to be dominant will depend on the characteristics of each individual case, where each possible alternative will be assessed on the basis of a multiplicity of criteria (Bengston, 1994, p. 525). No algorithm or axiomatization of choice is possible under these conditions. All that matters is that the decision process itself be well defined. In fact, as argued by Gowdy and Mayumi (2001), choices over multidimensions are conducive to states where the agent is unable to choose. The so-called indifferent states of neoclassical analysis, when it comes to multidimensional issues, are better interpreted as alternatives that agents 'cannot order without a great deal of hesitation or without some inconsistency' (Gowdy and Mayumi, 2001, p. 233; cf. Georgescu-Roegen, 1954, p. 522). Such choices generally will not be transitive. We may also wish to argue that a single individual may have several conflicting 'souls', and hence may reach different judgements, depending on the point of view, or dimension, which is being favoured (Steedman and Krause, 1986).

It seems to me that the weak comparability criterion advocated by Martinez-Alier et al. (1998) and Gowdy and Mayumi (2001) is very similar to the post-Keynesian principle of the separability of needs. This principle severely restricts the substitution effects that could arise between elements that belong to different groups of needs, but it does not totally eliminate them. One could presume that multi-criteria decision techniques that rely on weak comparability would still entertain substitution effects. If monetary compensations are high enough, they will win the day. Consumers will be swayed by a high enough monetary trade-off, even if they hesitate to do so. But several ecological economists have denied any role for substitution effects, at least in some circumstances for some categories of households. This is what Vatn and Bromley (1995) call 'choices without prices without apologies'.

Substitution effects are totally wiped out when lexicographic choices or choices of a lexicographic nature are entertained. This is tied to the post-Keynesian principle of the subordination of needs, or the irreducibility principle of Georgescu-Roegen. Lexicographic choices in the field of environment have been explicitly put forward by Edwards (1986), Stevens et al. (1991), Lockwood (1996), Spash and Hanley (1995), Spash (1998), van den Bergh et al. (2000), Gowdy and Mayumi (2001) and Kant (2003). The first five of these authors present a graphical representation of lexicographic choice, pointing out that it dismisses the neoclassical axiom of indifference, also called the Archimedes axiom or the axiom of gross substitution, which is so essential to price-based neoclassical environmental policies. These authors do not claim that all agents exhibit behaviour based on choices of a lexicographic nature. Rather they argue that a substantial proportion of the population – sometimes called ethicists or altruists – exhibit such a behaviour on matters tied to environment, and that neoclassical representations of these consumers are misleading, and lead to inadequate interpretation of surveys on the opinions of people about their environment. This applies in particular to the contingent valuation surveys.

The difference between standard neoclassical consumer analysis and the heterodox approach based on the separability and the subordination of needs, within the context of environmental issues, can be shown most clearly with the help of two diagrams, inspired by Spash (1998). Figure 7.1 illustrates standard neoclassical analysis, and possibly the principle of separability of needs with its associated region of hesitation. Income devoted to private goods is on the vertical axis, while the some environmental good (the size of a rain forest or of an old-growth forest, the area of wetlands, or ozone levels) is represented on the horizontal axis, as in the example provided by Lockwood (1996, p. 88). Consumers are assumed to

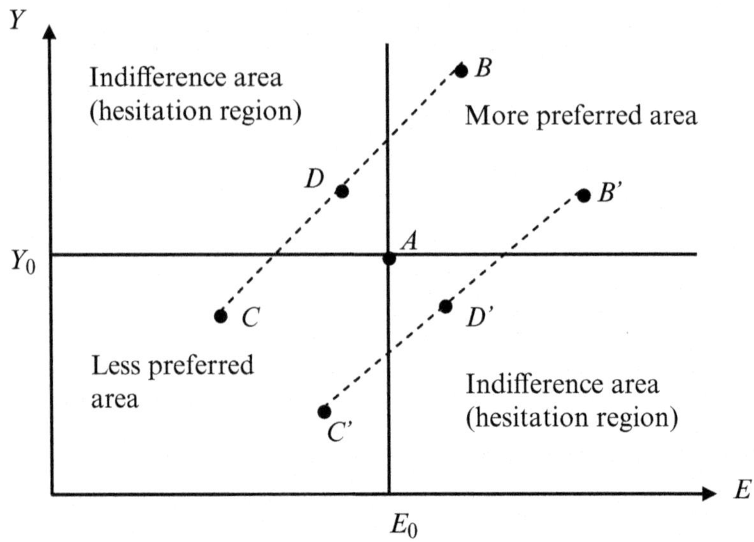

Figure 7.1 The neoclassical indifference approach and the hesitation region

be choosing between keeping up a certain provision level of environmental good on the one hand, and the income amount which they can devote to private good consumption on the other hand. The former is called *E* and the latter is *Y*. Suppose that the starting situation is one where the size of the forest is E_0, while income level is Y_0, which corresponds to point *A*. The plane can thus be divided into four quadrants, divided by the vertical and horizontal lines passing through the starting endowment. The north-east quadrant, including the two horizontal and vertical lines defining it, is an area that represents combinations of private consumption and forest size which are preferred, compared to bundle *A*. Symmetrically, the south-west quadrant, with its two line frontiers, represents an area of less preferred combinations, relative to *A*. On the other hand, the two remaining zones, the north-west and south-east quadrants, are areas of indifference. These are areas where some trade-off is assumed to be possible. It is possible to have more private consumption in exchange for a smaller forest, or some larger forest in exchange for a lesser amount of private consumption. The consumer is willing to make the trade-off, at some price, because if the terms of the trade-off are high enough, the trade-off will keep constant the satisfaction (the utility) of the consumer.

In each of the two areas of indifference, there will be a multiplicity of combinations that will keep constant the utility of the consumer. This locus of points, along with combination *A*, will define the neoclassical indifference curve. What the neoclassical axiom of indifference says, now called the axiom of continuity, is that if there exists a combination *B* which is preferred to the starting bundle *A*, while there is another combination *C* which is less preferred to *C*, as shown in Figure 7.1, then there must exist a combination *D* on the segment linking *B* to *C* which is indifferent to the initial bundle *A*. This segment is shown by the dashed line in Figure 7.1. Another such dashed line illustrates the axiom of continuity in the other area of indifference, in the south-east quadrant, with bundles *B*', *C*' and *D*'. The neoclassical indifference curve would then go through the three points *A*, *D* and *D*'.

A first criticism of this indifference curve construction is that of Gowdy and Mayumi (2001, pp. 232–4), as already outlined above. They assert that the two areas of indifference, when environmental issues are at stake, are instead areas of hesitation, which are likely to carry inconsistent and hence intransitive choices. These are caused by the high level of fundamental uncertainty associated with environmental issues. Inconsistency is the symptom of the lack of information about the future, and it also reflects the inability and the reluctance of consumers to compare bundles that include weakly comparable components.

The second critique of this neoclassical indifference curve construction is that based on the principle of subordination, and its associated choices of a lexicographic nature. This is illustrated with Figure 7.2, inspired by Spash (1998, p. 53). Once more, the individual consumer is assumed to start from bundle *A*. Let us suppose that the achieved bundle constitutes the thresholds levels that must be minimally obtained for the individual to retain the present level of satisfaction. Any combination that provides an income inferior to Y_0 would bring about a lower level of satisfaction, whatever the size of the environment good. Symmetrically, any combination that would reduce the environmental provisions below E_0, whatever the amount of private consumption, would also lead to a lower level of satisfaction. On the other hand, provided the threshold level of income Y_0 is attained, we presume that the primary determinant of the satisfaction of the consumer is the size of environmental goods *E*. For instance, bundles *B* and *B*' in Figure 7.2 would always be preferred to bundle *A* or *A*'. Only with bundles providing equal environmental goods would the income level *Y* become a (secondary) determinant of the combination choice. For instance *B* would be preferred to *B*'. The plane is thus divided into two zones (plus point *A*). The north-east quadrant, with its horizontal and vertical frontiers, is the area of more preferred combinations relative to *A*. The other three quadrants are all areas of less preferred combinations relative to the initial bundle *A*.

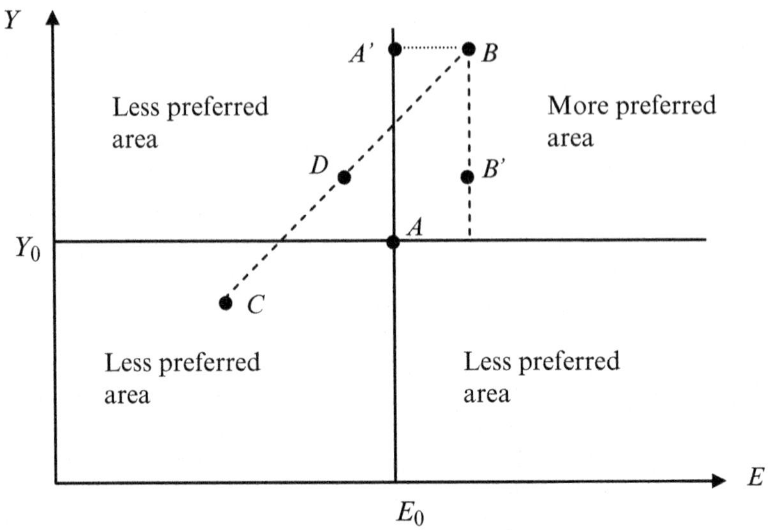

Figure 7.2 Choices of a lexicographic nature with thresholds

Such an alternative consumer behaviour does not fulfil the conditions of the axiom of continuity. As was done in Figure 7.1, we may draw in Figure 7.2 a dashed segment line connecting bundle *B*, which is preferred to *A*, and bundle *C*, which is less preferred than bundle *A*. However there does not exist any point *D* on this segment which corresponds to a bundle providing an amount of satisfaction which is equal to that of combination *A*. No combination of forest size and income level is indifferent to that of combination *A*. The axiom of continuity, or of indifference, does not hold any more, because of the lexicographic nature of choices. This implies that the Archimedes axiom, according to which everything has a price, does not hold anymore either.

IMPLICATIONS FOR THE CONTINGENT VALUATION METHOD

As is well known, within the standard neoclassical choice theory framework, the willingness to pay (WTP) and the willingness to accept (WTA) (or willingness to sell, WTS) are well-defined measures of the Hicksian consumer surplus, which should be equal to each other (small income effects aside). Still, numerous studies have shown that WTA assessments largely exceed those of WTP. The discrepancy is easily a factor of 3–10

(Knetsch, 1990, p. 228), and even a factor of 3–50 when environment issues are considered (Gowdy, 1993, p. 236). Lockwood (1996, p. 91) points out that these discrepancies are particularly large when there exist few substitutes for the good being valued, which is in line with the distinction that we have made about the separability of needs.

Various explanations have been offered for this phenomenon. The first obvious one is the non-independence principle, more precisely the heredity principle, according to which we hold on more dearly to something which we already have than to something which we never had (Knetsch, 1990; Gowdy, 1993). The second explanation has to do with lexicographic ordering. Consumers might be willing to give up a limited amount of money to improve their environment; but they would demand an unlimited amount of compensation to accept a reduction of the same environment. In fact, they might be unwilling to trade for any reduction in the quality of their environment.

This brings to the fore the large number of zero or infinite bids, as well as refusals to bid, that are encountered in contingent valuation studies. Zero bids or refusals to bid are often interpreted as signalling no interest in improving or preserving the quality of environment. On the other hand, bids that appear absurdly high are waved off, on the basis that they cannot fit the neoclassical theory of the consumer surplus. These anomalous responses, however, are anomalous only within the strict neoclassical framework. As was first pointed out by Edwards (1986, p. 149), the willingness to sell will be undefined for agents that hold preferences of a lexicographic nature whenever their income exceeds their minimum standard of living. In that case: 'an altruist committed to the welfare of wildlife and future generations is expected to protest against contingent markets when asked for minimum WTS by either refusing to bid, bidding zero dollars, or bidding an extremely high amount'.

Some researchers have investigated these possibilities. Lockwood (1996, p. 99) concludes that his pilot study shows 'that some individuals do have complex preference maps which include regions of lexicographic preference for the protection of native forests from logging'. Stevens et al. (1991, p. 398) claim that most respondents gave answers that were inconsistent with either the neoclassical trade-off approach or the lexicographic theory: 'However, 80 percent of the remainder gave responses that were consistent with lexicographic preference orderings.' Spash and Hanley (1995) have investigated the motives behind zero bids. They found that nearly none of the zero bids were given for reasons of zero value. Rather, some participants to the study said that they could not afford to pay anything, while most zero-bidders claimed that ecosystem rights ought to be protected at all costs, and hence should be protected by law. This is consistent

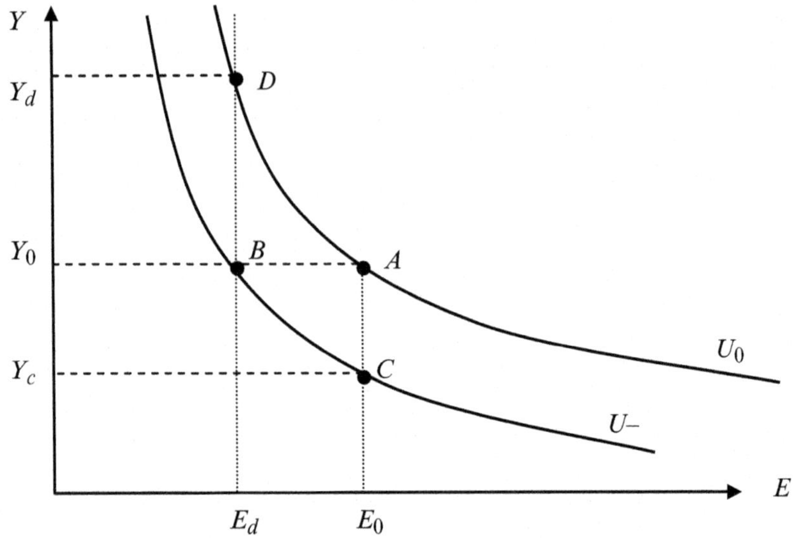

Figure 7.3 Neoclassical contingency value assessment with indifference curves

with Kahneman and Knetsch (1992, p. 69), who claim that participants to contingent evaluation are bound to respond with indignation to questions about accepting more pollution over existing pristine landscapes, this indignation being expressed by 'the rejection of the transaction as illegitimate, or by absurdly high bids'.

Once again we can give a graphical illustration of these difficulties for neoclassical choice theory. As a basis for comparison, let us start with the illustration of the standard neoclassical case, with indifference curves. Let us assume once again that consumers are concerned with the income level that they can devote to private consumption as well as the size of old growth forest. Figure 7.3 is inspired by the graph provided by Edwards's (1986) pioneer article. Assume the existence of two well-behaved indifference curves, with the consumer being initially located at combination *A* on the U_0 utility indifference curve. Suppose the size of the environmental good is projected to be reduced from E_0 to E_d. As is well known, willingness to accept (WTA) is measured by the distance $(Y_d - Y_0)$. The consumer will be indifferent to combinations *A* and *D*. As a trade-off for the reduction $(E_0 - E_d)$ in the size of the environmental good, the consumer is willing to accept a monetary compensation of $(Y_d - Y_0)$. Alternatively, if consumers need to pay to preserve the quality of their environment, the consumer may either forsake environmental goods, in which case the person moves horizontally from combination *A* to combination *B* (onto the lower indifference curve *U*-); or the consumer may be willing to pay (WTP) an amount ($Y_0 - Y_c$) to retain the quality of environment at E_0, in which case consumers move down vertically from point *A* to point *C* (on the same lower indifference curve *U*-). With well-behaved indifference curves, WTP and WTA would be approximately equal, save for the decreasing marginal rate of substitution, as they are drawn in Figure 7.3.

Let us now examine the case of choices of a lexicographic nature. Let us take the simplest case, beyond pure lexicographic choice. Assume the primary element of choice, until income level Y^* is achieved, is the level of income. This means that, for any income level below Y^*, the combination with the highest level of income will be preferred, regardless of the size of the environmental good. The secondary element of choice, the size or quality of the environmental good *E*, plays a role only with combinations that feature equal levels of income. By contrast, once the threshold level of income Y^* is achieved (Stevens et al., 1991, p. 398), the primary element of choice becomes the size of the environmental good, while private income reverts to a secondary element of choice, which plays a role only when combinations that feature equal forest sizes are being compared. This is tied with the principle of satiation. This algebraic example was proposed by Lockwood (1996, p. 89), and it corresponds to the graphical example provided by Edwards (1986, p. 148). Figure 7.4 illustrates this case.

In Figure 7.4, which illustrates the above preference framework of a lexicographic nature, there is not a single indifference curve. No two combinations carry equal satisfaction. Each point on this two-dimensional plane is ordered. The continuous lines with the arrows represent quasi-indifference lines, sometimes called behavioural curves (Lutz and Lux, 1979, p. 318). Below the level of income Y^*, these quasi-indifference lines are horizontal, implying that the consumer prefers higher private consumption to lower private consumption, regardless of how much of the environmental good is being provided (*D* is preferred to *F*). The higher the horizontal quasi-indifference curve, the happier the consumer is. However, for a given level of income, say Y_f, the person prefers more to less environmental goods (*F* is preferred to *G*). This is what the arrows are meant to represent, and this is how these quasi-indifference curves are differentiated from the standard flat or vertical indifference curves that would represent addictive behaviour.

When the threshold level of income Y^* has been attained, the size of the environmental goods becomes the primary ordering criterion. The quasi-indifference curves become vertical. The further to the right the quasi-indifference curve, the better off the consumer is (bundle *C* is preferred to *B*). But for a given amount of environmental goods, say E_0, the higher the

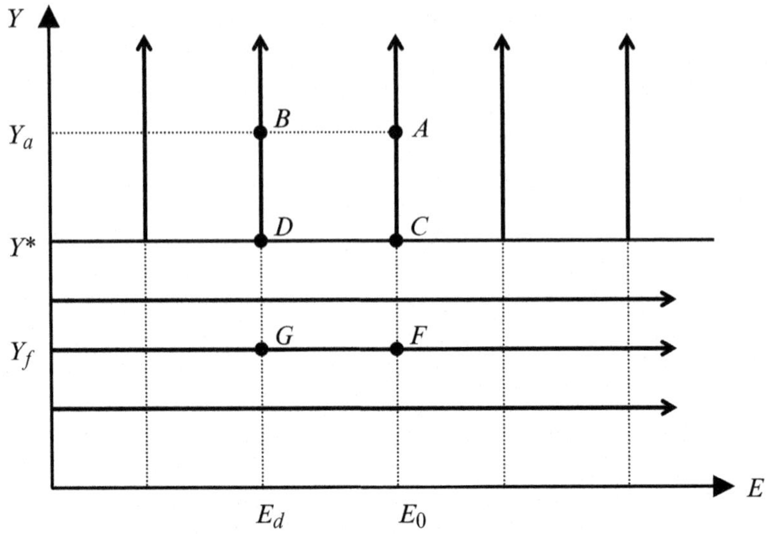

Figure 7.4 Contingency value assessment with choices of a lexicographic nature: quasi-indifference curves

income level the higher the satisfaction of the consumer (bundle A is preferred to C), which is what the arrows on each vertical quasi-indifference curve once again are meant to indicate.

What are the implications of such a preference set for contingency evaluation studies? Assume the consumer starts with combination A, with an income exceeding the minimum threshold. Suppose this consumer is being asked about a possible reduction in the size of the environmental good from E_0 to E_d. The likely willingness to pay (WTP) of this person will be $(Y_a - Y^*)$, that is, the entire discretionary income of the consumer, beyond the threshold income level. The consumer would wind up at combination C. Note however that the consumer is not indifferent between combination C and combination B, as was presumed in the neoclassical analysis of Figure 7.3. In Figure 7.4, the consumer still prefers combination C to combination B. The measured WTP thus underestimates the true value of environmental goods in the consumer mind. Note in addition that whatever the proposed reduction in the size of the environmental good, the income that can be given up remains the same, unless the reduction is so small that it does not trigger any negative feeling on the part of the consumer. On the other hand, if the consumer were to start with combination F, below the threshold level of income, WTP would be zero, or near zero, since more income is always preferred to less in this region.

What about the willingness to accept compensation (WTA)? Starting from the above-threshold combination *A*, the WTA is undefined, or it is infinite, since no amount of money will compensate for any loss in the quality of environment (Edwards, 1986, p. 148; Spash and Hanley, 1995, p. 193). Even an infinite amount of additional income would not procure enough compensation for the loss in the size of the environmental good to keep constant the consumer's level of satisfaction. Any reduction in the environmental good causes a reduction in the satisfaction of the consumer, since the environment is the primary criterion of choice.

Choices of a lexicographic nature thus demonstrate that contingent valuation studies that solicit WTP and WTA estimates can arrive at widely different estimates. The use of one method, when the other should be more appropriate, is not a matter of indifference. In addition, the WTP estimate does not correctly reflect the willingness to trade of the consumer. As Lockwood (1996, p. 92) points out:

> this sacrifice may not be regarded by the respondent as a transaction based on a free exchange, but as the payment of a ransom for recovery of a valued item. Ransom demands cannot be considered as Hicksian measures of economic welfare, because the person can never be indifferent between the value of the ransom paid and the value of the ransomed entity. The magnitude of the ransom is independent of the value of the entity, so the same payment may be offered for different quantity changes even though each increment in provision is valued.

Given all this, it is not surprising that several people surveyed in contingency valuation studies 'either refuse to participate in the survey, offer a protest response, try to play the game by inflating their response in an attempt to introduce their non-compensatory value into the process, or offer a WTP which is not a Hicksian measure of welfare change' (Lockwood, 1996, p. 91).

It would be possible to draw a wide variety of choices of a lexicographic nature. Lockwood (1996, pp. 90–92) presents an algebraic example where consumers revert to choices based on indifference curves when thresholds for income level and environment are achieved. This could be represented graphically, with the help of the apparatus developed in Figures 7.3 and 7.4. We could also assume, reciprocally, that compensating choices are made until thresholds are reached, at which point, consumers move on to non-compensatory choices. The principle of heredity could also easily be introduced, by assuming that consumers take as their new environment threshold the most recently experienced levels of environment quality.

CONCLUSION

The work of Georgescu-Roegen very much inspired Post-Keynesian renditions of consumer theory. Georgescu-Roegen himself was very much concerned with environmental issues, and was one of the earlier economics writers on the topic. Georgescu-Roegen criticized neoclassical choice theory and consumer theory because he felt it lacked realism. He did not want a theory to be based on axioms that provided 'a more convenient approach or lead to a simpler scheme'; rather he provided an alternative choice theory because he believed it offered 'a more adequate interpretation of the structure of our wants' (Georgescu-Roegen, 1954, p. 519). This was certainly the case of his heredity principle, or the non-independence principle. Improved realism of consumer theory is also the justification for the rejection of the postulate of indifference, and its replacement by the principle of irreducibility, which we associated with a combination of the principles of the separability and the subordination of needs (Georgescu-Roegen, 1968, p. 263). Indeed, all seven principles of consumer choice suggested here are designed to provide more realism in consumer theory. To develop a more realistic foundation for consumer choice also seems to be the goal of ecological economics (Gowdy and Mayumi, 2001, p. 234; van den Bergh et al., 2000, p. 44) and sustainable forest management (Kant, 2003, p. 40).

All theories require some degree of abstraction by necessity. Still, there is a need for realism, especially in the realm of environmental economics. I have shown that the principles of consumer behaviour which have been put forward by post-Keynesian economists have already been endorsed or put to use by some specialists of ecological economics. These principles help to explain some conundrums in empirical work, notably in the contingency valuation studies, and they help to question the relevance or the adequacy of these studies. They also offer a way forward to make future choices on difficult public issues. Environmental policy must be based on proper consumer foundations that will provide an appropriate agenda for environmental regulation.

REFERENCES

Arestis, P. (1992), *The Post-Keynesian Approach to Economics*, Aldershot, UK and Brookfield, VT, USA: Edward Elgar.

Arrous, J. (1978), 'Imperfection de l'information, incertitude et concurrence', Doctoral dissertation, Université de Strasbourg et Université des Sciences Sociales de Grenoble.

Bengston, D.N. (1994), 'Changing forest values and ecosystem management', *Society and Natural Resources*, **7**, 515–33.
Bird, J.W.N. (1982), 'Neoclassical and Post Keynesian environmental economics', *Journal of Post Keynesian Economics*, **4** (4), 586–93.
Crivelli, R. (1993), 'Hysteresis in the work of Nicholas Georgescu-Roegen', in J.C. Dragan, E.K. Seifert and M.C. Demetrescu (eds), *Entropy and Bioeconomics*, Milan: Nagard, pp. 10–129.
Drakopoulos, S.A. (1990), 'The implicit psychology of the theory of the rational consumer', *Australian Economic Papers*, **29**, 182–98.
Drakopoulos, S.A. (1992), 'Psychological thresholds, demand and price rigidity', *Manchester School of Economics and Social Studies*, **40** (2), 152–68.
Drakopoulos, S.A. (1994), 'Hierarchical choice in economics', *Journal of Economic Surveys*, **8** (2), 133–53.
Earl, P.E. (1983), *The Economic Imagination: Towards a Behavioural Analysis of Choice*, Armonk, NY: M.E. Sharpe.
Earl, P.E. (1986), *Lifestyle Economics: Consumer Behaviour in a Turbulent World*, Brighton: Wheatsheaf.
Edwards, S.F. (1986), 'Ethical preferences and the assessment of existence values: does the neoclassical model fit?', *Northeastern Journal of Agricultural and Resource Economics*, **15** (2), 145–50.
Eichner, A.S. (1987), *The Macrodynamics of Advanced Market Economies*, Armonk, NY: M.E. Sharpe.
Etzioni, A. (1988), *The Moral Dimension: Toward a New Economics*, New York: Free Press.
Galbraith, J.K. (1958), *The Affluent Society*, London: Hamish Hamilton.
Georgescu-Roegen, N. (1954), 'Choice, expectations and measurability', *Quarterly Journal of Economics*, **48** (4), 503–34.
Georgescu-Roegen, N. (1966), *Analytical Economics*, Cambridge, MA: Harvard University Press.
Georgescu-Roegen, N. (1968), 'Utility', in D.L. Sills (ed.), *International Encyclopedia of the Social Sciences*, Vol. 16, London: Macmillan, pp. 236–66.
Gintis, H. (2000), 'Beyond *Homo Economicus*: evidence from experimental economics', *Ecological Economics*, **35**, 311–22.
Gowdy, J.M. (1993), 'Georgescu-Roegen's utility theory applied to environmental economics', in J.C. Dragan, E.K. Seifert and M.C. Demetrescu (eds), *Entropy and Bioeconomics*, Milan: Nagard, pp. 230–40.
Gowdy, J.M. and K. Mayumi (2001), 'Reformulating the foundation of consumer choice theory and environmental valuation', *Ecological Economics*, **39** (2), 223–37.
Havard, G. and C. Vidal (2003), *Histoire de l'Amérique française*, Paris: Flammarion.
Holt, R.P.F. (2005), 'Post-Keynesian economics and sustainable development', *International Journal of Environment, Workplace and Employment*, **1** (2), 174–86.
Kahneman, D. and J.L. Knetsch (1992), 'Valuing public goods: the purchase of moral satisfaction', *Journal of Environmental Economics and Management*, **22** (1), 57–70.
Kant, S. (2003), 'Extending the boundaries of forest economics', *Forest Policy and Economics*, **5** (1), 39–56.
Knetsch, J.L. (1990), 'Environmental policy implications of disparities between

willingness to pay and compensation demanded measures of values', *Journal of Environmental Economics and Management*, **18** (3), 227–37.

Lancaster, K. (1991), 'Hierarchies in goods-characteristics analysis', *Modern Consumer Theory*, Aldershot, UK and Brookfield, VT, USA: Edward Elgar, pp. 69–80.

Lavoie, M. (1992), *Foundations of Post-Keynesian Economic Analysis*, Aldershot, UK, and Brookfield, VT, USA: Edward Elgar.

Lavoie, M. (1994), 'A Post Keynesian theory of consumer choice', *Journal of Post Keynesian Economics*, **16** (4), 539–62.

Lavoie, M. (2004), 'Post Keynesian consumer theory: potential synergies with consumer research and economic psychology', *Journal of Economic Psychology*, **25**, 639–49.

Lavoie, M. (2005), 'Post-Keynesian consumer choice theory for the economics of sustainable forest management', in S. Kant and R.A. Berry (eds), *Economics, Natural Resources, and Sustainability: Economics of Sustainable Forest Management*, Dordrecht: Kluwer, pp. 67–90.

Lockwood, M. (1996), 'Non-compensatory preference structures in non-market valuation of natural area policy', *Australian Journal of Agricultural Economics*, **40** (2), 85–101.

Lutz, M.A. and K. Lux (1979), *The Challenge of Humanistic Economics*, Menlo Park, CA: Benjamin-Cummings.

Martinez-Alier, J., G. Munda and J. O'Neill (1998), 'Weak comparability of values as a foundation for ecological economics', *Ecological Economics*, **26** (3), 277–86.

Nell, E.J. (1992), 'Demand, pricing and investment', *Transformational Growth and Effective Demand: Economics After the Capital Critique*, London: Macmillan, pp. 381–451.

Pasinetti, L.L. (1981), *Structural Change and Economic Growth*, Cambridge: Cambridge University Press.

Ravetz, J. (1994–95), 'Economics as an elite folk science', *Journal of Post Keynesian Economics*, **17** (2), 165–84.

Robinson, J. (1956), *The Accumulation of Capital*, London: Macmillan.

Roy, R. (2005), 'The hierarchy of needs and the concept of group in consumer choice theory', *History of Economics Review*, **42**, 50–56.

Schefold, B. (1997), *Normal Prices, Technical Change and Accumulation*, London: Macmillan.

Simon, H.A. (1962), 'The architecture of complexity', *Proceedings of the American Philosophical Society*, **106** (6), 467–82.

Simon, H.A. (1976), 'From substantive to procedural rationality', in S.J. Latsis (ed.), *Method and Appraisal in Economics*, Cambridge: Cambridge University Press, pp. 129–48.

Spash, C.L. (1998), 'Investigating individual motives for environmental action: lexicographic preferences, beliefs, attitudes', in J. Lemons, L. Westra and R. Goodland (eds), *Ecological Sustainability and Integrity: Concepts and Approaches*, Dordrecht, Netherlands: Boston, MA, USA and London, UK: Kluwer Academic Publishers, pp. 46–62.

Spash, C.L. and N. Hanley (1995), 'Preferences, information and biodiversity preservation', *Ecological Economics*, **12** (3), 191–208.

Steedman, I. and U. Krause (1986), 'Goethe's *Faust*, Arrow's possibility theorem and the individual decision-taker', in J. Elster (ed.), *The Multiple Self*, Cambridge: Cambridge University Press, pp. 197–231

Stevens, T.H., J. Echeverria, R.J. Glass, T. Hager and T.A. More (1991), 'Measuring the existence value of wildlife: what do CVM estimates really show?', *Land Economics*, **67**, 390–400.

van den Bergh, J.C.J.M., A. Ferrer-i-Carbonell and G. Munda (2000), 'Alternative models of individual behaviour and implications for environmental policy', *Ecological Economics*, **32**, 43–61.

Vatn, A. and D.W. Bromley (1995), 'Choices without prices without apologies', in D.W. Bromley (ed.), *The Handbook of Environmental Economics*, Oxford: Basil Blackwell, pp. 3–25.

Zamagni, S. (1999), 'Georgescu-Roegen on consumer theory: an assessment', in K. Mayumi and J.M. Gowdy (eds), *Bioeconomics and Sustainability: Essays in Honor of Nicholas Georgescu-Roegen*, Cheltenham, UK and Northampton, MA, USA: Edward Elgar, pp. 103–21.

8. Price-based versus standards-based approaches to reducing car addiction and other environmentally destructive activities

Peter E. Earl and Tim Wakeley

INTRODUCTION

Concerns about the impact of production and consumption on the environment have led to two different kinds of mitigating policies in recent years. One approach focuses on using taxes and markets for tradable pollution permits or credit offsets to bring relative prices more into line with social opportunity costs. The other is more redolent of the kinds of quantity rationing approach to resource allocation used in wartime planning. It involves imposing standards for maximum acceptable emissions (for example, grams of carbon dioxide – CO_2 – per kilometre travelled by a motor vehicle, or a sales-weighted average standard across a car manufacturer's entire product range) or for rates of resource usage (for example, litres of water per head per day in a household). This latter 'standards-based approach' goes against the grain of mainstream economic thinking: it seems to involve the arbitrary application of rules by bureaucrats and it limits opportunities for those who wish to pollute more to do deals with those who are willing to pollute less. However, from the standpoint of heterodox approaches to economics, it may be argued that standards-based policies are much more likely than price-based policies to be effective means towards meeting environmental challenges. This chapter attempts to mount precisely such an argument by using inputs mostly from Post Keynesian macroeconomics and economic psychology.

The rest of the chapter is structured as follows. In the next section, we critically examine the textbook justification for the prima facie appeal of market-based approaches and we also examine problems with market-based approaches from the macroeconomic standpoint, drawing parallels between conditions in carbon trading markets and the kinds of concerns that Post Keynesian monetary economists have about the workings of financial systems and foreign exchange markets. Next, we examine how structural adjustments to changing relative prices are inhibited by the presence of long-lived assets. The two subsequent sections show, respectively, how inputs from psychology can be used to understand how people avoid facing up to the environmental consequences of their choices, and how their addictions to environmentally harmful forms of consumption might be quelled. The penultimate section raises some issues concerning the interaction between compulsory standards and the economics of product development, while the final section offers some concluding reflections. Throughout the chapter we use the problem of reducing motor vehicle emissions as a focus for our analysis.

PARALLELS WITH MACROECONOMIC COORDINATION PROBLEMS

A key theme in Keynes's contribution to macroeconomics is the idea that adjustments to shocks in the economic environment could be deviation-amplifying. This view contrasts sharply with the mainstream economist's presumption that the effects of disturbances tend to dissipate, rather as happens when one hurls a brick into a pond: ripples spread out the effects of the shock and calm returns. Whereas in the mainstream view the policy focus is on making it easier for the price mechanism to generate an appropriate set of prices, Keynes (1936, Chapter 19) contended that freeing up relative prices was not guaranteed to solve macroeconomic coordination problems and might even exacerbate them. Because of this, more active government intervention could often be needed. These contrasting views about the economic environment seem also to have lessons for us about the economics of the environment.

Mainstream environmental economics essentially presumes that if we have environmental problems, these are due to market failures that result in decision-makers not facing appropriate sets of relative prices. If relative prices were adjusted to ensure that they properly reflected environmental costs, then optimal resource use would occur. Such a perspective is evident in the case of policies for limiting the emission of CO_2. Increasing volumes of CO_2 are ending up in the atmosphere and giving rise to an enhanced greenhouse effect because consumption of fossil fuels historically has not included any price for disposal of their gaseous by-products. If an appropriate limit is set for the volume of CO_2 emissions and energy users have either to purchase permits to emit CO_2 or demonstrate that they are taking steps, such as planting an appropriate number of trees, to sequester the CO_2 that they emit, then emissions will be bought under control. The rising cost of using energy will provide incentives to economize on energy consumption and the possibility of selling carbon credits will encourage resource owners to invest in schemes for carbon sequestration.

This kind of thinking appears to be fine in principle, and simple textbook models seemingly demonstrate its utility, but typically these models gloss over a number of problems which need to be addressed in their real-world application. The appeal of the carbon trading approach rests upon its use of market mechanisms and their theoretically demonstrated ability to produce Pareto-efficient outcomes. If we note that 'a *market* is a specific institutional arrangement consisting of rules and conventions that make possible a large number of voluntary transfers of property rights on a regular basis' (Ménard, 1995, p. 170) and that markets are themselves 'goods' in the sense that they have to be 'created by economic activity' (Loasby 1999, p. 118), we can see that a problem with the textbook view is that the results presuppose that fundamental decisions have already been taken by some authority prior to the market coming into operation.[1] This means that the outcome from the apparently apolitical working of market forces is in fact dependent upon a set of rules which have to be decided upon in advance of the market doing its work. Typically this rule-creating process is unavoidably political in nature since it involves making value-based decisions including the need to decide who the relevant stakeholders are, and as a result it may ignore affected parties if they do not have adequate representation for some reason or another – for example, non-human species (Costanza, 2004).

Having identified the relevant stakeholders (usually human society and firms) a set of property rights over the right to pollute is created by issuing permits to pollute up to a specified level of emissions (for example, tonnes of CO_2). Quite apart from the practical scientific problems of identifying a sustainable quantity of pollution, another problem is encountered here because some mechanism for distributing the newly created property rights among stakeholders must be established. How this is achieved matters because, as is well known, efficiency and fairness are not necessarily commensurate; it is perfectly possible to arrive at a Pareto-efficient allocation of resources which is perceived to be unfair by some coalitions, since the outcome of a market trading exercise depends strongly on the distribution of initial endowments of tradable goods (in this case, permits to pollute) between the respective parties. The issue of how to distribute permits in a fair and equitable manner has no easy solution and necessarily takes market-makers (Casson, 1997) into the difficult terrain of ethics and social choice theory as they grope for criteria by which to judge distributive justice (see Rawls, 1971; Nozick, 1974). It also renders the process open to political lobbying and the influence of powerful players as they try to protect their vested interests.

The success of the market solution also requires that everyone must participate and that an effective monitoring system must be established to ensure that there is no evasion of obligations to match emissions with permits or sequestration investments. Players might not like the changing pattern of relative prices but they would have to adapt to them or fall foul of the law.[2] Yet more problems become apparent when we start considering how the allowable overall level of CO_2 emissions is decided upon. Anything other than a policy of zero net global emissions per period is potentially problematic in ways that have striking parallels with the problems of coordinating saving, investment and borrowing recognized by Post Keynesian macroeconomists, and which similarly may be poorly handled by decentralized market processes.

From a free-market standpoint, it would not be essential to require zero net emissions in each time period, as the market for carbon permits and credits would permit optimal intertemporal allocations. The global economy could run a carbon deficit today in return for running a carbon surplus in the future. Polluters who did not buy current carbon permits would have to purchase claims on future carbon credits being issued by those who were planning to invest in carbon sequestration in future. The market for carbon permits would appear to work just like the foreign exchange market, with current permit prices being shaped by expected future permit prices and the rate of interest. Here, however, Post Keynesian concerns with the operation of speculative markets need to be raised.

One obvious concern is whether promises to invest in sequestration will be honoured. Firms engaging in net emissions today and offsetting this by purchasing carbon credits to be delivered at some point in the future may find that their money vanishes into the pockets of opportunistic agents who had no intention to plant forests. There will be incentives for carbon emitters to buy diversified portfolios of carbon credits to reduce the risks of being hit by such defaults.

Secondly, there is the risk that speculative trading of carbon credits will cause their prices to depart from levels that reflect underlying supply and demand fundamentals. Speculators who were not carbon emitters might purchase futures in carbon credits because they believed that they could sell them later for a profit. Such activities would affect signals to invest in sequestration projects. For the carbon market to work efficiently, players must have accurate knowledge of the underlying science of climate change and of the economics of carbon sequestration, in just the same way that, for the growth of foreign debt not to become a problem, currency traders need to have knowledge of the underlying fundamentals and processes of structural change taking place in economies that are running current account deficits. If a carbon debt is run up by current generations, it may have complex path-dependent environmental impacts with complex implications for how much of a carbon surplus needs to be generated in future periods. Similar problems could arise from using intertemporal permits trading to ensure sustainable fishing of particular species due to the complex biodynamics of fish populations. If deficits today cannot simply be repaid by investments in matching volumes of credits in the future, then state intervention would be needed, rather in the manner of central banks and monetary policy. In other words, if the authorities judge that pollution deficits being incurred today would need to be offset by more than 100 per cent in the future, then they would need to engage in open-market operations to bid up the price of future permits, thereby encouraging investment in sequestration and deterring today's decision-makers from polluting right now.

For the foreseeable future, we have neither within-period nor intertemporal zero emissions policies. Nor are there enforceable global limits to net annual emissions rates, with polluters able to bid for slices of a corresponding supply of emission permits on global permits markets. Instead, the policy regime is one of having tightening targets for overall levels of pollution (in some countries) combined with a mix of micro-level regulation of pollution levels for particular products such as cars, some taxes on carbon emissions and some trade in carbon credits through which liabilities for carbon taxes may be reduced. True, there are incentives for market players to study climate science and assess whether the overall levels of pollution being allowed today are too lax, for if they are, it would be likely that much tighter controls would be applied in future with corresponding impacts on asset values. The trouble is, the horizons involved may be much longer than investors are used to addressing, the uncertainties may be too great to assess and turning the clock back may be simply impossible: this is an exemplar case of what Post Keynesians such as Davidson (1994) would call 'fundamental uncertainty' and 'non-ergodicity'. Worse still, if consumers are willing and able to pay additional costs associated with carbon taxes there is nothing to hold overall emissions in check if this willingness to pay is underestimated by governments (or governments focus on short-term electoral considerations) and tax rates are set too low.

Spash (2002) explores in some detail the implications of fundamental or 'strong uncertainty' for environmental economics. Mainstream approaches to uncertainty typically focus on 'weak uncertainty' by characterizing possible future states of the world as a set of known probabilities. In doing so, they provide spurious precision to environmental calculations. Spash (2002, p. 122) argues that we inevitably have a lack of knowledge about the future behaviour of irreducibly complex systems like the climate: partial ignorance arises because we have to close our models artificially in order to understand them, while indeterminacy is generated by the unpredictable behaviour of other actors in the system. Environmental economic issues are thus firmly in the realm of strong uncertainty, with the normal objective science based on logical positivism revealed to be too narrow a platform from which to formulate policy prescriptions. This is the kind of situation that Shackle labels as 'un-knowledge'. As he observed: 'When there is knowledge we can, and must, apply reason and calculation. When there is un-knowledge, we have freedom for imagination and conjecture' (Shackle, 1972, p. 18). The implication here is that: 'Scientific progress requires a willingness to accept some ideas which cannot be established conclusively because they lie beyond evidence or logic' (Spash, 2002, p. 147). With this in mind, we now turn to a consideration of factors limiting the effectiveness of relative price changes as means of inducing changes in patterns of consumption.

PROBLEMS CAUSED BY DURABLE ASSETS AND LIFESTYLE COMMITMENTS

Within mainstream economics, change is something that is seen as happening readily, so long as relative prices give appropriate signals. This perspective appears to work if one thinks about how we substitute when buying fruit and vegetables. If there is a natural disaster that wipes out the supply of bananas, then prices rise sharply and we switch to alternative fruits. However, things are far less straightforward if consumption systems involve durable assets, the implications of whose widespread presence has long been a key theme in Post Keynesian thinking.

Now clearly, even in some cases where consumer durables are involved, we sometimes do see very rapid rejection of an outmoded way of doing things because there has been a change in relative prices. A recent example is the abandonment of film-based photography in favour of digital photography, but this involved much more than a simple change in average total cost per printed photograph: the digital revolution changed how images were stored and shared, along with radically changing consumers' photographic habits, in ways that depended fortuitously on home computing and the emergence of the Internet; technologies that did not exist when the first digital image processing chips were invented (see Earl and Wakeley, 2007). Though the information technology revolution is not without implications for the efficiency of public transport or the need to travel to work, it is unwise to rely on things working out in a parallel way in the case of changes in the relative costs of using durable assets with different environmental consequences.

Consider as an example the likely responses to a steep rise in the price of petrol. This may indeed encourage some people to work more from home, though differences between face-to-face and virtual interactions and problems in monitoring workers remotely will limit the extent of this. It is likely also to affect adversely the sales of vehicles that have poor fuel consumption (other things being equal). However, in most cases it will not rapidly force the existing stock of such vehicles off the roads. Rather, what will happen is that their second-hand values will fall sharply until their expected overall ownership costs (fuel, maintenance and depreciation) are seen as similar in non-pecuniary terms. The fuel-inefficient vehicles may then continue to be used for a decade or more despite the price increase of fuel having cost their initial owners dearly in terms of unexpected depreciation.

For a hike in petrol prices to cause the immediate scrapping of gas-guzzling vehicles on a large scale, either of two things needs to happen:

- the price increase for fuel must be so great that the running costs of such vehicles exceed the running and capital costs of their less thirsty counterparts (in other words, even if a gas-guzzling car is a free good, it is not worth running one); or
- the price increase for fuel must be indicative of an environmental problem that is seen as so serious that it becomes socially or morally unacceptable to run such vehicles, something that cannot be offset by their cheapness (even if they are being given away) or appeal in other terms, such as power and refinement.

The second point may sound as though it involves a breach in the axiom of gross substitution due to consumers employing a hierarchy of characteristic targets in the manner often suggested in Post Keynesian microeconomics (for example, Earl, 1986a; Lavoie, 1992, 2004). This would certainly be in line with the pioneering thinking of Bird (1982, p. 592), who signposted the potential significance of hierarchical satisficing models of choice for a Post Keynesian environmental economics a quarter of a century ago. However, depending on what is available to tempt the consumer in terms of price and non-price performance in non-environmental dimensions, it may also be possible to understand an overwhelming environmental concern in terms of a traditional trade-off-based choice model, such as that proposed by Lancaster (1966). (It is worth noting here that Etzioni's, 1988 attempt to highlight the significance of moral aspects of decision-making is essentially cast in terms of the standard perspective, rather than seeing the moral philosophies that people use to organize their lives as entailing personal standards that imply particular 'no-go' areas in terms of choices they will regard as possible.)

Though set out in respect of motor vehicles, precisely the same argument can be made in terms of aircraft, environmentally inefficient domestic appliances and industrial equipment, or energy-inefficient real estate into which resources have already been sunk (see Salter, 1960). It should also be noted that the capital losses that rising operating costs impose on owners of such assets also reduce the latter's ability to finance switching to more environmentally friendly technologies.

The presence of lifestyles based on complementarities between products and activities further enhances the significance of durable physical assets as barriers to phasing out environmentally costly forms of consumption. Consider, for example, the situation of consumers who have chosen to build their lives around living on large plots of land, a long drive from where they work, so that their children can enjoy horses, fresh air, and so on. If fuel costs rise sharply there is an incentive to give up this lifestyle and move closer to the city centre. There is also an incentive to redevelop properties closer to the city centre into higher-density forms. However, the change in incentives is unlikely to result in acreage properties being abandoned and the land turned back to farming. Rather, we should expect to see an adjustment in relative real estate prices between acreage and urban properties. Those on acreages will tend to suffer capital losses if they try to sell up, which will limit their ability to switch to an urban lifestyle. Normally one might expect that the floor to the fall in prices of such properties would be provided by their value for farming purposes, but it is possible for prices of some rural properties to fall below this if a family trying to sell up from within an area of acreage properties would be offering, in effect, an enclave of little use to a farmer.

It is not just changes in relative capital values of complementary assets that will take much of the leverage out of increases in prices of environmentally related products such as energy. We should also recognize the cognitive costs that consumers will have to incur if they abandon their hopes and dreams and set about constructing new lifestyles for themselves. A lifestyle is not just a bundle of assets and activities; it also consists of sets of assumptions, theories and 'do' and 'don't' heuristics for how to live, in much the same way that an approach to science is more than a laboratory, testing equipment and database (Earl, 1986a, 1986b). Making a radical switch of lifestyle, like making a radical switch in a scientific research programme or paradigm, can be a major source of anxiety: new ways of thinking need to be worked out and tested, and in the interim there may be great voids of unfamiliarity with which to contend. If the implications of change are drastic in these cognitive terms, then change is something to be avoided even if it is financially expensive to do so. Many people would find it devastating if they were suddenly told they were, say, medically no longer fit to drive, for this news would destroy many of their expectations about everyday life if they have built their lives around the freedom and flexibility that comes from being able to get around by car. They would suffer feelings of loss similar to, though probably not on quite the same scale, as they would suffer if they lost a loved one unexpectedly. From this perspective it is not surprising that environmentalists urging that we change our lifestyle and reduce our dependence on fossil fuels go unheeded.

CONFLICTING GOALS AND THE REDUCTION OF COGNITIVE DISSONANCE

If consumers are becoming increasingly affluent, they may be perfectly willing to pay more to consume more polluting products even if, ideally, they would prefer to be restrained in the costs they impose on the environment. Although, in principle, they might use their greater hourly earning power to permit them to engage in job-sharing or work part-time, in practice most consumers increase their consumption instead. We can understand this quite readily in terms of Maslow's (1954) contention that people have a hierarchy of needs, a view applied most extensively in economics by Lutz and Lux (1979, 1988) and Lux and Lutz (1986). Maslow argues that people tend to give a higher ranking to being able to achieve social esteem than they do to self-actualization, so if their budgets do not permit meeting both goals, then being true to their ideals is the one that will tend to give way. From a Maslowian perspective, it is wrong-headed to focus on making it more expensive to purchase consumer products that involve more pollution: the trick is to make it socially meritorious to be seen to be consuming products that are more environmentally friendly. If so, then consumers can simultaneously enjoy social standing and be true to their ideals. This, clearly, is a surprising twist on the concept of conspicuous consumption where, for once, its pursuit is not wasteful as Veblen (1899) originally contended. Indeed it may give rise to a new 'class' of consumer, the environmental class, whom others may aspire to emulate. To the extent that economic behaviour is socially embedded (Granovetter, 1985, 2005) this emulation may proceed at an increasing pace as more people join the social network.

The sales success of Toyota's growing range of hybrid petrol–electric vehicles may be readily understood from this standpoint. A Toyota Prius in real-world traffic conditions is not particularly more economical than turbo diesel versions of similarly priced rival products such as a VW Golf or Vauxhall/Opel Astra, but it makes a much more conspicuous statement of environmentally friendly intent than does a decision to opt for a diesel version of one of its rivals. This is because the Prius has a distinctive body design that is not shared with a 'regular' model. However, despite this well-aimed piece of marketing, it is clear that many consumers remain willing to spend even more and consume much less environmentally friendly vehicles as they do so, despite growing environmental consciousness. (So far, more upmarket Toyota hybrids, sold under the Lexus brand, have shared their bodies with standard petrol versions.) A theoretical analysis of how they do this without feeling emotionally torn adds further to the case for regulating environmental standards rather than just making it more expensive to be environmentally profligate.

Within mainstream economics, the question of how people resolve conflicts between their ideal behaviour and what they actually do is essentially a matter of how they make trade-offs within their budget constraints. From this standpoint, they can resolve these conflicts either by having more money, so that they can get better environmental performances without sacrificing anything else (which opens the door to the argument that economic growth is good for the environment), or by changing their weightings between different product characteristics. In reality, however, consumers may not be facing up to the fact that they could be making a better contribution to maintaining the quality of the environment. If there is a clash between their actions and their ideal behaviour, cognitive dissonance theory (Festinger, 1957; Earl and Wicklund, 1999) predicts that they will adjust their cognitions so as to remove it from their minds.

In some cases we may expect this to involve the consumer in a fallacy of composition between micro and macro issues. Clearly, some aspects of rising living standards may involve consuming bigger outputs of product characteristics and yet consuming fewer physical resources, because the products are increasingly made from knowledge, not from physical resources. Living standards rise in part because products can be made more cheaply via technological progress that results in fewer parts and miniaturization. At the level of the individual we may therefore appear in some parts of our lives to be reducing our consumption of physical resources even though we are getting a bigger flow of services for our money. The trouble is, more and more people are enjoying affluent lifestyles, so savings per product may be offset by a rise in the volume of products being made. It may also be the case that falling costs have more to do with environmental costs being incurred out of sight and hence out of mind, as with spectacularly cheap modern products pouring out of China.

In other cases, the affluent consumer faces a problem of justifying what at first sight appears to be more profligate behaviour. For example, suppose a consumer receives a major promotion and celebrates by buying a new car that serves very nicely as a symbol of their success but does nothing to reduce their overall greenhouse gas emissions, even though they profess to be interested in doing the right thing for the environment. Cognitive dissonance theory leads us to expect that the consumer will rationalize the choice as good for the environment – for example: 'Though it is a larger and more powerful car than what I used to drive, the BMW's engine has all the latest technology and its emissions are no worse', or: 'Actually I did think of buying the V8-powered model, since I can now afford it, but the six-cylinder one had quite enough power and is much more environmentally friendly'; rather than: 'You wouldn't know to look at it, but the diesel version I bought cost quite a bit more than a petrol one, but its overall emissions are way less.' Alternatively, they may conjure up reasons why the choice is going to have less of an environmental impact than might at first sight appear – for example: 'It's nice to have the BMW, though I doubt I'll be driving so much now, as I also splashed out on this brilliant bike and am going to get into shape by cycling to work some days.'

Scope for telling oneself that there is no real downside to a decision may even be exploited to justify choices in which rising affluence is associated with more environmentally profligate consumption – for example: 'Well, yes, I know that the LandCruiser's fuel consumption is far worse than what I used to drive, but this will be more than offset by us taking holidays exploring the Outback, rather than flying off to Europe as we used to do; a round-the-world flight uses as much fuel per passenger as the average motorist here uses in an entire year, you know.'

Whether or not the actions flagged as offsets to environmentally costly actions actually materialize may depend considerably on the extent of social inquisition that people face. Our thinking here is related to the 'economics of self-control' in which people are sometimes observed to offer hostages to ensure that they will have an incentive to carry out an action in the face of self-perceived weakness of will. One such hostage is the making of a public commitment, as when an academic submits an abstract of a conference paper as a means of ensuring their motivation to write the paper (see Elster, 1979). If the idea of the paper is kept private, failure to write it is not a source of embarrassment, unlike the case with a formally proposed conference paper.

If justifications of environmentally questionable choices are not offered publicly, then the extent of follow-up action may be rather limited and, if consumers recall their private justifications and notice they have not acted upon them, we should expect from cognitive dissonance theory that their minds will find another way of framing their actions to remove the inconsistency. This way of wriggling out of their original justification will be harder to use if the original argument was publicly voiced, and those with whom they interact keep reminding them of it as part of a process of social competition in which a person's credibility depends on whether history shows they mean what they say and stick to it. From the standpoint of the economics of self-control literature, a novel approach to environmental policy would be for consumers to be encouraged to log public pledges on a website about how they plan to become environmentally better citizens over a particular time horizon. The time horizon, it must be noted, would have to be well specified to preclude wriggling by those who failed to live up to their pledges. The pledge idea could be taken beyond a declaration of intent, for example, to making a financial commitment to donate a particular sum to an environmentally worthy cause in the event that they cannot prove they have done what they promised. This might be a rather effective way to foster environmental good citizenship as a means of conspicuous consumption (and possibly an environmentally more effective means of conspicuous consumption than, say, buying a Toyota Prius).

DEALING WITH THE ADDICTED CONSUMER

In the absence of policies that promote environmental self-control, the likelihood of people in effect turning a blind eye to the environmental consequences of their actions is increased by several factors that go against mainstream economic thinking. First, there is Ainslie's (1993) finding that tendencies towards addictive behaviour tend to go hand in hand with tendencies to discount the future hyperbolically rather than exponentially in that context. Making addictive products very expensive has a long history of being a very unsuccessful policy for curtailing addiction in the face of such tendencies. To escape from dysfunctional patterns of behaviour, addicts need to learn how to ascribe a higher relative weight to future situations.

If we see the modern consumer's attachment to energy-inefficient motor vehicles (along with energy-thirsty housing and international air travel and environmentally destructive holidays, and so on) as a kind of addiction, there may be lessons for environmental economists from the thinking that rehabilitation psychologists such as Ainslie employ to treat drug and alcohol addictions. The strategy used essentially involves trying to increase the focus of the addicts on foregoing the addictive behaviour right now since each act of abstinence serves as a precedent for them not indulging in the addictive consumption in the future: if they can abstain now they can more readily predict that they will abstain in the future, with the prediction tending to be self-confirming. One way to increase the chances of this strategy working is to short-circuit the hyperbolic discounter's tendency to try to single out particular occasions from events in general as occasions in which it is acceptable to have a lapse: if they are allowed occasional lapses, then they will look for, and find, occasions that can be classed as different and legitimate. A myriad of 'exceptions' will destroy their ability to think of themselves as being unlikely to succumb to the addictive behaviour in future.

Treatment of motoring addiction clearly runs into the problem that the diversity of occasions in which people use their cars opens up much scope for pointing out exceptions in which their car's use seems justifiable. For example, an academic might wish to use his car less and yet hold back from doing so via a series of arguments such as: 'I'm lecturing in the evening on Tuesdays and Wednesdays and the late buses are infrequent and unreliable/it isn't safe enough to cycle in the dark, whilst on Thursdays I have to pick up my son from his mother's place on the way home and take him to soccer training, and on Friday I do the shopping at the supermarket on the way home, so Monday is the only day when I can do as I'd like but that means I'm not really getting enough times on the bike to be fit enough for the journey not to be exhausting.' We can readily expect that if getting the bus on Mondays involves being awake and up earlier on that day alone, it is rather unlikely to happen in such a case. The probability of consumers getting into more environmentally appropriate habits might, however, be increased if they could be persuaded to rethink existing habits: doing the weekly shopping on Thursdays whilst the boy is doing soccer training diffuses the objection to leaving the car at home on Fridays, while taking an evening meal at work after late classes on Tuesday and Wednesday may reduce the urgency of getting home on these evenings and limit the extent to which existing bus schedules are a problem. Unfortunately, as with policies to stop drug and alcohol addiction, individual therapy is very expensive. It may be that obstructive policies, such as those which restrict parking or road access on particular days of the week, depending on registration plate numbers, are more realistic ways of getting people to shake their addiction to travelling by car.

It may be easier to shake addiction to gas-guzzling vehicles than to get consumers to forego the automobile altogether. Tilting the balance from thirsty cars today versus draconian restrictions on motoring in the future, to more economical vehicles both now and in the future may in large part simply be a matter of demonstrating to consumers that life with economical vehicles is not as terrible as it seems in prospect. The suggestions we offer here are somewhat inspired by the work of Katzev and Johnson (1983) in which 'foot in the door' psychology was used successfully as a non-price strategy for reducing electricity consumption. The idea behind their research project was to begin with a very simple request and then use its outcome as a basis for making bigger demands. Subjects were initially just asked to keep diaries of their energy consumption. From doing this they discovered the energy costs of various aspects of their lifestyles. They were then asked to see whether they could cut back their consumption by a percentage, given they now knew more about their energy use patterns. The response was typically willing and successful in meeting targets, and the targets were then successively ramped up as subjects discovered what they could do without and found it easy to handle in practice. The lesson is that major environmental costs might be avoidable if policies begin with the assumption that consumers suffer from bounded rationality that to some extent can be reduced via regulations that promote self-education (see Earl, 2007). Furthermore, rather than having immutable preferences, consumers choose via aspiration levels that are moveable: if they can get used to running central heating and hot water systems at lower temperatures, then they are likely also to be able to get used to smaller cars.

In the case of motoring, the problem is how to make this demonstration and get consumers to come around to thinking of themselves as potential owners of economical vehicles, modern examples of which probably have much more space, refinement and performance than they imagine. One way of doing this is to try to ensure that people who rent vehicles try out more economical ones than they normally drive, rather than treating themselves to something more profligate. Having experienced state-of-the-art small cars, consumers would then be more likely to downsize on their next purchase of a new car. The obvious non-price strategy is to impose emissions standards for rental company fleets that are tighter than those applied to the weighted averages of vehicles sold by individual manufacturers. This may, however, even be a case in which punitive taxes on gas-guzzling cars might also be quite effective. Emissions-based taxes would force rental car companies to engage in price discrimination by offering similarly fuel-frugal vehicles that differed in levels of quality. The literature on framing effects (see Kahneman et al., 1981) leads to the prediction that consumers would be much more likely to look at substitution possibilities with care in the case of a vacation rental vehicle in which the cost per week is clearly spelt out for different types of cars, compared with what happens when they actually buy their cars and the weekly cost is much more fuzzy. (This is so not merely because of the increasing tendency to finance vehicles on overdraft mortgages with no particular repayment schedules, but also because, unlike the case with clear alternative total quotation figures from a rental car firm, there is easy scope for cognitive dissonance reduction to twist calculations, as with, 'I'd probably end up keeping a larger car longer, as the bigger engine wouldn't wear out so quickly, which will reduce average cost per week over the time I own it.')

If the probability of a consumer experiencing more frugal vehicles through renting was not high enough to produce the desired impact, an additional strategy could involve requiring purchasers of new (or newer) vehicles to test at least one vehicle with emissions of no more than a particular level. If a legal requirement were not seen as politically feasible, an obvious alternative would be to provide a financial incentive to try such vehicles. Again, framing effects might be expected to result in this policy having a bigger impact than one that had a similar fiscal cost but was achieved by reducing taxes on the favoured class of vehicles. Part of a framing and aspiration-shaping strategy in this context might be the use of star-rating systems for fuel economy, in much the same way as washing machines and dishwashers are often required to be displayed with prominent stickers rating them in terms of energy and water use efficiency: labelling a vehicle as, say, worth only two stars on a five-star scale may seem to carry quite different connotations from having a windscreen sticker that states its fuel consumption and rate of carbon emission.

STANDARDS AND THE ECONOMICS OF PRODUCT DEVELOPMENT

To the extent that consumers continue to take a short-term view of their situations and ascribe higher weighting (or priority) to product features pertaining to status and non-environmental safety, regulating product standards is a vital part of environmental policy. Politicians deal with a 'lack of telescopic faculty' in the context of saving up for retirement by introducing compulsory superannuation schemes, for otherwise there may be serious budgetary problems with state pensions in an ageing population. In the case of motoring, they are increasingly dealing with poor product safety or the fallibility of users by a plethora of regulations, such as compulsory fitment of airbags, anti-lock braking systems (and, possibly soon, electronic stability controls) in cars, and requirements regarding pedestrian impact safety. (Some of these regulations, it needs to be added, have negative environmental consequences: fuel economy of vehicles would have improved far more in the last decade or so if changes to vehicle safety requirements had not led to increasing weight.) They do not leave it to the market and presume far-sighted, well-informed consumers with good self-control will necessarily buy products from manufacturers who chose to incorporate such features voluntarily.

When faced with legislated standards, manufacturers inevitably complain, for these add to their costs and limit their freedom to compete as they wish. But the practicalities of dealing with such impositions are not particularly different from dealing with situations in which customers impose standards by using similar checklists of requirements when they shop, as per the Post Keynesian view of consumer choice, rather than being prepared to consider the merits of any combination of product attributes. We have elsewhere set out the economics needed to solve the resource allocation problem presented by product development decisions (Earl and Wakeley, 2006, 2007), so here we will merely raise some additional points of relevance in this context.

Firstly, by concentrating an entire industry on making improvements in particular product characteristics, a standards-based policy may accelerate the pace of technological change through learning curve effects within firms and external economies of scale between them as the pool of capabilities and demand for particular kinds of inputs grows. If the standards are challenging, the competitive pressure to crack them first and/or in the most economical manner is conducive to experimentation and Schumpeterian competition (Schumpeter, 1934).

Secondly, giving a clear timetable of increasingly tight environmental standards enables firms to make better-informed choices about which product development path to follow. Given that the performance levels offered by different generations of technology may overlap over some of their ranges, but all are prone to suffer from diminishing returns, it can sometimes be rational to stick to a current technology genre, at a higher cost per performance increment than seems likely from the next-generation technology, in order to jump to a third-generation technology capable of meeting standards that the second generation will be hard pressed to meet. (A car maker, for example, might find it better to improve economy in the immediate future by introducing automatic engine cut-out/fire-up technology and pull-away assistance from an enlarged starter motor, as some European manufacturers are doing, rather than going the whole hog of copying Toyota's hybrid system, but then jump straight to fuel-cell power.) If they make the coordination of complementary investments easier to achieve, standards-based policies may also help investment planning, in ways that price-based policies cannot: it may be relatively easy to design cars to use alternative sources of energy, but far harder to ensure there is an infrastructure to feed that energy source to them.

Finally, we note that imposing environmentally based standards can have pay-offs in helping to raise other standards, so the sequencing of standards is an important issue in public policy, just as it is in allocating research and development budgets when a firm is trying to match its offerings to changing customer templates. An example here is the connection between vehicle safety and vehicle emissions. Tighter emissions standards encourage car makers to experiment with lighter materials and to be cleverer in combining safe construction with lighter designs. Such standards may also cut the number of obese sport utility vehicles (SUVs) and thereby make motorists more willing to downsize to smaller, more economical vehicles because the perceived risk of being hit by heavyweight vehicles is reduced. But likewise, the imposition of tougher active safety standards (in contrast to the passive safety standards that have promoted the recent bloating of many ranges of cars) could have beneficial effects on fuel economy if SUVs were unable to meet them due to their rollover-producing higher centres of gravity.

CONCLUSION

In the presence of strong uncertainties about technology and environmental science, and without the moral dimension coming in to break the principle of gross substitution, the price mechanism will be a poor means of getting rapid changes in the way that economic activities impinge on the environment. What is needed is the imposition of standards, either by the state (emission standards, water-efficiency standards, and so on) or by consumers and firms incorporating increasingly tough environmental requirements into their decision-making processes. If politicians are to get away with forcing higher environmental standards on society, then they may need to combine them with grants to ease the cost of replacing assets whose trade-in values are being wiped out.

This kind of situation is not merely one in which, as Keynes (1937, p. 214) put it: 'there is no scientific basis on which to form any calculable probability whatever. We simply do not know.' It is also a situation in which in the long run, humanity will be dead or, at the very least, life might be very unpleasant if market forces take an overly optimistic view of how economic activities are going to affect the biosphere. Policies that may potentially involve catastrophic irreversible consequences should not be designed using probabilistic decision methods. Rather, as Shackle-inspired Post Keynesians would recognize (see Young, 2001), the focus needs to be on working out the bounds of possibility under different policy scenarios. This is much easier to do if the policy focus is on how far it is necessary to go in setting standards to which economic actors will be required to adhere, rather than on adaptations that they might make to relative prices that the market might throw up or which might be induced by the State.

Quite apart from the greater scope they offer for meeting environmental objectives, standards-based policies also win in terms of equity. For example, if one tries to solve a shortage of water by charging whatever it takes to ensure that reservoirs do not run dry, it is perfectly possible to have a situation in which the most wealthy consumers continue to fill their pools and irrigate gardens that they have chosen to stock with plants that are native to wetter areas, whilst poorer consumers find that what little discretionary income they used to have is now diverted into meeting basic needs for drinking and personal hygiene. Standards that make environmentally harmful conspicuous consumption harder and result in people from all walks of life having to mingle with each other are likely to bring reinforcing improvements in environmental conditions and social capital. Public transport is likely to continue to offer unreliable and often sordid services, and walking along the streets may continue to be seen as unsafe, so long as the rich can get about by cocooning themselves inside their prestigious gas-guzzlers.

NOTES

1. The identity of this authority depends upon the level at which the policy is being implemented. If it is a domestic policy the job falls to the nation's government; if it is an international policy the job falls to a coalition of all member nations' governments. If reaching consensus in the domestic case is difficult, then in the latter case it is more so, as demonstrated by the problems associated with the ratification of the Kyoto Protocol.
2. In an international agreement setting, the extent to which governments have an incentive to police their own nation's performance relative to targets is an issue here (see McKibbin and Wilcoxen, 2007).

REFERENCES

Ainslie, G. (1993), *Picoeconomics: The Strategic Interaction of Successive Motivational States within the Person*, Cambridge: Cambridge University Press.

Bird, P.J.W.N. (1982), 'Neoclassical and post Keynesian environmental economics', *Journal of Post Keynesian Economics*, **4** (Summer), 586–92.

Casson, M. (1997), *Information and Organization: A New Perspective on the Theory of the Firm*, Oxford: Oxford University Press.

Costanza, R. (2004), 'Changing visions of humans' place in the world and the need for an ecological economics', in E. Fullbrook (ed.), *A Guide to What's Wrong with Economics*, London: Anthem Press, pp. 237–46.

Davidson, P. (1994), *Post Keynesian Macroeconomic Theory*, Aldershot, UK and Brookfield, VT, USA: Edward Elgar.

Earl, P.E. (1986a) *Lifestyle Economics: Consumer Behaviour in a Turbulent World* Brighton, UK: Wheatsheaf, and New York, USA: St Martin's.

Earl, P.E. (1986b), 'A behavioural analysis of demand elasticities', *Journal of Economic Studies*, **13** (3), 20–37.

Earl, P.E. (2007), 'Consumption X-inefficiency and the problem of market regulation', in R. Frantz (ed.), *Renaissance in Behavioural Economics: Essays in Memory of Harvey Leibenstein*, London: Routledge, pp. 176–93.

Earl, P.E. and T. Wakeley (2006), 'The economics of product development: a marginalist/evolutionary synthesis', paper presented at the 2006 Conference of the Association for Heterodox Economics, 14–16 July, University College London/London School of Economics; available at: http://espace.library.uq.edu.au/view.php?pid=UQ:8482.

Earl, P.E. and T. Wakeley (2007), 'Conjectures about future wants: some insights from evolutionary economics with reference to digital photography', *International Journal of Technological Intelligence and Planning*, **3** (1), 24–38.

Earl, P.E. and R.A. Wicklund (1999), 'Cognitive dissonance', in P.E. Earl and S. Kemp, (eds), *The Elgar Companion to Consumer Research and Economic Psychology*, Cheltenham, UK and Northampton, MA, USA: Edward Elgar, pp. 81–8.

Elster, J. (1979), *Ulysses and the Sirens: Studies in Rationality and Irrationality*, Cambridge: Cambridge University Press and Paris: Maisons des Sciences de l'Homme, revised edition 1984.

Etzioni, A. (1988), *The Moral Dimension: Toward a New Economics*, New York, USA: Free Press, and London, UK: Collier-Macmillan.

Festinger, L. (1957), *A Theory of Cognitive Dissonance*, Stanford, CA: Stanford University Press.

Granovetter, M. (1985), 'Economic action and social structure: the problem of embeddedness', *American Journal of Sociology*, **91** (3), 481–510.

Granovetter, M. (2005), 'The impact of social structure on economic outcomes', *Journal of Economic Perspectives*, **19** (1), 33–50.

Kahneman, D., P. Slovic and A. Tversky (eds) (1981), *Judgement Under Uncertainty: Heuristics and Biases*, Cambridge: Cambridge University Press.

Katzev, R.D. and T.R. Johnson (1983), 'A social psychological analysis of residential electricity consumption: the impact of minimal justification techniques', *Journal of Economic Psychology*, **3**, 267–84.

Keynes, J.M. (1936), *The General Theory of Employment, Interest and Money*, London: Macmillan.

Keynes, J.M. (1937), 'The general theory of employment', *Quarterly Journal of Economics*, **51**, 209–23.

Lancaster, K.J. (1966), 'A new approach to consumer theory', *Journal of Political Economy*, **74**, 132–57.

Lavoie, M. (1992), *Foundations of Post Keynesian Economic Analysis*, Aldershot, UK and Brookfield, VT, USA: Edward Elgar.

Lavoie, M. (2004), 'Post Keynesian consumer theory: potential synergies with consumer research and economic psychology', *Journal of Economic Psychology*, **25**, 639–49.

Loasby, B.J. (1999), *Knowledge, Institutions and Evolution in Economics*, London: Routledge.

Lutz, M.A. and K. Lux (1979), *The Challenge of Humanistic Economics*, Menlo Park, CA: Benjamin Cummings Publishing Company.

Lutz, M.A. and K. Lux (1988), *Humanistic Economics: The New Challenge*, New York: Bootstrap Press.

Lux, K. and M.A. Lutz (1986), 'Economic psychology: the humanistic perspective', in A.J. MacFadyen and H. MacFadyen (eds), *Economic Psychology: Intersections in Theory and Applications*, Amsterdam: North-Holland, pp. 383–424.

Maslow, A.H. (1954), *Motivation and Personality*, New York: Harper and Row.

McKibbin, W.J. and P.J. Wilcoxen (2007), 'A credible foundation for long-term international cooperation on climate change', in J.E. Aldy and R.N. Stavins (eds), *Architectures for Agreement: Addressing Global Climate Change in the Post-Kyoto World*, Cambridge: Cambridge University Press, pp. 185–208.

Ménard, C. (1995), 'Markets as institutions versus organizations as markets? Disentangling some fundamental concepts', *Journal of Economic Behavior and Organization*, **28**, 161–82.

Nozick, R. (1974), *Anarchy, State and Utopia*, Oxford: Basil Blackwell.

Rawls, J. (1971), *A Theory of Justice*, Cambridge, MA: Harvard University Press.

Salter, W.E.G. (1960), *Productivity and Technical Change*, Cambridge: Cambridge University Press.

Schumpeter, J.A. (1934), *The Theory of Economic Development*, Cambridge, MA: Harvard University Press (translated by R. Opie from 1912 German edition, Leipzig: Duncker & Humblot).

Shackle, G.L.S. (1972), *Epistemics and Economics: A Critique of Economic Doctrines*, Cambridge: Cambridge University Press.

Spash, C.L. (2002), *Greenhouse Economics: Values and Ethics*, London: Routledge.

Veblen, T. (1899), *The Theory of the Leisure Class*, New York: Macmillan.

Young, R.A. (2001), *Uncertainty and the Environment*, Cheltenham, UK and Northampton, MA, USA: Edward Elgar.

9. The socio-psychology of achieving sustainable consumption: an example using mass communication

Lucia Reisch, Clive L. Spash and Sabine Bietz

INTRODUCTION

Changing consumption patterns to be more environmentally friendly or sustainable is becoming a major issue but has been a recognized problem for some time. Various threads of thought came together in the second half of the twentieth century, and these formed the basis for the modern critique by ecological economists of standard economic growth as a means for increasing human welfare. The idea that more consumer goods increase absolute levels of well-being was attacked theoretically by Hirsch's (1977) social limits to growth and empirically by Easterlin (1974). The physical constraints on material throughput were made evident by the work of Georgescu-Roegen (1971) and Kneese et al. (1970) on incorporating the laws of thermodynamics into economic models. This led Daly (1977) to recommend a steady-state economy which respects the need for limits to the scale of human activity. However, achieving such a state would mean addressing the role of corporations in promoting consumerism as evident in the works of Kapp (1950, 1978) and Galbraith (1958, 1967).[1] The idea of the consumer being sovereign in the marketplace and so determining what is produced is then debunked (Mishan, 1969). Thus, sustainability policy emphasizes the need to develop practical approaches by which consumption behaviour can be changed (Reisch, 2004).

The complete picture as sketched above is far from having been adopted in political or policy circles despite the concept of 'sustainable consumption' moving to the international policy agenda (for example, OECD, 1997). Rather than controlling consumption, recycling materials and increasing production efficiency have tended to be the dominant means supposed to decouple environmental degradation from economic growth. The point that even very efficient economies can be massive per capita and absolute consumers of resources seems to have been missed. Growth of income and material throughput by means of industrialization and mass consumerism remains the basic economic aim of Western democracy. This obsession with growth is regarded as a success story in terms of the 'development' of modern economies; this is in spite of persistent inequitable distribution within and between nations, and the expanding scale of environmental problems. The North–South divide in terms of resource consumption is meant to be addressed by more consumption for all, despite the massive resource imports needed to maintain current Northern consumption patterns. The growing economies of China and India are following the same route to 'success'. Thus, control of the most politically dominant and globally pervasive environmental problem of recent years, the enhanced greenhouse effect, has been framed as a 'pro-growth strategy' rather than a major barrier to continued orthodox economic growth (Spash, 2007a). The question of consumption 'for what' is not one that mainstream economists or politicians wish to ask, let alone answer.

This leaves the policy agenda on sustainable consumption in danger of becoming a merely rhetorical reflection of concern. On the one hand there is an increasing recognition of the need to control consumption and even a sense of urgency, while on the other the characteristics, scale and scope of the problem of unsustainable consumption are substantively left unexplored. Røpke (2006) identifies five research questions for ecological economists: (1) How can consumption be conceptualized? (2) What are the environmental impacts of consumption? (3) What are the driving forces behind growing consumption? (4) How does consumption relate to the quality of life? and (5) How can consumption patterns be changed? This last question is perhaps the most challenging because it raises questions as to the role of individual choice in the modern structure of political and economic systems. Addressing that question is the aim of this chapter.

The emphasis of writers like Kapp and Galbraith upon the institutions of the market as controlling behaviour have more recently been supplemented by theories on the psychology of consumption behaviour. Socio-psychological explanations of consumption focus upon humans as embedded in specific social relationships. This adds a behavioural explanation of consumption to the socio-economic aspects related to the institutional set-up of the economy, and the historical socio-technological formation of lifestyles (Røpke, 1999). There is then a concern as to the role that consumption activities play in defining human self-identity. From the catchphrase 'you are what you eat,' to brand images and open display of brand labels, to 'keeping up with the Joneses', modern consumerism emphasizes the construction of a self-image and a social role. This means that individuals are not just manipulated by corporations but have become complicit in their own manipulation.

Some green non-governmental organizations have then attempted to break this loop with explicit recognition of the psychology of consumption. Perhaps the best example in this regard is the publication *Adbusters* which employs market advertising approaches in satirical ways to promote anti-consumerism and raise individual awareness. Governments face the same problem if they are to remove and control activities creating pollution, destroying ecosystems and causing biodiversity loss. However, attempts at reaching the disinterested mass of the population with a sustainable consumption message seem relatively rare or restricted to crisis (for example, energy or water shortages). There is thus a lack of research as to the potential means and their effectiveness.

In this chapter we explore how behavioural change in everyday consumption patterns might be addressed. The theoretical basis is described in the next section in terms of the psychological aspects of consumerism. This emphasizes the importance of positive and emotive messages channelled through media relevant to a target social group. Next, a case-study is presented where such an approach was implemented. Specifically we report on the attempt by Project Balance[2] to improve interest in sustainable behaviour in Germany amongst the disinterested and poorly educated (see also, Reisch, 2006; Reisch and Bietz, 2007). This employed a mass communication strategy using broadcast TV reports on a popular science show. This was combined with linked multiple media to allow follow-up by interested viewers. The project involved collaboration between media, science, corporations, sustainability actors and consumer watchdogs. The aim was to raise the level of engagement with sustainable consumption issues. This was monitored and analysis was conducted from media, marketing and consumer research perspectives. Initial consumer research results are reported. We conclude by discussing some of the implications.

UNDERSTANDING SOCIO-PSYCHOLOGICAL ASPECTS OF CONSUMPTION

Since the late 1980s, consumer research has investigated individual and institutional limits preventing sustainable consumption behaviour ('barriers'), and factors enabling the achievement of more sustainable lifestyles ('drivers'). Until the 1990s, this research was conducted under the labels of 'environmental' and 'pro-social' behaviour (Reisch and Røpke, 2004). Following this route, empirical work on attitudes by social psychologists led to the development of various attitudinal scales by which specific behaviour might be explained on the basis of pro-environmental attitudes.

An early and still popular pro-environmental scale is the New Ecological

Paradigm (NEP) designed by Dunlap and Van Liere (1978) using 12 statements, with which respondents agree or disagree on a Likert-type (four-point) scale, to capture key aspects of environmentalism. This has been applied to monitor changing environmental awareness and in the prediction of economic behaviour for example, using the NEP to measure pro-environmental attitudes to help explain willingness to pay for environmental improvements (Kotchen and Reiling, 2000). The NEP and pro-environmental attitudes have been linked to value orientations (biospheric, social altruistic and egoistic) by Stern (2000). This value-belief-norm model of human behaviour generalizes Schwartz's (1977) norm activation theory by postulating that adverse consequences to valued objects activate personal norms, such as a sense of obligation to take pro-environmental actions. Thus, for example, people who value other species highly will be concerned about environmental conditions that threaten such species (biospheric value orientation) while those who care about other people will be concerned for their health and well-being as a result of changing environmental quality (social altruism). The aim of such work is to explain the motives and beliefs underlying specific actions.

In terms of consumption behaviour the engagement of individuals in the framing of the environment as an aspect of the marketplace becomes important. If the environment, or aspects of it, can be regarded as just a commodity then economists can limit their policies to market-based instruments, that is, valuing change in monetary terms, spreading markets to new areas (for example tradable carbon permits) and using monetary incentives to achieve desired behaviours. Evidence on the problems associated with this outlook has then arisen from employing motivational measures in hypothetical markets. For example, pro-environmental attitudes have been hypothesized to be determinants of willingness-to-pay (WTP) leading to protest bidding by environmentalists because they are more likely to hold deontological or rights-based beliefs which reject economic consequentialist and utilitarian positions (Spash, 1997). Such trade-off rejection is consistent with holding lexicographic preferences (Spash, 2000), and confronts the consumerist approach to valuing the environment with a belief system which rejects notions of commensurability (Aldred, 2006). This creates problems for economists trying to extend commoditization to the environment, because individuals may not just refuse to engage but may also give monetary values unrelated to trade prices (Spash, 2006). Psychological motivations then become key to understanding behaviour and designing policy instruments. Thus, simple economic approaches using taxes or subsidies as incentives to change behaviour can have unexpected consequences and crowd out moral and norm-based motives to action (Frey and Jegen, 2001).

Clearly then, in developing effective intervention strategies, knowledge about underlying psychological variables is indispensable. Research has addressed the role of stable dispositions as well as specific environmental cognitions and emotions (Kals and Maes, 2002). The explanatory power of generalized personality traits and broad beliefs (for example general perceptions of control, altruism and social responsibility) on various sustainable behaviours has proven to be low and inconsistent (for example Bamberg, 2003). However, specific environmental cognitions – morals, ecological awareness, control beliefs and justice appraisals – exert strong stabilizing effects on sustainable behaviour (Montada and Kals, 2000). Following Shaver's (1985) model of responsibility, the attribution of ecological responsibility to oneself, as well as to external agents (for example politicians, corporations), is based upon a general awareness of ecological risks (for example pollution of soil, air and water; consequences of the greenhouse effect; the risks of damage to the ozone layer; decrease of biodiversity) and belief in one's ability to reduce those risks effectively. Moral reasoning and normative messages over what constitutes a right or wrong action is a proven motivational basis for overcoming various factors (for example, interest shifts, social traps, lock-ins and high-cost perceptions) (Cialdini, 2003; Cialdini et al., 2006). This provides at least two entry points for intervention programmes. First, they can aim at creating risk awareness via providing information and knowledge. Second, they can provide solutions in order to increase an individual's perceived behavioural control (for example, showing concrete, low-cost, alternative behaviours).

While useful, this approach neglects the impact of various categories of emotions. This omission can be explained by the prevalence of rational choice-based action theories such the Theory of Reasoned Action (Ajzen and Fishbein, 1980), the Theory of Planned Behaviour (Ajzen, 1991), and the Theory of Trying (Bagozzi and Warshaw, 1990). A core element in these models is the proposition that individuals are motivated to act on the basis of beliefs about consequences, cost and benefits, and importance. The basic theoretical characterization, with respect to individual psychology, is of humans as restricted, resourceful, expecting, evaluating and maximizing (Coleman and Fararo, 1992). The model has been informed and influenced by mainstream economic theory.[3] Emotions seem incompatible with such a characterization of humans and so are absent. Only since the 2000s have a significant number of studies in consumer research appeared in the literature that involve emotions (for an overview see Laros and Steenkamp, 2005).

The emotional foundations of sustainable (environmental) behaviour can be observed in negative and positive ways. Examples of negative emotions are expressing indignation about other peoples' lack of pollution control, anger about too much pro-environmental decision-making, and guilt about one's own unsustainable consumer decisions. Positive emotions may be expressed as affinity or simply love of nature. Whereas certain emotions can be traced back to moral cognitions, feelings of love toward nature appear to be based upon experiences made with significant others (McShane, 2007; Montada and Kals, 2000). In contrast, ecological fear and experienced ecological burdens appear less important. As Kals and Maes (2002, p. 113) state:

> With regard to the socio-ecological dilemma, the significance of a moral base makes sense, as there is only little direct personal benefit derived from sustainable behaviour. This moral dimension is reflected not only cognitively, but also experienced emotionally . . . Sustainability should not only be appraised cognitively but also as an internalized norm, which is interconnected with personal experiences and even feelings of love.

Indeed, the emotional dimension of sustainable behaviours can be taken into account in intervention programmes where the experience of positive emotions plays a key role.

The characteristics of environmental problems are particularly challenging in terms of designing interventions to change behaviour, that is: visible costs and invisible benefits and consequences; benefits to geographically and temporally remote third parties; intangibles that are difficult to portray; the need for long-term engagement due to large amounts of complex information; the need to change basic values; and the need to get outside opinion leaders on board. Following the work of Andreasen (1995), approaches to induce behavioural change in consumers can be regarded as forming five strategies:

1. Education: bearing the risk of 'boomerang effects', that is, behavioural responses exactly opposite to those desired (for example, Ringold, 2002). Anger, defiance, denial and other negative responses might occur since consumers often do not want to be 'lectured' on their behaviour (for example, Wolburg, 2006).
2. Persuasion: as used in social advertising. The focus is on arguments and motivational 'cues' to change behaviour. This 'selling approach' can be perceived as too pushy.
3. Behaviour modification: as found in behavioural theory which stresses learning by reward and punishment. The approach can be very costly, which restricts its application to individuals or small groups. The underlying psychological model is also narrow and the connotations of enforced behaviour may be politically contentious.

4. Social influence: using campaigns directed at influencing community norms and collective behaviour. While promising, the approach requires situations in which social issues are well understood and norms accepted. Effectiveness will be determined by the pressures to conform. The behaviour to be influenced needs to be socially important (for example, health) and visible (for example, smoking). Appeals to group norms may be less effective the more individualism is emphasized in society.
5. Social marketing: combining features from the above four approaches in a comprehensive and integrated manner. It uses the 'Four P's' (product, place, price, promotion) of marketing as tools, and relies on market research with careful segment targets (for example, Kotler et al., 2002; Smith, 2006). Andreasen (1995, 2001) provides empirical evidence supporting the potential of social marketing to influence consumers, particularly in the context of human health.

The use of a social marketing concept based on positive emotions and entertaining features – 'ecotainment' (Lichtl, 1999) – is hypothesized to be more effective than both the hitherto predominant fact-oriented style of consumer information, as well as negatively framed fear and threat approaches. Positive emotional appeals enable a target audience to move from non-interest and ignorance to contemplation of behavioural change (Monahan, 1995). In contrast, appeals to fear prove counterproductive – provoking defence mechanisms and inattention (Hale and Dillard, 1995). Prior research has shown that a fact-oriented style at best reaches the 'usual suspects' (that is, the more educated, information-prone and interested consumers) but not the poorly educated.

DESIGNING AND CONDUCTING AN EMPIRICAL APPLICATION IN GERMANY

Project Balance was set up as both a trendsetting initiative to stimulate sustainability communication amongst the public, and an academic research project to assess factors of success and failure. In its dual approach, the project design resembled what was termed 'action research' in the 1970s (Isaac and Michael, 1987). The project was designed with partners from academia, the media and media research that is, both practitioners and theorists.[4] The research was conceptualized as an iterative and ongoing process, rather than a one-way activity with a neatly defined beginning and end. This then resembles more an upward spiral of exploration: planning, structuring, pre-testing, implementing, monitoring and replanning. Figure 9.1 sketches the design of the project.

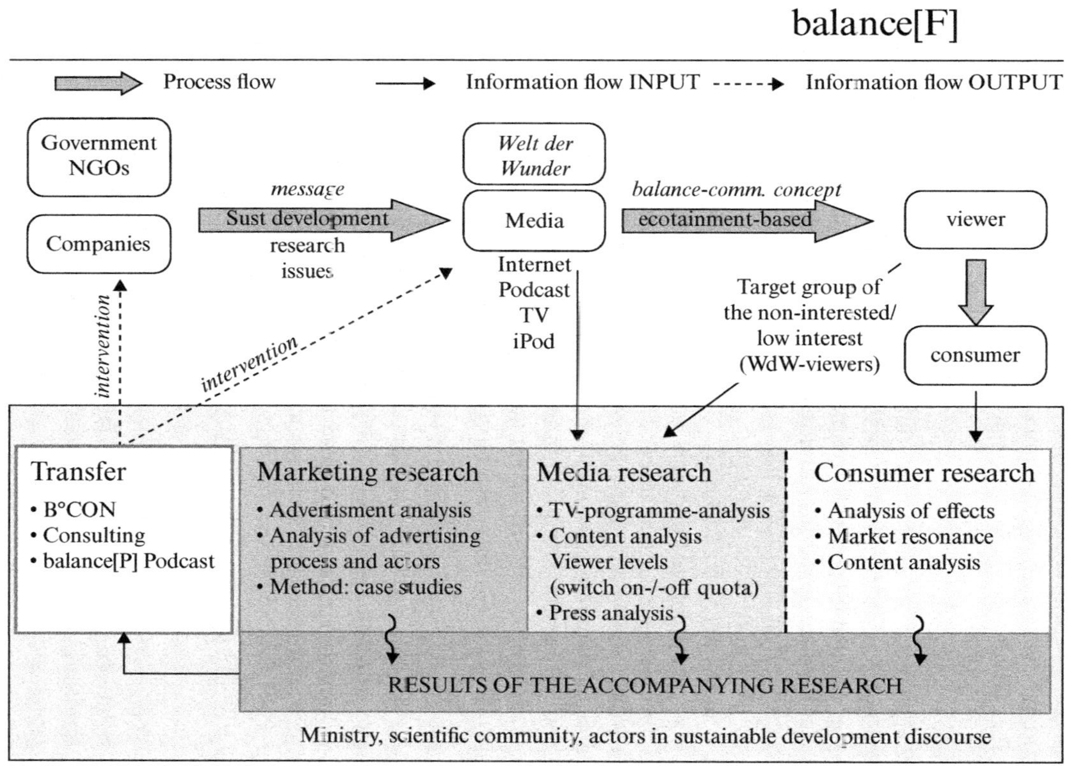

Figure 9.1 Overview of the project design

THE TREND-SETTING INITIATIVE

Permanent information overload is a problem in modern economies. For example, Kroeber-Riel and Weinberg (2003) estimate that less than 5 per cent of actively sent corporate communication directed to consumers is received. TV viewer research shows that 'zapping' or channel changing, and other advert avoidance strategies, are widely employed (for example, Gunter et al., 1995; Siddarth and Chattopadhyay, 1998). Overall, consumers show less interest in classic corporate one-sided 'push-communication'. Hence the rise of the alternative 'pull-media', such as the Internet, where recipients select customized content and have a dialogue option to exchange views and voice their opinions (Web 2.0 communication).

Project Balance aimed for public engagement and discourse on sustainable consumption and production using a range of push- and pull-media. Various TV reports were employed as teasers aiming to redirect viewers to become users, readers and finally 'doers'. The basic hypothesis was that the use of emotionalized and entertaining messages directed at the disengaged 'broad masses' could successfully promote attention, interest, positive attitudes and knowledge-seeking, and change behavioural intentions regarding sustainable consumption. The approach involved two steps: first, gaining viewers' attention, interest and sympathy via social marketing tools triggering (mostly) positive emotions; and second, transmitting convincing cognitive messages informing and confirming prior attitudes towards behavioural change.

In consumer behaviour research, high-involvement behaviours such as the ones discussed in this chapter are conceptualized as being developed through definable stages. Several models of behavioural change have been proposed (Maibach and Cotton, 1995). Project Balance selected the Transtheoretical Model of Behaviour Change (Prochaska and DiClemente, 1984), which has undergone considerable field testing mainly in the public health domain (for example, Mohr et al., 2001). The model describes five stages:

- Stage 1: Pre-contemplation, in which consumers do not think of the behaviour as being appropriate for them. This can be due to pure ignorance, presumed irrelevance or, more difficult to change, principles and norms.
- Stage 2: Contemplation, in which consumers think about and evaluate recommended behaviours, and also look for more information.
- Stage 3: Preparation, in which consumers have decided to act and prepare; for example, search for brands and stores.
- Stage 4: Action, in which consumers initiate a new behaviour.

- Stage 5: Confirmation, in which consumers are committed to the behaviour and have no desire or intention to return to the earlier behaviour.

Ideally, intervention strategies target consumers as classified by the five groups. Communication tasks appropriate to each are thus to create awareness and interest, change values, motivate behavioural change, create action and maintain change, respectively (Andreasen, 1995). The aim is to move consumers to their respective next stage, rather than attempt to bring everyone to 'confirmation'. General media may achieve early-stage transformation while the latter stages are more likely be reached with tailored messages and media such as print, Internet and podcasts.

While the five stages provide a conceptual framework, in practice Stages 2 and 3 are closely intertwined and separating individuals is difficult. Moreover, consumers may be in different stages with respect to different consumption domains, for example food and travel. Bearing these limitations in mind, a questionnaire was administered to aid classification by stage. This included questions regarding subjects' knowledge about the concept of sustainability, their viewing preferences and interests (that is, interest in TV programmes on environmental and social issues), their general view on the environmental debate and their individual responsibility, as well as their attitudes and behaviour towards 'green' and 'fair' consumption.[5] The results were then compared with available data from representative survey results on 'green' and 'average' German consumers.[6] This allowed a crude classification according to the five stages, but proved sufficient to evaluate the impact of project communication stimuli.

Project Balance focused on the initial stages, namely the generation of interest, attention and attitude formation amongst people who have no or low interest in sustainability issues. In order to achieve maximum target group exposure, the sustainability messages had to be placed in media channels that the target audience would normally choose. Channels were carefully selected regarding core viewer characteristics, reach, frequency, impact and cost. During the project, cross-media spin-offs – a website, a print magazine and a podcast show – were developed and target group exposure was increased.[7]

Short TV 'Balance Reports' were co-developed by the project team and TV editorial staff. These were aired between September 2004 and October 2006 on the TV show *Welt der Wunder* (World of Wonders). On each show, one of six reports was a Balance Report, introduced by the show's host. *Welt der Wunder* was the first and, at the time, one of the most popular science programmes of its kind aired on commercial television in Germany. Its motto was 'Science made easy – fascinating stories delivered with a dash of levity'.[8] During the project, the show was running weekly on a commercial TV channel at prime time on Saturday evenings and being rerun on Sunday afternoons and Monday late nights. Additionally, the show appeared three times per week on a news channel (N-TV). In addition, from 2006, the Balance Reports were aired once per week on the call-in TV show *Welt der Wonder – Schau dich schlau!* (World of Wonders–Watch yourself Smart!), a half-hour version of the full-hour evening show.

Altogether, 34 Balance Reports were aired and each reached about 2 to 3 million viewers per week. The Balance Reports fell into two categories. First, there were those which presented companies committed to sustainable production or services; here, specific branded sustainable products or services were showcased (for example organic baby food, a new type of childcare, alternative living in a tree house, biofuel, renewable resource loans, alternative paving and alternative oil filter for cars). Second were a variety of reports on sustainability that were not company-specific but showcased sustainable products or product use in general, such as fair trade coffee, hybrid cars, organic meat, fuel-saving driving, sustainable timber, detergent or the sustainable cultivation of apples.

The reasons for such a design and the cooperation with *Welt der Wunder* can be summarized as follows:

1. Free access was provided to detailed audience research data – collected by the prestigious German Gesellschaft für Konsumforschung (GfK) in Nuremberg – on the basis of non-profit cooperation with the producer of *Welt der Wunder*. Usually such data are too expensive for academic researchers to access. This enabled tracking viewers' switch-on switch-off behaviour for every second of the programme and advertisements.
2. Market research showed that *Welt der Wunder* and RTL II's core audience matched the target desired, being both less educated and less interested in environmental and social issues than the average German TV viewer. During the project this was verified based on GfK's viewer profiles.
3. *Welt der Wunder* was to date the most popular science programme on German TV with about 4 million viewers per show. The show was aired weekly during prime time and repeated several times during the week on different channels.
4. The show host was also the producer and had, in the past decade, become a well-known celebrity and himself a 'brand' in Germany. His high credibility encouraged audiences to pay particular attention to messages delivered and presented by him. The host was motivated by

personal beliefs about the necessity of a more sustainable lifestyle and so added to the information presented in the TV reports.

5. Last but not least, the editorial staff, scriptwriters and the producer were open-minded and interested enough to embrace the project group's continuous 'sustainability coaching' efforts. In practice, this is highly relevant since the freedom of the press forbids external intrusion in the production of a programme. The content and design of TV reports are the full responsibility of the broadcasters. After recent heated public debate and legal conflicts at national and European level on surreptitious TV advertising, product placement, and issue placement journalists and programme makers have become very sensitive to undue influence in their work.

Research into the effectiveness of health communication has shown that the more effective campaigns use multiple media and repetition of a single message either in the form of retransmission of the original message or in slight variations on the basic theme. Also, the use of the news media as a means of increasing visibility has been shown to be successful (Backer et al., 1992). Hence, it was expected that a 'hook-up' cross-media strategy transmitting multiple repeated messages on multiple channels, tailored to the different subtarget groups, would be effective in creating attention and knowledge. The aim was also to redirect TV viewers to the more informative website, the magazine, or – especially for the young age group – to podcast shows on sustainability issues.

THE RESEARCH PROJECT

The accompanying research was split into three modules: media research, consumer research and marketing research. There was close interaction between these research groups, in particular between media and consumer components. Figure 9.1 sketches the project modules and their core research methods.

Various data were collected from public participants prior to the start of Balance Report TV broadcasting. First, there was a public sample (N = 440) of focus group participants; and second, there was a convenience sample of Internet users (N = 881). The focus groups were preselected to represent the typical *Welt der Wunder* viewer, that is, younger, less educated and less interested in environmental issues than the average German TV viewer. This sample was screened to select only those who had not previously watched the Balance Reports. The Internet users came from the

Welt der Wunder website, could participate in an online game, and were then exposed to Balance Reports. The stage separation questionnaire, mentioned above, was administered to the focus group sample prior to any Balance Report exposure.

Focus groups were carried out between February and November 2006. The target group members were specifically selected according to their similarity to the project's target group profile from groups such as students of vocational schools, secondary school teenagers, driving schools, but also hospital administrators, non-professional sports teams and, as a control group, university graduates. For the focus group discussion, a standardized questionnaire was designed to measure emotional appeal, attractiveness, acceptability and relevance of the Balance Reports, and to collect socio-demographic data. Recall of the reports' information was also tested.

Consumer research carried out reception analysis and content analysis. Reception analysis used both direct (for example questionnaires) and proxy measures (for example switch-on switch-off data). Data were retrieved mainly from focus group discussions, expert group discussions, individual interviews, case-studies with companies (on their sustainable marketing strategies) and market response analysis. Content analysis addressed the perceived contents of the messages in the TV reports. This was investigated in focus groups as well as via computer-assisted qualitative data analysis (CAQDA), performed with ATLAS.ti. Moreover, in web-based questionnaires, viewers were profiled via available GfK data and standardized instruments measuring their propensity to environmental and socially conscious consumption. The criteria of analysis were: comprehensibility of the message, attractiveness (measured by polarity profiles and direct questions), emotional appeal (before and after design), acceptability and relevance (with the proxy measure of remembrance of content and emotions).

Special attention was given to the measurement of emotions. While lately there has been a significant increase in research into affective processes in consumer behaviour (Richins, 1997), information about the nature of emotions and their measurement is still scarce. In the consumer research module of Project Balance, the measurement of emotions was performed with the German version (Krohne et al., 1996) of the PANAS questionnaire (Watson and Clark, 1988). Furthermore, split-second data from both media research (switch-on switch-off) and the computer-assisted qualitative data analysis via ATLAS.ti of the reports proved extremely useful. This allowed viewers' reactions to be related to tiny bits of narration or format so that patterns and correlations in the data could be discerned (Schwender et al., 2007, 2008).

Results

The results reported in this chapter focus on the early stages of behavioural change. This is in line with the main challenge of Project Balance which was to stimulate interest and attitude change in consumers with limited interest in and/or knowledge of sustainable lifestyles.[9] Moreover, the results are initial and are hence presented on a less detailed level than will be found in later publications.

CREATING AWARENESS AND INTEREST

Following the rough classification approach described above, about half of the focus group study subjects were classified as being in the stage of pre-contemplation. For example, in 7 out of 11 focus groups, not one participant could roughly define the term 'sustainability'. This is below average for Germany. Also, interest in organic and fair trade goods as well as in respective media programming was below average. Addressing this group requires showing and explaining the relevance of new behavioural possibilities, for instance, to try an alternative 'fair trade' coffee. The aim was to communicate that there is an alternative to conventional products and that the latter bear problems of sustainability (knowledge), as well as that the proposed behaviour is not antithetical to the values of the majority of society, or may even be fashionable. The behaviour is then to be associated with potential for improved well-being by presenting benefits in a frame that creates positive emotions and attitudes.

Online viewer surveys conducted on the project website straight after a Balance Report was aired, as well as focus group results, showed that the Balance Reports were overwhelmingly regarded as interesting, informative and attractive. Thus, the disinterested target group was engaged despite the Balance Reports dealing with issues more challenging than the other standard items in the show. Evidence from switch-off analysis revealed that the fear (aired by TV officials in the early phases of Project Balance) of an immediate switch-off reaction when such 'difficult' topics were presented, proved to be unfounded. On a more technical note, the clips were rated by viewers (via polarity profiles) as 'authentic, modern and clear'. Most importantly for this project, the majority of the clips were able to create the positive emotions which were intended. The qualitative analysis (CAQDA, focus groups) showed that, in a nutshell, the emotional value of the reports was much more decisive than the content.

CHANGING PERSPECTIVES AND MOTIVATING ACTION

As explained above, Stages 2 and 3 are so closely interlinked that, in practice, it was neither possible nor sensible to distinguish the two. More than a third of the focus group study subjects could be classified as currently fitting into these stages, where proposed behaviours are considered and evaluated and action is taken to seek more information on alternatives.

In Stage 2, explaining the benefits and reducing the perceived costs of behavioural alternatives are important. For example, one TV report showed the thrifty use of compact detergent, and focused on the individual benefits (cost, environment, health) of 'washing correctly'. At the same time, it conducted explicit 'demarketing' by emphasizing the individual and environmental cost of the common alternative (filler-boosted washing powder). This specific report was rated as interesting and motivating in both polarity profiles and focus groups. Focus group sessions revealed that it gave viewers new perspectives and made them think about alternatives.

For those consumers who have reached the preparation stage, it is important to provide easily accessible information and hands-on service guidance in order to reduce transaction costs to a minimum. Moreover, consumers at this stage are ready for a more extended information search in different media. The three- to eight-minute TV report is limited as an information carrier.

A solution was to guide viewers explicitly, via prompts from the show's host, to the website where additional material (for example, on the European 'wash right' campaign, a voluntary initiative by the large washing detergent producers) and service tools (for example a service module that computed the optimal amount of detergent when the user entered their postcode) were provided. Log file analysis showed that about half of the online users of the Balance website made use of its offers of more detailed information. About 10 per cent of this group opted for re-viewing the Balance Reports of the latest shows, and then actively searched for more information on the *Welt der Wunder* homepage. Also, an analysis of email reactions and requests (which were collected by the programme producer within two weeks of each report being aired), showed that viewers did engage in active information searching, some asking for product-specific information and distributors.[10] Another indicator was the good Internet user participation rate (N = 881) in the 'sustainability quiz' designed and employed as an online education tool.

In all these interactions, the one-way passive TV information was supplemented by an active and selective information search process with the option of two-way communication. This is of the utmost importance.

Consumers do not make their decisions in a social vacuum; rather, they are part of families and peer groups, colleagues at work, virtual communities, and neighbourhoods. These groups act as 'communication buffers' in commenting on and evaluating information, attitudes and consumption decisions of the individual. They can act as facilitators, as sources of (contradictory or supporting) information, and as sources of social pressure. Relevant others – people from these communities, or celebrities – can act as role models and opinion leaders. These tendencies were also exploited in Project Balance by actively involving the (already existing) virtual *Welt der Wunder* community and by trying to stimulate discussions.

In a market reaction analysis carried out with the public relations and/or marketing departments of companies showcased by *Welt der Wunder*, it was reported that employees of companies in the TV reports had liked the presentation of their company as a sustainability leader and appreciated being approached by friends and family who had also watched the programme. Such 'halo-effects' can be expected to have positive motivational and identity building impacts both internally (for employees) and externally (for consumers). Moreover, as we found in the surveys and focus groups, viewers often remembered small interesting facts presented in the TV reports, which they then passed on as 'conversation pieces' and status markers to others. This shows some of the possibilities for advancing sustainability issues in public discourse.

CONCLUSION

Reaching the mass of disinterested consumers who are busy in their everyday lives of work, family and relationships is a major challenge. There appears some good potential for the 'ecotainment' approach, at least for the early stages of a consumer behavioural change process. The hypothesis that stimulating positive emotions can act as a motivator has been supported, it seems. However, whether emotion works to increase consumers' interest in and liking of more sustainable consumption alternatives seems to depend heavily on whether the target group relates to the themes presented, clip design chosen, wording and music used. A credible and appealing sender of the sustainability message also proved important. This is actually bad news for most governmentally driven consumer information on sustainable consumption.

There are also a number of pitfalls associated with the approach for serious communication on sustainability issues with the public by companies or government. Sustainability communication is a highly complex and even risky activity that needs careful strategic planning and genuine stakeholder input. Research and practice have shown that, if not practiced in a sophisticated and culturally adapted manner, consumers might easily feel misled (Becker-Olsen et al., 2006). The 'trendsetting module' of the project could be seen as jeopardizing the serious content of sustainability science by summarizing and 'dumbing down' the messages. Yet, reaching the disinterested masses requires some innovation in communication and conception of policy instruments. The 'ecotainment' approach should then be seen as a possible element in a much broader range of policy tools – from price incentives to deliberative participatory processes.

In attempting to address the modern problems of consumerism via the means used by corporations, the same problems as identified by Galbraith and Kapp seem to recur. That is, marketing and the psychology of advertising aim to manipulate the consumer to a behavioural act, that is, purchase. An approach like that of Project Balance may then be regarded as aiming to manipulate viewers. The fact is that corporate behaviour has been challenged in this respect and needs constant review by social organizations which have the power and authority to challenge them. Repeating a corporate approach that is recognized as problematic is something to avoid. For example, even if forms of 'stealth marketing' were deemed effective, they appear inadvisable; such as subliminal messaging that relies on the forces of the unconscious. The charge of manipulation is substantiated if viewers/consumers are unaware of and fail to realize that they are being marketed to and influenced, or the visibility of the sender/company is hidden. In Project Balance the sender was clearly identified in the opening credits of the TV show, sometimes also in the teasers and moderation, as well as on the website and all other media channels. In addition, the aim was to raise active engagement in the issues and debate in society, not merely push a product purchase.

While from a utilitarian perspective the end may justify the means, from a deontological one there is the need to define clear limits in terms of the ethics of communication. Basically, manipulation profoundly counteracts the ideas of transparency, trust and authenticity that are fundamental to sustainable consumption and its communication. Indeed the ecological economics literature on sustainability is concerned with making explicit problems of justice and ethical treatment of others as well as exposing the role played by dominant institutions in society in creating the economic and environmental problems we face.

Explicit reference to ethical conduct is clearly necessary in all public policy, whether economic cost–benefit analysis conducted behind closed doors or open public engagement. Manipulation is just as feasible in the former (Spash, 2008) as in the later (Spash, 2007b). Both ecological and Post Keynesian economists aim beyond a focus on a narrow set of mainstream economic instruments of public policy, but in doing so need to pay attention to researching their implications. This requires being aware that institutions of public policy are framed within the context of our political economy.

The challenge is therefore to design institutions which achieve the multiple goals desired. Yet within the structures of modern society there will by definition be a struggle for power. If society is to move towards a more sustainable footing which addresses the unsustainable rate of modern material throughput and energy use, then the cycle of mass consumerism will need to be addressed. That means finding democratic means of addressing the masses and changing consumption patterns.

NOTES

1. Kapp's concern was more clearly with the manipulation of marketing and advertising and the waste of resources involved. Galbraith in his 'revised sequence' has a broader theory of political economy in which corporation and state work together to ensure that there is adequate aggregate demand as well as management of specific consumer demand by the firm.
2. Project Balance was set up as a trendsetting initiative to enforce sustainability communication in the German general public and as an academic research project that accompanied this trendsetting initiative and evaluated its outcomes. The name was chosen to denote a sustainable lifestyle which aims to balance economic, ecological and social goals. The term 'sustainability' was rejected as fuzzy and difficult to comprehend. Sustainable consumption was intentionally framed as well-being within a balanced lifestyle; resembling what is now termed lifestyle of health and sustainability (LOHAS), see www.lohas-com. However, LOHAS predominantly targets higher-status socio-economic and income groups while the 'balance lifestyle' also targets lower ones.
3. Viewing consumers as much more than just the mainstream economists 'rational' decision-maker has also been supported and strengthened by a variety of research relating economics and psychology. Gintis (2000) provides an overview of experimental results in this regard. Earl (1990) distinguishes different interactions between the two disciplines and explains how 'psychological economics' challenges economists seeking to limit the use made of ideas from psychology. He sees inputs from psychology as enhancing the understanding of, and improving the ability to predict, behaviour normally viewed as the preserve of economics.
4. Project Balance was funded by the German Ministry of Research and Education (Project No.07BAL01). It ran from 2004 to 2007 with a budget of €1.5 million. Main researchers were Clemens Schwender (Jacobs University of Bremen), Lucia Reisch (Copenhagen Business School) and Martin Kreeb (Hohenheim University). In order to receive ongoing feedback from other stakeholders, a Consultancy Board of Advisors was established composed of academic experts from environmental psychology, sustainable development, green marketing, ethics and communications research, as well as of practitioners from non-governmental organizations (NGOs), consumer organizations, the German Council of Sustainable Development, and the leading German media research institution Grimme Institut, among others.
5. Questionnaires, in German only, available from the lead author.
6. The major source profiling the 'average' German is the biannual survey of environmental awareness, concern and attitude of German consumers (Kuckartz and

Rheingans-Heintze, 2004, 2006). Among other relations it shows the strong correlation between awareness level and level of education; it also provides data on the average knowledge of the concept of sustainability and other green issues.
7. For more detail and statistics, see Reisch and Bietz (2008). As regards the other media employed: the *Welt der Wunder* magazine has been discontinued as was the podcast.
8. See the show's website at http://weltderwunder.de.msn.com.
9. Monitoring and measurement of actual behavioural change – let alone its stabilization into a routine – was outside the remit of a design where data could only be derived indirectly from company interviews and market response analysis. This more ambitious task would require a panel design or a form of ethnographic research, although the later stages might be approximated using measurement of behavioural intentions.
10. For instance, one report showcased a new oil filter with which car owners can retrofit their cars and save drastically on oil change costs in passenger vehicles. This report created about 400 emails within several days and almost 200 direct requests to the producer of the oil filter.

REFERENCES

Ajzen, I. (1991), 'The theory of planned behaviour: some unresolved issues', *Organizational Behavior and Human Decision Processes*, **50**, 179–211.

Ajzen, Icek and Martin Fishbein (1980), *Understanding Attitudes and Predicting Social Behaviour*, Englewood Cliffs, NJ: Prentice Hall.

Aldred, J. (2006), 'Incommensurability and monetary valuation', *Land Economics*, **82** (2), 141–61.

Andreasen, Alan R. (1995), *Marketing Social Change: Changing Behavior to Promote Health, Social Development, and the Environment*, San Francisco, CA: Jossey-Bass.

Andreasen, Alan R. (2001), *Ethics in Social Marketing*, Washington, DC: Georgetown University Press.

Backer, Thomas E., Everett M. Rogers and Pradeep Sopory (1992), *Designing Health Communication Campaigns: What Works?*, Newbury Park, CA: Sage.

Bagozzi, R.P. and P. Warshaw (1990), 'Trying to consume', *Journal of Consumer Research*, **17**, 127–40.

Bamberg, S. (2003), 'How does environmental concern influence specific environmental related behaviours? A new answer to an old question', *Journal of Environmental Psychology*, **23**, 21–32.

Becker-Olsen, K., B.A. Cudmore and R.P. Hill (2006), 'The impact of perceived corporate social responsibility on consumer behaviour', *Journal of Business Research*, **59**, 46–53.

Cialdini, R.B. (2003), 'Crafting normative messages to protect the environment', *Current Directions in Psychological Science*, **12**, 105–9.

Cialdini, R.B., L. Demaine, B.J. Sagarin, D.W. Barrett, K. Rhoads and P.L. Winter (2006), 'Managing social norms for persuasive impact', *Social Influence*, **1** (1), 3–15.

Coleman, James S. and Thomas J. Fararo (eds) (1992), *Rational Choice Theory: Advocacy and Critique*, Newbury Park, CA: Sage.

Daly, H.E. (1977), *Steady-State Economics*, San Francisco, CA: W.H. Freeman.

Dunlap, R.E. and K.D. Van Liere (1978), 'The "New Environmental Paradigm"', *Journal of Environmental Education*, **9** (4), 10–19.

Earl, P.E. (1990), 'Economics and psychology: a survey', *Economic Journal*, **100** (402), 718–55.

Easterlin, R.A. (1974), 'Does economic growth improve the human lot? Some empirical evidence', in P.A. David and M.W. Reder (eds), *Nations and Households in Economic Growth: Essays in Honor of Moses Abramovitz*, New York: Academic Press, pp. 98–125.

Frey, B.S. and R. Jegen (2001), 'Motivation crowding theory', *Journal of Economic Surveys*, **15** (5), 589–611.

Galbraith, J.K. (1958), *The Affluent Society*, Boston, MA: Houghton Mifflin.

Galbraith, J.K. (1967), *The New Industrial State*, New York: New American Library.

Georgescu-Roegen, N. (1971), *The Entropy Law and the Economic Process*, Cambridge, MA: Harvard University Press.

Gintis, H. (2000), 'Beyond *Homo economicus*: evidence from experimental economics', *Ecological Economics*, **35** (3), 311–22.

Gunter, B., A. Furnham and Z. Lineton (1995), 'Watching people watching television: what goes on in front of the TV set?', *Learning, Media and Technology*, **21** (3), 165–91.

Hale, Jerold L. and James P. Dillard (1995), 'Fear appeals in health promotion campaigns: too much, too little, or just right?', in Edward W. Maibach and Roxanne Louiselle Parrott (eds), *Designing Health Messages*, Newbury Park, CA: Sage, pp. 65–80.

Hirsch, F. (1977), *Social Limits to Growth*, London: Routledge & Kegan Paul.

Isaac, S. and W.B. Michael (1987), *Handbook in Research and Evaluation for Education and the Behavioural Sciences*, San Diego, CA: Edits Publisher.

Kals, Elisabeth and Jürgen Maes (2002), 'Sustainable development and emotions', in Peter Schmuck and Wesley P. Schultz (eds), *Psychology of Sustainable Development*, Norwell, MA: Kluwer Academic Publishers, pp. 97–122.

Kapp, K.W. (1950), *The Social Costs of Private Enterprise*, New York: Shocken.

Kapp, K.W. (1978), *The Social Costs of Business Enterprise*, 3rd edn, Nottingham: Spokesman.

Kneese, A.V., R.U. Ayres and R.C. d'Arge (1970), *Economics and the Environment: A Materials Balance Approach*, Washington, DC: Resources for the Future.

Kotchen, M.J. and S.D. Reiling (2000), 'Environmental attitudes, motivations, and contingent valuation of nonuse values: a case study involving endangered species', *Ecological Economics*, **32** (1), 93–107.

Kotler, P., N. Roberto and N. Lee (2002), *Social Marketing: Improving the Quality of Life*, Thousand Oaks, CA: Sage.

Kroeber-Riel, W. and Peter Weinberg (2003), *Konsumentenverhalten*, 8th edn, Munich: Vahlen.

Krohne, H.W., B. Egloff, C.-W. Kohlmann and A. Tausch (1996), 'Untersuchungen mit einer deutschen Version der "Positive and Negative Affect Schedule" (PANAS)', *Diagnostica*, **42** (2), 139–56.

Kuckartz, Udo and Anke Rheingans-Heintze (2004), *Umweltpolitik. Umweltbewusstsein in Deutschland 2004*, Berlin: Bundesministerium für Umwelt, Naturschutz und Reaktorsicherheit (BMU).

Kuckartz, Udo and Anke Rheingans-Heintze (2006), *Trends im Umweltbewusstsein: Umweltgerechtigkeit, Lebensqualität und persönliches Engagement*, Wiesbaden: VS-Verlag.

Laros, F. and J.-B. Steenkamp (2005), 'Emotions in consumer behaviour: a hierarchical approach', *Journal of Business Research*, **58**, 1437–45.

Lichtl, Martin (1999), *Ecotainment: der neue Weg im Umweltmarketing*, Vienna and Frankfurt: Wirtschaftsverlag.

Maibach, Edward W. and David Cotton (1995), 'Moving people to behaviour change: a stages social cognitive approach to message design', in Edward W. Maibach and Roxanne L. Parott (eds), *Designing Health Messages*, Newbury Park, CA: Sage, pp. 41–64.

McShane, K. (2007), 'Anthropocentrism vs. nonanthropocentrism: why should we care?', *Environmental Values*, **16** (2), 169–86.

Mishan, E.J. (1969), 'The myth of consumers' sovereignty', in E.J. Mishan, *Growth: The Price We Pay*, London: Staples Press, pp. 89–96.

Mohr, L.A., D.J. Webb and K.E. Harris (2001), 'Do consumers expect companies to be socially responsible? The impact of corporate social responsibility on buying behaviour', *Journal of Consumer Affairs*, **35**, 45–72.

Monahan, Jennifer L. (1995), 'Thinking positively: using positive affect when designing health messages', in Edward Maibach and Roxanne L. Parott (eds), *Designing Health Messages*, Thousand Oaks, CA: Sage, pp. 81–113.

Montada, L. and E. Kals (2000), 'Political implications of environmental psychology', *International Journal of Psychology*, **35** (2), 68–176.

OECD (1997), *Sustainable Consumption and Production*, Paris: OECD Publications.

Prochaska, James O. and Carlo C. DiClemente (1984), *The Transtheoretical Approach: Crossing the Traditional Boundaries of Therapy*, Homewood, IL: Dow Jones-Irwin.

Reisch, Lucia A. (2004), 'Sustainable consumption as a consumer policy issue', in Lucia A. Reisch and Inge Røpke (eds), *The Ecological Economics of Consumption*, Current Issues in Ecological Economics, Cheltenham, UK and Northampton, MA, USA: Edward Elgar, pp. 175–89.

Reisch, Lucia A. (2006), 'CSR consumer information: the case of balance project', in Mette Morsing and Suzanne C. Beckmann (eds), *Strategic CSR Communication*, Copenhagen: Copenhagen Business School Press, pp. 185–211.

Reisch, L.A. and S. Bietz (2007), 'How to convince the inconvincible? A mass mediated approach to communicate sustainable lifestyles to a low-interest target group', *International Journal of Innovation and Sustainable Development*, **2** (2), 192–200.

Reisch, Lucia A. and Sabine Bietz (2008), 'Kommunication des Nachhaltigen Konsums für die Massen? Ergebnisse der Konsumforschung im Projekt balance[f]', in Clemens Schwender, Werner F. Schultz and Martin Kreeb (eds), *Medialisierung der Nachhaltigkeit: Das Forschungsprojekt balance[f]: Emotionen und Ecotainment in den Massenmedien*, Marburg: Metropolis, p. 315–35.

Reisch, Lucia A. and Inge Røpke (eds) (2004), *The Ecological Economics of Consumption*, Cheltenham, UK and Northampton, MA, USA: Edward Elgar.

Richins, M.L. (1997), 'Measuring emotions in the consumption experience', *Journal of Consumer Research*, **24** (September), 127–46.

Ringold, Debra Jones (2002), 'Boomerang effect: in response to public health interventions: some unintended consequences in the alcoholic beverage market', *Journal of Consumer Policy*, **25** (1), 27–63.

Røpke, I. (1999), 'The dynamics of willingness to consume', *Ecological Economics*, **28** (3), 399–420.

Røpke, I. (2006), 'Consumption and environment: ecological economic perspectives', PhD thesis, University of Roskilde, Denmark, Department of Environment, Technology and Social Studies.
Schwartz, S.H. (1977), 'Normative influences on altruism', in L. Berkowitz (ed.), *Advances in Experimental Social Psychology*, 10th edn, New York: Academic Press, pp. 221–79.
Schwender, C., D. Mocigemba and S. Otto (2007), 'Der "Ecotainment"-Index. Ein Instrument zur Messung kognitiver und emotionaler Wirkung von TV-Beiträgen', *Zeitschrift für Medienpsychologie*, **19** (2), 46–57.
Schwender, C., D. Mocigemba, S. Otto, L.A. Reisch and S. Bietz (2008), 'Learning from commercials – communicating sustainability issues to new audiences: why emotions matter', in Theo Geer Ken, Arnold Tukker, Carlo Vezzoli and Fabrizio Ceschin (eds), *Proceedings of the SCORE! Conference 'Sustainable Consumption and Production: Framework for Action: Refereed Sessions III–IV'*, pp. 353–72, Conference of the Sustainable Consumption Research Exchange (SCORE!) Network, Brussels, 10–11 March 2008, available at http://www.score-network.org/files//24121_CF2_session_3-4.pdf (accessed 23 June 2009).
Shaver, Kelly G. (1985), *The Attribution of Blame: Causality, Responsibility, and Blameworthiness*, New York: Springer.
Siddarth, S. and A. Chattopadhyay (1998), 'To zap or not to zap: a study of the determinants of channel switching during commercials', *Marketing Science*, **17** (2), 124–38.
Smith, W.A. (2006), 'Social marketing: an overview of approach and effects', *Injury Prevention*, **12**, 38–43.
Spash, C.L. (1997), 'Ethics and environmental attitudes with implications for economic valuation', *Journal of Environmental Management*, **50** (4), 403–16.
Spash, C.L. (2000), 'Ecosystems, contingent valuation and ethics: the case of wetlands re-creation', *Ecological Economics*, **34** (2), 195–215.
Spash, C.L. (2006), 'Non-economic motivation for contingent values: rights and attitudinal beliefs in the willingness to pay for environmental improvements', *Land Economics*, **82** (4), 602–22.
Spash, C.L. (2007a), 'The economics of climate change impacts à la Stern: novel and nuanced or rhetorically restricted?', *Ecological Economics*, **63** (4), 706–13.
Spash, C.L. (2007b), 'Deliberative monetary valuation (DMV): issues in combining economic and political processes to value environmental change', *Ecological Economics*, **63** (4), 690–99.
Spash, C.L. (2008), 'Contingent valuation design and data treatment: if you can't shoot the messenger, change the message', *Environment and Planning C: Government and Policy*, **26** (1), 34–53.
Stern, P.C. (2000), 'Toward a coherent theory of environmentally significant behaviour', *Journal of Social Issues*, **56** (3), 407–24.
Watson, D. and L.A. Clark (1988), 'Development and validation of brief measures of positive and negative affect: the PANAS scales', *Journal of Personality and Social Psychology*, **54** (6), 1063–70.
Wolburg, Joyce (2006), 'College students' responses to antismoking messages: denial, defiance, and other boomerang effects', *Journal of Consumer Affairs*, **40** (2), 293–323.

PART IV

Structuring Systems of Production

10. Incorporating biophysical foundations in a hierarchical model of societal metabolism

John Gowdy, Mario Giampietro, Jesus Ramos-Martin and Kozo Mayumi

INTRODUCTION[1]

Economic theory is currently in a state of disarray after the collapse of neoclassical welfare economics (NWE) – the organizing framework that dominated economic theory and policy for the 50-year period following the Second World War (Albert and Hahnel, 1990; Bowles and Gintis, 2000; Colander et al., 2004; Davis, 2006). Devastating theoretical critiques of the Walrasian system have been made for decades. Indeed one could argue that the critics have won decisively every major theoretical battle (King, 2002). Yet until recently the NWE model continued its dominance because its supporters simply ignored the mounting theoretical paradoxes and inconsistencies that helped ultimately to undermine the system. The overwhelming dominance of neoclassical economists in the most prestigious universities and on editorial boards of the most prominent journals also helped to maintain the oligopoly of Walrasian theory throughout the later part of the twentieth century (Hodgson and Rothman, 1999).

The NWE model finally began to crumble in the face of overwhelming empirical evidence that the basic behavioral model, *Homo economicus*, offered a poor description of actual human behavior (Gintis, 2000; Henrich et al., 2001; Sen, 1977) and that it led to erroneous predictions and policy disasters (Kahneman, 1994; Stiglitz, 2002). The empirical assault was ultimately more successful than the theoretical one because it confronted the neoclassical paradigm on its own terms using its own criteria (Gowdy, 2004). It is fair to say that the majority of top economic theorists today reject the core assumptions of the NWE model. Most recent winners of the Nobel Prize in Economics were chosen because their work moved beyond the simple assumptions of rational economic man and perfect competition – two assumptions necessary to hold the NWE system together.

An important reason for the success of behaviorist criticism was that NWE contained a model of human behavior. Even though it was a poor representation of actual behavior, *Homo economicus* did provide a starting point for empirical testing. Production theory provides a much more difficult challenge. As many Post Keynesian economists have pointed out, there is no neoclassical theory of production. Historically, NWE was developed as a description of how consumers allocate limited income to get the maximum satisfaction from spending on consumer goods. This model of allocation in consumption was simply transferred to production to describe how firms with limited budgets optimally allocate 'inputs' to maximize production or profits. So although NWE has a rudimentary theory of the origin of 'wants' (people are greedy, hedonistic, self-centered and self-regarding), it contains nothing whatsoever about the origin of inputs (factors of production). There is no concept in NWE of production as a physical system requiring the transformation of nature, including human labor power, into commodities. Developing realistic models of economic production, including the role of inputs from nature and the influence of human institutions, is one of the greatest challenges facing economists today. This chapter is a modest step toward the goal of developing a biophysical approach to the analysis of economic production.

The remainder of the chapter is organized as follows. The next section gives a brief history of production theory documenting the abandonment of real production by NWE. The third section presents some existing alternatives to neoclassical production theory including the work of Pasinetti, Sraffa and Steedman. We then present a new model of production developed by Giampietro and Mayumi (2000a, 2000b) based on Georgescu-Roegen's (1984) flow-fund model. The following section uses this model to examine the growth of the Chinese economy, 1980–99. The last section concludes.

THE ABANDONMENT OF PRODUCTION IN ECONOMIC THEORY

For the classical economists – Smith, Ricardo, Malthus, Mill, Marx – production was central to economic analysis. Adam Smith provided insights into the social and physical reasons for increasing returns to scale, the division of productive income among social classes, and the relationship between wages and the subsistence requirements of workers (Smith, 1937 [1776]). His first major work, *The Theory of Moral Sentiments* (1976 [1759]), was in some ways a more 'modern' work than *The Wealth of Nations* since its themes of social interaction and cooperation are echoed in contemporary work in behavioral economics. Ricardo wrote extensively on the topic of diminishing returns to scarce natural resources (coining the term 'rent'). Malthus's (1926 [1798]) insights into the relationship between population growth and agricultural production are still being debated today. Marx (1959 [1878]) made a critical distinction between 'wealth' and 'value' and recognized that nature was the ultimate source of all wealth (Gowdy, 1988).

After the marginalist revolution, beginning in the 1870s, economists all but abandoned questions of physical production and distribution and focused on the mathematical representation of the utility of isolated individuals. In response to the political implications of Marx's labor theory of value, economists such as Böhm-Bawerk and Menger developed a theory of commodity value based on marginal utility and an analogous theory of distribution based on the value of the marginal product (Campus, 1987).

In the last decades of the nineteenth century Edgeworth, Pareto and Walras developed an elaborate mathematical system of value and utility optimization based on notions borrowed from mechanics, most notably, equilibrium within a field of forces (Mirowski, 1989). To some extent Pareto and Walras built on earlier utilitarian notions of human nature, drawing on a line of reasoning from Hobbes, Smith and Mill based on the idea of 'natural man' independent of society.[2] Utility theory also had a testable model of human behavior embodied in 'economic man' (although this model is clearly falsified by contemporary behavioral research).

The thermodynamic model of equilibrium in a field of forces was adopted by economists in the 1870s and by the 1890s, through the work of Wicksell and Wicksteed (Mirowski, 1989). That model was applied to production by merely relabeling the contents of the utility model. Instead of consumers exchanging a fixed amount of goods to maximize utility, firms exchanged a fixed amount of inputs to maximize production. Rather than building on classical theories of production, neoclassical economists discarded the work of earlier economists like Smith, Ricardo and Jevons who gave a central place to the role of natural resources in economic production. The result was not a model of production but rather a model of the efficient allocation of an existing collection of productive inputs and a predetermined allocation of these inputs. Pasinetti (1977, pp. 25–6) writes of the Walrasian model:

> The model clearly has nothing to do with the phenomenon of production. The problem it deals with is the optimal allocation, through exchange, of a certain initial endowment and distribution of resources . . . It became necessary to shape a theory of production (which by its very nature is concerned with *flows*) in such a way as to meet the requirements of a preexisting theory concerning the optimal 'allocation' of certain *stocks* of resources. This feature of marginal theory has proved itself to be of crucial importance for subsequent theoretical

developments, because it has inevitably contributed to keeping the phenomenon of production in a secondary and subordinate position.

The neoclassical theory of production was a clear break with classical economics. The fact that production requires physical inputs (natural resources and labor) subject to decreasing physical returns was not really compatible with the notion of 'equilibrium within a field of forces' and over the course of the twentieth century the categories 'land' and 'labor' were more or less banished from the theory of production. Every input became a kind of capital and the engine of economic growth became 'technology', an amorphous concept more in tune with the abstraction 'utility' than with the physical reality of production. This is clear in the notion of the neoclassical production function. Consider the still widely used Cobb–Douglas function: $Q = AK^{\alpha}L^{1-\alpha}$ where $1 > \alpha > 0$. The parameter A is considered to be 'pure technological change', independent of productive inputs. Technology in the neoclassical system is some sort of amorphous force that can increase the productive power of the economy without limit. If one assumes that there are no diminishing returns to technology, then there is no need to worry about the scarcity of any particular productive input. Any particular scarcity can be overcome through substitution and by applying more technology. In the core Walrasian model, not only is utility independent of society and the biophysical world, but so is production. Not only is the agent of consumption a 'homogeneous globule of desire' (Veblen, 1898); that desire can be satisfied by a 'homogenous globule of technology' independent of time and space.

Neoclassical 'growth theory' models merely duplicate the Edgeworth Box of exchange by allocating growth rates of inputs, or ratios of growth rates, instead of the inputs themselves (see Solow, 1956; Romer, 1986). These models do not depict production in any engineering, physical sense. They have no notion of time[3] as an unfolding historical phenomenon or actual physical production processes (Shaikh, 1974). As is often the case with neoclassical theory, more is claimed for these models than they can actually deliver. For example, Samuelson (1972, p. 174) states:

> Until the laws of thermodynamics are repealed, I shall continue to relate outputs to inputs – i.e. to believe in production functions. Until factors cease to have their rewards determined by bidding in quasi-competitive markets, I shall adhere to (generalized) neoclassical approximations in which relative factor supplies are important in explaining their market remunerations.

The fact that 'output' requires 'inputs' does not justify ignoring real time, or assuming constant returns to scale and the near perfect substitutability that the Walrasian production function requires. Nor does it justify ignoring political power, market power, and social and economic history by assuming that competitive markets alone determine factor prices.

When the neoclassical production function is applied to the issues of environmental and social sustainability the results are predictably sterile. In the Walrasian framework particular problems have nothing to do with absolute scarcity (economic production within a finite world), but only relative scarcity (the static allocation of known quantities of productive inputs). For example, the standard economic analysis of global climate change says nothing about potential social or environmental disruption unless it affects the output of market goods. Moreover, in neoclassical models of sustainability the future time path of technological innovation and its effect on production is assumed to be known, the social discount rate and its time path (usually straight-line discounting) is known, and it is assumed that the socially optimal mix of consumption and investment at all future time points can be determined and fixed at a particular point in time (the present) (Nordhaus, 2001). Within the NWE framework it is justifiable to invest in climate change prevention only if we increase market consumption by doing so, that is, investing in climate change prevention increases the discounted flow of gross domestic product (GDP). Only total GDP matters so the importance of any economic activity is measured solely by its percentage of GDP. Incredibly, respected economists argue that since the only sector likely to be affected by climate is agriculture, and since that sector only represents 3 percent of GDP, we need not worry about its impact (see the quotes by Nordhaus, Beckerman and Schelling in Daly, 2000).

The assumption that only totals matter, one good or one input is as good as another, also clouds neoclassical analysis of critical productive inputs such as energy and labor. For example, in a classic essay about the role of energy in the economy, Manne (1978) argues that energy shortages cannot have a large effect on the economy since energy costs only represent about 5 percent of production costs. The production function approach with its exclusive focus on allocation and its implicit assumption that everything is substitutable has little to say about critical outputs (food) or critical inputs (energy and labor). Again, in these models technology is a solution to everything. Physical reality plays no important role in the standard production function approach.

ALTERNATIVE APPROACHES TO PRODUCTION ANALYSIS

During the long heyday of the neoclassical synthesis not all economists abandoned insights of classical economics. Piero Sraffa (1960), building on the work of Ricardo, constructed a logically tight and consistent model that accomplished two all-important goals: (1) it solved the problem of finding an invariant measure of value; and (2) it provided a devastating critique of neoclassical capital and distribution theory. Sraffa's work was the inspiration for the 'Cambridge criticisms' of neoclassical capital theory developed by Joan Robinson and others (for a thorough discussion see Harcourt, 1972). The Cambridge criticisms were in a sense based on the physical nature of capital as inherently heterogeneous and impossible to aggregate in any realistic sense. Unlike primary inputs like labor and energy it must be measured in monetary units which necessarily depend upon prices and distribution. Sraffa's short book *Production of Commodities by Means of Commodities* (1960) stands as one of the great intellectual achievements of the twentieth century and has spawned several ongoing lines of research extending classical economic thought (Kurz, 2006; Roncaglia, 1991).

Michał Kalecki's work also reflects the classical concern with production. One of his major contributions was to develop a cost-of-production theory of prices – in contrast to the neoclassical demand-determined theory of price. Another major contribution of Kalecki was his emphasis on class conflict and the battle over the proportion of the economic surplus going to owners and workers. Relevant to the issues covered here is Steedman's (1992) criticism of Kalecki for ignoring the reality of production processes that necessarily involve vertical integration and joint production. Most goods produced are neither 'finished goods' nor 'raw materials' but rather intermediate commodities. The notion of vertical integration is a central feature of modern industrial economies and is critical to understanding the importance of primary inputs in economic activity.

Pasinetti's (1977, 1981) basic model of vertical integration has been extended in an input–output framework by Rymes (1983, 1986), Gowdy and Miller (1990), Miller and Gowdy, 1998) and others to take full account of intermediate production and the reproducibility of capital inputs. Indeed, although not normally considered to be a 'theory', input–output analysis offers a well-developed alternative to the neoclassical production function. Dynamic input–output models may be cast in an equilibrium framework but the input–output and 'computable general equilibrium' approaches are distinctly different. An input–output table can be seen as a snapshot of a particular economy at a particular point in time. It need not be interpreted as an equilibrium model in the sense of optimization, stability or having a tendency to return to equilibrium if disturbed. Input–output analysis has been criticized for its fixed coefficient assumption, but evidence suggests that this is a more accurate representation of actual production than the twice-differentiable isoquant of Walrasian theory. Researchers have found that average variable cost curves exhibit constant returns to scale and that firms use the services of capital and labor in fixed proportions even though capital stock is fixed (Miller, 2000). Recent studies by the Federal Reserve Banks and the Bureau of the Census document the ubiquity of fixed proportions in manufacturing (Corrado and Mattey, 1997). These studies found that plants typically change production levels by increasing or decreasing all inputs together by shutting down or reopening entire plants or portions of plants, not by changing the number of hours worked.

Ecological economists have used various forms of input–output to describe the relationship between economic activity, social institutions and environmental features. The extended version of input–output (IO) analysis, the social accounting matrix (SAM), gives a concise view not only of economic flows but also of the interconnections between production sectors, households and primary inputs. In this way, it becomes possible to characterize those complementary aspects of the economic process associated with consumption. This is important because in order to be able to consume more, a socio-economic system has to invest more in the consuming sector in terms of both capital goods and human activity (Zipf, 1941). A further extension using natural resource accounts (NRAs) provides for a supporting environmental or natural resource base in terms of productive inputs required directly from nature and outputs that affect environmental quality. Economic, social, and environmental transactions are captured by IO, SAM and NRAs, respectively. With a quantitative description of these flows, a SAM–NRA model can be used to analyze complex scenarios of economic, social and environmental change.

The expanded IO system is superior to the production function approach in depicting a real economy in actual social and environmental context. Still missing, however, are several critical features necessary for analyzing real-world economic–biosphere interactions. Among these are the scale of the human system, vis-à-vis the carrying capacity of the earth's natural systems, and a realistic representation of economic dynamics including synergy, innovation and novelty.

One of the most complete representations to date of an economic–social–biophysical system is Georgescu-Roegen's (1984) flow-fund model. His model is essentially an IO–SAM–NRA model but one that takes into account time duration and irreversible qualitative change. Briefly, Georgescu-Roegen distinguishes between flow coordinates and fund coordinates. Flow coordinates are elements that enter but do not exit the production process or, conversely, elements that exit without having entered the process (for example, a new product). Flow coordinates include matter and energy *in situ*, controlled matter and energy, and dissipated matter and energy. Fund coordinates (capital, people, and Ricardian land) are agents that enter and exit the process, transforming input flows into output flows. Fund coordinates can only be used at a specified rate and must be periodically renewed. Georgescu-Roegen's model can account for scale and time duration and also addresses the question of whether or not a given technology is viable. A technology is viable if and only if an economic system it represents can operate steadily, as long as environmental flows of available energy and matter are forthcoming in necessary amounts in relation to the set of constraints determined by the characteristics of the fund elements (for a more complete explanation of Georgescu-Roegen's model see Mayumi, 2001, Chapter 6).

The essence of Georgescu-Roegen's model is that it recognizes the finiteness and time dependence of the production process. It recognizes that the provision of labor power is a social as well as bioeconomic phenomenon and that energy is a critical input in powering industrial society. An empirical model of production that captures these last two insights is briefly described in the next section and applied to the Chinese economy. The goal of the third section is to illustrate a particular approach that addresses and integrates biophysical and economic aspects across different scales.

MULTI-SCALE INTEGRATED ANALYSIS OF SOCIETAL METABOLISM (MSIASM): AN OVERVIEW OF THE MODEL

The methodology described here is called the Multi-Scale Integrated Analysis of Societal Metabolism (MSIASM). It was formalized by Giampietro and Mayumi (2000a, 2000b) and more systematically investigated by Giampietro (2003). Empirical analyses based on this approach are available for several countries including Ecuador (Falconi-Benitez, 2001), Spain (Ramos-Martin, 2001) and Vietnam (Ramos-Martin and Giampietro, 2005). The basic structure of the MSIASM system is shown in Figure 10.1.

Like Georgescu-Roegen's flow-fund model, the MSIASM model is a bioeconomic model of economic production addressing the biophysical constraints imposed by: (1) the characteristics of those economic elements for the simultaneous activities of production and consumption; (2) the process of capital accumulation; (3) the process of demographic adjustments; and (4) the environmental loading resulting from the metabolism of society and the supply and sink capacity of the ecosystem embedding it. The MSIASM approach looks at the structure of the human economy in terms of two primary inputs: human activity and exosomatic energy.

Human activity has the characteristics of a fund element, requiring

Level n		
FUND ELEMENT		FLOW ELEMENT
Total human activity (THA)	←→	Total exosomatic throughput (TET)
Level $n-1$		
FUND ELEMENT		FLOW ELEMENT
HA_{PW} (paid work)	← production →	ET_{PW} (paid work)
HA_{HH} (household)	← consumption →	ET_{HH} (household)
Level $n-2$		
Subsectors of HA_{PW} (paid work)	←→	Subsectors of ET_{PW} (paid work)
FUND ELEMENT		FLOW ELEMENT
HA_{AG} (agriculture)	←→	ET_{AG} (agriculture)
HA_{PS} (production)	←→	ET_{PS} (production)
HA_{GS} (government and services)	←→	ET_{GS} (government and services)

Figure 10.1 The MSIASM system of accounts

investment in reproduction and determining a social and biophysical constraint on the supply and demand of labor time. The total budget of human activity represents, on the time scale of one year, the given endowment of hours for which the two complementing compartments of production and consumption compete. Total human activity (THA) is the total time available for the whole population (the size of population times 24 hours times 365 days).

Exosomatic energy has the characteristics of a flow element mapping onto the level of economic activity in each economic compartment. Exosomatic energy input is measured in joules per year. The total exosomatic throughput (TET) represents, again on the time scale of one year, the total energy dissipated by a socio-economic system for supporting the activities of production and consumption. TET is calculated by the 'joules equivalent' of a particular type of reference energy source (for example oil equivalent) per year used by the economy.

Each of these two primary inputs (THA and TET) defined at the level of the whole socio-economic system (level n) is disaggregated further – at the level $n-1$ – into two compartments: (1) production – which is measured by the fraction of the total (both of human activity and energy) invested in economically productive activity; and (2) consumption – which is measured by the fraction of the total (both of human activity and energy) invested in household activity. The compartment of productive activity – as defined at the level $n-1$ – is further disaggregated, at the level $n-2$, into three broad sectors: agriculture, production, and services and government. The same disaggregation can be done for the components of consumption.

From these accounts the following relationships between human activity, energy throughput and economic output can be calculated:

1. The annual average exosomatic metabolic rate: $EMR_{SA} = TET / THA$ (the amount of energy used per total available human labor time) – at the level n.
2. The sectorial exosomatic metabolic rate: ET_i / HA_i (EMR for each sector) – for levels below level n.
3. The saturation index of human labor: $SI = HA_{PW} / THA$ (the ratio of human labor time used for paid work) – this index characterizes the split of human activity between production and consumption. In this system of accounting the compartment of consumption includes the overhead of human activity, which is required for the reproduction of the fund element human activity, which is supplying labor power (that is, it determines the dependency ratio in the population).
4. The saturation index of exosomatic energy: ET_{PW} / TET (the ratio of exosomatic energy used for paid work) – this index characterizes the split of the total exosomatic throughput consumed by the economy between production and consumption. In this system of accounting the compartment of production includes the overhead of energy, which is consumed for the reproduction of the productive sector.

These relationships can be used to characterize the exosomatic energy metabolism of a society by linking these variables belonging to different hierarchical levels and scales. The term 'societal metabolism' indicates that this biophysical characterization of the economic process refers to the overall pattern of production and consumption. This characterization is obtained by mapping a key flow element (in this example 'exosomatic energy consumption') against a key fund element (in this example 'human activity'). Such a mapping is obtained simultaneously on different hierarchical levels: (1) at the level n over the whole economy; (2) at the level $n-1$ over the two categories of production and consumption; and (3) at the level $n-2$ – for the major subsectors of the productive sector. With this breakdown the MSIASM approach allows for comparisons between elements of a given economic system operating at different hierarchical levels. One can compare, for example, how the amount of energy used per total available human labor time (EMR) of an agricultural sector compares with the average EMR of the whole economy. Comparison can also be made between elements belonging to different economic systems, even of different sizes, but operating at the same hierarchical level (for example, how the EMR of the agricultural sector of China compares with that of Mexico). It is also possible to study mutual constraints determined by the combined characteristics of the relative funds and flow elements at various hierarchical levels.

IMPLEMENTING MSIASM: THE CASE OF CHINA: 1980–99

In the 20-year period analyzed in this study, the Chinese economy has seen an increase in both total energy consumption and energy efficiency (OECD, 2002, 2004). The total primary energy supply rose from 24767 PJ in 1980 to 45493 PJ in 1999 for an average annual growth rate of 3.09 percent. The energy intensity (EI) (MJ/$), that is, the amount of energy per dollar of GDP, decreased from 33.3 MJ/$ in 1980, to 10.4 MJ/$ in 1999 or by an average of 6 percent per year. This is the first peculiarity in the behavior of the Chinese economy.

Even though China is still a developing country having a very low level of GDP per capita and other low levels of economic development indicators, the energy intensity of its economy has been decreasing. It is instructive to look at the effects associated with changes in demographic variables. The Chinese population increased from 841 million people in 1980 to 1253 million in 1999 – an increase of almost 410 million or an average of 2 percent per year. The exosomatic energy metabolism of the society, EMR_{SA}, increased from 2.8 MJ/h in 1980 to 4.1 MJ/h in 1999. These values are still much lower than those for world average (7.8 MJ/h) and considerably lower than the Organisation for Economic Co-operation and Development (OEDC) average of 22.3 MJ/h. The growth rate of population is not so high, but since the number 410 million is so huge, a tremendous amount of energy is required for such a population increase. China represents a case where demographic variables play a decisive role in explaining its lagging structural development.

The MSIASM approach makes it possible to see the evolution of the distribution of THA between paid work activities and non-paid work activities. The allocation of THA to paid work is related to securing the proper function and growth of the system in the short term. The allocation to non-paid work represents the net dissipative aspect of the economy, that we capture in the household sector (HH) that includes non-working people (young and elderly) and non-working or non-paid time of the active population (sleeping, leisure, personal care, education, and so on). This is an overhead required for the reproduction of the fund element human activity, required for the supply of labor power.

The fraction of paid work time in China rose from 14 percent of total available time in 1980 to 18.4 percent in 1999. Therefore, not only did China experience a huge increase in population in absolute terms, but also a growing fraction of its THA was directed to paid work activities. This phenomenon implied an additional challenge in terms of capital accumulation of the economy. In fact, the level of capital accumulation of the Chinese economy had to keep pace not only with the absolute increase of population size, but also with the peculiar demographic trend associated with China's one-child birth control policy, boosting the pace of growth of the workforce. A wave of adults entered the workforce in the period soon after the policy was implemented. Thus, the degree of increase in the extensive variable HA_{PW} was driven by the combined effect of an increase in the extensive variable THA from population growth and by the increase in the fraction of paid work time (the intensive variable SI_{HA}). More capital was required by China not only to deliver more goods, services and infrastructure to the growing population, but also to maintain the previous level of fossil energy input used per hour of paid work (EMR_{PW}) for a growing working population.

Another important aspect of our analysis is to explain the existing profile of distribution of this huge increase of working time in the paid work sector over the different sectors of China's economy. Starting from the data we can say that the fraction of the population working in industry, energy and mining has remained more or less constant, 18 percent of HA_{PW} in 1980 with a slight decrease to a 17 percent of HA_{PW} in 1999. By contrast, the fraction of human activity allocated in agriculture has dramatically decreased. This decrease from 68 percent in 1980 to 47 percent in 1999 implied huge side-effects for the Chinese economy. Abandoning agriculture goes hand in hand with emigration to cities. In turn this requires more infrastructure to cope with the needs of an increasing urban population. However, in spite of this huge demand for new infrastructure, it was the service sector that absorbed this massive shift away from agriculture. In fact, during this time period the percentage of time spent in paid work in the service sector went from 14 percent in 1980 to 36 percent in 1999. Considering China's population growth in this period, and the dramatic increase in the time per person devoted to paid work, this is a phenomenal change.

Why are the industry, energy and mining sectors not absorbing the massive flow of working time escaping the agricultural sector, at a time when more infrastructure and more consumer goods are necessary? This would be the typical path of countries undergoing rapid industrialization

Table 10.1 Exosomatic energy metabolism by sector, 1980 and 1999

	1980 (MJ/hour)	1999 (MJ/hour)
EMR_{PW}	18	15.8
EMR_{PS}	92.9	80.9
EMR_{SG}	4.6	3.0
EMR_{AG}	1.0	1.3

in the history of developed economies. In order to answer this question we have to check both the relative levels of exosomatic energy metabolism of the different sectors in the Chinese economy and their evolution over time.

Looking at Table 10.1 we can recognize two points. The three different sectors do have very different metabolic rates, as was expected. Therefore, the general benchmark value for $\mathrm{EMR_{PW}}$ does not provide much information about typologies of metabolism of lower-level sectors. Rather, such a value is determined by: (1) the characteristic value of $\mathrm{EMR_i}$ of the subsectors; and (2) by the profile of distribution of the workforce over the subsectors.

An increase in EMR_{PW} would imply that the country is accumulating capital per worker by increasing the amount of exosomatic devices and consumption of energy invested per hour of working time in the productive sectors over time. Actually, this has not been happening in China. In fact, for the economy as a whole EMR_{PW} has dropped from 18 MJ/h in 1980 to 15.81 MJ/h in 1999. This same tendency is observed in the industry, energy and mining sector, where EMR_{PS} moved from 92.9 MJ/h in 1980 to 80.9 MJ/h, and in the services and government sector, where $\mathrm{EMR_{SG}}$ moved from 4.6 MJ/h in 1980 to 3 MJ/h in 1999. The only sector that showed an increase – even if very slightly – with respect to its exosomatic metabolic rate, is the agricultural sector. It moved from an EMR_{AG} of 1 MJ/h in 1980 to an EMR_{AG} of 1.3 MJ/h in 1999. However, this benchmark value remains absolutely low when compared with international standards (for example much lower than the metabolism of the household sector in developed countries; see for instance Ramos-Martin, 2001). This slight increase can easily be explained by the massive reduction of the working population within the agriculture sector, whereas the area in production and relative input use in agriculture was not reduced proportionally.

How is it possible that China, one of the fastest-growing economies of the world, despite the huge increase in energy consumption in the period considered, is reducing the level of biophysical capitalization – indicated by the level of EMR – of its more strategically important sectors (industry, energy and mining; services and government) over time? We gave a partial answer to this question earlier, when mentioning the effect of demographic changes. But there is another important aspect to be considered before arriving at a more plausible explanation.

Looking at the relative value of EMR of these three sectors (Table 10.1) we can immediately see that moving an hour of human activity from the agriculture sector to the industry, energy and mining sector requires a dramatic increase of the rate of exosomatic metabolism. Not only does this imply a dramatic increase of energy consumption per hour of work, but it also requires investing to provide the capital capable of amplifying the use of energy per hour of work. This explains why the massive move away from agriculture, for the moment, is absorbed by the services and government sector. In fact, such a transfer implies 'only' an increase in EMR of 2.4 times (from 1.3 MJ/hour in the agriculture sector to 3.1 MJ/hour in the services and government sector), whereas a move from the agriculture sector to the industry, energy and mining sector implies an increase in EMR of 62.2 times (from 1.3 MJ/hour in EMR_{AG} to 80.9 MJ/hour EMR_{PS}). Therefore, it is no wonder that China has not had considerable increases in the relative value taken by HA_{PS}. Actually, the slight decrease of this sector over time seems to indicate that for the moment it is a continuous increase in productive efficiency that makes it possible to hold such a value constant (the economic investments in this sector are associated with better technology reducing the requirement for labor).

At this point we can clearly see a combined effect of three factors: (1) population growth – an absolute increase in THA; (2) the extraordinary growing fraction of working population within the given THA – that in China is now almost 60 percent (versus the 50 percent value level found in Australia, the United States and Canada, and the 40 percent value level of many European countries); (3) the massive switch of working activity away from the agricultural sector, which has the lowest exosomatic metabolic rate, toward the relatively more energy-intensive services and government sector. The combination of these three factors generated a 'mission impossible syndrome' for increasing the level of energy metabolized per worker in the two sectors SG – services and government; and PS – industry, energy and mining. In spite of the formidable increase in energy consumption and the wave of investment in the different sectors which occurred in China in the period 1990–1999, the increase in the supply of exosomatic devices and input of energy in these two sectors has not been able to match the pace of increase in the size of the labor force (HA_{PS} and HA_{SG}). This is why the characteristic benchmarks of the exosomatic metabolic rate of these two sectors – EMR_{PS} and EMR_{SG} – have been falling, as shown in Table 10.1.

China has been burdened by its large population, resulting in a very low return per hour of labor for agricultural activities based on farms of less than 1 hectare (Giampietro et al., 1999), and by demographic trends induced by the one-child policy aimed at reducing population growth. From the above analysis it is clear that China faces a daunting dilemma. To become a modern economy, the country has to invest huge amounts of money and energy: (1) to build infrastructure for the rapidly growing urban population; (2) to develop new industries to increase the level of accumulated capital so that the increase in labor productivity can be based not only on low-cost labor but also on technological productivity; and (3) to increase domestic final consumption in order to improve the material standard of its population. From an economic point of view, the latter is also necessary for helping build up an internal market large enough to make the Chinese economy more robust, stable and resilient to fluctuations in the US dollar.

In spite of its spectacular rate of economic growth in the period 1980–1999, China faces an uncertain future. Looming energy shortages and terrible environmental degradation threaten to undermine the economic progress made so far. Growing social unrest has been kept in check so far only by increasingly repressive measures by the government. China's rapid growth in military spending is an increasing source of tension with its international trading partners. Tackling this complex set of issues requires a characterization of its economic development which must be capable of considering different dimensions of analysis based on different typologies of constraints and different scales. It is our opinion that empirical models which address and integrate biophysical and socio-economic analysis across different scales can provide more robust and useful insights and indications than models based on conventional economic analysis.

CONCLUSION

A great contribution of Post Keynesian economics has been to provide a systematic critique of the Walrasian model of production. Post Keynesians and related schools of thought incorporated the classical concepts of commodity production, the class conflict over the annual social surplus, and the importance of real physical costs. Theoretically consistent production models based on the work of Pasinetti, Rymes, Sraffa and others using vertically integrated input–output relationships have proved to be powerful tools in characterizing the structure of modern economies. In this chapter we have extended the model of production to the whole pattern of production and consumption in addition to capital accumulation characterized on different hierarchical levels, in order to emphasize the biophysical nature of human activity. The energy and mineral bonanza of the twentieth century put the issue of biophysical limits on the back burner for neoclassical and heterodox economists alike. The simple relationships between human activity, energy use and economic production derived from the MSIASM approach can shed a great deal of light on comparative economic systems and the historical development of selected economies. The case of China is particularly interesting in terms of both its recent rapid development, and its looming challenges in making the transition to a sustainable, modern economy. In the coming years it will be interesting to see if the predictions of the MSIASM system come to pass.

NOTES

1. Two different versions of our chapter were presented at two conferences: (a) the 6th International Conference of the European Society for Ecological Economics in Lisbon, 14–17 June 2005; and (b) the 15th. International Conference on Input–Output Techniques, Renmin University of China, Beijing, China, 27 June–1 July, 2005. Kozo Mayumi would like to acknowledge financial support from the Zengin Foundation for Studies on Economics and Finance in Japan.
2. '[Let us] . . . return again to the state of nature, and consider men as if but even now sprung out of the earth, and suddenly (like mushrooms), come to full maturity, without any kind of engagement with each other' (Thomas Hobbes, 1651, quoted in Bowles, 2004, p. 93).
3. 'Once the equilibrium has been established in principle, exchange can take place immediately. Production, however, requires a certain lapse of time. We shall resolve the second difficulty purely and simply by ignoring the time element at this point' (Walras, *Elements of Pure Economics*, 1977 [1874], p. 242).

REFERENCES

Albert, M. and R. Hahnel (1990), *A Quiet Revolution in Welfare Economics*, Princeton, NJ: Princeton University Press.

Bowles, S. (2004), *Microeconomics: Behavior, Institutions, and Evolution*, Princeton, NJ: Russell Sage Foundation.

Bowles, S. and H. Gintis (2000), 'Walrasian economics in retrospect', *Quarterly Journal of Economics*, **115**, 1411–39.

Campus, A. (1987), 'Marginalist economics', in J. Eatwell, M. Milgate and P. Newman (eds), *The New Palgrave Dictionary of Economics*, Vol. 3, London: Macmillan, pp. 320–22.

Colander, D., R.P.F. Holt and J.B. Rosser (2004), *The Changing Face of Economics: Interviews with Cutting Edge Economists*, Ann Arbor, MI: University of Michigan Press.

Corrado, C. and J. Mattey (1997), 'Capacity utilization', *Journal of Economic Perspectives*, **11**, 151–67.

Daly, H. (2000), 'When smart people make dumb mistakes', *Ecological Economics*, **34**, 1–3.
Davis, J. (2006), 'The turn in economics: neoclassical dominance to mainstream pluralism?', *Journal of Institutional Economics*, **2**, 1–20.
Falconi-Benitez, F. (2001), 'Integrated assessment of the recent economic history of Ecuador', *Population and Environment*, **22** (3), 257–80.
Georgescu-Roegen, N. (1984), 'Feasible recipes and viable technologies', *Atlantic Economic Journal*, **12**, 21–30.
Giampietro, M. (2003), *Multi-Scale Integrated Analysis of Agroecosystems*, New York: CRC Press.
Giampietro, M., S. Bukkens and D. Pimental (1999), 'General trends of technological changes in agriculture', *Critical Reviews in Plant Sciences*, **18**, 261–82.
Giampietro, M. and K. Mayumi (2000a), 'Multiple-scale integrated assessment of societal metabolism: introducing the approach', *Population and Environment*, **22** (2), 109–53.
Giampietro, M. and K. Mayumi (2000b), 'Multiple-scale integrated assessment of societal metabolism: integrating biophysical and economic representations across scales', *Population and Environment*, **22** (2), 155–210.
Gintis, H. (2000), 'Beyond *Homo economicus*: evidence from experimental economics', *Ecological Economics*, **35**, 311–22.
Gowdy, J. (1988), 'The entropy law and Marxian value theory', *Review of Radical Political Economics*, **20**, 34–40.
Gowdy J. (2004), 'The revolution in welfare economics and its implications for environmental valuation and policy', *Land Economics*, **80**, 239–57.
Gowdy, J. and J. Miller (1990), 'Harrod–Robinson–Read measures of primary input productivity: theory and evidence from US data', *Journal of Post Keynesian Economics*, **12**, 591–604.
Harcourt, G. (1972), *Some Cambridge Controversies in the Theory of Capital*, Cambridge: Cambridge University Press.
Henrich, J., R. Boyd, S. Bowles, C. Camerer, E. Fehr, H. Gintis and R. McElreath (2001), 'In search of *Homo economicus*: behavioral experiments in 15 small-scale societies', *American Economic Review*, **91**, 73–8.
Hodgson, G. and H. Rothman (1999), 'The editors and authors of economics journals: a case of institutional oligopoly?', *Economic Journal*, **109**, F165–F186.
Kahneman, D. (1994), 'New challenges to the rationality assumption', *Journal of Institutional and Theoretical Economics*, **150**, 18–36.
King, J. (2002), *A History of Post Keynesian Economics since 1936*, Cheltenham, UK and Northampton, MA, USA: Edward Elgar.
Kurz, H. (2006), 'The agents of production are the commodities themselves: on the classical theory of production, distribution and value', *Structural Change and Economic Dynamics*, **17**, 1–26.
Malthus, T. (1926 [1798]), *An Essay on the Principle of Population*, London: Macmillan.
Manne, A. (1978), 'The fable of the elephant and the rabbit?', in C.J. Hitch (ed.), *Energy Conservation and Economic Growth*, AAAS Selected Symposium 22, Westview, CT: Westview Press.
Marx, K. (1959 [1878]), 'Critique of the Gotha Program', in L.S. Fever (ed.), *Marx and Engels: Basic Writings on Politics and Philosophy*, New York: Anchor Books.
Mayumi, K. (2001), *The Origins of Ecological Economics: The Bioeconomics of Georgescu-Roegen*, London: Routledge.

Miller, J. and J. Gowdy (1998), 'Vertically integrated measures of the rate of profit in the United States, 1950–1990', *Review of Income and Wealth*, **44**, 555–64.
Miller, R. (2000), 'Ten cheaper spades: production theory and cost curves in the short run', *Journal of Economic Education*, Spring, 119–30.
Mirowski, P. (1989), *More Heat than Light*, Cambridge: Cambridge University Press.
Nordhaus, W. (2001), 'Global warming economics', *Science*, **294**, 1283–4.
OECD (2002), *OECD Statistical Compendium on CD-ROM*, Paris: OECD.
OECD (2004), *OECD Employment Outlook 2004*, Paris: OECD.
Pasinetti, L. (1977), *Lectures on the Theory of Production*, New York: Columbia University Press.
Pasinetti, L. (1981), *Structural Change and Economic Growth: A Theoretical Essay on the Dynamics of the Wealth of Nations*, Cambridge: Cambridge University Press.
Ramos-Martin, J. (2001), 'Historical analysis of energy intensity of Spain: from a "conventional view" to an "integrated assessment"', *Population and Environment*, **22** (3), 281–313.
Ramos-Martin, J. and M. Giampietro (2005), 'Multi-scale integrated analysis of societal metabolism: learning from trajectories of development and building robust scenarios', *International Journal of Global Environmental Issues*, **5**, 225–63.
Romer, P. (1986), 'Increasing returns and long-run growth', *Journal of Political Economy*, **99**, 1002–37.
Roncaglia, A. (1991), 'The Sraffian schools', *Review of Political Economy*, **3**, 187–219.
Rymes, T.K. (1983), 'More on the measurement of total factor productivity', *Review of Income and Wealth*, **29**, 297–316.
Rymes, T.K. (1986), 'The measurement of multi-factor productivity in an input–output framework: new Canadian estimates', in A. Franz and N. Rainer (eds), *Problems of Compilation of Input–Output Tables*, Vienna: Orac-Verlag.
Samuelson, P.A. (1972), *The Collected Scientific Papers of P.A. Samuelson*, J.E. Stiglitz (ed.), Cambridge, MA: MIT Press.
Sen, A. (1977), 'Rational fools: a critique of the behavioral foundations of economic theory', *Philosophy and Public Affairs*, **6**, 317–44.
Shaikh, A. (1974), 'Laws of production and laws of algebra: the HUMBUG production function', *Review of Economics and Statistics*, **56**, 115–20.
Smith, A. (1937 [1776]), *The Wealth of Nations*, New York: Modern Library.
Smith, A. (1976 [1759]), *Theory of Moral Sentiments*, Oxford: Clarendon Press.
Solow, R.M. (1956), 'A contribution to the theory of economic growth', *Quarterly Journal of Economics*, **70**, 65–94.
Sraffa, P. (1960), *Production of Commodities by Means of Commodities*, Cambridge: Cambridge University Press.
Steedman, I. (1992), 'Questions for Kaleckians', *Review of Political Economy*, **4**, 125–51.
Stiglitz, J. (2002), *Globalization and its Discontents*, New York: W.W. Norton.
Veblen, T. (1898), 'Why is economics not an evolutionary science?', *Quarterly Journal of Economics*, **12**, 373–97.
Walras, L. (1977 [1874]), *Elements of Pure Economics*, Fairfield, CT: A.M. Kelley.
Zipf, G.K. (1941), *National Unity and Disunity: The Nation as a Bio-Social Organism*, Bloomington, IN: Principia Press.

11. Theoretical and policy issues in complex Post Keynesian ecological economics

J. Barkley Rosser, Jr

INTRODUCTION

Post Keynesian economics contains competing approaches (King, 2002). One group draws on Keynes (1936) to emphasize the role of fundamental uncertainty in economics, that which cannot be characterized by a known probability distribution (Davidson, 1982–83, 1994). Another focuses more on specific models of macroeconomic dynamics, or macrodynamics, often relying upon non-linear relations in the economy that can lead to complex endogenous fluctuations. This group often looks to the work of Kalecki (1935, 1971) for its inspiration, although such figures as Kaldor (1940), Goodwin (1951) and even Hicks (1950) played important roles in its development.

I (Rosser, 2006) have proposed that the fact that each of these approaches draws partly from, or has influenced the perspective of complex economic dynamics, may provide some degree of unity in the conflicts between these schools. Complexity underlies uncertainty, which deeply drives the policy issues, which becomes especially clear for the case of the most dramatic of ecological economics issues, that of global warming (Spath, 2002).

This chapter extends this argument, with the focus now being more specifically on ecological economic systems and their forms of dynamic complexity. On the one hand foundational ideas of dynamic complexity have arisen from the study of ecological systems. On the other, the interlinkages of ecological with economic systems can be seen to be a special source of complex dynamics in the combined systems. An example of an idea from ecology that directly influenced macrodynamic theory is that of the predator–prey model, first applied to macroeconomics by Goodwin (1967). Predators overeat prey, whose declining population then drives down the predator population, which then allows the prey population to recover, which allows the predator population to increase, which in turn again pushes down the prey population, in a cyclical dynamic. An example of the latter is the variety of complex dynamics that can arise in fisheries through the interaction of non-linearities in the biodynamics of fish populations with non-linearities in the behavior of the fishers (Hommes and Rosser, 2001), which can also be seen ultimately as predator–prey dynamics, with humans the predators.

WHAT ARE COMPLEX DYNAMICS?

The Massachusetts Institute of Technology (MIT) physicist, Seth Lloyd, famously collected at least 45 different definitions of 'complexity' (Horgan, 1997, p. 303, footnote 11), with many of these involving some form or variation of algorithmic or other computationally related definitions of complexity. Some have long advocated the use of such definitions in economics (Albin with Foley, 1998), with a recent upsurge of such advocacy (Markose, 2005; Velupillai, 2005). While these approaches may involve more rigorous definitions than other approaches, they are less useful for the analysis of ecological economic systems than more explicitly dynamic definitions. Indeed, some of the critics of dynamic approaches criticize them precisely because of their dependence on biological analogies and concepts (McCauley, 2004, Chapter 9).

We shall stick with the dynamic definition I (Rosser, 1999) adopted from Day (1994), given its usefulness for models involving ecology. This definition is that a system is dynamically complex if it endogenously does not converge on a point, a limit cycle, or an explosion or implosion,[1] or more generally that the system's endogenous and deterministic dynamics exhibit some degree of irregularity such as sudden discontinuities or an apparently random pattern that is not really random. A characteristic of such dynamically complex systems is that they usually involve some non-linearity, although the presence of non-linearity is no guarantee that a system will be dynamically complex. This is true for a single equation system, although Goodwin (1947) showed that a system of coupled linear equations with lags might behave in the manner described here as complex, even though the uncoupled, normalized equivalent is non-linear.

I (Rosser, 1999) characterized this definition as a 'broad tent' one, which included within itself the 'four Cs':[2] cybernetics, catastrophe theory, chaos theory and 'small tent' complexity, associated with heterogeneous interacting agents models. These four approaches appeared on the scene publicly decade after decade, one after the other, even though the mathematical roots of each had been developing over much longer periods of time. Arguably, the first of these has become folded into the last of these currently, while the other two continue to develop on their own separate paths, with numerous applications in pure biology and ecology. Broadly speaking, catastrophe theory studies endogenous discontinuities in certain kinds of dynamical systems that arise as given control variables change continuously, while chaos theory focuses on systems that exhibit sensitive dependence on initial conditions, also known as 'the butterfly effect'. Regarding 'small tent complexity', this originated in models from the 1970s (Schelling, 1971; Föllmer, 1974) in which immediate neighbors affect each other without necessarily directly affecting an entire system, even though these local effects can lead to broader systemic effects through complex emergence.

COMPLEX ECOLOGIC–ECONOMIC DYNAMICS AND (POST) KEYNESIAN UNCERTAINTY

The Debate

Paul Davidson (1994) is the acknowledged leader of what he calls the 'Keynes Post Keynesian' school of economic thought, which emphasizes particularly the role of fundamental uncertainty from the work of Keynes (1921, 1936). A long-running debate between Davidson (1996) and other Post Keynesians (Rosser, 2006) has involved the relationship between complexity theory and the concept of Keynesian uncertainty. While Davidson has rejected complexity theory as not providing an ontological foundation for Keynesian uncertainty, which he insists must be accepted on axiomatic grounds, others have argued that indeed the ubiquity of complex dynamics in economic systems can provide a theoretically and empirically valid foundation for the concept. We shall not regurgitate the details of this debate here further. Rather, we shall consider some ecologic–economic systems that exhibit forms of dynamic complexity that this observer at least believes imply a reasonable form of Keynesian uncertainty. Indeed, the problem of non-quantifiable uncertainty has been one of the biggest issues facing both standard environmental as well as more heterodox ecological economists for some time, with many of these uncertainties deriving from the limits of our scientific knowledge about the environment. These uncertainties lie at the heart of the policy issues confronting ecological economics, such as global warming or the preservation of species in dynamically complex systems.

Catastrophically Discontinuous Ecologic–Economic Systems

Even without interactions with human beings and their economically driven conduct in relation to the natural environment, strictly ecological systems are known to exhibit dynamic discontinuities on their own. Some are known to exhibit multiple equilibria with discontinuities appearing as systems move from one basin of attraction to another dynamically, even without any human input, including the periodic mass suicides of lemmings (Elton, 1924), coral reefs (Done, 1992; Hughes, 1994), kelp forests (Estes and Duggins, 1995), and potentially eutrophic shallow lakes (Schindler, 1990). The latter can be exacerbated by human input as well in combined systems, as humans can flip such a lake from a clear oligotrophic state to a murky eutrophic state by loading phosphorus from fertilizers or other sources (Carpenter et al., 1999; Brock et al., 2002; Wagener, 2003).

A famous example of a cyclical pattern involving two species interacting in which the explosion of population of one leads to a catastrophic collapse of the other is the spruce–budworm cycle of about 40 years in Canadian forests (Ludwig et al., 1978). There is a substantial degree of predictability in this system, given its roughly periodic nature. However, human intervention can affect it in various ways. In particular, human efforts to avoid or overcome the cycle can actually lead to greater discontinuities and larger catastrophic collapses, an observation that underlay Holling's (1973) innovation of the concept of a trade-off between stability and resilience in ecosystems. Furthermore, Holling (1986) has argued that this system can be substantially impacted by small changes in quite distant ecosystems, as for example the draining of wetlands in the mid-US that can lead to fewer birds arriving in Canada from Mexico that eat the budworms and help keep their population under control, an example of 'local surprise, global change'.

The dynamics of this system are given as follows, from Ludwig et al. (1978). Let B equal the budworm population, r_B their natural population growth rate, K_B the budworm carrying capacity (determined by the amount of leaves on the spruce trees), α the predator saturation parameter (a proportion of the budworm carrying capacity), β the maximum rate of predation on the budworms, and u^* the equilibrium leaf volume, then the budworm dynamics in their early stages are given by:

$$dB/Dt = r_B B(1 - B/K_B) - \beta B^2/(\alpha^2 + B^2). \qquad (11.1)$$

Nonzero equililbria are solutions of

$$(r_B K_B/\beta) = u^*/[(\alpha/K^2) + u^{*2})(1 - u^*)]. \qquad (11.2)$$

The set of solutions implied by this system contains a zone of multiple equilibria and associated catastrophic hysteresis loops representing an infected forest.[3] This system is a variation on a predator–prey system, which we shall discuss further below, but note here that the original predatory–prey models studied by Lotka (1920, 1925 [1945]) and Volterra (1926, 1931) showed smooth, interconnected cycles rather than discontinuities, which is somewhat more like what the first empirically studied predatory–prey cycle, that of the Arctic hare and lynx, also tends to show, albeit with some variations.

A classic system subject to multiple equilibria and sudden, catastrophic changes due to human activity is in desert ecosystems, especially in cases where cattle grazing of fragile grasslands is involved (Noy-Meir, 1973; Ludwig et al., 2002; Rosser, 2005). In such cases, fragile rangelands can be overtaken by woody vegetation quite suddenly after an episode of overgrazing. Of course, this is linked to the classic problem of open access, which reflects an institutional failure in the face of certain technological conditions.

Yet another system in which catastrophic declines of populations can happen with this clearly being the result of human activities interacting with the ecosystem, is in fishery dynamics, especially in the famous case of an open-access fishery subject to a backward-bending supply curve (Copes, 1970). Collapses of fisheries are a global problem of enormous consequence and importance, with many such happening, including among others: Antarctic blue and fin whales, Hokkaido herring, Peruvian anchoveta, Southwest African pilchard, North Sea herring, California sardines, Georges Bank herring (and more recently, cod[4] also), and Japanese sardine (Clark, 1985, p. 6), with Jones and Walters (1976) specifically studying the collapse of the Antarctic blue and fin whales using catastrophe theory. A more general approach is provided by Clark (1990), Rosser (2001) and Hommes and Rosser (2001), which is summarized below.

Let x = fish biomass, r = intrinsic fish growth rate, k = ecological carrying capacity, t = time, h = harvest and $F(x) = dx/dt$, the growth rate of the fish without harvest (but limited by the carrying capacity). Then a sustained yield harvest, drawing on Schaefer (1957) is given by:

$$h = F(x) = rx(1 - x/k). \tag{11.3}$$

Let E = catch effort in standardized vessel time, q = catch ability per vessel per day, c = constant marginal cost, p = price of fish, and δ = the time discount rate. Then the basic harvest yield is:

$$h(x) = qEx. \tag{11.4}$$

Hommes and Rosser (2001) show that the supply curve for optimizing fishers is given by:

$$x_\delta(p) = k/4\{1 + (c/pqk) - (\delta/r) + [(1 + (c/pqk) - (\delta/r)^2 + (8c\delta/pqkr)]^{1/2}\}. \tag{11.5}$$

This entire system is depicted in Figure 11.1, with the backward-bending supply curve in the upper right and the yield curve in the lower right. The degree of backward bending is linked to the discount rate, and if it is less than about 2 percent, there is no backward bend, with the curve simply asymptotically approaching the maximum sustained yield of the fishery as the price rises. However, the maximum backward bend occurs when δ is infinite, which gives the case equivalent to the open access case studied by Gordon (1954).

The basic story of fishery collapse is depicted also in the upper right quadrant, where it is presumed that there is a gradual increase in demand, which eventually triggers a sudden increase in price and decrease in the steady-state harvest yield as the system passes through a single equilibrium zone into a three equilibria zone and finally into the single equilibrium zone associated with high price and low harvest yield.

Regarding the implications for Post Keynesian uncertainty theory, while some of these systems have elements of predictability, such as the approximately 40-year periodicity of the spruce–budworm cycle, others do not at all, such as the sudden collapses of overgrazed grasslands or overfished fisheries. The general existence of ecological thresholds is a ubiquitous phenomenon (Muradian, 2001), with the locations of these thresholds generally unknown. Rosser (2001) proposes using the precautionary principle in such cases, and Gunderson et al. (2002) see this as a fundamental problem for maintaining the resilience of threatened ecosystems around the world. This is not to say that extremal events cannot be modeled or their probability come to be known (Embrechts et al., 2003). But a critical threshold of global significance that has not been crossed before with the relevant probability distribution unknown, such as the danger of Greenland or Antarctic ice sheets sliding off suddenly due to global warming, remains subject to and reinforces the problem of Keynesian uncertainty, even if Lloyd's of London is writing catastrophic insurance contracts on beachfront housing against massive flooding. This problem becomes more serious when there is irreversibility within the system (Kahn and O'Neill, 1999).

Chaotic and Other Complex Dynamics in Ecologic–Economic Systems

It was actually from the study of population dynamics in ecology that the term 'chaos' first came to be used for endogenously erratic dynamical systems that exhibit sensitive dependence on initial conditions (May, 1974). Soon after this, actual chaotic dynamics was observed in laboratory

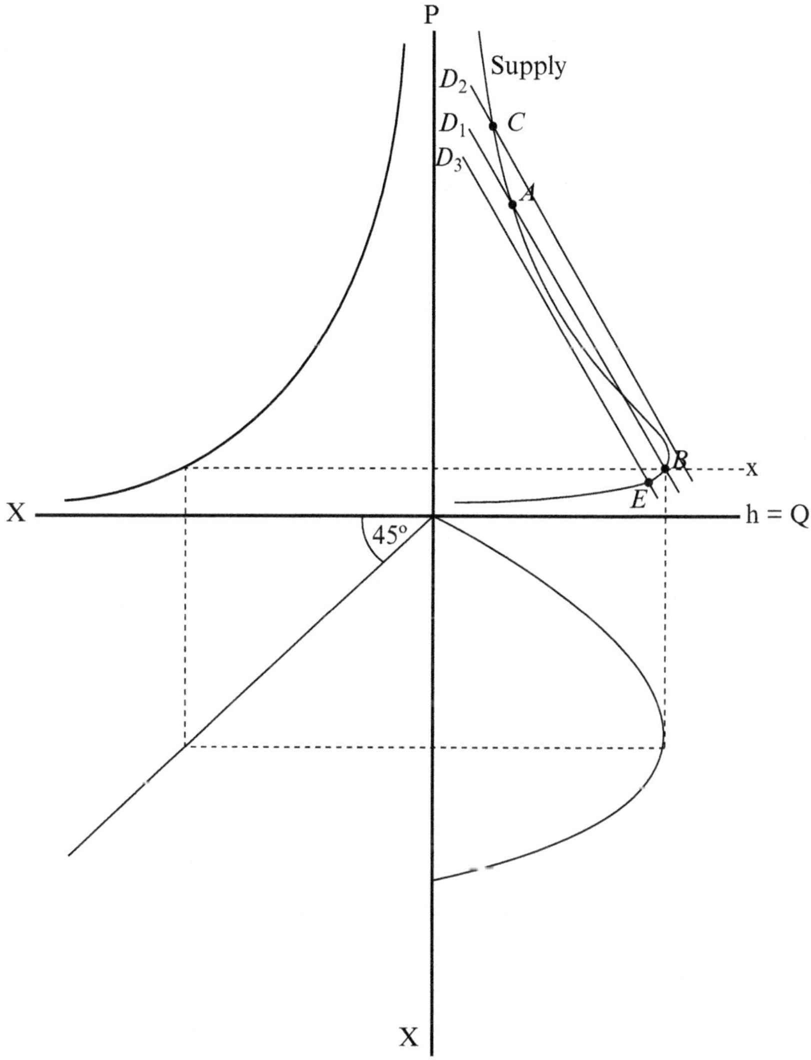

Figure 11.1 Gordon–Schaefer–Clark fishery model

populations of sheep blowflies (Hassell et al., 1976). It has since been argued that one is less likely to observe actual chaotic dynamics in natural populations because of the presence of statistical noise, while at the same time such noise is likely to increase the amplitude of fluctuations that do occur (Zimmer, 1999).

The Gordon–Schaefer–Clark fishery model of Hommes and Rosser

(2001) described above can also be shown to exhibit chaotic dynamics under certain not unreasonable conditions. Letting the demand function be linear of the form:

$$D(p) = A - Bp_t, \quad (11.6)$$

then letting agents follow naive expectations of the form that next period's price will be the same as this period's price leads to cobweb[5] adjustment dynamics of:

$$p_t = D^{-1}S_\delta(p_{t-1}) = [A - S_\delta(p_{t-1})]/B. \quad (11.7)$$

For the case where $B = 0.25$ and A is given a value such that consumer demand will equal the maximum sustained yield at the minimum possible price, Hommes and Rosser (2001) show that as δ increases past 2 percent the supply curve will bend backward and the system will gradually undergo period-doubling bifurcations. Chaotic dynamics will occur in a range for δ between about 8 percent and 10 percent, with the system simply going to the high price, low yield equilibrium for discount rate higher than 10 percent.

Hommes and Rosser then follow earlier work of Hommes and Sorger (1998), who in turn followed an argument due to Grandmont (1998), which shows that in a chaotic environment, agents following a relatively simple adjustment rule might be able to 'learn to believe in chaos' and adjust to follow the underlying chaotic dynamic according to a consistent expectations equilibrium.

The possibility of chaotic dynamics in fisheries has been studied by others as well, with Conklin and Kolberg (1994) showing it for reasonable parameters in the case of a halibut fishery when the supply curve is bending backwards. Furthermore, Doveri et al. (1993) have shown the possibility of chaotic dynamics in a multiple-species aquatic ecosystem.

The fishery model laid out above and studied by Hommes and Rosser (2001) can also be shown to exhibit yet another complex phenomenon that increases the difficulty of making clear forecasts and of experiencing sudden changes in the dynamic pattern of a system. This is the phenomenon of the coexistence of multiple basins of attraction in which the boundaries between these basins may have a fractal shape, leading to a complex interpenetration of one basin by another or by several others. This phenomenon has been demonstrated for the Hommes–Rosser model by Foroni et al. (2003). The possibility of such dynamics in a purely economic model was first demonstrated by Lorenz (1992) for a variation of the Kaldor (1940) macroeconomic model. With such fractal boundaries, small changes in parameter values can push the system from one basin of attraction into another with little predictability.

Finally, we move to a much grander scale perspective to consider the possibility of chaotic dynamics involving the combined, global economic–climatic system. Chen (1997) has shown the possibility of such chaotic dynamics at such a level. In his model, he has two sectors, agriculture and manufacturing. Global temperature is a linear function of the level of manufacturing, but agriculture is a quadratic function of global temperature. With some assumptions regarding price-setting between the two sectors, he is able to show the possibility of chaotic dynamics in both global temperature as well as the sectoral levels of output and prices.

At this point we need to remind ourselves that chaotic dynamics most thoroughly undermine any form of simple forecasting. Slight changes in initial points or parameter values can lead to substantial changes in dynamic paths. This is one way in which the possibility of complex dynamics provides a conceptual foundation for the concept of fundamental Keynesian uncertainty.

ECOLOGICAL FOUNDATIONS OF COMPLEX POST KEYNESIAN MACRODYNAMICS

We have already noted the fact that the early Post Keynesian economics models involving non-linear relations in investment or other macro relations were the foundation of realization for economics more broadly of the possibility of endogeneity of macro fluctuations (Rosser, 2006), a development initiated by Kalecki (1935). These earlier Post Keynesian models (not labeled as such when they first appeared), which contained non-linear elements, usually in the relevant investment equation, would later be shown to imply the possibility of complex dynamics. These later manifestations of their inherent complexity came to play an important role in the more general recognition that non-linearity can lead to endogenously complex dynamics in macroeconomic models.

Among the most important of those involved in these efforts was Richard Goodwin (1947, 1951, 1967), with Strotz et al. (1953) showing the first chaotically dynamic economic model, based on Goodwin (1951) with its non-linear accelerator, even as they did not understand what they had discovered. His 1967 model more explicitly drew on ecological predecessors in the form of the predator–prey model of Lotka (1920, 1925) and Volterra (1926, 1931). Ironically for the old Marxist, Goodwin, in his model it is the workers with their wage demands who play the role of the 'predators', with their wage demands bringing about the reversal of the investment-driven capitalist expansion. Goodwin's (1967) model of business cycles is given by the following, where W = wages. Y = national GDP, with $W/Y = \omega$, the workers' share, L = employed workers, N = population of labor force, hence L/N = the rate of employment, which is given by λ, with $P(\lambda)$ being a linear Phillips curve relation between the rate of employment and the rate of changes of wages, K = the capital stock, $v = K/Y$, the accelerator relation, α is the rate of technological change, and β is the rate of population growth. From all of this the Goodwin (1967) model can be given as

$$d\omega/dt = \omega[\, P(\lambda) - \alpha], \tag{11.8}$$

$$d\lambda/dt = \lambda[(1 - \omega)/v - \alpha - \beta] \tag{11.9}$$

While Goodwin initially only studied the endogenous limit cycle easily implied by these equations, Pohjola (1981) would show that with certain parameter values in a discrete form, this model can generate chaotic dynamics, extending a version of the model developed by Desai (1973), with Goodwin (1990) himself later fully examining these implications.

A similar history has occurred with regard to the predator–prey model itself in ecology, one of the most important and widely used models of population dynamics among species. The original formulation due to Lotka and Volterra only generated simple oscillations, limit cycles. Given their regular periodicity, these seemed to fit available field data, for example from the famous Arctic hare and lynx cycle from Canada for which the Hudson Bay Company had compiled a several centuries-long data set, which showed a cycle of about 10–11 years in length of the two interrelated populations, based on pelts sold to the company by Indians who hunted the species.

However, a complication is that whereas in the simple theoretical model amplitude is constant from period to period, this is not the case in the field data. Such fluctuations of amplitude with a roughly constant period are consistent with chaotic or semi-chaotic variation of the predator–prey model, which can arise with appropriate lagging or further non-linearities. Such non-linearities can enter in through the recognition of the role of other species, for example in the hare–lynx model recognizing that when the hare population is sufficiently low, the lynx will switch to pursuing other species. This was the extension that led Schaffer (1984) to be the first to propose the possibility of chaotic dynamics within the hare–lynx cycle, with Solé and Bascompte (2006, pp. 38–42) providing an overview. Shortly, after Schaffer, Brauer and Soudack (1985) showed the possibility of chaotic dynamics in predator–prey fisheries systems with high harvest thresholds. The dynamics of lemmings and Finnish voles have also been seen to be possibly chaotic, or at least semi-chaotic, with periods of unstable chaotic dynamics interspersing with periods of convergence (Ellner and Turchin, 1995; Turchin, 2003). We note the curiosity here that whereas it was from biology that the study of chaotic dynamics entered into economics, with regard to predator–prey models, it was economics that discovered the possibility of chaotic dynamics prior to the ecologists (Pohjola, 1981; Shaffer, 1984).

More recent work has shown the possibility of various other forms of complex dynamics arising with predator–prey systems. Thus, the phenomenon of fractal basin boundaries between multiple basins of attraction has been studied by Gu and Huang (2006) for predator–prey models. Kaneko and Tsuda (2001) provide an even broader array of forms of complex dynamics that can arise in coupled dynamical systems.

Finally, the discussion of predator–prey dynamics has moved to a higher level of macroevolution where chaotically oscillating patterns of phenotype and genotype variation occur over the long periods of evolutionary change within a predator–prey context (Solé and Bascompte, 2006; Sardanyés and Solé, 2007). This pattern in some respects reflects the chaotic long-wave evolutionary dynamics studied by Goodwin (1986).

POLICY IMPLICATIONS

The existence of complex dynamics in ecologic–economic systems complicates policy-making considerably. Rosser (2001) argued that two well-known principles are more important in the face of the threats of possible sudden discontinuities or more erratic dynamic patterns: the precautionary principle and the scale-matching principle. The first is pretty obvious. The existence of thresholds beyond which catastrophic outcomes can occur should induce considerable caution, especially when irreversibilities are involved. How we deal with discovering where those thresholds are and what to do about them remains a problem that veers into that of Keynesian uncertainty, even though some do make efforts to estimate probabilities in these situations. In some cases, such as with the various reports on global warming, probabilities are estimated, but they are done so while ignoring the probabilities of these more disturbing potentially catastrophic events.

Scale-matching is another matter that involves making sure that any policy action is directed at the appropriate level of the ecological hierarchy. Global problems should be dealt with globally; local ones locally. This may seem obvious, but it becomes less obvious when decision-making must interact with the assignment or assessment of property rights. These two must align themselves relevantly with the environmental or ecological effects of a policy or an action (Rosser and Rosser, 2006). It should be kept in mind that mere ownership is not sufficient, as implied by such analysts of the 'common property resource problem' as Gordon (1954). Control of access is the key, and the assignment of property rights must align itself with the ability to control access and achieve environmentally sustainable outcomes.

CONCLUSION

Just as argued by Rosser (2006) that there was an important influence from Post Keynesian economics on the development of complexity theory, so too here we see some elements of influence on more specifically ecological–economic complex systems theory. Indeed, the influence has been both ways as was seen with the role of predator–prey models in Post Keynesian macrodynamics. Many of the deepest themes of the various schools of Post Keynesian economics are most clearly seen in the cases of complex ecologic dynamics, with these themes manifesting themselves most clearly in policy terms in the form of the problem of fundamental Keynesian uncertainty.

NOTES

1. Day (2006, p. 63) has since moved toward favoring a more general definition of complexity taken from the *Oxford English Dictionary*: 'a group of interrelated or entangled relationships'. This more general definition contains the dynamic one that we focus on here, but is perhaps less useful given that the link between Post Keynesian uncertainty and ecological economics is clearest in such dynamically complex systems.
2. This phrase was introduced along with the term 'chaoplexity' by Horgan (1997) to ridicule these ideas.
3. See Rosser (2005) for further discussion of issues related to complex forestry dynamics.
4. See Ruitenback (1996) for a discussion of the collapse of the once great cod fishery off Newfoundland.
5. Chiarella (1988) showed for a wide class of cases that chaotic dynamics can arise with cobweb dynamics. Such dynamics are widespread in agriculture, and various cycles in agriculture, including cattle and pigs, have been argued to be possibly chaotic. For an overview of possible chaotic dynamics in various sub-parts of agriculture, see Sakai (2001).

REFERENCES

Albin, Peter S. with Duncan K. Foley (1998), *Barriers and Bounds to Rationality: Essays on Economic Complexity and Dynamics in Interactive Systems*, Princeton, NJ: Princeton University Press.

Brauer, Fred and A.E. Soudack (1985), 'Optimal harvesting in predator–prey Systems', *International Journal of Control*, **41**, 111–28.

Brock, William A., Karl-Göran Mäler, and Charles Perrings (2002), 'Resilience and sustainability: the analysis of nonlinear dynamic systems', in Lance H. Gunderson and C.S. Holling (eds), *Panarchy: Understanding Transformations in Human and Natural Systems*, Washington, DC: Island Press, pp. 261–89.

Carpenter, Stephen R., Donald Ludwig and William A. Brock (1999), 'Management of eutrophication for lakes subject to potentially irreversible change', *Ecological Applications*, **9**, 751–71.

Chen, Z. (1997), 'Can economic activity lead to climate chaos? An economic analysis on global warming', *Canadian Journal of Economics*, **30**, 349–66.

Chiarella, Carl (1988), 'The cobweb model: its instability and the onset of chaos', *Economic Modelling*, **5**, 377–84.

Clark, Colin W. (1985), *Bioeconomic Modelling and Fisheries Management*, New York: Wiley InterScience.

Clark, Colin W. (1990), *Mathematical Bioeconomics: The Optimal Management of Renewable Resources*, 2nd edn, New York: Wiley InterScience.

Conklin, James E. and William C. Kolberg (1994), 'Chaos for the halibut?', *Marine Resource Economics*, **9**, 153–82.

Copes, Parzival (1970), 'The backward-bending supply curve of the fishing industry', *Scottish Journal of Political Economy*, **17**, 69–77.

Davidson, Paul (1982–83), 'Rational expectations: a fallacious foundation for studying crucial decision-making processes', *Journal of Post Keynesian Economics*, **5**, 182–97.

Davidson, Paul (1994), *Post Keynesian Macroeconomic Theory*, Aldershot UK and Brookfield, VT, USA: Edward Elgar.

Davidson, Paul (1996), 'Reality and economic theory', *Journal of Post Keynesian Economics*, **18**, 479–508.

Day, Richard H. (1994), *Complex Economic Dynamics: An Introduction to Dynamical Systems and Market Mechanism, Volume I*, Cambridge, MA: MIT Press.

Day, Richard H. (2006), 'The complex problem of modelling economic complexity', in Mark Setterfield (ed.), *Complexity, Endogenous Money and Macroeconomic Theory. Essays in Honour of Basil J. Moore*, Cheltenham, UK and Northampton, MA, USA: Edward Elgar, pp. 63–73.

Desai, Meghnad (1973), 'Growth cycles and inflation in a model of class struggle', *Journal of Economic Theory*, **6**, 527–45.

Done, T.J. (1992), 'Phase shifts in coral reef communities and their ecological significance', *Hydrobiology*, **247**, 121–32.

Doveri, F., M. Scheffer, S. Rinaldi, S. Muratori and Y. Kuznetsov (1993), 'Seasonality and chaos in a plankton–fish model', *Theoretical Population Biology*, **43**, 159–83.

Ellner, S. and Peter Turchin (1995), 'Chaos in a noisy world: new methods and evidence from time series analysis', *American Naturalist*, **145**, 343–75.

Elton, Charles S. (1924), 'Periodic fluctuations in the number of animals: their causes and effects', *British Journal of Experimental Biology*, **2**, 119–63.

Embrechts, Paul, Claudia Küppelberg and Thomas Mikosch (2003), *Modelling Extremal Events for Insurance and Finance*, Berlin: Springer.

Estes, J.A. and D. Duggins (1995), 'Sea otters and kelp forests in Alaska: generality and variation in a community ecological paradigm', *Ecological Monographs*, **65**, 75–100.

Föllmer, Hans (1974), 'Random economies with many interacting agents', *Journal of Mathematical Economics*, **1**, 51–62.
Foroni, Ilaria, Laura Gardini and J. Barkley Rosser, Jr (2003), 'Adaptive and statistical expectations in renewable resource markets', *Mathematics and Computers in Simulation*, **63**, 541–67.
Goodwin, Richard M. (1947), 'Dynamical coupling with especial reference to markets having production lags', *Econometrica*, **15**, 181–204.
Goodwin, Richard M. (1951), 'The nonlinear accelerator and the persistence of business cycles', *Econometrica*, **19**, 1–17.
Goodwin, Richard. M. (1967), 'A growth cycle', in C.H. Feinstein (ed.), *Socialism, Capitalism and Economic Growth: Essays Presented to Maurice Dobb*, Cambridge: Cambridge University Press, pp. 54–8.
Goodwin, Richard M. (1986), 'The economy as an evolutionary pulsator', *Journal of Economic Behavior and Organization*, **7**, 341–9.
Goodwin, Richard M. (1990), *Chaotic Economic Dynamics*, Oxford: Oxford University Press.
Gordon, H. Scott (1954), 'Economic theory of a common property resource: the fishery', *Journal of Political Economy*, **62**, 124–42.
Grandmont, Jean-Michel (1998), 'Expectations formation and stability of large socioeconomic systems', *Econometrica*, **66**, 741–81.
Gu, En-Guo and Yibing Huang (2006), 'Global bifurcations of domains of feasible trajectories: an analysis of a discrete predator–prey model', *International Journal of Bifurcations and Chaos*, **16**, 2601–13.
Gunderson, Lance H., C.S. Holling, Lowell Pritchard, Jr and Garry Peterson (2002), 'Understanding resilience: theory, metaphors, and frameworks', in Lance H. Gunderson and Lowell Pritchard, Jr (eds), *Resilience and the Behavior of Large-Scale Systems*, Washington, DC: Island Press, pp. 3–20.
Hassell, M.P., J.H. Lawton and R.M. May (1976), 'Patterns of dynamical behavior of single-species populations', *Journal of Animal Ecology*, **45**, 471–86.
Hicks, John R. (1950), *A Contribution to the Theory of the Trade Cycle*, Oxford: Oxford University Press.
Holling, C.S. (1973), 'Resilience and stability of ecological systems', *Review of Ecology and Systematics*, **4**, 1–24.
Holling, C.S. (1986), 'Resilience of ecosystems: local surprise and global change', in W.C. Clark and R.E. Munn (eds), *Sustainable Development of the Biosphere*, Cambridge: Cambridge University Press, pp. 292–317.
Hommes, Cars H. and J. Barkley Rosser, Jr (2001), 'Consistent expectations equilibria and complex dynamics in renewable resource markets', *Macroeconomic Dynamics*, **5**, 180–203.
Hommes, Cars H. and Gerhard Sorger (1998), 'Consistent expectations equilibria', *Macroeconomic Dynamics*, **2**, 287–321.
Horgan, John (1997), *The End of Science: Facing the Limits of Scientific Knowledge in the Twilight of the Scientific Age*, New York: Broadway Books.
Hughes, T.P. (1994), 'Catastrophes, phase shifts, and large-scale degradation of a Caribbean coral reef', *Science*, **265**, 1547–51.
Jones, Dixon D. and Carl J. Walters (1976), 'Catastrophe theory and fisheries regulation', *Journal of the Fisheries Resource Board of Canada*, **33**, 287–300.
Kahn, James R. and Robert V. O'Neill (1999), 'Ecological interaction as a source of economic irreversibility', *Southern Economic Journal*, **66**, 391–402.

Kaldor, Nicholas (1940), 'A model of the trade cycle', *Economic Journal*, **50**, 78–92.

Kalecki, Michał (1935), 'A macrodynamic theory of business cycles', *Econometrica*, **3**, 327–344.

Kalecki, Michał (1971), *Selected Essays on the Dynamics of the Capitalist Economy*, Cambridge: Cambridge University Press.

Kaneko, Kunihiko and Ichiro Tsuda (2001), *Complex Systems: Chaos and Beyond, a Constructive Approach with Applications in Life Sciences*, Berlin: Springer-Verlag.

Keynes, John Maynard (1921), *Treatise on Probability*, London: Macmillan.

Keynes, John Maynard (1936), *The General Theory of Employment, Interest and Money*, London: Macmillan.

King, John E. (2002) *A History of Post Keynesian Economics since 1936*, Cheltenham, UK and Northampton, MA, USA: Edward Elgar.

Lorenz, Hans-Walter (1992), 'Multiple attractors, complex basin boundaries, and transient motion in deterministic economic systems', in Gustav Feichtinger (ed.), *Dynamic Economic Models and Optimal Control*, Amsterdam: North-Holland, pp. 411–30.

Lotka, Alfred J. (1920), 'Analytical notes on certain rhythmic relations in organic systems', *Proceedings of the National Academy of Sciences, United States*, **6**, 410–15.

Lotka, Alfred J. (1925), *Elements of Physical Biology*, Baltimore, MD: Williams & Williams; reprinted in 1945 as *Elements of Mathematical Biology*.

Ludwig, Donald, Dixon D. Jones and C.S. Holling (1978), 'Qualitative analysis of insect outbreak systems: spruce budworm and forest', *Journal of Animal Ecology*, **47**, 315–32.

Ludwig, Donald, Brian H. Walker, and C.S. Holling (2002), 'Models and metaphors of sustainability, stability, and resilience', in Lance H. Gunderson and Lowell Pritchard, Jr (eds), *Resilience and Behavior of Large-Scale Systems*, Washington, DC: Island Press, pp. 21–48.

Markose, Sheri M. (2005), 'Computability and complexity: markets as complex adaptive systems (CAS)', *Economic Journal*, **115**, F159–F192.

May, Robert M. (1974), 'Biological populations with non-overlapping generations: stable points, cycles, and chaos', *Science*, **186**, 645–7.

McCauley, Joseph P. (2004), *Dynamics of Markets: Econophysics and Finance*, Cambridge: Cambridge University Press.

Muradian, R. (2001), 'Ecological thresholds: a survey', *Ecological Economics*, **38**, 7–24.

Noy-Meir, I. (1973), 'Desert ecosystems: environment and producers', *Annual Review of Ecology and Systematics*, **4**, 353–64.

Pohjola, Matti T. (1981), 'Stable, cyclic, and chaotic growth: the dynamics of a discrete time version of Goodwin's growth cycle', *Zeitschrift für Nationalökonomie*, **41**, 7–38.

Rosser, J. Barkley, Jr (1999), 'On the complexities of complex economic dynamics', *Journal of Economic Perspectives*, **13** (4), 169–92.

Rosser, J. Barkley, Jr (2001), 'Complex ecologic-economic dynamics and environmental policy', *Ecological Economics*, **37**, 23–37.

Rosser, J. Barkley, Jr (2005), 'Complexities of dynamic forest management policies', in Shashi Kant and R. Albert Berry (eds), *Economics, Sustainability, and Natural Resources*, Dordrecht: Springer, pp. 191–206.

Rosser, J. Barkley, Jr (2006), 'Complex dynamics and post Keynesian economics', in Mark Setterfield (ed.), *Complexity, Endogenous Money and Macroeconomic Theory: Essays in Honour of Basil J. Moore*, Cheltenham, UK and Northampton, MA, USA: Edward Elgar, pp. 74–98.

Rosser, J. Barkley, Jr and Marina V. Rosser (2006), 'Institutional evolution of environmental management under global economic growth', *Journal of Economic Issues*, **40**, 421–9.

Ruitenback, H.J. (1996), 'The great Canadian fishery collapse: some policy lessons', *Ecological Economics*, **19**, 103–6.

Sakai, K. (2001), *Nonlinear Dynamics and Chaos in Agricultural Systems*, Amsterdam: Elsevier.

Sardanyés, Josep and Ricard V. Solé (2007), 'Chaotic stability in spatially-revolved host–parasite replicators: the *Red Queen* on a lattice', *International Journal of Bifurcations and Chaos*, **17**, 589–606.

Schaefer, M.B. (1957), 'Some considerations of population dynamics and economics in relation to the management of marine fisheries', *Journal of the Fisheries Resource Board of Canada*, **14**, 669–81.

Schaffer, W.M. (1984), 'Stretching and folding in lynx fur returns: evidence for a strange attractor in nature?', *American Naturalist*, **124**, 796–820.

Schelling, Thomas C. (1971), 'Dynamic models of segregation', *Journal of Mathematical Sociology*, **1**, 143–86.

Schindler, D.W. (1990), 'Experimental perturbations of whole lakes as tests of hypotheses concerning ecosystem structure and function', *Oikos*, **57**, 25–41.

Solé, Ricard V. and Jordi Bascompte (2006), *Self-Organization in Complex Ecosystems*, Princeton, NJ: Princeton University Press.

Spath, Clive L. (2002), *Greenhouse Economics: Value and Ethics*, London: Routledge.

Strotz, Robert H., J.C. McAnulty and Joseph B. Naines, Jr (1953), 'Goodwin's nonlinear theory of the business cycle: an electro-analog solution', *Econometrica*, **21**, 390–411.

Turchin, Peter (2003), *Complex Population Dynamics: A Theoretical/Empirical Synthesis*, Princeton, NJ: Princeton University Press.

Velupillai, Kumaraswamy Vela (2005), 'Introduction', in K.V. Velupillai (ed.), *Computability, Complexity and Constructivity in Economic Analysis*, Victoria: Blackwell, pp. 1–14.

Volterra, V. (1926), 'Fluctuations in the abundance of a species considered mathematically', *Nature*, **118**, 558–600.

Volterrra, V. (1931), *Leçons sur la ThéorieMathématique de la Lutte pour la Vie*, Paris: Gauthier-Villars.

Wagener, Florian O.O. (2003), 'Skiba points and heteroclinic bifurcations with applications to the shallow lake system', *Journal of Economic Dynamics and Control*, **27**, 1533–61.

Zimmer, C. (1999), 'Life after chaos', *Science*, **284**, 83–6.

12. Environmental innovation: a Post Keynesian interpretation

James Juniper

INTRODUCTION

This chapter draws on Porter and van der Linde's article, 'Green and competitive', which addresses the potential for corporations that are increasingly required to meet stringent environmental regulations to achieve sustainable improvements in their competitive advantage. Porter's arguments are employed to weave together two strands of research. On the one hand there is the literature on 'smart' or 'responsive' regulation that is largely derived from a juridical framework. This strand of research posits that we are currently witnessing the evolution of a 'third way' to both develop and implement systems of regulation and corporate governance. On the other hand there is the chartalist literature, which places emphasis on the role of government in creating net financial assets through deficit spending, which can be applied to the task of achieving full employment through the provision of largely full-time jobs within the public sector. More recently, on chartalist grounds, Mitchell and Juniper (2007) have advocated a 'spatial Keynesian' form of employment creation to be achieved through a regionally implemented job guarantee. This policy intervention has an advantage over traditional Keynesian expansionary programmes (without positing the necessity for any mutual exclusion), which require large-scale investment in public infrastructure; insofar as employment opportunities can be specifically targeted at regions of high unemployment.

The first of these strands is subject to criticism on the basis of an alternative theoretical framework developed by William Lazonick and Mary O'Sullivan. While their notion of the 'social conditions of the innovative enterprise' provides a Chandleresque critique of the corporate governance literature (Chandler, 1977), it also recognizes that macroeconomic conditions can exercise a significant influence over the choices firms make between strategies of innovation or adaptation. An articulation of this interrelationship from a policy-oriented perspective represents the major concern of this chapter.

To set the scene, the next section of the chapter examines the issues raised by Porter and van der Linde's 1995a *Harvard Business Review* article on competitive advantage and environmental regulation. Although the arguments made in this paper are persuasive, it will be argued in the third section that Porter and van der Linde do not possess a cogent and comprehensive theory that relates corporate governance to innovation in general, and environmental innovation in particular. The fourth section of the chapter draws on the work of Lazonick and O'Sullivan as an alternative framework for addressing the influence of corporate governance over innovation. However, these authors underplay the macroeconomic role of government in supporting innovation. These diverse strands of theory are woven together in the fifth section of the chapter, which provides an overview of the spatial Keynesian paradigm, and focuses on the macroeconomic constraints over innovation and regional development. Policy implications and conclusions are addressed in the seventh and final section of the chapter.

THE *HARVARD BUSINESS REVIEW*'S ENVIRONMENTAL DEBATE

Michael Porter's analysis of innovation and regional development is grounded in his earlier research on industrial organization. Initially Porter's approach was based on a fairly orthodox interpretation of the structure–conduct–performance paradigm, which placed emphasis on entry barriers, the threat of substitution from rival products and services, the bargaining power of buyers, the bargaining power of suppliers, and rivalry amongst incumbents.

In contrast, Michael Porter's key theoretical argument in his 1990 text on *The Competitive Advantage of Nations* is that firms (and nations) create advantages by developing institutional mechanisms (both public and private) for creating specialized factors or discovering new ways to produce and market goods and services. He suggests that there are systemic influences behind competitive success arising from interactions between factor conditions, demand conditions, clusters of related and supporting industries, and individual patterns of firm rivalry, structure and strategy. Porter cautions that the Ricardian theory of comparative advantage has become less relevant in globalized industries where firms are increasingly decoupled from the factor endowments of host-nations and can gain access to internationally traded resources and factors (including capital and information). At the same time, he observes that modern technology nullifies the importance of specific factors of production. Moreover, many nations with markedly divergent industry and trade compositions now have relatively comparable pools of factors (for example skills and infrastructure). Finally, he notes that specific factor disadvantages within a region or nation can act as a spur to the development of compensatory mechanisms, which in time come to serve as new and sustainable sources of global competitive strength.[1]

It is within this theoretical context that Porter and van der Linde (1995a, p. 120) commence their investigation of environmental innovation, beginning with a discussion of business attitudes towards environmental regulations. While most businesses evince a grudging acceptance of the need for regulation, they suggest that this is complemented by a belief in the existence of a necessary trade-off between ecology and related social benefits, on the one hand, and economy and related private costs, on the other hand. Thus, policy-makers are condemned to oscillate between periods of more or less regulation. Porter and van der Linde complain that this view reflects a largely static conception, which holds as if fixed technology, consumer needs, products and processes, so that any regulation would automatically increase cost. However, Porter and van der Linde argue the contrary position: if properly designed, environmental standards could change things by triggering innovation. Costs could be lowered and the value of products increased by enhancing 'resource productivity' within the firm or region.

To bolster their claims, Porter and van der Linde (1995a, p. 121) turn to a well-used case study: that of the Dutch flower industry. In the early post-world-war two period this industry was characterized by cultivation in small plots, where contamination of soil and groundwater by pesticides was common. Subsequently, a 'closed-loop' system was developed based on greenhouse technology where plants were grown in a rock wool substrate. This technology breakthrough, they argue, led to lower risk of infestation, lower variation and, thus, improved quality.

Naturally, Porter and van der Linde (1995a, p. 122) ask whether this example represents an exception or a general rule. Deciding in favour of the universal, they establish a general principle: Pollution = Inefficiency. Inefficiencies are manifold, including hidden costs 'buried' in the life cycle of products and services and overall resource inefficiencies. The former are manifest in the form of energy cost, resource wastes and discards, while the latter most commonly obtain in the form of incomplete material utilization, poor process control, waste, defects and storage costs.

One reason why these inefficiencies are not detected is that most companies focus on pollution control through better identification, processing and disposal. However, as with total quality management (TQM), Porter and van der Linde argue that quality-minded companies such as Du Pont can eliminate hazards, hard-to-handle materials and unneeded activities. A litany of examples and cases, across a wide variety of industries, are presented in support of their contentions – many of them drawn from studies conducted in collaboration with the US Management Institute for Environment and Business.

This evidence leads Porter and van der Linde (1995a, p. 125) to ask an obvious question: if so many opportunities are available to achieve environmental solutions, why the need for regulation in the first place? Their answer amounts to a rejection of the presumption – one that is paradoxically a mainstay of modern finance theory – that all competitive opportunities are automatically exhausted (that is, there are no $10 bills lying on the ground waiting to be picked up). The reason for this rejection is the usual one of market failure: firms do not have perfect information, face adequate incentives or have the ability to exercise appropriate timing. In the corporate sector, environmental interventions are in a transitional phase where both companies and consumers lack experience. For example, due to apparently free discard many customers are unaware of hidden packaging costs. Thus, Porter and van der Linde (1995a, p. 128) conclude that regulation is therefore needed to provide pressure for innovation pressure, to promote environmental aspects of process innovation, to compensate for lack of customer perception, and to impose a level playing field during the period of transition. Once again, they refer to the diffusion of TQM methods in Japan, which was supported by government promotions such as the Deming Prize.

Porter and van der Linde go on to highlight what they refer to as the costs of a 'static mind set', which is most obviously expressed in the current adversarial climate of wasteful power struggles between regulators and industry. Here, they cite a 1992 study by the RAND Institute for Civil Justice (Acton and Dixon, 1992), in which it was noted that 88 per cent of company costs arose due to litigation, whereas only 12 per cent were related directly to site clean-up. Nevertheless, the authors acknowledge that legitimate controversy sometimes arises. For example, the social benefits of removing pollution have often been overstated. In addition, the private costs to companies are often unnecessarily high despite the social benefits of reduction due to poorly designed regulations. Porter and van der Linde stress that usually the degree of strictness of regulations is not the problem so much as the focus on clean-up rather than prevention. At the same time, liability exposure can discourage risk-taking on the part of firms, while enforcement rigidity remains a problem (for example, a 95 per cent reduction in pollution impact may still result in the offending company paying the full penalty).

Accordingly, Porter and van der Linde (1995a, p. 124) argue for innovation-friendly regulation where the focus is on outcomes rather than technologies, where concern is with stable and predictable interventions rather than laxity, with high levels of industry involvement, market incentives, and harmonization of regulations across both fields and countries. An end-user focus, they suggest, can often promote upstream improvements. Governments should ensure that regulators acquire high levels of technical competence so that less time and resources are spent on regulatory enforcement and resistance.

Porter and van der Linde (1995a, p. 130) go on to consider the implications of their analysis for companies. They instance the case of fuel emission standards in the USA in comparison with West Germany and Japan, first observing that managers frequently 'dig their heels in' to the detriment of their own industry competitiveness. They suggest that one reason for this resistance is that environmental issues in the USA are still the province of consultants rather than specialists internal to the industry (Porter and van der Linde, 1995a, p. 131). This organizational feature promotes both a legalistic and adversarial approach, and 'end-of-pipe' solutions, which neglect issues of resource productivity. Porter and van der Linde observe that often, these same consultants are vendors for 'end-of-pipe' equipment. And even when expertise is internalized, those responsible often lack line management authority. Porter and van der Linde (1995a, p. 132) urge US companies to be more vigilant in measuring and monitoring pollution impact, and highlighting unused inventory and emitted or discarded resources. Globalization, they contend, heightens the importance of resource productivity. They warn managers against ignoring the opportunity cost of underutilization and overestimating the requisite risk adjustments that should be made to the cost of capital for environmental investments. Furthermore, they suggest companies should trace information on own- and user-resource usage back to the design stage. At the same time, they argue that managers should develop proactive relationships with regulators (Porter and van der Linde, 1995a, p. 133).[2]

A cogent critique of Porter's competitive advantage framework is afforded by dynamic competency theorists. The grounds for this critique are examined in the next section of the chapter, which draws on Teece et al. (1997) and Australian research on 'smart' regulation.

A CRITIQUE OF PORTER AND VAN DER LINDE'S APPROACH

Porter and van der Linde advocate an approach to governance that is informed by 'smart' regulation. This aspect of regulation has been promoted by an active group of Australian researchers largely working within a juridical framework, whose members variously discuss the attributes of 'smart' (Gunningham and Grabosky, 1998) or 'responsive' regulation (Ayres and Braithwaite, 1992). This approach can supposedly overcome the limitations associated with both top-down systems of 'command-and-control' regulation and neoliberal processes of voluntary self-regulation. Instead, a responsive or 'smart' regulation approach is advocated because it has the capacity to distinguish between virtuous and rational agents, non-virtuous though rational agents and non-virtuous and irrational agents, so that regulators can selectively intervene, drawing on a variety of carefully designed mechanisms correlated with each class of agents, ranging respectively from persuasion, through punitive sanction, to ultimate incapacitation.

The EU's end-of-life vehicle legislation serves as a convincing example of responsive regulation that goes beyond dichotomy between command-and-control (Stalinist) and voluntary self-regulation (Neoliberal) systems of governance. Making the car the property of the automotive producer at the end of its useful life in the context of highly costly landfill and toxic waste disposal foists upon the company the urgent necessity to reduce environmental costs through design for ease of disassembly and design for low pollution impact, including design for recyclables and toxic waste reduction. The impetus behind such changes is reinforced by requirements for both producers and their major suppliers to be third-party accredited in the ISO 14001 standard pertaining to environmental management systems. The latter requires documentation of life-cycle analysis and of resulting strategies that have the aim of eliminating pollution impact. The Australian advocates of responsive regulation turn to juridical and psychological research for support. Unfortunately, these sources ignore the all-important politico-economic drivers of effective governance.

As Teece et al. (1997, p. 511) have argued, the orthodox analysis of industrial organization regards some industries as more attractive than others because they afford more opportunities to restrain competitive forces. As economic rents are derived from imperfectly competitive industry structures, the choices to invest in one rather than another sector will therefore depend on opportunities for erecting or preserving 'impediments' to competition. Obstacles to interfirm rivalry within a given sector of industry can be constructed either through the exploitation of 'reputation' effects, or because incumbent firms in these industries can openly engage in predatory pricing or, perhaps more diplomatically, can signal their intentions to others (warning them off in advance). In the latter case firms must 'second-guess' the moves of rivals while acting in accordance with the principle, 'do unto others before they do unto you'.

Teece et al. turn to resource-based theory and dynamic competencies theory for an alternative explanation of relative performance. In these theoretical approaches, emphasis is placed on the development, accumulation, combination and protection of unique skills and capabilities. Congruent with changes in the external environment, firm competencies must not only be deployed, but also coordinated and constantly renewed. Teece et al. (1997, p. 516) draw a further distinction between core competencies (which define a firm's fundamental business and can be enhanced through the development or acquisition of complementary assets) and dynamic capabilities (the purpose of which is to build, integrate and reconfigure existing competencies to address the rapidly changing environment). Accordingly, the key step for strategy is the foundation of distinctive, difficult-to-replicate advantage. In this light it is understandable that Teece et al. (1997, p. 517) feel obliged to reject the neoclassical notion of the firm as a nexus of contracts, along with its Coasian counterpart (Coase, 1937), which views the firm as either a 'quasi-market' or an organizational form that has entirely displaced the market.

Teece et al. (1997, p. 518) point to the fact that market incentives are far from exhaustive and can function in such a manner as effectively to destroy cooperative activity and learning. Essentially, this is because there is no basis on which individual effort can be calibrated with joint effort. Rather, the essence of capabilities is that they cannot be assembled using markets (that is, they are untraded) and, as such, they require various forms of decentred rather than unilateral coordination. In sum, the balance sheet is not equivalent to the organization, and organizations entail both hierarchy and integration. Organizational processes, they suggest, are remarkably diverse, including internal and external mechanisms of coordination, integration, learning and reconfiguration. The firm must take a position in both traded and untraded assets of a technological nature, while investing in complementary assets that can be financial, structural, institutional, market-related and reputation-based (Teece et al., 1997, p. 522). In addition, technological opportunities draw not only on basic science, but also on aspects of the national, regional and industrial innovation system in which firms are embedded. For all these reasons, history (in the form of path-dependent processes) matters.

It would seem that dynamic competencies theory affords a robust alternative to the strategic analysis of Porter and van der Linde. Although Porter (1990) himself draws on work by Teece it seems to be marginal to his preferred analytical framework.

AN ALTERNATIVE PERSPECTIVE ON CORPORATE GOVERNANCE

The literature on corporate governance tends to be more narrowly focused than its regional development counterparts. To finance economists and accountants: 'Corporate Governance deals with the ways in which suppliers of finance to corporations assure themselves of getting a return on their investment' (Shleifer and Vishny, 1997, p. 737). Corporate governance is the system by which business corporations are directed and controlled. The corporate governance structure specifies the distribution of rights and responsibilities among different participants in the corporation, such as the board, managers, shareholders and other stakeholders, and spells out the rules and procedures for making decisions on corporate affairs.

During the early 1990s business economists (Porter, 1992; Prowse, 1990) were fearful that the USA would soon be overtaken by Japan and Germany due to the fact that 'bank-based' capital markets in these latter nations encouraged investors to adopt longer-term or more patient horizons (for UK evidence on the same phenomenon, see Miles, 1995; Satchell and Damant, 1995; Cuthbertson et al., 1997). These fears of a US eclipse abated during the 'dot-com' boom of the later 1990s, only to be reinvigorated after the 2001 crash, in the light of revelations about the illegal practices on the part of companies such as Sunbeam, Enron and Xerox.

At the height of the 'dot-com' boom US researchers started to reassess Anglo-American capital markets in a positive light. Neoclassical financial economists such as La Porta et al. (2002) focused on transactions costs, including imperfect information – which are seen to operate as barriers to successful deal-making – from a more juridical perspective. In the corporate sector, a raft of legal rights and obligations were seen to influence the levels of risk faced by providers of external finance. However, these orthodox and largely juridical readings of corporate governance have been questioned by authors such as William Lazonick and Mary O'Sullivan.

Lazonick (1991, p. 19) complains that orthodox approaches to issues of governance, including that of Shleifer and Vishny (1997) and Williamson's (1985) transaction cost theory, do not address the fundamental question of how productive resources are developed within an innovating enterprise. In viewing strategy solely as a form of predatory behaviour, the enterprise can only be conceived as a 'market imperfection' impeding free flow of resources. Moreover, markets are viewed as a cause rather than as a consequence of economic development. From this market-based perspective, firms are advised to create 'high-powered' incentives with no obligation for the sharing of returns: instead, salaries merely serve to segment and separate remuneration out from productive effort. In the work of

Coasians such as Oliver Williamson, the role of firms is confined to that of 'working things out', that is, to optimizing subject to technological (asset specificity), behavioural (guileful opportunism), and cognitive (bounded rationality) constraints.

In particular, Lazonick (1991, p. 195) argues that for transaction cost theory there is no concept of the dynamics of capitalist development, nor of business as a value-creating organization. Instead, the focus is on 'adaptive, sequential decision-making' in the face of 'disturbances', which economizes on bounded rationality (Lazonick, 1991, p. 209). The core presumption is that 'in the beginning there were markets', and '[o]nly as market-mediated contracts break down are the transactions in question removed from markets and organized internally' (Williamson, 1985, p. 143). In contrast, Lazonick argues that bounded rationality can be transformed into collectivized forms of rationality through organizational innovation and learning, while high-powered incentives can transform opportunism into collective purpose (Lazonick, 2002, p. 3065). There is little or no understanding on the part of transaction cost theorists of the role business enterprises play in the innovation process, specifically the basis on which firms allocate resources for innovation. For Lazonick, this is fundamentally an issue of organizational rather than market control.

Lazonick even extends this line of complaint to dynamic capabilities theory, saying that it has nothing to say about such issues as the location of strategic control, the allocation of financial returns, the re-integration of learning and strategy, and how to develop a strategic response to new competitors and environments when firms are confronted with the obsolescence of existing asset positions (Lazonick, 2002, p. 3069). No doubt this overstates the case (especially in regard to the last point), but it does highlight what is cogent and unique about the theoretical framework that Lazonick (and his erstwhile collaborator, Mary O'Sullivan) have constructed.

In recognition of the value of this theoretical context, Lazonick and O'Sullivan were commissioned to advise the EU on a range of matters regarding effective corporate governance. Lazonick and O'Sullivan (2002) outline a theoretical framework, which they call the social conditions of the innovative enterprise (SCIE). In their reports to the EU, they describe how institutional factors interact with industrial conditions (technology- and market-related) and organizational conditions (strategic, cognitive and behavioural) to influence the SCIE.

Lazonick (1991, pp. 198–206) presents a cogent summary of his theory of the innovative organization. He argues that the crucial problem faced by business organizations is that of fixed costs. Because neither production nor sale are certain or instantaneous, firms must choose between two opposing strategies. On the one hand, they can be innovative, developing productive capabilities and resources. On the other hand, they can be adaptive, staying with known technical specifications and existing capabilities. This choice is made in the context of two forms of uncertainty. 'Productive uncertainty' is concerned with the internal organization of firm, while 'competitive uncertainty' concerns rivalry on the part of other firms. Both forms of uncertainty obtain over the two sequential stages of development and utilization of capabilities.

Lazonick (1991, pp. 203–4) emphasizes the fact that higher levels of innovation imply more uncertainty as the firm must invest in vertically integrated activities, research and development (R&D), planning and coordination. These costs are minimized for the adaptive firm, which maintains a lower level of fixed commitments. The innovative enterprise must invest in management capabilities, the development and coordination of specialized skills, coordination mechanisms that increase the speed of throughput, and higher levels of backward and forward integration. All these activities are associated with the transformation of both variable into fixed costs, and competitive uncertainty into productive uncertainty. Nevertheless, the firm can exercise more control over the process by trading-off a higher risk of failure against enhanced opportunities for growth (Lazonick, 1991, p. 201). Moreover, Lazonick cautions that even late movers face some uncertainty over their ability to manage the requisite investments and, more often than not, they are exposed to an increased threat of 'creative destruction'. Accordingly, oligopolies always confront the dangerous temptation of relaxing into regimes of adaptation. At the same time, Lazonick (1991, p. 206) notes that effort-saving technological change creates opportunities for achieving high throughput. However, this imposes the need for extensive backward and forward integration, the conversion of variable into fixed costs, the conversion of competitive into productive uncertainty, and the successful exploitation of both scale and scope economies so that fixed costs can be spread over larger production volumes.

Governance issues play an essential role in influencing aspects of organizational renewal, processes of technological diffusion and the commercial outcomes of innovation-related activity. Lazonick (2003, pp. 35–6) also briefly addresses the issue of how developmental states can influence the SCIE. However, these interactions are not examined in any detail.[3] The motivation for the next section of the chapter is the desire to explain the nature of these interactions before examining the implications of macroeconomic settings for developments in environmental and other forms of innovation. It will be argued that macroeconomic policies that successfully achieve full utilization of capacity are highly conducive to innovation at the level of the individual enterprise.

MACROECONOMIC ELEMENTS FOR A NEW THEORETICAL PERSPECTIVE

In arguing that the SCIE are a tool for the systematic study of the diversity of institutional and organizational conditions across nations and industries, and over time, Lazonick acknowledges the importance of both enterprises and nation states in promoting innovation and development (Lazonick, 2003, p. 25). He notes in particular that each can adopt different modes of 'accessing' foundational finance.

Unfortunately, Lazonick does not provide a detailed account of how macroeconomic considerations influence enterprise innovation. Nevertheless, from the preceding analysis it should be obvious that policies designed to achieve high levels of effective demand, capacity utilization and full employment will encourage firms to adopt innovative rather than adaptive strategies. A buoyant economy will support strategies of backward and forward integration and high throughput, which results in the spreading of fixed costs over larger volumes.

From the chartalist perspective advocated by economists as diverse as Keynes, Schumpeter and Abba Lerner, the demand for currency is induced by the necessity of paying taxes that the government imposes on the private sector.[4] The issue of currency through public spending enables the government to gain control over resources, products and services that have been produced by the non-government sector (including both the rest of the world and the private sector).

Accordingly, given the non-government sector's desire to net save, unemployment may arise when monies withdrawn through taxation are greater than those injected into the economy. Deficit spending is necessary to create net financial assets required to meet this desire for net saving because net financial assets cannot be created within the non-government sector. This is because every asset created on the balance sheet of the non-government sector is matched by a corresponding liability. The net wealth of the non-government sector thus reflects cumulative deficit spending on the part of the federal government.[5]

To spend, the government merely credits the exchange settlement accounts of the central bank. When taxes are paid, these same accounts are debited. The national government then sets the interest rate by absorbing any net liquidity remaining in the banking system through the sale of bonds. Thus bond sales are not required to 'finance' government spending. Their task is to absorb excess liquidity so that interest rates can be determined. As shown in Japan, a chosen interest rate can be selected and maintained by the government, irrespective of how large the budget deficit becomes. In this light, the long-term maintenance of government surpluses destroys jobs and leads to a continual reduction in the net wealth of the national economy (Mitchell and Juniper, 2007).

From this chartalist perspective governments do not face any budget constraint on their spending. The government spends by crediting private sector bank accounts at the central bank. Moreover, this process occurs independently from the accumulation of revenue by the government. What is frequently referred to as a 'constraint' is in actual fact an ex post accounting identity (Bell and Wray, 2002–03).

In Juniper (2007), the insights gleaned from this 'spatial Keynesian' and chartalist perspective on macroeconomics are combined with Lazonick and O'Sullivan's conditions of the innovative enterprise framework to arrive at a rigorous interdisciplinary framework for the analysis of centrally coordinated regional innovation and regional development policy. In particular, it articulates the often-overlooked linkage between (spatially articulated) macroeconomic policies of full employment, infrastructure development, training, and regional innovation policy, before examining opportunities for empirical analysis that are afforded by this integrative approach.

The first argument is that, in fostering high levels of effective demand, national governments also promote higher rates of innovation.[6] While most macroeconomists recognize the existence of a strong causal link between aggregate demand and both tangible and intangible forms of investment, Lazonick and O'Sullivan's theoretical framework focuses attention on the need for high rates of throughput at the enterprise level both to spread the burden of fixed capital charges and to cushion against the uncertainties that are engendered by more innovative rather than adaptive strategies.

The second argument is related to the Post Keynesian principle that the provision of a 'buffer stock' of secure, public sector jobs that pay an appropriate minimum wage for those who would otherwise be unemployed affords better protection against inflation than would be provided through the maintenance of unemployment or, for that matter, through the increasing prevalence of precarious employment. This is because those who are actively employed are work-ready and can readily move into the private sector if and when more jobs become available. Nevertheless, over and above these anti-inflationary advantages, the maintenance of an employment buffer stock also promotes innovation. This because prospective employers in the non-government sector must attract buffer stock employees through an offer of better pay, improved conditions, career paths, better working conditions or more challenging work opportunities. In contrast, neoliberal strategies based on the promotion of labour market flexibility actively discourage innovation because inefficient firms can simply force the pecuniary and non-pecuniary forms of remuneration down for their unfortunate workforces.

The third argument is related to the view that governments have an all-important role in the provision of nominal anchors for both the overall level of prices and rates of return.[7] The former can be achieved through the determination of an appropriate minimum wage for buffer stock employees, while the latter can be achieved through the government's ability to determine short-term rates of interest. Under neoliberal regimes that privilege monetary policy over fiscal policy, the stability of the latter nominal anchor is clearly undermined. However, it should also be acknowledged that the achievement of stable nominal anchors determines the base so that a mildly escalating sequence of wage relativities in different occupations and sectors can evolve to reflect and drive productivity differentials. This too fosters higher rates of innovation. The implications of these insights into the linkages between macroeconomics and innovation will be articulated in the concluding section of the chapter.

POLICY IMPLICATIONS AND CONCLUSION

While the literature on 'smart' or 'responsive' regulation, including the work of Porter and van der Linde, has made a valuable contribution to our understanding of corporate and environmental legislation and governance, the above arguments imply that it must be embedded within a broader theoretical framework that draws on both macroeconomic insights and a more comprehensive understanding of the institutional conditions of the innovative enterprise. To support the development and implementation of successful innovation policies – environmental or otherwise – will require a blurring of traditional demarcations between microeconomic and macroeconomic theory.

From the preceding discussion it should be apparent that end-of-life vehicle legislation conforms closely to the defining characteristics of 'smart' regulation (Aalders and Wilthagen, 1997, pp. 431–4). For one thing, it takes advantage of intermediary structures, such as industry networks, in promoting environmental management practices and forms of environmental contracting along the supply chain. For another, it actively encourages corporate social responsibility through the internalization of external goals and values. In part, this is achieved through the requirement for firms to gain third-party accreditation in the ISO 14001 environmental management quality assurance standard. This monitoring by third parties, backed by legislative enforcement, compensates for the limited inspectorate capacity of government regulators.

When viewed from the Chandlerian perspective of Lazonick and O'Sullivan, it is evident that design for disassembly and recyclability will be both costly and fraught with uncertainty for firms in the automotive sector. No doubt, a range of microeconomic and institutional support mechanisms would encourage firms to adopt innovative rather than merely adaptive strategies. These mechanisms could include the construction of strong research links between the science sector and industry, the provision of patient and dedicated finance to encourage less tangible forms of environmental investment, the provision of government-funded bureau services to advise firms about life-cycle analysis (pollution impact and frequency, rates of resource usage and energy consumption) and the prospective gains that might be achieved through investment in best-practice technologies (including through recycling), and the establishment of educational facilities to train graduates in the requisite environmental management techniques and related engineering skills.

However, above and beyond this familiar suite of microeconomic forms of intervention, this chapter has emphasized the importance of macroeconomic influences over environmental investment and innovation. In current economic conditions the automotive industry is caught between two pincers. On the one hand, customers are demanding more fuel-efficient vehicles in the face of rising fuel costs. On the other hand, firms are confronting a global situation of excess supply for cars and trucks, aggravated by the sub-prime crisis and subsequent economic downturn in world economic growth. In this context, national governments are engaging in a war of subsidies and rebates with the aim of encouraging domestic automotive producers to manufacture within their own national boundaries or at the very least, plan, design and coordinate offshore production of the current generation of fuel-efficient and hybrid vehicles. Similar arguments can be applied to other sectors of industry.

On the basis of a detailed analysis of the uneven duration and persistence of regional unemployment, Mitchell and Carlson (2003, p. 12) recommend what they term a 'spatial Keynesian' policy regime combining demand expansion to remove the spending gap occasioned by the desire of the private sector to net save, spatial distribution of public sector employment creation, and regionally directed public sector infrastructure and industry policy. This spatial Keynesian policy regime has been described in more detail in Mitchell and Juniper (2007). At the same time, although overarching strategies can be developed and communicated they must be supported by effective coordination mechanisms linking together both centre and periphery, and integrating labour market programmes that promote full employment with training, science and technology policies, and spending on infrastructure and less tangible, innovation-related capital works. While all investment activity is exposed to high levels of uncertainty and problems of irreversibility, environmental investments are particularly susceptible to these factors, due to both the complexities associated with environmental processes, and high levels of uncertainty about likely national and international policy responses (Juniper, 2007).

The opportunities afforded by 'smart' regulation will not be adequately pursued by firms that are confronted with low and volatile levels of effective demand, nor will they be taken up by firms characterized by hierarchical forms of organization.[8] Demand-side macroeconomic policies and microeconomic corporate governance mechanisms must be brought together to privilege innovation over adaptation. Firms can always choose to withdraw from undesirable product lines, and may even move offshore to avoid environmental controls.

Five main principles of policy development can be extracted from the above synthesis of Post Keynesian macroeconomics and theories of governance. First, recognition of the complementarity between macroeconomic policies of demand management and microeconomic policies promoting innovation (both general and environmental in nature) will require a reversal of the orthodox wisdom on the need to construct sound microeconomic foundations for macroeconomic analysis. Instead, more emphasis must be accorded to macroeconomic influences and constraints over enterprise-level phenomena. Second, in achieving macroeconomic objectives of low inflation, the arguments presented above suggest that the implementation of a spatially coordinated job guarantee would afford greater advantages than either their non-accelerating inflation rate of unemployment (NAIRU) or precariousness-based counterparts in combating inflation. Third, privilege should be restored to (spatially oriented) fiscal rather than monetary policy in promoting the objectives of macroeconomic growth and stability. Fourth, monetary policies aimed at lowering nominal interest rates and achieving a 'euthanasia of rentier' will be seen to boost innovation and productivity growth. Fifth, the kinds of balance-of-payments or budget-deficit pessimism evinced by certain traditions in economics, economic geography and sociology – including regulation theory (see Brenner and Glick, 1991) – should be firmly rejected. In this regard, the monetary autonomy associated with floating exchange rates is advantageous for those wishing to embrace programmes of full employment. Finally, it is important to realize that a raft of environmental policies can be directly integrated with those that offer public sector employment. This is especially the case for developing countries wishing to develop sustainable, low-input but high-yield, agricultural sectors.

In national economies that are characterized by high levels of labour force precariousness (such as Australia and the USA) and neoliberal policies of macroeconomic restraint, innovative activity has been hindered. Confronted with declining profit margins and heightened competitive pressure, companies operating within precarious labour markets frequently responded by transferring plant and equipment to countries where the labour force is cheaper though no less docile and environmental controls are weaker. Despite this, the new raft of environmental regulations governing automotive production are succeeding in their transformative goals largely because they are being implemented within two of the largest automotive consumer-markets in the world, namely, the EEU and the state of California. However, this chapter has argued that microeconomic interventions should be complemented by those of a more macroeconomic nature.

NOTES

1. More recently, Porter has become an advocate of cluster-based regional development predicated on an earlier recognition (Porter, 1990, p. 120) that the intensity of interaction between firms within the 'competitive diamond' could be heightened if firms are geographically localized. For a hard-hitting critique of this regional agenda see Martin and Sunley (2003, p. 7).
2. Porter and van der Linde's article and subsequent papers published in the *Journal of Economic Perspectives* (see Porter and van der Linde, 1995b, 1995c) provoked a series of rejoinders, including articles and letters (in particular see Palmer et al., 1995; Portnoy, 1995).
3. The critique of the 'new regionalist' agenda mounted by economic geographers such as MacLeod and Jones (1999) also highlights the importance of macroeconomic policies coordinated at the national level for regional development.
4. The concept of money described here as 'chartalism' was introduced to the world by a German economist named Georg Friedrich Knapp. Knapp (1924, p. 32) chose the term 'chartalism' to convey the notion, widespread since the seventeenth century, that money is a symbol, rather than a thing. In other words, all means of payment are 'pay-tokens, or tickets used as means of payment'. He argued that money is a creation of the state and that whatever it is that the state accepts in payment for the taxes that it levies on the non-government sector, determines both the nature of money and its ultimate value. In his text *A Treatise on Money*, John Maynard Keynes (1976, pp. 4–5) endorsed Knapp's chartalist perspective. He was also instrumental in having the work translated into English and subsequently published.
5. A formal treatment of these issues is set out in a recent paper by Godley and Lavoie (2007) where a stock-flow consistent macroeconomic modelling framework is used to explain how governments create net-financial assets through deficit spending.
6. Post Keynesians (Harcourt, 1972; Arestis and Sawyer, 1997) argue that the capital debates of the 1930s and 1970s, though rarely discussed in mainstream economics journals, which undermine the aggregative 'parables' of neoclassical economics (that is, the marginalist theories of income distribution), also serve to question any faith in the self-correcting forces of the 'invisible hand'.
7. This insight is one of the important contributions made by Piero Sraffa during the capital controversies. Sraffa demonstrated the impossibility of constructing a Ricardian standard commodity that would be invariant both to changes in income distribution and to shifts in effective demand, in the presence of increasing or decreasing returns to scale (see Andrews, 1996). This insight justifies the chartalist conviction that governments must exert control over nominal anchors such as the money rate of interest (to stabilize prospective rates of return) and the minimum wage (to stabilize the level of prices). Both

of these phenomena relating to the inseparability of real aspects of the economy from nominal aspects serve to question the conventional policy division between microeconomic analysis of market failures and macroeconomic problems of inflation and unemployment, forestalling any formal separation of the real sector of the economy from the nominal sector: a process referred to as 'block recursivity' in the neoclassical synthesis models described by Thomas Sargent (1979).

8. In this regard see O'Sullivan (2000) for detailed commentary on what she calls the principles of financial commitment, organizational integration and insider control.

REFERENCES

Aalders, M. and J. Wilthagen (1997), 'Moving beyond command and control: reflexivity in the regulation of occupational safety and health and the environment', *Law and Policy*, **13**, 415–43.

Acton, Jan Paul and Lloyd S. Dixon (1992), 'Superfund and transaction costs: the experiences of insurers and very large industrial firms', Working Paper, Rand Institute for Civil Justice, Santa Monica, California.

Andrews, David R. (1996), 'Nothing is hidden: a Wittgensteinian interpetation of Sraffa', *Cambridge Journal of Economics*, **20**, 763–77.

Arestis, P.G.P. and M. Sawyer (1997), *Capital Controversy, Post-Keynesian Economics and the History of Economic Thought*, London and New York: Routledge.

Ayres, I. and J. Braithwaite (1992), *Responsive Regulation: Transcending the Deregulation Debate*, Oxford: Oxford University Press.

Bell, Stephanie and Randy Wray (2002–03), 'Fiscal effects on reserves and the independence of the Fed', *Journal of Post Keynesian Economics*, **25** (2), 263–71.

Brenner, R. and M. Glick (1991), 'The regulation approach: theory and history', *New Left Review*, **1** (188), 45–119.

Chandler, A. (1977), *The Visible Hand: The Managerial Revolution in American Business*, Cambridge, MA: Harvard University Press.

Coase, Ronald, H. (1937), 'The nature of the firm', *Economica*, November, 386–405, reprinted in J.B. Barney and W.G. Ouchi (eds) (1988), *Organizational Economics*, San Francisco, CA: Jossey-Bass.

Cuthbertson, K., S. Hayes and D. Nitzke (1997), 'The behaviour of UK stock prices and returns: is the market efficient?', *Economic Journal*, **107**, 986–1008.

Godley, W. and M. Lavoie (2007), 'Fiscal policy in a stock-flow consistent (SFC), model', Levy Economics Institite, Working Paper No. 494, April, http://www.levy.org.

Gunningham, N. and P. Grabosky (1998), *Smart Regulation: Designing Environmental Policy*, Oxford: Clarendon Press.

Harcourt, G. (1972), *Some Cambridge Controversies in the Theory of Capital*, Cambridge: Cambridge University Press.

Juniper, J. (2007) 'Environmental investment and valuation: a Keynesian (and Freudian) perspective', *International Journal of Environment, Workplace and Employment*, **3** (3–4), 230–47.

Keynes, John Maynard (1976 [1930]), *A Treatise on Money. Volume I: The Pure Theory of Money*, New York: Harcourt Brace Jovanovich.

Knapp, G.F. (1924), *The State Theory of Money*, abridged edn, H.M. Lucas and J. Bonar (trans.), London: Macmillan & Co.

La Porta, Rafael, Florencio Lopez de Silanes, Andrei Shleifer and Robert W. Vishny (2002), 'Investor protection and corporate valuation', *Journal of Finance*, **57**, 1147–70.
Lazonick, W. (1991), *Business Organization and the Myth of the Market Economy*, Cambridge: Cambridge University Press.
Lazonick, W. (2002), 'Theory of innovative enterprise', *International Encyclopedia of Business and Management Handbook of Economics*, 2nd edn, London: Thomson Learning, pp. 3055–76.
Lazonick, W. (2003), 'The theory of the market economy and the social foundations of innovative enterprise,' *Economic and Industrial Democracy*, **24** (1), 9–44.
Lazonick, W. and M. O'Sullivan (2002), 'Corporate governance, innovation, and economic performance in the EU: Project Policy Report', Research Report funded by the Targeted Socio-Economic Research Programme of the European Commission (DGXII), under the Fourth Framework Programme.
Martin, R. and P. Sunley (2003), 'Deconstructing clusters', *Journal of Economic Geography*, **3**, pp. 5–35.
MacLeod, G. and M. Jones (1999) 'Reregulating a regional rustbelt: institutional fixes, entrepreneurial discourse, and the "politics of representation"', *Environment and Planning D: Society and Space*, **17**, 575–605.
Miles, D. (1995), 'Testing for short-termism in the UK stock market: a reply', *Economic Journal*, **105** (September), 1224–7.
Mitchell, W.F. and E. Carlson (2003), 'Why do disparities in employment growth across metropolitan and regional space occur?', Working Paper No. 03-09, Centre of Full Employment and Equity, the University of Newcastle, http://e1.newcastle.edu.au/coffee.
Mitchell, W.F. and J. Juniper (2007) 'Towards a spatial Keynesian macroeconomics', in Philip Arestis and Gennaro Zezza (eds), *Advances in Monetary Policy and Macroeconomics*, Houndsmill: Palgrave Macmillan, pp. 192–211.
O'Sullivan, M. (2000), 'The innovative enterprise and corporate governance', *Cambridge Journal of Economics*, **24**, 393–416.
Palmer, K., W.E. Oates and P.R. Portney (1995), 'Tightening environmental standards: the benefit–cost or no-cost paradigm', *Journal of Economic Perspectives*, **9** (4), 119–32.
Porter, M.E. (1990), *The Competitive Advantage of Nations*, London: Macmillan and New York: Free Press.
Porter, M.E. (1992), 'Capital disadvantage: America's failing capital investment system', *Harvard Business Review* (September–October), 65–82.
Porter, M. and C. van der Linde (1995a), 'Green and competitive: ending the stalemate', *Harvard Business Review*, **73** (5), 120–34.
Porter, M. and C. van der Linde (1995b), 'Reply to Portnoy's critique of Porter and van der Linde (1995), "Green and competitive: ending the stalemate"', *Harvard Business Review*, **73** (6), 206–8.
Porter, M. and C. van der Linde (1995c), 'Towards a new conception of the environment–competitiveness relationship', *Journal of Economic Perspectives*, **9** (4), 98–118.
Portnoy, P.R. (1995), 'Critique of Porter and van der Linde (1995a), "Green and competitive: ending the stalemate"', *Harvard Business Review*, **73** (6), 204–6.
Prowse, Stephen D. (1990), 'Institutional investment patterns and corporate

financial behaviour in the United States and Japan', *Journal of Financial Economics*, **27**, 43–66.
Sargent, T.J. (1979), *Macroeconomic Theory*, New York: Academic Press.
Satchell, S.E. and D.C. Damant (1995), 'Testing for short-termism in the UK Stock market: a comment', *Economic Journal*, **105**, 1218–23.
Shleifer, A. and R.W. Vishny (1997), 'A survey of corporate governance', *Journal of Finance*, **52** (2), 737–83.
Teece, D.J., G. Pisano and A. Shuen (1997), 'Dynamic capabilities and strategic management', *Strategic Management Journal*, **18** (7), 509–33.
Williamson, O.E. (1985), *The Economic Institutions of Capitalism*, New York: Free Press.

13. The sustainable economic development of traditional peoples

James Kahn and Alexandre Rivas

INTRODUCTION

There have been many models of economic growth advanced through the years, all of which put some degree of emphasis on investment and the development of capital stocks. However, in addition to the degree of emphasis on investment, an important distinction between Post Keynesian and neoclassical models is that neoclassical models assume path-independence and Post Keynesian models assert path-dependence. One potential contribution of ecological economics and discussions of sustainable development to the Post Keynesian perspective is that the consideration of environmental capital and the potential of irreversible destruction of environmental capital during the growth process lend strong support to the idea that growth is path-dependent. Neither the lack of policy prescriptions of the neoclassical model nor the conventional policy prescriptions of Post Keynesian models will assure the proper preservation of environmental capital. The problem of choosing a growth path becomes even more severe when considering growth of the informal sector, particularly among traditional peoples. The protection of environmental capital and the development of appropriate social capital through policy interventions are critically important. This question of the appropriateness of capital becomes even more pressing when dealing with traditional populations in rural areas. If capital accumulates according to market forces, the capital will concentrate in industrial centers and not in the rural communities. Unfortunately, traditional Post Keynesian models do not pay much attention to the distributional aspects of growth policy, particularly to the regions populated by traditional peoples. Under either type of policy, the only options available to rural dwellers are to move to the industrial centers (which often already have high levels of unemployment) or to engage in more intense extraction to supply the urban and industrial areas, which may have important consequences for environmental degradation and sustainability of these communities.

However, the spirit of the Post Keynesian approach to economic growth is more amenable to addressing these issues, and a blending of Post Keynesian and ecological economics can lead to appropriate changes to policy recommendations that can steer these communities onto a realistic and sustainable growth path through the protection of environmental capital and the development of other types of capital. This chapter develops the theory of sustainable development in remote rural areas and develops policies based upon these theories. The discussion is illustrated with examples from the state of Amazonas in Brazil, some of which have already been implemented and some of which are still in search of funding. Our conclusions are that national development plans will often bypass traditional communities, unless specific development plans are implemented that are appropriate for these communities. The scale of the projects must be appropriate to the size of the communities, but appropriate scale is not sufficient. The capital investments must be tailored to the unique circumstances of these communities in a fashion that is qualitatively different than would be the case for national development plans. Conventional development projects or unplanned growth can lead to irreversible environmental degradation and the loss of ecological services.

Sustainable development is a goal that has been widely adopted but remains poorly understood. The typical definitions that arise from the early Brundtland Report (World Commission on Environment and Development, 1987) articulate that sustainable development increases the well-being of the current generations without reducing the prospects of future generations, but this genre of definitions has two flaws. First, it is a conceptual goal with no specification of operational goals where one can determine whether one is meeting the constraint of not reducing the prospects of future generations. Second, this genre of definitions does not address the question of the equity of the development pattern within the current generation or within a particular future generation. In other words, a development path could be considered sustainable even though it left certain sectors of the population in perpetual poverty. In particular, throughout the world, national development plans bypass traditional rural peoples, and often generate environmental, economic and social changes that reduce the quality of life of these communities.

This chapter examines these two problems in the context of sustainable development of subsistence communities in rural Amazonia. The chapter examines whether the typical pattern of market forces and government policies focused on the rapid growth of gross domestic product (GDP) will improve or impoverish these rainforest communities, in both the short run and the long run. The next step is to suggest alternative types of policies that can improve the quality of life of these communities in both the short run and the long run, and generate truly sustainable development. We will show that sustainable development of the rainforest communities requires policies that augment community social, human-made and human capital while preserving environmental capital. Neither neoclassical economics nor Post Keynesian economics adequately address the role of environmental capital and the importance of ecological services that environmental capital provides. Ecological economics stresses the role of ecological services, which are not generally market goods. Ecological economics, like Post Keynesian economics, recognizes the importance of non-market forces, but emphasizes the need to generate policies that extend past the simple stimulation of the national economy. The incorporation of environmental capital into models of growth and development is critical in developing guidance for these types of policies. Before discussing the theory of sustainable development and our experience in Amazonas, we introduce the Rio Negro region of the state of Amazonas, Brazil. The third section presents the theory of sustainable development, while the fourth section relates these concepts to differences between the neoclassical and Post Keynesian approach. The fifth section looks at the relationship between the national economy and rainforest communities in Amazonas. We then discuss different types of capital shortfalls in sustainable development and how these can be rectified with appropriate policies. The final section presents our conclusions.

THE RIO NEGRO REGION

Although it is common to begin a chapter such as this with the theoretical model, we will begin by describing the region that has motivated both our conceptual and our applied work. This will provide a context in which to evaluate the applicability of our conceptual model. The geographic area in which we base our discussion in this chapter is the Rio Negro drainage in the state of Amazonas, Brazil, from the municipality[1] of Novo Ayrão upstream to the municipality of São Gabriel dos Cachoeira, at the border with Venezuela.[2] This region is not well integrated into the national economic system, but has tremendous potential for sustainable development and is important in terms of the overall preservation of the Amazonian basin and its biodiversity resources. This region of the Amazon has not undergone the disturbances and deforestation of other Amazonian areas. In fact, the four municipalities in this region have close to 100 percent of their land area in the original forest.

This area of the Rio Negro drainage is immense. The four municipalities of Novo Ayrão, Barcelos, Santa Isabella do Rio Negro and São Gabriel dos Cachoeira have a combined area of a little over 332 278 km^2 (IBGE, 2007), 30 percent larger than the whole country of Ecuador, approximately the size of Belgium. The area is almost entirely undisturbed rainforest, extremely high in biodiversity and increasingly vulnerable to potential damage from unsustainable logging, commercial fishing and illegal mining of gold. As the situation worsens in neighboring states and countries in terms of the presence of loggers and other unsustainable extractionists (as well as drugs), the more likely these activities are to spread into the Rio Negro area. Since the area is relatively sparsely populated – 82 053 people (IBGE, 2007) with a density of approximately 0.25 of a person per square kilometer – it could be extremely vulnerable to intra-Amazonian migration or immigration from coastal Brazil.

The people in this area are entirely traditional peoples. Traditional peoples in the Amazon area are defined by the Brazilian government as indigenous in lifestyle but not completely indigenous in their genetics. These people are known as Caboclos or *ribeirinhos*.[3] They are of mixed Portuguese and Indian (and sometimes African) descent. Indigenous production technologies and indigenous culture are a part of their lives. Hunger tends not to be a problem in the region, as fish and fruit are abundant, and manioc is grown sustainably by making small clearings in the forest which revert to forest within four or five years. This sustainable type of agroforestry has been practiced in the region for thousands of years.

The population is principally literate, although only a small fraction of the population has more than four years of schooling. Better access to further schooling is often cited as an important factor in improving quality of life. Some small communities have health clinics funded by the state or municipality, but increased access to health care is also cited as an important need (Casey et al., 2008). Some communities have electric generators, but only sufficient diesel fuel (usually provided by state or municipal government) to run the generators for a few hours per day.

The generation of cash income in this region is extremely difficult because of the great distances to the principal markets in Manaus and across the borders in Columbia and Venezuela. In addition, obstacles are created by the market power of the people who control the middleman activities. For example, one of the principal economic activities is the live capture of *piabas*, or ornamental fish (fish for freshwater aquaria). The *piabeiros* who capture these fish only make a fraction of a cent, and refer to themselves as slaves to the middlemen who have their headquarters in Barcelos. These middlemen send the fish to several firms in Manaus who export to the distributors in Miami and Europe. It is interesting to note that even though middlemen are responsible for the extremely low ornamental fish prices that the producers receive, the fish gatherers would not be able to market their fish without this distribution service, as they have no way of transporting live fish to Manaus.

This area of the Amazon is pristine, but currently has only 4.7 percent of its area in officially protected conservation units or reserves. The sustainable development and environmental preservation of the four municipality areas is important because it constitutes a huge gap in the protection of the central Amazon. In the southern portion of this area, there are many legally (and effectively) protected areas, including the contiguous system formed by the Mamirauá Sustainable Development Reserve, the Amanã Sustainable Development Reserve and the Jaú National Park (see Figure 13.1). This comprises the largest contiguous protected area in the world. Other protected areas in the southern part of the region include the Anavilhanas Biodiversity Reserve, a short distance upstream of Manaus. In the northern part of this region are the large indigenous reserves and national parks along the borders with Venezuela and Columbia.

Although the huge area in the middle of the central part of this region is unprotected, sustainable development initiatives can help preserve the rainforest by enabling communities more effectively to govern resources, work with each other cooperatively and exclude outsiders. Voluntary resource management agreements, when formally approved by state and federal agencies, can be very effective conservation tools.

Although this four-municipality tract of the Rio Negro drainage is pristine, there are threats to the preservation of the rainforest and aquatic resources. Although it is unlikely that major roads, agricultural investments or other capital-intensive projects will be implemented there, other threats exist. In this area, every subsistence fisherman is a potential clear-cutting farmer, logger, gold miner or commercial fisherman. Although the population of the area is relatively small for such a big region, the combined impact of a massive switch from traditional activities to commercial extractivism could have terrible consequences. An even more likely threat comes from a lack of ability of communities to prevent outsiders such as commercial fishermen and industrial loggers from coming to the region. Moreover, there is the great danger that migration from other areas could bring unsustainable small-scale farmers and gold miners from other parts of Brazil, leading to significant losses of this important biodiversity resource. This migration of people and destructive economic activity to the region may be difficult to prevent because of the lack of ability of the municipal governments and individual communities to prevent the outsiders from entering. Poor economic and social conditions in other regions of Brazil create these pressures to enter the region.

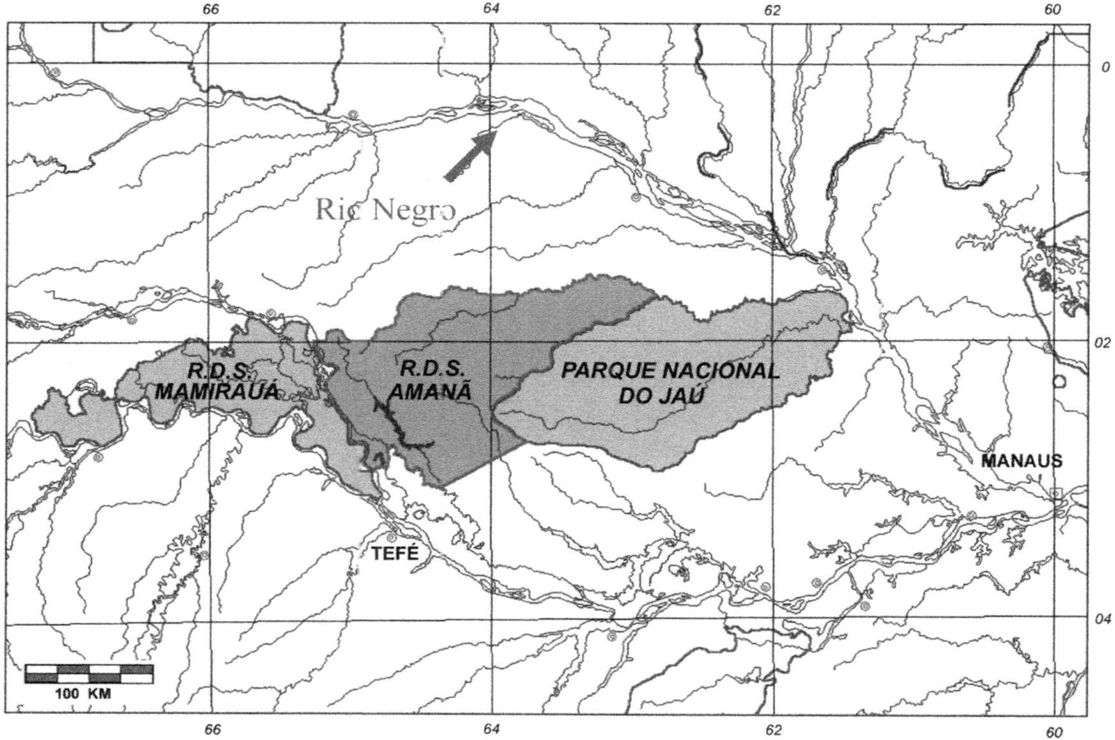

Base cartográfica: Diagnóstico Ambiental da Amazônia Legal IBGE/DGC/DERNA - DEGEO - DECAR

Figure 13.1 *Protected areas to the southwest of the Rio Negro*

WHAT ARE THE CONDITIONS FOR SUSTAINABLE DEVELOPMENT?

There has been considerable discussion in the literature on the conditions that are necessary for sustainable development. Much of the more neoclassical literature, such as papers by Pezzey (1989), Pezzey and Withagen (1998), Hartwick (1993) and others focus on whether human-made capital (*K*) can accumulate quickly enough to offset the loss of what they call natural capital (*N*).[4] This type of approach views natural capital as exhaustible resources (such as coal, iron or oil) and views GDP to be a function of human-made capital and natural resources as in equation (13.1):

$$GDP = f(K, R), \frac{\partial GDP}{\partial K} > 0, \frac{\partial GDP}{\partial N} > 0, R = -\frac{\partial N}{\partial t} \qquad (13.1)$$

Under these conditions, and if human-made capital is a perfect substitute for natural capital, then an increase in the stock of human-made capital can compensate for depletion in the stock of natural capital and sustainable development is possible. This conception of the interplay between human and capital formation and natural capital depletion has been at the heart of the debate about the consequences of growth and scarcity, since Barnett and Morse's classic study in 1967. However, there has been a series of articles on environmental economics, ecological economics and Post Keynesian economics that present alternative models of growth[5] and sustainable development.[6] In this version of growth, GDP is recognized to be a function of additional types of capital. One aspect of this discussion highlights the importance of human capital and social capital, where human capital reflects the quantity and quality of our human resources, and social capital reflects the status of our social institutions. Another aspect of this discussion is the separation of natural capital into two types of capital, natural resources and environmental resources.

In this chapter, we define natural capital as those provisions of nature from which we extract part of the stock of the resource in our economic or social activities. For example, we would remove barrels of oil or tons of coal from the ground. In contrast, environmental capital is the collection of environmental systems from which we obtain a flow of ecological services. In this process, we do not consume the capital stock in the process of utilizing these flows. Ecological services would include flows such as nutrient cycling, maintenance of atmospheric chemistry, protection of water resources, flood protection, soil formation, and pollination. Note that it is possible for an environmental system, such as a forest, to provide both natural resources (such as wood) and environmental resources (that provide ecological services such as carbon sequestration and biodiversity). Natural resources arising from ecosystems can also be labeled as a 'provisioning service' of the ecosystem.

The inclusion of environmental capital in the production function (in contrast to focus on undifferentiated natural capital) as a type of capital substantially changes the perspective on resource scarcity and growth. The reason for this is that while it is reasonable to assume that human-made capital is a good substitute for natural capital (for example more fuel-efficient engines compensate for the increasing scarcity of oil), it is simply not realistic to suggest that the same assumption holds with respect to environmental capital. Human-made capital simply cannot provide ecological services at the same scale as environmental systems (Kahn and O'Neill, 1999; Batabyal et al., 2003). Two recent examples from the United States demonstrate this very well, with both examples related to the Mississippi system. The first example follows the loss of the flood control services of the wetlands in the upper Mississippi watershed. These wetlands were converted into agricultural holdings, and society attempted to deal with these losses of flood control services by the construction of a series of levees and dams along the Mississippi River system. However, the massive flood of 1993 illustrates the inability of the human-made systems to provide the same degree of flood protection, as a 25-year rain (a rain of intensity that is expected once in 25 years) caused a 100-year flood (a flood of intensity that one expects once in every 100 years). How does a 25-year rain cause a 100-year flood? The answer is simple: loss of the wetlands that store the rainwater and gradually release it into the tributaries and the Mississippi River. Similarly, the storm surge generated by Hurricane Katrina was much more devastating than it would have been 50 years in the past, because of the loss of coastal wetlands to absorb, slow and buffer the storm surge. These examples were chosen because flood control and storm protection are probably the ecological services for which engineering best replicates nature, and still they were inadequate. If we begin to think about the ability of human systems to sequester carbon at the same level as the rainforests, preserve biodiversity at the same level of coral reefs, or form soil at the same rate as a prairie or temperate forest, the importance of preserving environmental capital becomes apparent. Franceschi and Kahn (2003) argue that the key to sustainable growth lies with accumulating human-made capital, social capital and human capital at the same time that stocks of environmental capital are protected.

The importance of the role of environmental capital is even more pronounced when sustainable development is viewed in the Brundtland perspective as an increase in the social welfare of the current generation without reducing the prospects for future generations. An increase in social welfare is not generated solely by an increase in GDP. Rather, social welfare is a function of many variables, including the health of the population, social justice and environmental quality. For example, social welfare can be written as a function of GDP, health of the population (*HPop*), environmental quality (*EQ*) and social justice (*SJ*) as in equation (13.2).

$$SW = g(GDP, HPop, SJ, EQ) \tag{13.2}$$

The implication is that protecting environmental quality is important when talking about generating sustainable growth of GDP, but even more important when talking about sustainable development of the overall quality of life or standard of living. The same argument can be made concerning the importance of social capital and human capital. So, as one talks about sustainable development in terms of overall quality of life, the accumulation of a broad portfolio of capital (while protecting environmental capital) becomes an even more critical condition. Thus, in general terms, we view the process of sustainable development to be a process of accumulating non-environmental capital while protecting environmental capital.

It may seem strange that we are focusing a discussion of capital accumulation and sustainable development on a rural region such as these four municipalities in Amazonas state. How can the discussion of the sustainable development of a region with less than one-tenth of 1 percent of the national population inform the issue of sustainable development or macroeconomic growth? We focus on these rural regions because we feel that they are often left behind by economic development policies, particularly policies that focus on rapid growth of national GDP. In addition, short-run maximization of the growth of GDP often leads to environmental degradation of rural areas, lowering both quality of life and the ability of rural communities to engage in both subsistence and market activities. The existence of this phenomenon in the rural areas of Amazonas is discussed later in this chapter.

Despite this apparent disconnect between the potential development of rural areas and the more urban, formal sectors of the economy, the causal relationship between the accumulation of capital and sustainable development holds for both sectors of the economy. It is just that in the remote rural regions, different types of capital investments are needed.

Two types of social capital are crucial to the focus of our concept for the implementation of sustainable development in rural communities. The first type of social capital is that which provides better governance of environmental resources. The second type of capital is that which permits a greater portion of the value of the final product to accrue to the community. One aspect of this is the displacement of middlemen who are not part of the community. As is often the case with extractive resources, the communities who are dependent on these resources receive pennies on the dollar, while the middlemen make monopoly profits. It should be noted that sometimes social capital itself is not enough and that appropriate human and human-made capital must be developed to help communities fulfill this intermediary step between production and the final sale of these products. In addition, appropriate human capital, human-made capital and social capital must be developed so that a larger proportion of the production chain takes place in the communities. The combination of adding value, controlling a greater portion of the distribution chain, and developing governance which excludes outsiders and prevents intercommunity open-access exploitation can go a long way in improving the community standard of living and protecting the ecosystem. We illustrate this with specific examples from Amazonas, but the general concepts are applicable to many remote regions that are dependent on ecological resources for both subsistence and income.

The discussion above outlines the importance of both social capital and environmental capital. The role that these types of capital play in growth is not articulated in the traditional neoclassical perspective. Social capital may be recognized through discussions of the importance of property rights, but this is the extent of the discussion. Although the importance of institutions is often stressed in Post Keynesian approaches, environmental capital has been largely ignored. However, the consideration of environmental capital and its interaction with social capital supports some of the major conclusions of Post Keynesian models, such as the importance of an explicit growth policy and the likely path-dependency of growth.

Setterfield (2001) contrasts some of the major differences in both the structure and implications of Post Keynesian and neoclassical growth models. He notes that since many of the neoclassical models assume a type of Say's Law, the implication is that a focus on aggregate supply is sufficient to generate growth and no further growth policy is necessary. However, we argue that because of potential irreversibilities and associated path-dependence, spatially oriented growth policies are essential.

The other contribution of our discussion to the Post Keynesian approach is related to the Post Keynesian assertion that growth is likely to be path-dependent. Equation (13.1) can be rewritten to include social, environmental and human capital as inputs to the production process. This revised production function can be used to construct a typical (neoclassical style[7]) maximization problem, where the goal is to maximize the sum of the present value of output over some planning horizon. The goal would be to maximize:

$$\int_{s=i}^{n}\int_{t=0}^{t_1} GDP[K(s,t), S(s,t), E(s,\gamma,t), HC(s,t), N(s,t)]e^{-rt}dt \qquad (13.3)$$

where K refers to human-made capital, S to social capital, E to environmental capital, HC to human capital, N to natural capital, γ (or $\partial E/\partial t$) is the recovery rate of E, and s the scale of human activity. This maximization would be subject to a set of constraints, co-state equations and state equations. If certain types of environmental degradation are irreversible, then γ is likely to be quite small and could be negative. In other words, there is an upper bound on how quickly environmental capital can recover from degradation. This has been demonstrated to be the case with many types of ecosystems such as the Amazonian rainforest (Lovejoy, 1986, Lovejoy et al., 1986). Note that $\partial^2 E/\partial s \partial t$ is highly likely to be negative, implying that γ will decline with s, and will eventually become negative. The inability to regenerate E is likely to generate path-dependence, and will generate path-dependence if the neoclassical assumption that E and K are perfect substitutes is rejected. This path-dependence will exist over a wide range of values of γ, s and the elasticity of substitution between K and E. Franceschi and Kahn (2003), Kahn and O'Neill (1999) and Batabyal et al. (2003) discuss the reasons for, and the significance of irreversibility, thresholds and non-linearity in the relationships between E and GDP (and social welfare) that govern the values of the above parameters. The potential irreversibility of losses of social capital is also important to consider, especially social capital that governs human interaction with environmental resources.

In summary, the implications of our model reinforce several of the important Post Keynesian critiques of the neoclassical macroeconomic growth models. In particular, growth policy must pay attention to the protection of environmental capital, as well as the protection of existing social capital and the creation of new social capital. Additionally, policy must help to develop human-made capital and human capital that works in concert with the environmental and social capital in the region. The market, left to its own devices, will not do this. Furthermore, macroeconomic growth policy that focuses on aggregate macroeconomic variables cannot do this and is likely to eliminate potentially desirable growth paths.

THE MACROECONOMIC INTERACTION BETWEEN THE URBAN AND RURAL AREAS IN AMAZONAS STATE

Amazonas state is one of the wealthier states of Brazil, primarily because of its extensive manufacturing center. In the 1960s, an assembly industry was created by special incentives that allowed the imports of parts without the payment of duties. This was followed by other types of economic incentives, most importantly reductions in the state and federal corporative income tax. The assembly industry gradually transformed itself into a manufacturing center, with Manaus now being the electronics center of Brazil. Leading products include cellular telephones, televisions, other electronics and motorcycles.

However, this economic development has not directly impacted the interior regions of the state. Amazonas state is a large state (equivalent to 20 percent of the area of the lower 48 United States) and the interior regions are quite distant from the capital city of Manaus. With the exception of the Urucu oil fields 700 km upstream of Manaus on the Rio Solimoes and the Pitinga tin mine to the northeast, economic activities in rural areas are largely subsistence with very few commercial agricultural activities.

The economic development of the Manaus does not necessarily imply improvements for the rural areas for several reasons. First, it can lead to migrations from the rural regions to the city, leaving a sparsely populated rural region even more sparsely populated. Second, as Manaus grows, its need for products from the rural regions increases. For example, the demand for fish and wood both will increase proportionately to the population of the Manaus. At first, it might seem as if increased production of wood and fish are good for the rural communities, but these activities do not generate much income for the residents of the rainforest communities. The extractive activities are controlled by firms operating out of Manaus, and laborers are paid trivially low prices for their output. More importantly, these commercial activities, particularly the commercial harvest of fish, are in direct conflict with subsistence activities. In many areas commercial fishing has depleted fish populations to the point where rural communities have difficulty harvesting sufficient fish for their own consumption, and fish are the primary source of protein in this region. Other negative environmental impacts are associated with the harvest of wood. Thus, the demand for inputs generated by a growing industrial sector, or the demand for goods created by a growing urban population is unlikely to have a beneficial impact on *ribeirinho* communities. 'Trickle-down' simply does not work for the rural sector. In other words, although programs to develop the urban and industrial centers obviously create important benefits for the urban areas and the nation as a whole, this type of development path largely bypasses rural areas, and as mentioned, can reduce the quality of life in rural communities through environmental and social change.

Large rural development projects have been implemented in many regions of the world, but have often proven unsuccessful. One of the chief reasons for this lack of success has been the immigration to rural areas that these programs generate. Large mining, forestry and agricultural projects tend to draw immigrant labor from among the unemployed and underemployed in large urban areas. This immigrant population competes with the traditional population for resources, often appropriating their land, and generating environmental degradation that reduces the quality of life for the traditional populations. Other social problems, such as crime, violence, increase in prevalence of diseases associated with environmental degradation (malaria, schistomiasis, leshmaniasis, and so on), prostitution and increases in incidence of sexually transmitted diseases often develop. This pattern of development can be found in many regions of the world, and is present in Brazilian states such as Pará, Mato Grosso and Rôndonia, in the area of the Brazilian Amazon often called the 'arc of deforestation'. However, this development pattern has not yet appeared to a significant extent in the state of Amazonas, and the state retains 96 percent of its original forest cover.

The problem of path-dependency and irreversibility can be best understood by comparing two income paths, one for sustainable and the other for unsustainable activities, as depicted in Figure 13.2. Unsustainable activities would include those that result in clear-cutting, causing irreversible loss of the rainforest, with associated consequences for the productivity of the land. Examples include small farms cleared by immigrant (from coastal Brazil) farmers, industrial agriculture (soy bean, corn and sugar), clear-cutting for timber and mining activities.

Both general national development policies and unplanned market growth would lead the economic development of the rainforest to the unsustainable path, because of the significantly higher income in the short run. Unfortunately, irreversibility of destruction of the rainforest implies a path-dependency that makes it impossible to change paths and move from point A to point B.

For this reason, growth policies need to encourage people to choose the sustainable path, or growth will eventually crash due to the loss of environmental resources. Appropriate growth policies can shift the sustainable path upwards, raising the plateau of the sustainable curve relative to the peak of the unsustainable path. This would also serve to shift the intersection between the two paths to the left, reducing the period of time

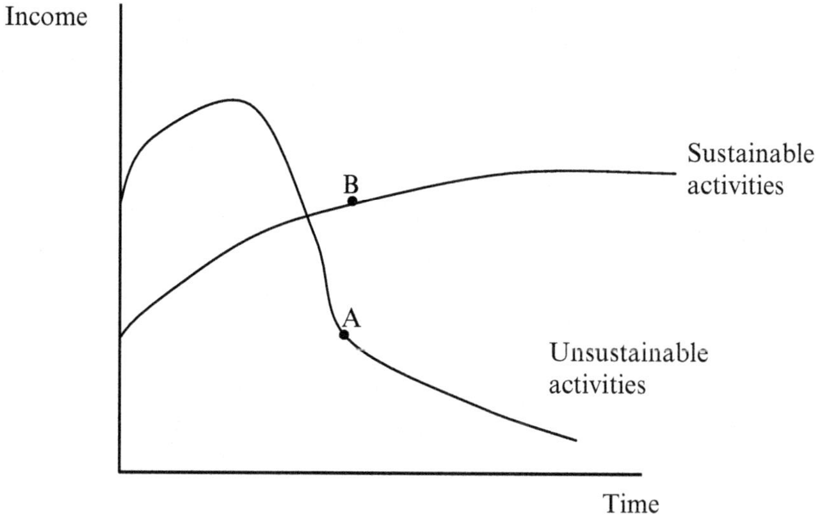

Figure 13.2 Alternative income paths

in which unsustainable activities yield higher annual income than sustainable activities. Our case studies focus on how investment in human capital, social capital and human-made capital, while maintaining environmental capital, can shift the sustainable curve upward in our case-study region.

Reiterating, the crucial policy question is: 'How can sustainable development be stimulated among traditional communities?' The answer is that plans need to be created specifically for the rural regions, most appropriately focused on small groups of neighboring communities or even at the level of the individual community. These types of development projects are often overlooked by national governments or by large lending agencies such as the World Bank or International Monetary Fund, because they tend not to have a measurable impact on national GDP.[8] Plans based on increasing national GDP are unlikely to improve the quality of life in these regions for the reasons articulated above. In tandem with national development policies it is essential to implement community-based programs. As we will demonstrate in our discussion of the Rio Negro region, the successful plans are most likely to be based on the sustainable harvest of extractive resources and ecological services. Our preliminary analysis of the situation in *ribeirinho* communities of the Rio Negro suggests that a successful development path has the following characteristics:

1. The development of social institutions that allow communities to manage the resources in and around their communities.

2. The development of social institutions such as cooperatives that displace exploitive middlemen.
3. The development of appropriate human capital, social capital and human-made capital to increase the value-added of products made in rainforest communities.
4. The development of new products made from rainforest inputs.
5. The development of new markets for products produced in rainforest villages.

SOCIAL INSTITUTIONS FOR BETTER CONTROL AND MANAGEMENT OF ENVIRONMENTAL RESOURCES

The fragility of Amazonian rainforests to large-scale deforestation has been well documented in the literature (Lovejoy, 1986, Lovejoy et al., 1986). However, even in areas with low-density populations of traditional peoples, open-access externalities can lead to environmental degradation and negative impacts on income, nutrition and quality of life. The conflict among users can take many forms, including conflict by users from the same community, conflict between similar users from different communities, and conflicts between community users and outsiders engaging in commercial extraction activities.

One of the most important types of conflict occurs when people from outside the region enter the areas surrounding the communities to extract resources. This could take the form of industrial activities, such as large-scale logging or commercial fishing. It could also take the form of small-scale activities, including artisanal mining (*garimpos*), forestry or farming.

Another important type of conflict arises when traditional residents of the community switch from traditional sustainable forms of production to non-sustainable extraction activities. Each and every subsistence fisherman in each and every *ribeirinho* community is a potential small-scale gold miner, logger or clear-cutting farmer. This is one of the reasons why it is so crucial to increase the income associated with sustainable activities, thereby reducing the economic pressure to pursue unsustainable extraction activities.

There are many ways to control resource use and mitigate open-access conflicts, such as regulation by the state or federal government. However, in Brazil, environmental law tends to be written more to control large-scale activities and is based on direct controls (Biller, 2003). These types of laws do not function well in terms of providing positive incentives for sustainable activities and also are not appropriate for resolving conflicts among different types of users, particularly when one of the user groups functions at the subsistence level. Moreover, in the vast expanses of Amazonia, monitoring and enforcement by a central authority can be quite difficult.

The need for better institutions to manage resources more effectively can readily be illustrated with fisheries in the Rio Negro region. For example, the conflict among the fisheries in Rio Unini[9] was quite pronounced, with conflicts between all four types of users. The four types of fisheries include sport fishing for peacock bass (*tucunaré*), commercial fishing for catfish, subsistence fishing for a wide variety of species, and live capture of *piabas* (ornamental aquarium fish).

Some of the conflicts are quite obvious, as the pursuit of the same species leads to open-access exploitation and diminution of the stocks. Other types of conflict are less obvious, such as between *piabeiros* and sport fishermen, who are pursuing entirely different species. In this case, the mega-horsepower outboard engines of the bass boats of the sport fishermen create wakes that damage and displace the wicker fish traps of the *piabeiros*. It should be noted that in this river, most of the potential income lies with sport fishing, where American fishermen pay $3000 per week to participate in the world-class fishing opportunities there, which many regard to be the most productive (in terms of size and quantity of big fish) peacock bass fishery in the world.

A project was developed[10] that negotiated a voluntary fishery management agreement among the involved parties. The river was divided into three sections: the area around the communities was designated for subsistence fishing only, the upper reaches of the river were designated for 'catch and release' sport fishing, and the middle stretch of the river was designated for commercial fishing. Subsistence fishing could also take place in the sport and commercial fishing stretches, but these tended to be further from the villages and there was not any significant pressure. Sport fishing was limited to clients of two companies who were signatories to the agreement and these firms agreed to recruit and train their workforce from the local communities (as opposed to Manaus or other larger cities). The companies also agreed to provide additional development aid to the communities, such as drilling wells.

The voluntary agreement was approved by state and municipal authorities. Non-signatories to the agreement were prohibited from exploiting fishery resources in the region. Monitoring is provided by the sport fishing enterprises, the communities and graduate students conducting research in the area. If violations are observed, government authorities are notified for enforcement. This arrangement has been sufficient to keep non-signatory commercial fishermen and non-signatory sport fishing enterprises from harvesting fish from the Rio Unini.

In the first and second year of the agreement, research was conducted to determine the impact of this agreement on communities, how the agreement could be modified in the future to increase further the benefits for all participants, and how fish populations are being affected. Although not enough data have been collected to test hypotheses concerning the impact of the agreement statistically, preliminary indications are that it was successful, and that all the user groups support its continuation. Barcelos municipality is working with our group to extend the arrangement to other tributaries. Unfortunately, the project was forced to end, as the Rio Unini became part of an extractive reserve, administered by the federal government. The federal government has prohibited all fishing activities until a new management plan is developed. It is unclear whether this successful project will be reinitiated in the future. However, the project team is pursuing funds to implement it in tributaries that are not covered by extractive reserves and other protected areas.

THE DEVELOPMENT OF SOCIAL INSTITUTIONS TO DISPLACE EXPLOITIVE MIDDLEMEN

Rural inhabitants in general, and traditional and indigenous people in particular, often receive very little compensation for the resources they extract. There are several reasons for this. First, they often do not have direct access to firms who use the extractive outputs to produce a final output. Second, when the resource is sold in markets as harvested, the resource extractors do not have access to urban markets, exporters or retailers. This function is often appropriated by middlemen whose gateway position between extractors and markets allows them to accrue all the economic rents associated with the resource. As long as these middlemen control the distribution of the resource, the traditional and indigenous people earn trivially low incomes from their extractive activities, creating pressure to satisfy their income needs by overexploiting the ecosystem.

This problem has been recognized in a number of development situations. For example, since the mid-1990s, this problem has begun to be well addressed for coffee growers, and 'fair trade' coffee offers growers a greater share of the ultimate retail value of the coffee.

In the Rio Negro region, this problem manifests itself primarily in fisheries. *Ribeirinhos* are often subcontracted by commercial fishermen, and are only paid a few cents per kilogram of fish. In contrast, these fish retail at $2–$10 per kilogram. *Ribeirinhos* are unable to bring the fish to markets in Manaus or smaller cities such as Barcelos, because they lack the ice-making facilities, fuel and proper boats to transport the fish hundreds of kilometers to market. A similar type of problem is found in the ornamentals fishery. We will illustrate this problem with the ornamentals fishery and then talk further about commercial fishing below.

One of the principal activities of *ribeirinhos* in this region is the live capture of *piabas*, or ornamental fish (fish for freshwater aquaria). The *piabeiros* who capture these fish only make a few pennies on the dollar, and refer to themselves as slaves to the middlemen who have their headquarters in Barcelos. These middlemen send the fish to several firms in Manaus who export to the distributors in Miami and Europe. While it would be difficult for the people in the region to take over the whole export chain all the way to Miami, cooperatives of *piabeiros* could displace the middlemen in Barcelos, allowing more income to reach the rainforest communities. However, these cooperatives do not yet exist and cannot be successful without the cooperation of the exporters. Our feeling is that the exporters are uncomfortable with the economic exploitation of the *piabeiros*, and would be willing to work with cooperatives of *piabeiros* in the same way that large coffee distributors have been willing to work with cooperatives of small-scale coffee growers. Thus, one of the central thrusts of the project team's future work in the Rio Negro region will be helping the *ribeirinhos* to develop these cooperatives and creating resource management agreements to support the cooperatives. The development of these cooperatives is an example of investment in social capital that fills a critical need in the sustainable development of these rainforest communities.

INVESTMENT ACTIVITIES TO INCREASE VALUE-ADDED

The development of institutions to give the communities control over resources and bypass middlemen is based on the development of social capital. As important as these investments are, taken alone they cannot achieve the highest sustainable development path. Additional value-added must be created by increasing the amount of processing activity that takes place in the villages. This change in the type of economic activity that goes on in *ribeirinho* communities requires investments in human and human-made capital in addition to social capital. We will illustrate this process with fishery activity and handicrafts in the Rio Negro region.

Fisheries provide the primary source of protein for the people in this region, and also a source of income. Unfortunately, the income associated with selling the catch is extremely low. The primary source of the low income is the fact that *ribeirinhos*, for the most part, do not have good access to markets. Although those that live near the municipal capital cities can sell in these markets, most *ribeirinhos* would have to transport their fish over 100 km to reach the market. The *ribeirinhos* do not have fast boats or ice-making facilities, and even if they had this infrastructure, the market price of whole fish may not support the fuel cost of the transportation and ice-making. The alternative would be to work as subcontractors to firms that have these facilities (and export to Manaus, southern Brazil and Europe), but the *ribeirinhos* have no economic power in these subcontract relationships and only earn pennies per kilogram of fish that they catch. The wholesalers are often in Columbia, and sell the fish, particularly catfish, to the European market. This currently has a higher value than regional markets such as Manaus, but the fishermen can not bypass the wholesalers and sell the fish directly to Europe. Selling the fish directly in Manaus does not work because of the lack of ice-making and transportation infrastructure. Somehow, a way must be found to bypass the wholesalers to Europe with a profitable income to the local fishermen. This is important in another dimension because it is widely believed by knowledgeable people that the wholesalers are involved in the laundering of money for the Columbian narcotics industry, inflating the prices they say they are receiving and using that as a way to slide drug money into the legitimate economy. The less fish that wind up in the hands of these wholesalers, the less drug money they will be able to launder and the greater the sustainability of the greater Amazonian region.

The Instituto Piatam[11] plans to help the fishing communities by developing value-added products that can be sold directly to supermarkets in Manaus and large cities in south Brazil. Fishing cooperatives would be developed, and voluntary fishery management agreements for various stretches of the rivers and tributaries. As with our previous projects, these agreements would be presented to state and federal governments for ratification so that they would have the power of law behind them and be more effective in excluding non-participants. Increasing income potential without limiting access will only lead to increased environmental degradation without increasing the income of the communities. Outsiders must be excluded through the development of these fishery cooperatives and the fishery management plans.

In addition, the development of new technologies to generate new fishery products with higher value-added (than simply selling whole fish to wholesalers) is an important component of the plan. We would help them implement packaging and flash-freezing facilities to make fish fillets ready to go directly onto the freezer (or fresh-thawed) shelves of supermarkets in Manaus (and eventually São Paulo, Rio de Janeiro, Miami, and so on). The fillets would be packaged in sauce or spice, including local dishes such as fish with *tucupi* sauce, or international dishes such as Cajun or Thai. These could be sold by the cooperatives directly to the supermarkets and could obtain a better price for fishermen then simple whole fish. The cooperative as a whole would be able to support the fast boats to bring the fish to Manaus. Alternatively, they could be shipped as airfreight from the municipal capital cities to Manaus. We would seek to develop a branding mechanism to signify the contribution to forest preservation of these fish products. In addition to developing an 'eco-label' we would also develop a 'fair trade label' as currently seen in coffee markets to indicate that these products pay a fair price to small-scale primary producers.

Product diversity is also important because a sole reliance on fisheries could lead to either insufficient income or too much pressure on the fish stocks. In addition, it is important to find sources of income for women, who are not as involved in the fishery industry as men. One way to do this is to develop products made from non-timber forest products. A variety of possibilities exist, including: frozen juice and smoothie concentrates; sweets made from rainforest fruits and nuts; and soaps, lotions and other cosmetic items made from nuts, aromatic barks, roots, fruits and non-nut oils. The discussion of non-timber forest products will focus on jewelry and handicrafts, an area in which we have already begun projects.

Traditional and indigenous communities have always produced jewelry and other handicrafts. Seeds, fibers and shaped pieces of wood can make very attractive jewelry, boxes, combs and other handicrafts. The traditional residents of these regions have developed very strong skills in working with these materials to produce attractive jewelry and handicrafts. However, there are several technical and marketing problems that prevent these activities from reaching their full income potential.

For example, seeds that become beads for necklaces, bracelets and earrings have a high moisture content and eventually degrade from within from bacteria or fungus. When this happens to local women, they simply discard the items and fashion new ones. However, when a young woman in Manaus, let alone Rio de Janeiro or New York, sees the contamination on the beads and it gets on her skin or clothes, she will never buy another and will tell her friends not to buy them. These seeds need to be kiln-dried at a critical heat to reduce their moisture content, kill existing bacteria and fungi, and then be sealed to prevent the reabsorption of moisture. Similarly, wood beads, small boxes and other handicrafts tend to have a high moisture content due to the natural humidity of the rainforest. When moved to a drier environment, such as a temperate location or an air-conditioned apartment, they tend to warp. Again, there is a need to develop a drying technology and a method for sealing the wood.

Marketing is also an issue. The styles that traditional women make for themselves would simply not be acceptable for a 20-something-year-old woman to wear with high heels and a 'little black dress' to an urban nightclub. However, the same rainforest materials, when arranged according to a different fashion sense, can be very exciting to that same consumer. We are currently working with traditional women to help them develop appealing fashions and appropriate technologies.[12]

An important aspect of the development of markets is the creation of a price premium for sustainably produced products that reduce pressure to deforest the rainforest. Unfortunately, a credible and well-recognized certification authority does not exist for these types of products. It is critical to develop such certification authority or brand-name recognition of these products. One aspect of a sustainable development process for this region (and similar regions around the world) would be to develop a marketing program that creates the appropriate consumer awareness and increases the demand for these products, thereby creating a price premium and greater benefits to the communities for engaging in these sustainable activities.

CONCLUSION

The economic growth and sustainable development of nations are complex processes. In the modeling of these processes, neither neoclassical nor Post-Keynesian models consider adequately the importance of environmental capital, and they do not adequately address the differential spatial patterns of growth and development. In particular, subsistence-level populations in rural areas do not benefit from the national growth process, and are often left worse off due to environmental degradation associated with the growth process.

Our ecological economics model focuses on the preservation of environmental capital, in part by developing social capital to allow communities the ability to govern the environmental resources in their region. Examples from current and planned projects in the Rio Negro system also emphasize the importance of developing social capital, human-made capital and human capital to reduce the role of exploitive middlemen and to increase value-added in the communities.

Our ecological economics approach also reinforces two themes underlying the Post Keynesian approach. The first of these focuses on the importance of path-dependence. Since ecological services are critically important to both economic growth and improvements in social welfare, and since destruction of environmental capital may be irreversible, both growth and development will be path-dependent. The second theme focuses on the importance of policy. In this regard, our ecological economics approach goes beyond the need for macroeconomic growth policy, and demonstrates the need for environmental policy as well as specific policies designed to meet the capital investment needs of the communities in the informal or subsistence sector. These capital investments needs include social capital, human capital and human-made capital. Although we illustrate our discussion with case studies from the Rio Negro region of Amazonas, Brazil, our approach is applicable to the subsistence sector in other regions and in other developing countries.

NOTES

1. Note that in Brazil, the names of the municipality (the county) and the names of the capital city of the municipality are the same. We will differentiate between the capital city and the municipality when appropriate.
2. The project team has also been working extensively in Rio Solimões between Coari and Manaus, but the ecological economics approach taken in this chapter focuses on Rio Negro communities.
3. Caboclo is a Tupi-Guarani word meaning 'an Indian who lives in a white man's house'. *Ribeirinho* is a Portuguese word meaning 'little river dweller'.
4. Much of the neoclassical literature does not differentiate among the various provisions of nature, calling every stock of natural resources 'environmental capital'. We believe it very important to differentiate between natural capital and environmental capital. Natural capital is what is ordinarily viewed as reserves of extractive resources. Humans extract a portion of the stock to satisfy their consumption or production needs. In contrast, we define environmental capital as those environmental systems that produce ecological services. Humans receive benefits from this flow of services without diminishing the stocks of environmental capital. Ecological services include flows such as nutrient cycling, carbon sequestration, maintenance of the hydrological cycle, soil formation and so on. A good discussion of the importance of ecological services to the economic process and to the question of development can be found in the Millennium Ecosystem Assessment (2005).
5. We define growth as a unidimensional concept focused on GDP. Development is multidimensional focusing on social welfare. Both growth and development can be sustainable or unsustainable. Much of the neoclassical literature (see Pezzey (1989) and Hartwick(1993)) only focus on growth when examining sustainability and do not deal with the more complex dimensions of development.
6. See Pearce and Warford (1993), Franceschi and Kahn (2003) and Stern (1997) for a sample of this literature.
7. It might seem strange that we are using a strictly neoclassical tool to address our points about the importance of a heterodox approach. However, the casting of our arguments in the structure of these models highlights the difference between a neoclassical and ecological economics approach.
8. This is not to say that these types of development plans are completely absent. In particular, micro-lending programs have been very successful in community development in recent years, and there are many examples of community forestry, ecotourism and similar programs that have been successful. However, these types of programs tend not to be an integral part of national development strategies.
9. The Rio Unini is a tributary of the Rio Negro in Barcelos municipality.
10. Project directors are Professors Alexandre Rivas and Carlos Freitas. Funding was provided by FAPEAM (Amazonas State Science and Technology Foundation).
11. The Instituto Piatam is a non-governmental research organization comprised of researchers from the Amazonian area.
12. Renata Mourão is the principal investigator of this part of the project.

REFERENCES

Barnett, Harold and Chandler Morse (1967), *Scarcity and Growth*, Washington, DC: Resources for the Future.

Batabyal, Amit, James R. Kahn and Robert O'Neill (2003), 'On the scarcity value ecosystem services', *Journal of Environmental Economics and Management*, **46**, 334–52.

Biller, Dan (2003), 'Environmental impact assessment in Brazil', in David Irvin, James Kahn and Marie Livingston (eds), *Does Environmental Policy Work? The Theory and Practice of Outcomes Assessment*, Cheltenham, UK and Northampton, MA, USA: Edward Elgar, pp. 114–30.

Casey, James, James Randall Kahn and A.A.F. Rivas (2008), 'Willingness to accept compensation for the environmental risks of oil transport on the Amazon: a choice modeling experiment', *Ecological Economics*, **67**, 552–9.

Franceschi, Dina and James R. Kahn (2003), 'Beyond strong sustainability', *International Journal of Sustainable Development and World Ecology*, **10**, 211–20.

Hartwick, John (1993), 'The generalized R% rule for semi-durable exhaustible resources', *Resource and Energy Economics*, **15**, 147–52.

IBGE (Instituto Brasileiro de Geografia e Estatistica) (2007), http://www.ibge.gov.br/estadosat/perfil.php?sigla=am, accessed 13 June 2007.

Kahn, James R. and Robert V. O'Neill (1999), 'Ecological interaction as a source of economic irreversibility', *Southern Economic Journal*, **66** (2), 391–402.

Lovejoy, Thomas (1986), 'Conservation planning in a checkerboard world: the problem of the size of natural areas', in F.T. Last, M.C.B. Hotz and B.G. Bell (eds), *Land and its Uses, Actual and Potential: An Environmental Appraisal*, New York: Plenum Press, pp. 289–301.

Lovejoy, Thomas, R.O. Bierregaard, Jr, A.B. Rylands, J.R. Malcolm, C.E. Quintela, L.H. Harper, K.S. Brown, Jr, A.H. Powell, G.V.N. Powell, H.O.R. Schubart and M.B. Hays (1986), 'Edge and other effects of isolation on Amazon forest fragments', in M.E. Soule (ed.), *Conservation Biology: The Science of Scarcity and Diversity*, Sunderland, MA: Sinauer Associates, pp. 257–85.

Millennium Ecosystem Assessment (2004), 'Millennium Ecosystem Assessment: Ecosystems and Human-Wellbeing', www.Millenniumassessment.org/documents.

Millennium Ecosystem Assessment (2005), *Ecosystem and Human Well-being: Synthesis*, Washington, DC: Island Press.

Pearce, David W. and Jeremy J. Warford (1993), *World Without End*, Washington, DC: Oxford University Press for the World Bank.

Pezzey, John (1989), 'Economic analysis of sustainable growth and sustainable development', Working Paper 15, World Bank, Environment Department.

Pezzey, John and Cees A. Withagen (1998), 'The rise, fall and sustainability of capital-resource economies', *Scandinavian Journal of Economics*, **100** (2), 513–27.

Setterfield, Mark (2001), 'Macrodynamics', in R.P.F. Holt and S. Pressman (eds), *A New Guide to Post Keynesian Economics*, New York: Routledge, pp. 92–101.

Stern, David (1997), 'The capital theory approach to sustainability: a critical appraisal', *Journal of Economic Issues*, **31**,145–73.

World Commission on Environment and Development (1987), *Our Common Future*, The Brundtland Report, Oxford: Oxford University Press.

14. Optimize versus satisfice: two approaches to an investment policy in sustainable development[1]

Jerry Courvisanos

INTRODUCTION

There are two broad approaches to sustainable development. The first, adopted by both neoclassical and ecological economics, focuses on optimality. The second is the satisficing approach, which is based on Post Keynesian and institutionalist principles. This chapter argues that there is a fundamental weakness in the optimality approach, and that this weakness undermines any effective investment policy towards sustainable development. Because Post Keynesian economists take uncertainty and cumulative causation into account, they are in a better position to deal with sustainable development and develop appropriate investment policy. The satisficing approach thus provides an opportunity for Post Keynesian economists to make a major contribution in the area of sustainable development (Winnett, 2003).

From the neoclassical perspective, environmental concerns are resolved through optimal cost–benefit algorithms. Ecological economics sees the economy as a subset of the global ecosystem, requiring an optimal scale of resource use. From this vantage point, optimality is the only policy approach to resolving environmental issues that has generally been considered. However, these optimality strategies fail to address two problems identified by Post Keynesian economists: fundamental instability in economic activity (Kalecki, 1971), and inappropriate use of technology (Lowe, 1976).[2] These failures lead to suboptimal solutions.

A superior alternative to the optimality approach comes out of a dynamic Post Keynesian non-optimal (satisficing) framework for sustainable development based on the work of Adolph Lowe and Michał Kalecki.

DEFINING SUSTAINABLE DEVELOPMENT

Sustainable development became popular in 1987 after the publication of the Brundtland Report (WCED, 1987) and the World Bank (1987) environment pamphlet.[3] Both define sustainable development as economic development that 'meets the needs of the present without compromising the ability of future generations to meet their own needs' (WCED, 1987, p. 8). Many actions can promote sustainable development. Organizations (especially businesses) and governments can develop policies for energy efficiency, recycling, reducing obsolescence and improving public transportation. However, the key element underlying sustainable development is the technology in plant and equipment that enables the above actions to be effective. Such investment is the focus of this chapter. The specific policy definition of sustainable development adopted in this chapter comes from Vercelli (1998, p. 268) where he states that economic development is 'considered sustainable only when future generations are guaranteed a set of options at least as wide as that possessed by the current generation'. Vercelli goes on to specify that:

> If the set of available options is too small, their survival could be jeopardized, or could be of a very low quality, as is suggested by what happens today in the poorest areas of the world. In addition, any reduction in the available set of options would imply a reduction in the liberty of choice of future generations. (p. 269)

NEOCLASSICAL OPTIMALITY

The standard economic position on optimality has changed considerably over the post-World War II period. Until the mid-1970s, Keynesian macroeconomics aimed to stabilize the business cycle (Fusfeld, 1994, p. 155). Governments used a combination of fiscal, monetary and incomes policies to counter the business cycle and mitigate macroeconomic uncertainty. This allows private investment decisions to be based on better information, and lowers the amplitude of cyclical peaks and troughs. Countercyclical fiscal policy by governments offset fluctuations in private investment with public investment (Kalecki, 1945, pp. 89–90).

Cost–benefit analyses of environmental market failure at the microeconomic level operated in tandem with Keynesian macro-stabilization policy. Government use of taxes and charges to internalize the social costs of production allows optimal private investment decisions to be based on full marginal costs when calculating rates of return benefits on specific investment projects (Helm and Pearce, 1991). This leads to the adoption of the most appropriate cost-effective indicator in determining outcomes for policy decisions affecting the environment (Hoehn and Randall, 1987).[4]

Beginning in the early 1980s, however, as the free market approach came to dominate the profession, the orthodox neoclassical position shifted away from government control and towards greater market control. On this approach, governments only set broad parameters within which the private sector operates. At the macroeconomic level, the government sets medium-term targets for fiscal (balanced budgets) and monetary (minimum inflation) policy, so that market forces can respond flexibly to market signals. Coupled with this, deregulation fosters a private investment strategy that moves away from protected mature industries to growth industries with higher value-added. This approach seeks to provide investment decision-makers with better market information, while removing interventionist public policies that distort market information. For environmental protection, this approach recognizes the efficiency gains from market-based instruments (tradeable resource and pollution permits) over direct regulation (Godal and Klaassen, 2006). It allows private decision-makers to incorporate environmental costs as a marginal adjustment to the scale and form of investment projects, rather than as a fixed regulated cost. However, most applied market-based instruments 'have been grafted onto existing regulatory regimes rather than introduced as an alternative to such regimes' (Eckersley, 1995, p. 15).

Free market environmentalism views environmental externalities as 'the *absence* of markets and property rights' (Eckersley, 1995, p. 15). In this context, investment strategy returns to private decision-makers once government has converted 'the commons' into private property rights. Entrepreneurial initiative will respond to rising environmental demands by investing in new technologies that internalize external costs (Anderson and Leal, 1991). Public investment should only be contemplated when transaction costs are extreme, and then only in alliance with the private sector (through outsourcing, joint ventures, leasing, and so on).

Both the Keynesian and anti-Keynesian versions of the neoclassical approach are based on a static model within which private investment decisions are made. Stable private investment results from benchmark competitive conditions that are established by the state. These conditions let price signals arise, and let private entrepreneurs respond to these prices. Intricate equilibrium modelling of incentives towards strategic investment in environmentally based technology is induced by regulatory standards and the market signals that emerge.[5] The dynamic aspect of this orthodox position is the exogenous element of technological innovation (capital stock with embodied technical progress). Such technology, it is assumed, will come forward under correct market signals and will solve environmental problems. Thus, innovation is seen as arising through investment, but with no theory as to how it happens. Empirical evidence on technical change comes forth as only a 'residual' to all the basic internal static economic factors that are explicitly price-responsive, a position that has not altered since Denison (1962) identified it.

Benchmarking begins from the premise that human agency responds to market signals by tending towards a known (or knowable) stable equilibrium. The critical response to this is that technology itself, within the context of volatile market signals, generates uncertainty about future expectations, and this leads to cumulative short-run instability and cumulative long-run systemic change. Two Post Keynesian analyses, Minsky (1982) on financial instability and Crotty (1992) on the growth–safety trade-off in capital goods investment, show the volatility arising from market signals to investment (financial in Minsky's case and physical in Crotty's case). Research on the technology embodied in investment has shown strong cumulative cyclical expansions whenever new technological systems predominate, followed by cumulative cyclical contractions.[6] Furthermore, Joan Robinson's notion of historical time allows Post Keynesians to identify the capital stock inherited from the past and the expectations embodied in the path-dependence of this capital stock (Setterfield, 1995). This means that past decisions inordinately shape future investment decisions. Myopic selection pressures emerge that make it impossible for the price mechanism to allow an ecologically sustainable technology to come forth (Rip and Kemp, 1998, pp. 372–9).

From this critique, optimal allocation is not an option. The instability of investment and the path-dependence of technological innovation limit the neoclassical approach to environmental social costs. This is true of both the welfare (cost–benefit) and free market versions of the neoclassical approach. Both practical and conceptual concerns arise (see Stanfield, 1995, pp. 26–7).

At the practical level, there are the intractable problems of identifying and measuring social costs when calculating rates of return for investment projects extending into the unknowable future. Market signals do not provide the necessary data and do not prevent myopic selection pressures. Public investment strategies based on optimality cannot resolve these problems, unless public investment dominates the market as in the 'military–industrial complex', but this leads to a 'socialization of investment' of the sort advocated by Keynes and Kalecki, a position that is anathema to neoclassical economics.

At the conceptual level, ecological market failures are pervasive and interdependent in an uncertain world. Technological change embodied in new investment alters 'the extant institutional configuration' (Stanfield,

1995, p. 27), which is taken as given in neoclassical economics. Substantive (unbounded) rationality drives market decisions in neoclassical economics, but this assumes the absence of systemic mistakes and failures *ex post*. Yet in technological embedded investment, an evolutionary focus that is endogenous to entrepreneurial investment decisions makes such substantive rationality inoperable. Technical change defies any static equilibrium solution to ecological market failures, and propels it to the centre of the endogenous process of instability. Technology cannot be some *deus ex machina* that generates a market solution to the ecological disasters that accompany economic growth.

New neoclassical growth theory has taken the work of Kamien and Schwartz (1968) on induced innovation by firms and then endogenized technical change within growth models. Technical change, from research and development (R&D) expenditure and human capital accumulation, is modelled as a stock variable with positive externalities. This creates a divergence between optimal and equilibrium growth. Various environmental factors have been modelled in an effort to identify the form of the growth–environment dilemma.[7] A major achievement of these models is to reject the neutrality of money (Aghion and Howitt, 1998, p. 269), thereby opening the door for government intervention to improve economic welfare. However, the two Stanfield concerns remain: an inability to measure the size of intervention, and an inability to fix the existing configuration of institutional specifications (Verspagen, 1992, p. 652). Without such measures and fixes, optimality through intervention is impossible.

The new growth models support the position in this chapter of failure arising out of cyclical instability and inappropriate technology. Instability implies large cyclical swings in output, which increase uncertainty and lead to delays or suspension of investment and R&D (Aghion and Howitt, 1998, p. 269). This can increase environmental degradation, even in a zero economic growth scenario (Byrne, 1997). Ecologically inappropriate technology implies additional environmental spillover costs that need to be accounted for in the divergence of equilibrium from optimality. Types (but not exact size) of incentives for firms to do research under different scenarios are the minimal policy prescriptions that come out of these models (Rip and Kemp, 1998, p. 355). Benhaïm and Schembri (1996, p. 131) explain that neoclassical optimality prevents new growth models from providing any guidance for public or private investment strategies despite acknowledging systemic failures. Equilibrium optimality constructions cannot perceive sustainable development 'other than a state to reach' within very restrictive settings. Evolution of the system through technical change in historical time is impossible under optimality conditions. This neoclassical optimality approach assumes that today's economy is merely a scaled-up version of yesterday's economy;[8] it neglects the evolution of institutions with different technological trajectories and investment dynamics that effectively alter the path of economic development.

The overwhelming impression one gets from this overview of neoclassical environmental economics is one of microeconomic optimality. Research concentrates on valuation, types of instruments and resource constraints within particular regulatory regimes, allowing market signals to provide the appropriate environmental response. Sustainable development is assumed in the macro perspective as a future state that the economy reaches. As Bortis (1997, p. 15) explains: 'neoclassical economists interpret reality in terms of deviations from these ideal (or hypothetical) states of the world'. But sustainable development is a state that is never analysed; it is taken as given. Thus, it can only be assumed that the appropriate environmental market signals will elicit efficient allocative decisions to ensure sustainable development. Modelling hypothetical states provides the neoclassical research basis to identify both cost–benefit valuations (for example, Considine and Larson, 2006 on cap and trade permits in the Acid Rain Program), and various obstructions to the ideal sustainable development state (for example, Costello and Ward, 2006 on the reluctance to invest in biodiversity protection).

STEADY-STATE OPTIMALITY

Another approach to sustainable development comes from ecological economics, based on the seminal work of Herman Daly (1977 [1991]). Daly argues that sustainable development can only be achieved through optimal ecological resource use, derived from a 'biophysical equilibrium'. This equilibrium determines the optimal scale of production that balances material and energy throughputs into the economy, and maintains flows from the ecosystem at a constant and sustainable level. This is the optimal steady-state economy (SSE).[9] Daly (1977 [1991], p. 17) considers innovation as essential for this type of economy to improve the quality of society without adding to the stock of human artefacts that would distort the biophysical equilibrium. Market-based instruments of the sort supported by neoclassical economists are the public policy tools used to achieve this steady state. Daly (1996, p. 31) explains that in an SSE: 'the aggregate throughput is constant, though its allocation among competing uses is free to vary in response to the market'. This incorporates private incentives in optimal allocation to achieve collective control at the optimal scale of production. Daly's path-breaking analysis continues to dominate ecological economics. For example, Lawn (2007) argues that a transition to a steady-state economy is necessary to achieve sustainable development.

Georgescu-Roegen's application of the entropy law on material and energy flow to economic growth is the basis of Daly's steady-state economy optimal rule, and is the crucial unifying concept for ecological economics (Faber et al., 1996). All versions of sustainable development relying on flow analysis aim to keep the use of environmental and resource stocks constant over time. This can be achieved by keeping all natural stocks in their original state (strong sustainability) or only maintaining a constant aggregate sum of all stocks (weak sustainability).[10] Two constraints are needed to implement such optimal rules: one is the carrying capacity of the environment, and the other is the ability to close the economic–ecological system within which the strategy is being developed (van den Bergh, 1996, pp. 36–49). Both raise serious concerns regarding how the market economy can determine the biophysical equilibrium path of development. Sustainable development in ecological economics is thus not an assumed future equilibrium state as in neoclassical economics, but instead identified as the future macro-optimal equilibrium steady-state economy that environmental policy must be assessed against to determine their appropriateness (Söderbaum, 2007).

The steady-state economy is a sort of 'constrained market environmentalism'; the investment process operates the same as in neoclassical economics but with the crucial pre-analytic setting of an optimal scale of production. The size of investment projects is predetermined, yet there exists market-based encouragement to develop ecologically sustainable technology. Pearce and Atkinson (1993, p. 104) begin their discussion with: 'To do this we adopt a neoclassical stance and *assume* the possibility of substitution between "natural" and "man-made" capital".' This analytical device assumes overriding steady-state optimality and is adopted by ecological economists. The approach reaches its nadir with Sim (2006), where the neoclassical 'IS-LM' model is extended to include an 'EE' environmental equilibrium constraint that represents all interest rate–output combinations such that the economy's use of environmental services is exactly equal to the ability of the natural environment to supply them. Sim (2006, p. 401) admits that 'the model imposes a strong assumption that the policymaker has perfect knowledge of what the environment constraint is', but more puzzling is the implication that standard macroeconomic policy can induce supply of the natural environment. Varying the interest rate is a blunt and inefficient macroeconomic policy for the economy, so it is improbable that such rate variations can also induce appropriate environmental outcomes.

A citation analysis of published articles in *Ecological Economics* supports this market-based view of ecological economics. It notes that: 'due to the large number of citations to mainstream economics journals, neoclassical economics is clearly an important component of ecological economics' (Ma and Stern, 2006, p. 505).[11] Thus optimality, if redefined as a steady state, is the 'holy grail' that ties ecological economists to neoclassical environmental economists.[12]

Galbraith, coming from an alternative perspective, rejects this steady-state optimality. 'I have never quite agreed with the advocates of zero growth', for it would add to social tension as lower income groups would be severely disadvantaged (Galbraith and Salinger, 1981, p. 155).

A steady-state economy based on environmental market constraints reduces the influence of exogenous factors on investment cycle susceptibility, making these cycles more strongly endogenous. The crucial variables in Kalecki's investment cycle analyses are aggregate demand, profitability, debt levels and excess capacity (Courvisanos, 1996); they all continue to vary endogenously in a market-based, steady-state economy, except that the trend growth rate over the business cycle would be targeted at zero. The instability of investment then creates the endogenous uncertainty-based problems that were raised above with neoclassical economics. Vercelli (1998) argues that these uncertainty problems make any optimization algorithm based on substantive rationality impossible to express with operational significance. The irreversibility and complexity that arise over historical time require an adaptive procedure, or bounded rationality. This means that the objective of sustainable development can only be achieved in a cumulative process of learning-by-doing and acquiring knowledge through adaptive (non-optimal) conventions and rules.[13]

In a steady-state economy there is market-based investment instability and technical change. These are processes of cumulative change through time, not some stable equilibrium set by the market. Free market environmentalism does not have the analytics to deal with cumulative change in the ecological domain. As Stanfield (1995, p. 19) points out, discontinuities of threshold levels exist in the environment so that 'there is no smooth curve of residuals disposal and environmental deterioration'. Ecology mutates as it grows out of qualitative change. Optimal scale is undefined in the context of the two systemic failures of unstable business cycles and inappropriate technology. Instability leads to uncertainty as is experienced in speculative financial markets (for example, the sub-prime crisis), while inappropriate technology leads to technology lock-in (for example, the use of the automobile).

Some ecological economists have attempted to incorporate an evolutionary view of technical change and sustainable development. Carrillo-Hermosilla (2006, p. 731–2) proposes an agent-based model to consider the problem of technology lock-in as only 'potentially significant' and then explores a precautionary approach that is 'complementary to conventional equilibrium oriented environmental polices'. But this approach is a non sequitur due to the inoperability of conventional equilibrium as a concept.

A corporate investment strategy suited to innovation needs a stable business environment (Kay, 1993). A stable but adaptive evolutionary and incremental approach to investment is necessary for innovation that is ecologically supportive. However, static corporate and public policies in a steady-state optimal ecological framework cannot accommodate fundamental uncertainty. Ecological economics begins with Krutilla (1967) where he has an opening quote from Pigou stating that there is a case for some 'artificial encouragement to investment' by competent governments since returns appear well into the future, but this stance by Krutilla is made without acknowledging fundamental uncertainty. This has resulted in ecological investment strategies that maintain existing technological competence with 'end of pipe' add-on environmental solutions (Yarime, 2003) or technology that limits natural resource exploitation on a 'profit-maximizing sustained-yield basis' (Costanza and Daly, 1992, p. 44). Neither will deliver sustainable development unless market uncertainty can be ameliorated through public investment strategies that create a predictable but strategic focus to induce innovation that is cumulatively changing towards an ecologically sustainable investment programme.[14]

Ecological economics, unlike neoclassical economics, is made up of diverse and often incompatible approaches that are connected by the issue of sustainable development. Despite the links of steady-state economics to neoclassical market analysis as described above, the general recognition of uncertainty, evolution and 'open systems far from equilibrium' (Faber et al., 1996, p. 108) allows more 'room to move' in relation to how ecological economics can address sustainable development and investment policy. Further, technical progress is seen as permitting humankind to survive the movement to higher entropy more efficiently, and as such should be part of a conceptual framework towards sustainable development (Faber et al., 1996, pp. 127–34). There is a need to link all this together in an open system and sustainable development framework that incorporates insights from the physical and social sciences, as well as the broad heterodox economics community. Although writers in the field of ecological economics have argued for such a transdisciplinary approach to research, the theoretical framework has not been developed (see Hirsch Hadorn et al., 2006), and from an empirical investigation, the journal *Ecological Economics* seems to be 'less genuinely interdisciplinary than it would appear from the crude journal level data' (Ma and Stern, 2006, p. 505). Of greater concern, given the open systems approach these writers profess, is that heterodox economics journals are rarely cited (Ma and Stern, 2006, p. 497).

POST KEYNESIAN SATISFICING FRAMEWORK[15]

Holt (2005) argues cogently that the Post Keynesian worldview is compatible with the concerns of ecological economists and sustainable development. Further, Dunn and Pressman (2006–07) explicate how Post Keynesian economics, building on the work of Galbraith, has the potential to integrate with institutional economics, especially on environmental degradation.[16] The following is presented as a policy framework in the area of investment and innovation to a sustainable development future divorced of the optimality chimera, but compatible with the concerns of ecological economists and the procedural principles of institutionalists.

Post Keynesian economics can contribute in two significant ways to sustainable development, and in the process complement the field of ecological economics with a policy framework for investment and technical progress that eschews neoclassical market environmentalism and optimality scenarios.[17] First, it provides a bounded rationality (or satisficing) approach to the ecosystem and its links to the economy, yielding an iterative process towards sustainable development. Second, it contains a policy approach based on establishing sustainable development customs and norms, and the need for growth in demand.

The policy framework is aimed to operate in a Post Keynesian world of fundamental uncertainty (see Davidson, 1991) and cumulative change (see Kaldor, 1966) within the context of an innovative and sustainable environment. With policy action, the framework has satisficing (rather than optimizing) objectives as first espoused by Simon (1976) and then adopted in Post Keynesian behavioural analyses (Earl, 1989). Vercelli (1998, p. 273) has argued that satisficing is required for efficiency and ethical reasons due to fundamental uncertainty, irreversible processes and strategic learning. He concludes with the need for a 'designing rationality' that is 'aimed at designing a project of harmonious interaction between economic development and the natural environment and able to specify a strategy for its implementation'. The Post Keynesian satisficing framework outlined below is based on this designing rationality. It is broadly rational in economic terms and also ecologically sustainable in handling ecosystem dilemmas.

As a policy framework, the political economy of the environment and investment needs to deliver an innovation strategy within a long-run sustainable development framework. The satisficing approach needs to be cumulative and iterative in the short run, developing a strong market share and effective demand for sustainable development-based innovations.[18] As more information and knowledge are acquired, the policy can be recalibrated towards a more sustainable long-run outcome. The framework sets up guiding principles for the transition to sustainable development.[19] Transition to a new path of economic development is known as a 'traverse' and requires adopting: (1) leading-edge knowledge; (2) new practices; and (3) different social organizations.[20]

The procedural framework begins with identifiable goals and then develops a strategy of public intervention to meet Vercelli's definition of sustainable development specified at the start of this chapter.[21] Vercelli (1998, p. 274) explains why long-run goals have to be established:

> One of the main reasons for the deterioration of environmental problems may be ascribed precisely to the myopia of economic agents increasingly obsessed by very short-run objectives. Short-run rationality produces a profound irrationality in the longer run. Only a broader long-run rationality may produce a process of sustainable development avoiding deep regrets.

The framework is based on the work of Lowe and Kalecki on traverse economics, which defines the movement of an economy outside equilibrium,[22] and aims at overcoming myopic selection pressure. These principles provide a major shift in policy away from the standard optimizing approach. Lowe's supply-side instrumental analysis shows how to use instruments to achieve agreed goals. Lowe (1976) establishes an analytical framework enabling rules of formal logic to be applied to economic cause-and-effect sequences over historical time. This framework is aimed at using such cause-and-effect principles to set up structural adjustment policies that can deliver a sustainable, equitable and ecologically supportive economic environment. It requires a paradigm shift away from existing technological solutions. Lowe (1976, pp. 11–12)[23] calls this: 'the search for the economic means suitable for the attainment of any stipulated end. To this procedure I have assigned the label of instrumental analysis.' Forstater (1999) refers to this as 'retroduction', a search procedure that works backwards from ends (in this case sustainable development) to means (in this case planning).

Lowe argues that instrumental policy analysis must concentrate on investment, which is the central element of any growth path. Thus, any path to sustainable development must concentrate on the type of capital stock that, via effective demand, will carry the economy forward. Analysis and evidence show that uncertainty causes investment instability and undermines any smooth path to economic growth (Courvisanos, 1996, pp. 190–92).[24] Further, Lowe explains that in market-based regions, or nations lacking supportive physical and social infrastructure, there is insufficient order and coherence to impel the creation of innovative ecologically sustainable investment projects by the private sector. A structural adjustment policy with appropriate infrastructure spending is needed to underpin the path to sustainable development.

Second is the demand-side perspective planning of Kalecki (1986). This generates an investment strategy where there is motivation and voluntary conformity toward ecologically appropriate goals. A path of dynamic diffusion of new technology systems needs to be set up that is conducive to innovation in investment for sustainability. This requires a long-run investment strategy as well as an approach to adjust planning according to altered perspectives. To achieve this it is necessary to specify practical short-run targets that induce, through effective demand, innovation in investment that will lead to the specified long-run goals. Targets need to be monitored and plans must be assessed at regular points to see if it is necessary to revise the goals and the strategy for reaching the long-run sustainable vision. A perspective plan with these goals is set up to form a specific investment programme in consort with agreed ecological rules that deliver the type of ecological sustainability determined by the instrumental analysis.

Kalecki (1963) identifies two resource-saving parameters that provide ecological-efficient criteria for rules formulation. One is the coefficient of real depreciation. The goal here is to reduce this coefficient by proper maintenance and repair systems to equipment and infrastructure. The other is the coefficient of better utilization of existing productive capacity. Kalecki (1963, p. 16) points out: 'Greater output may be obtained from existing plant due to improvements in the organization of labour, more economical use of raw materials, elimination of faulty products, etc.' thus reducing the coefficient's value. Together these resource-saving coefficients provide a sound basis for ecological rules in a sustainable investment strategy.

Barbier (1989) developed some ecologically sustainable rules that could form the basis of any Lowe–Kalecki planning approach. These rules deal with rates of both exploitation of natural resources and generation of wastes that ecosystems can assimilate for long-run 'carrying capacity' sustainability. The problem is that different stakeholders (or interest groups) in the economy use alternative load-carrying capacity measures in relation to the ecosystem. Within the context of tourism, Hoffmann (1998) identifies three carrying capacity measures that can be applied to the ecosystem in general:

1. physical capacity as the absolute limit that a resource can cope with;
2. ecological or real carrying capacity as the level beyond which there are unacceptable ecological impacts for ecologists;

3. social or effective carrying capacity as the level beyond which unacceptable change occurs in the production of the good or service in terms of overcrowding and altering social behaviour.

Large businesses tend to support (1). Small and local businesses, public environmental bureaucracies and ecologists tend to support (2). The direct service providers 'on the ground' (for example, national park rangers, local environment groups, low-impact ecosystem-based services) tend to support (3). Kalecki's resource-saving coefficients can be applied to all three capacity measures.

The perspective planning approach first needs to set up a dialogue among all stakeholders on how to achieve a deeper ecosystem-sensitive market in any region or country using structural adjustment policies that plan to alter the economic base of that area. The aim is investment, not in 'end of pipe' solutions to the ecosystem, but in an innovative proactive strategy that significantly alters the operation of the economy using new information and communication technology (ICT) tools. This requires an understanding of the possible means to develop the economy with ICT investment, and an appreciation of the value of all three carrying capacity indicators as rules for monitoring, evaluating and developing each stage in the plan. Networking among all stakeholders over the goals and means must be rapid and continuous. Then processes need to be arranged where constructive dialogue concentrates on the means of achieving the goals based on the data available and rules used to assess this data. Once an investment plan is developed, there must be continual re-evaluation of these rules over time so that they are not static, but reflect the latest innovative technological changes. This ensures a flexible and adaptive investment strategy.

When setting up rules within either the planning process (for example, low-emission public transport system), or regulating the market (for example, emissions trading scheme), Hodge (1995, p. 56) explains that to maintain confidence in these rules: 'any prescriptions will have to embrace a wide range of capital assets and precautionary rather than optimising approaches'. This supports the satisficing rather than the optimizing approach to sustainable development. A satisficing framework can provide sufficient confidence so that rules can be adhered to. Such confidence induces innovation in investment, leading to revisions both in carrying capacities and economic growth for future re-evaluations of the perspective plan through the social learning process. This complexity-based cumulative and feedback process can establish precautionary rules to meet the goal of sustaining the ecosystem, while regularly evaluating and revising the rules for getting there.[25]

Since it is impossible to define with any certainty what sustainability requires, a risk-averse investment strategy not based on a static optimizing scale of production needs to be initially introduced. This points to effective carrying capacity rate as the critical measure. Over time, sustainability requires a 'shifting target' that depends on new information and technology becoming available, and on changing attitudes and expectations adopted by the generation that has democratic public control (Hodge, 1995, p. 56). Democratic control implies grassroots input from people who understand and operate within the fragile ecosystem, together with ability to influence directly the goals and means used to develop the ecologically sensitive economy. This approach rejects the bland superficial notion of democracy as some occasional voting for representative leaders, and embraces a more participatory process that requires significant appreciation of the life support systems that need to be taken into account (see Hirsch Hadorn et al., 2006).

In achieving sustainability, Hoffmann (1998) argues for strategic alliances and innovation networks among stakeholders. There are vast ideological and economic differences among all stakeholders, especially with regards to their support for different carrying capacity rules. So alliances and networks will be tenuous, if not impossible. Democratic control requires networking across all parties with specific details of the stipulated sustainable ends, but then decisions on the plans and implementation must be arrived at by majority support. The minority, even if more economically powerful, must accept the need to act within the bounds of the majority-based plan and policies.

Borrowing from the cumulative causation literature (Ricoy, 1987), the Lowe–Kalecki ecological framework provides for demand-led growth based on sustainability rules that establish certainty within which innovative investment by the private sector can flourish. Continual re-evaluation of the investment plan encourages further innovation, leading to more acceptable and internationally competitive sustainability rules. This creates a 'self-reinforcing internal dynamics' that induces strong international competitiveness, growth and employment.

In summary, this framework has three crucial elements consistent with Post Keynesian principles:

1. Cumulative effective demand that establishes a strong market share (demand-oriented stimulation).
2. Ecological rules that ensure capital investment is resource-saving with long-run carrying capacities which are sustainable (conventions under fundamental uncertainty).
3. Iterative, flexible and risk-averse investment strategy with democratic control (investment planning and management).

THE FUTURE

The future of our planet depends on meeting the ecological challenge. There are massive costs of inaction (Ackerman and Stanton, 2006). Ecological problems face our world from advanced economies, which have been at the forefront of ecological damage, and also from rapidly developing economies like China and India, which are currently driving very strong economic growth. Only a satisficing approach has the ability to mount this twin challenge and achieve genuine sustainable development.

This chapter has critiqued the optimality approaches of both neoclassical and ecological economics by exposing their inability to meet the ecological challenges of the future. Both approaches have something to contribute. Neoclassical economics has effective microeconomic tools to evaluate environmental projects and their impact on micro-ecological systems. Ecological economics has expertise in pollution controls and green accounting. But these schools cannot identify future system goals so that an effective investment regime with sustainable development and technological innovation can traverse to a long-run sustainable world. A traverse to such a new world requires that ecological economists abandon optimality and adopt the Post Keynesian satisficing framework. Planning is necessary for public investment infrastructure and private investment to dovetail into effective demand for capital stock that will deliver sustainable development. This chapter has taken on the challenge by using Galbraith (1973)'s notion of public and private planning for the public purpose in order to set up the Lowe–Kalecki sustainable development investment framework.

This is a satisficing framework that guides and supports broad economic–ecological institutional settings. Clear long-run ecological goals are a prerequisite.[26] These goals will be different for different regions, countries and cultures. Decisions need to be made on what sort of sustainable economy should exist 50 to 100 years from now. These goals then act as the focus of public and private investment planning decisions, 'working backwards' to the present. It is easier to start from where you want to be and work backwards than to hit a target goal from where you are currently. It also removes the tendency to favour the myopic status quo when one starts from the current situation.[27]

Courvisanos (2005) provides some examples of how the satisficing approach has been used in advanced economies. Each country needs to address its future goals in terms of investment towards solar-thermal, geothermal, wind power or nuclear technologies, in order to have these technologies 'proved up' (innovation) for future planned investment. Goals towards sustainable development are no longer an option, they are a necessity for survival. The science of global warming (or climate change) has become clear: 'The body of evidence and the growing quantitative assessment of risks are now sufficient to give clear and strong guidance to economists and policy-makers in shaping a response' (Stern, 2006, p. 1).[28]

The science is clear, and the economics of sustainable development has developed clear methodologies and guidelines. Goals can be set that are not mathematically accurate, but provide satisficing targets to aim for. Sustainable development technologies exist, albeit not fully proven on a mass scale. Demand for sustainable development on all levels, from recycling to wind power, has developed to a sophisticated level. The time has arrived to set up Post Keynesian investment planning, and accompanying infrastructure spending, for sustainable development that can be monitored, evaluated and adjusted based on agreed long-run goals that can themselves be altered as we get further into the unknowable future. For our planet to survive and provide options for our grandchildren, the challenge of meeting the future via the Post Keynesian approach outlined above must begin immediately.

NOTES

1. Research and writing of this chapter was largely undertaken in early 2007 while on professional development leave as Visiting Fellow at the Centre for Strategic Economic Studies (CSES), Victoria University, Melbourne, Australia. The facilities and staff of CSES were most helpful during the development and writing of this chapter. Special thanks to Ainsley Jolley from CSES for his great wisdom and experience in the economics and technology of sustainable development. Also, thanks to Ric Holt and Steven Pressman for insightful comments and strong editing.
2. Schumacher (1974) located inappropriate technology in the context of underdeveloped economies using advanced technology that was expensive, complex to operate by the poor, and destructive of the environment. Lowe (1976) located inappropriate technology in the context of advanced economies suffering structural disproportionalities due to production lags and excess capacities that emerge with investment decisions in capital goods. Schumacher worked with Kalecki in the Oxford University Institute of Statistics during the Second World War, co-writing a journal article on the organization of the post-war international financial system (Kalecki and Schumacher, 1943), and both writing a chapter each in a volume on *The Economics of Full Employment* (Burchardt, 1944). Lowe sees Kalecki as supporting his concerns on the instability of capitalist investment in the functioning of economic growth (see Courvisanos, 1996, p. 52). Thus, all three writers can be seen to reflect the particular Robinsonian perspective of Post Keynesian economics as identified in Harcourt (1981 [1985]) and Bortis (1997, p. 10).
3. For a short account of the genealogy of the term, see Vercelli (1998, pp. 267–8).
4. For an explanation of why the contingent valuation approach in neoclassical environmental economics is invalid, see the Marc Lavoie chapter in this volume (Chapter 7).
5. See, for example, Hart (2004), Greaker (2006), Puller (2006).
6. Courvisanos (1996) has combined the Minsky and Crotty analyses to develop a 'susceptibility cycle' of investment at the agency behavioural level involving technological innovation. Empirical studies have provided support for the clustering of innovation and consequent bunching of investment; see Freeman and Perez (1988) and Courvisanos and Verspagen (2004).

7. See the Appendix in Gastaldo and Ragot (1996, p. 84) for a tabulation of such studies and their results.
8. 'As was noted by Aghion and Howitt about endogenous growth: "the economy is always a scaled down version of what it was years ago" (1992:29)' (Benhaïm and Schembri, 1996, pp. 131–2).
9. Towards the end of a more recent book, Daly (1996, p. 223) clearly recognizes the optimality of his steady-state economy version of sustainable development: 'The optimal scale, following our basic ethic, would be the one that maximizes lives ever lived over time at a sufficient level of per capita resource use for a good life.'
10. For details on issues related to policy implementation of such optimal rules, see Costanza (1994), van den Bergh (1996, pp. 53–79), and Parts II and III of Faucheux et al. (1998).
11. Ma and Stern (2006, p. 492) explain that the journal *Ecological Economics* provides a representative sample of work within the field of ecological economics.
12. This strong tie between ecological economics and neoclassical environmental economics is supported by reference to the strongly neoclassical Pearce and Atkinson (1993) piece which is reported by Ma and Stern (2006) as the sixth-most-cited article in *Ecological Economics* (EE) articles from 1994 to 2003. It has always been cited in favourable terms. Yet, Pearce and Atkinson does not appear in the Top 30 cited articles in the neoclassical *Journal of Environmental Economics and Management* (JEEM). Its macro sustainable development perspective made it appropriate for EE but not JEEM (as argued in the previous section).
13. This procedural rationality has been recently adopted in resource management literature under the title 'social learning'. 'Social learning is an iterative and ongoing process that comprises several loops and enhances the flexibility of the socio-ecological system and its ability to respond to change' (Pahl-Wostl and Hare, 2004, p. 195). This process 'is not a search for the optimal solution to one problem but an ongoing learning and negotiation process where a high priority is given to questions of communication, perspective sharing and development of adaptive group strategies for problem solving' (Pahl-Wostl and Hare, 2004, pp. 193–4).
14. In fact Costanza and Daly (1992, p. 45) acknowledge that: 'Uncertainty itself is one of the critical factors that must be addressed in designing sustainable policies', suggesting that a natural capital depletion tax with some form of refundable assurance scheme to handle uncertainty. The problem is that this type of scheme will be subject to the same speculative pressures arising from capitalist uncertainty that occurs with any market-based approach.
15. This section is a revised and extended version of Section 3 of Courvisanos (2005) under the title 'eco-sustainable framework'. Both this chapter and Courvisanos (2005) are the outcome of a much larger research project presented in an embryonic form in Courvisanos (2000).
16. Galbraith recognized environmental degradation in terms of loss of public amenities in Galbraith (1958). He then argued for cleaning up and regulating this degradation through public planning in Galbraith (1973). Galbraith identified infrastructure and technology as possible elements in this degradation, but had no concept of public and private investment in sustainable development.
17. Winnett (2003) identifies integration of resource extraction and environmental assets in a monetary production economy with uncertainty in future stocks as a fertile area for Post Keynesian environmental economics, as none currently exists.
18. The hybrid car is a recent example of how demand ensures growing market share for an innovation. The problem is that this demand has come belatedly out of large petrol price rises (market signals). The technology has been around for a long time, but there has not been any sustainable development planning process to introduce it earlier into the capitalist economies. Up until the 2009 Great Recession, advanced capitalist economies' support for neoliberal *laissez-faire* economic policies prevented consideration of any such sustainable development planning procedures advocated in this chapter. With the recession has come a re-orientation towards more regulatory economic policies, and thus greater 'room to move' in relation to 'satisficing' environmental objectives.
19. See Kemp and Rotmans (2004) on the concept of transition to sustainability.

20. Examples of past transitions are: sailing to steam ships (1850–1914), gas to electric power (1878–1900), high to low death rates (1850-1900), residential coal to natural gas (1960-75), typewriters to computers (1970–90). The first three in the list co-evolved; see Geels (2005) for more details.
21. Goals, and targets, are crucial in any sustainable development planning project. Appreciation of the current systems that need to be transformed to achieve the appropriate sustainable development goals is a basic approach in all ecological economics towards sustainability (see Hirsch Hadorn et al., 2006).
22. See Kriesler (2003) on the traverse, which defines the movement of an economy outside equilibrium.
23. See the excellent exposition of Lowe in Oakley (1987).
24. See Richardson (1960) for details on lack of coordination in markets for investment and the systemic failures that this creates. Richardson explains how investment coordination through information agreements and industrial concentration can assist in developing micro-goals in policy-oriented strategies.
25. For details on Post Keynesian complexity analysis and its relationship to ecological economics, see the Barkley Rosser, Jr chapter in this volume (Chapter 11).
26. Goals can be either specific target reductions of pollution or greenhouse emitting (as in the Kyoto Protocol), or can be broad aims to introduce specific forms of new ecologically efficient technologies by a particular date.
27. Australia is a large coal and other commodities exporter, and also one of the largest per capita greenhouse emitting countries in the world. As an example of how difficult it is for political leaders to grasp the need for significant shift towards goals related to sustainable development rather than fiddle with fine-tuning the myopic status quo, Australia's Prime Minister from 1996 to 2007, Mr John Howard, said in a February 2007 TV interview: 'I think to start working backwards from a mathematically precise scenario 94 years from now, or 93 years from now, is a bit unrealistic and I don't think it's of any benefit to you or your viewers and I don't know that it gets us anywhere. I think what does get us somewhere is to say, "What can we do now, in a sensible way, that doesn't hurt us, to reduce carbon emissions?"' (ABC, 2007).

    The election in December 2007 of the slightly left-leaning Australian Labor Party, on an electoral promise to ratify Kyoto, has ended this unyielding position.
28. IPCC (2007) is a report from the leading world scientists on global warming which further adds support to the Stern (2006) statement.

REFERENCES

Ackerman, F. and E. Stanton (2006), 'Climate change – the costs of inaction: report to the Friends of the Earth England, Wales and Northern Ireland', Global Development and Environment Institute, Tufts University, MA, USA, 11 October; http:ase.tuffs.edu/gdae/pubs/rp/climate-costsofinaction.pdf, accessed 12 August 2009.

Aghion, P. and P. Howitt (1998), *Endogenous Growth Theory*, Cambridge, MA: MIT Press.

Anderson, T. and D. Leal (1991), *Free Market Environmentalism*, San Francisco, CA: Pacific Research Institute for Public Policy.

Australian Broadcasting Corporation (ABC) (2007), 'Howard on global warming, water, Hicks', *Lateline*, Broadcast 5 February, available at http://www.abc.net.au/lateline/content/2006/s1840963.htm.

Barbier, E. (1989), *Economics, Natural-Resource Scarcity and Development*, London: Earthscan.

Benhaïm, J. and P. Schembri (1996), 'Technical change: an essential variable in the choice of a sustainable development trajectory', in S. Faucheux, D. Pearce and J. Proops (eds), *Models of Sustainable Development*, Cheltenham, UK and Brookfield, VT, USA: Edward Elgar, pp. 123–50.
Bortis, H. (1997), *Institutions, Behaviour, and Economic Theory: A Contribution to Classical-Keynesian Political Economy*, Cambridge: Cambridge University Press.
Burchardt, F. (ed.) (1944), *The Economics of Full Employment: Six Studies from the Oxford University Institute of Statistics*, Oxford: Basil Blackwell.
Byrne, M. (1997), 'Is growth a dirty word? Pollution, abatement and endogenous growth', *Journal of Development Economics*, **54** (2), 261–84.
Carrillo-Hermosilla, J. (2006), 'A policy approach to the environmental impacts of technological lock-in', *Ecological Economics*, **58** (4), 717–42.
Considine, T. and D. Larson (2006), 'The environment as a factor of production', *Journal of Environmental Economics and Management*, **52** (3), 645–62.
Costanza, R. (1994), 'Three general policies to achieve sustainability', in A. Jansson, M. Hammer, C. Folke and R. Costanza (eds), *Investing in Natural Capital: The Ecological Economics Approach to Sustainability*, Washington, DC: Island Press, pp. 392–407.
Costanza, R. and H. Daly (1992), 'Natural capital and sustainable development', *Conservation Biology*, **6** (1), 37–46.
Costello, C. and M. Ward (2006), 'Search, bioprospecting and biodiversity conservation', *Journal of Environmental Economics and Management*, **52** (3), 615–26.
Courvisanos, J. (1996), *Investment Cycles in Capitalist Economies: A Kaleckian Behavioural Contribution*, Cheltenham, UK and Brookfield, VT, USA: Edward Elgar.
Courvisanos, J. (2000), 'Optimise vs satisfice: the uncontested battle of investment planning for sustainable development', paper presented at the International Society of Ecological Economics (ISEE) Conference, Australian National University, Canberra, 5–8 July.
Courvisanos, J. (2005), 'A post-Keynesian innovation policy for sustainable development', *International Journal of Environment, Workplace and Employment*, **1** (2), 187-202.
Courvisanos, J. and B. Verspagen (2004), 'Innovation and investment in capitalist economies 1870–2000: Kaleckian dynamics and evolutionary life cycles', in L.R. Wray and M. Forstater (eds), *Contemporary Post Keynesian Analysis*, Cheltenham, UK and Northampton, MA, USA: Edward Elgar, pp. 205–26.
Crotty, J.R. (1992), 'Neoclassical and Keynesian approaches to the theory of investment', *Journal of Post Keynesian Economics*, **14** (4), 483–96.
Daly, H. (1977), *Steady-State Economics*, San Francisco, CA: W.H. Freeman; 2nd edn, 1991, Washington, DC: Island Press.
Daly, H. (1996), *Beyond Growth: The Economics of Sustainable Development*, Boston, MA: Beacon Press.
Davidson, P. (1991), 'Is probability theory relevant for uncertainty? A Post Keynesian perspective', *Journal of Economic Perspectives*, **5** (1), 129–43.
Denison, E. (1962), *The Sources of Economic Growth in the US*, New York: Committee for Economic Development.
Dunn, S. and S. Pressman (2006–07), 'The lasting contributions of John Kenneth Galbraith: 1908–2006', *Journal of Post Keynesian Economics*, **29** (2), 179–90.
Earl, P. (1989), 'Bounded rationality, psychology and financial evolution: some behavioural perspectives on post-Keynesian analysis', in J. Pheby (ed.) *New*

Directions in Post-Keynesian Economics, Aldershot, UK and Brookfield, VT, USA: Edward Elgar, pp. 165–89.

Eckersley, R. (1995) 'Markets, the state and the environment: an overview', in R. Eckersley (ed.) *Markets, The State and The Environment: Towards Integration*, South Melbourne: Macmillan, pp. 7–45.

Faber, M., R. Manstetten and J. Proops (1996), *Ecological Economics: Concepts and Methods*, Cheltenham, UK and Brookfield, VT, USA: Edward Elgar.

Faucheux, S., M. O'Connor and J. van der Straaten (eds) (1998), *Sustainable Development: Concepts, Rationalities and Strategies*, Dordrecht: Kluwer Academic Publishers.

Forstater, M. (1999), 'Working backwards: instrumental analysis as a policy discovery procedure', *Review of Political Economy*, **11** (1), 5–18.

Freeman, C. and C. Perez (1988), 'Structural crises of adjustment, business cycles and investment behaviour', in G. Dosi, C. Freeman, R. Nelson, G. Silverberg and L. Soete (eds), *Technical Change and Economic Theory*, London: Pinter, pp. 38–66.

Fusfeld, D. (1994), *The Age of the Economist*, 7th edn, New York: HarperCollins.

Galbraith, J.K. (1958), *The Affluent Society*, Boston, MA: Houghton Mifflin.

Galbraith, J.K. (1973), *Economics and the Public Purpose*, Boston, MA: Houghton Mifflin.

Galbraith, J.K. and N. Salinger (1981), *Almost Everyone's Guide to Economics*, Harmondsworth: Penguin Books.

Gastaldo, S. and L. Ragot (1996), 'Sustainable development through endogenous growth models', in S. Faucheux, D. Pearce and J. Proops (eds), *Models of Sustainable Development*, Cheltenham, UK and Brookfield, VT, USA: Edward Elgar, pp. 73–85.

Geels, F. (2005), *Technological Transitions and Systems Innovations: A Co-evolutionary and Socio-Technical Analysis*, Cheltenham, UK and Northampton, MA, USA: Edward Elgar.

Godal, O. and G. Klaassen (2006), 'Carbon trading across sources and periods constrained by the Marrakesh Accords', *Journal of Environmental Economics and Management*, **51** (3), 308–22.

Greaker, M. (2006), 'Spillovers in the development of new pollution abatement technology: a new look at the Porter-hypothesis', *Journal of Environmental Economics and Management*, **52** (1), 411–20.

Harcourt, G. (1981), 'Post Keynesianism: quite wrong and/or nothing new?', Thames Papers in Political Economy, Summer; reprinted in P. Arestis and T. Skouras (eds) (1985), *Post Keynesian Theory: A Challenge to Neoclassical Economics*, Brighton: Wheatsheaf, pp. 125–45.

Hart, R. (2004), 'Growth, environment and innovation: a model with production vintages and environmentally oriented research', *Journal of Environmental Economics and Management*, **48** (3), 1078–98.

Helm, D. and D. Pearce (1991), 'Economic policy towards the environment: an overview', in D. Helm (ed.), *Economic Policy Towards the Environment*, Oxford: Blackwell, pp. 1–24.

Hirsch Hadorn, G., D. Bradley, C. Pohl, S. Rist and U. Wiesmann (2006), 'Implications of transdisciplinarity for sustainability research', *Ecological Economics*, **60** (1), 119–28.

Hodge, I. (1995), *Environmental Economics: Individual Incentives and Public Choices*, London: Macmillan.

Hoehn, J. and A. Randall (1987), 'A satisfactory benefit cost indicator from

contingent valuation', *Journal of Environmental Economics and Management*, **14** (3), 226–47.
Hoffmann, H. (1998), 'The tourism industry and the evolving need for strategic alliances: a DoZana perspective', paper presented at the Seventh International Greening of Industry Network Conference, Rome, November.
Holt, R. (2005), 'Post-Keynesian economics and sustainable development', *International Journal of Environment, Workplace and Employment*, **1** (2), 176–86.
Intergovernmental Panel on Climate Change (IPCC) (2007), *Climate Change 2007: The Physical Science Basis*, Contribution of working group I to the Fourth Assessment Report of the Intergovernmental Panel on Climate Change, edited by S. Solomon, D. Qin, M. Manning, Z. Chen, M. Marquis, K.B. Averyt, M. Tignor and H.L. Miller, Cambridge and New York: Cambridge University Press; also available from http://www.ipcc.ch/publications and data/publications_ipcc_Fourth_assessment_report_wgl_report_the_physical_science_basis.htm, accessed 12 August 2009.
Kaldor, N. (1966), *Causes of the Slow Rate of Economic Growth in the United Kingdom*, Cambridge: Cambridge University Press.
Kalecki, M. (1945), 'Full employment by stimulating private investment?', *Oxford Economic Papers* (Old Series), **7** (March), 83–92.
Kalecki, M. (1963), *Introduction to the Theory of Growth in a Socialist Economy* (in Polish), reprinted (in English) in J. Osiatyński (ed.) (1993), *Collected Works of Michał Kalecki, Volume IV: Socialism – Economic Growth and Efficiency of Investment*, Clarendon Press: Oxford, pp. 3–110.
Kalecki, M. (1971), *Selected Essays on the Dynamics of the Capitalist Economy, 1933–1970*, Cambridge: Cambridge University Press.
Kalecki, M. (1986), *Selected Essays on Economic Planning*, Cambridge: Cambridge University Press.
Kalecki, M. and E. Schumacher (1943), 'International clearing and long-term lending', *Bulletin of the Oxford University Institute of Statistics*, **5** (Suppl. 5), 29–39.
Kamien, M. and N. Schwartz (1968), 'Optimal "induced" technical change', *Econometrica*, **36** (1), 1–17.
Kay, J. (1993), *Foundations of Corporate Success: How Business Strategies Add Value*, Oxford: Oxford University Press.
Kemp, R. and J. Rotmans (2004), 'Managing the transition to sustainable mobility', in B. Elzen, F. Geels and K. Green (eds), *System Innovation and the Transition to Sustainability: Theory, Evidence and Policy*, Cheltenham, UK and Northampton, MA, USA: Edward Elgar, pp. 137–67.
Kriesler, P. (2003), 'Traverse', in J. King (ed.), *The Elgar Companion to Post Keynesian Economics*, Cheltenham, UK and Northampton, MA, USA: Edward Elgar, pp. 355–9.
Krutilla, J. (1967), 'Conservation reconsidered', *American Economic Review*, **57** (4), 777–86.
Lawn, P. (2007), *Frontier Issues in Ecological Economics*, Cheltenham, UK and Northampton, MA, USA: Edward Elgar.
Lowe, A. (1976), *The Path of Economic Growth*, Cambridge: Cambridge University Press.
Ma, C. and D. Stern (2006), 'Environmental and ecological economics: a citation analysis', *Ecological Economics*, **58** (3), 491–506.
Minsky, H.P. (1982), *Can 'It' Happen Again?*, Armonk, NY: M.E. Sharpe.

Oakley, A. (1987), 'Introduction: Adolph Lowe's, contribution to the development of a political economics', in A. Lowe, *Essays in Political Economics: Public Control in a Democratic Society*, New York: New York University Press, pp. 1–24.
Pahl-Wostl, C. and M. Hare (2004), 'Processes of social learning in integrated resources management', *Journal of Community and Applied Social Psychology*, **14** (3), 193–206.
Pearce, D. and G. Atkinson (1993), 'Capital theory and the measurement of sustainable development: an indicator of "weak" sustainability', *Ecological Economics*, **8** (2), 103–8.
Puller, S. (2006), 'The strategic use of innovation to influence regulatory standards', *Journal of Environmental Economics and Management*, **52** (3), 690–706.
Richardson, G. (1960), *Information and Investment: A Study in the Working of the Competitive Economy*, Oxford: Oxford University Press.
Ricoy, C. (1987), 'Cumulative causation', in J. Eatwell, M. Milgate and P. Newman (eds), *The New Palgrave: A Dictionary of Economics*, Vol. 1, London: Macmillan, pp. 730–35.
Rip, A. and R. Kemp (1998), 'Technological change', in S. Rayner and E. Malone (eds), *Human Choice and Climate Change, Volume 2: Resources and Technology*, Columbus: Battelle Press, pp. 327–99.
Schumacher, E. (1974), *Small is Beautiful: A Study of Economics as if People Mattered*, London: Abacus/Sphere Books.
Setterfield, M. (1995), 'Historical time and economic theory', *Review of Political Economy*, **7** (1), 1–27.
Sim, N. (2006), 'Environmental Keynesian macroeconomics: some further discussion', *Ecological Economics*, **59** (4), 401–5.
Simon, H. (1976), 'From substantive to procedural rationality', in S. Latsis (ed.), *Method and Appraisal in Economics*, Cambridge: Cambridge University Press, pp. 129–48.
Söderbaum, P. (2007), 'Issues of paradigm, ideology and democracy in sustainability assessment', *Ecological Economics*, **60** (3), 613–26.
Stanfield, J. (1995), *Economics, Power and Culture: Essays in the Development of Radical Institutionalism*, London: Macmillan.
Stern, N. (2006), *Stern Review on the Economics of Climate Change*, London: HM Treasury, 30 October, available at http://www.sternreview.org.uk.
van den Bergh, J. (1996), *Ecological Economics and Sustainable Development*, Cheltenham, UK and Brookfield, VT, USA: Edward Elgar.
Vercelli, A. (1998), 'Sustainable development, rationality and time', in S. Faucheux, D. Pearce and J. Proops (eds), *Models of Sustainable Development*, Cheltenham, UK and Brookfield, VT, USA: Edward Elgar, pp. 259–76.
Verspagen, B. (1992), 'Endogenous innovation in neo-classical growth models: a survey', *Journal of Macroeconomics*, **14** (4), 631–62.
Winnett, A. (2003), 'Environmental economics', in J. King (ed.), *The Elgar Companion to Post Keynesian Economics*, Cheltenham, UK and Northampton, MA, USA: Edward Elgar, pp. 122–6.
World Bank (1987), 'Environment, Growth and Development', Progress Report for the Development Committee Pamphlet 14, Washington, DC: World Bank.
World Commission on Environment and Development (WCED) (1987), *Our Common Future*, Oxford: Oxford University Press.
Yarime, M. (2003), 'From end-of-pipe technology to clean technology', PhD dissertation, University of Maastricht.

Index

Index prepared by Donna Reeder.

Printed by Printforce, United Kingdom